Secrets of the Space Age

Part One

The Sacrifices and Struggles to Get to the Moon

Part Two

The Aftermath: What Happened after Lunar Mission, Intrigue and United States Space Heroes Betrayed

by William E. Winterstein, Sr.
Lt. Col., Army (Ret.)

Robert D. Reed Publishers • Bandon, OR

Copyright © 2005 by William E. Winterstein, Sr.

All rights reserved.

Robert D. Reed Publishers
P.O. Box 1992
Bandon, OR 97411
Phone: 541-347-9882 • Fax: -9883
E-mail: 4bobreed@msn.com
web site: www.rdrpublishers.com

Typesetter: **Barbara Kruger**
Cover Designer: **Grant Prescott**

ISBN 1-931741-49-2

Library of Congress Catalog Control Number 2004097949

Manufactured, typeset and printed in the United States of America

Dedication

I dedicate this book to the German Rocket Team that was led by Dr. Wernher von Braun. This close-knit group of former German citizens had come to the U.S. at the end of World War II; its members became dedicated and patriotic American citizens in the mid-'50s. At Peenemünde, Germany, they had developed the very first long range, high altitude precision rocket, the A-4 (later called the V-2). In this country, they developed the first American long range rocket missiles— Redstone (250 nm), Jupiter (1500 nm), and Pershing (400-600 nm)—for the U.S. Army. After the U.S. had suffered defeat from the Russians in space exploration in 1957 with the launching of Sputnik, the von Braun team was the very nucleus of thousands of technical personnel in Huntsville, Alabama, and the Jet Propulsion Laboratory which developed and launched Explorer I, the first American satellite. This groundbreaking work of von Braun's rocket team led to the greatest technological achievement of the 20th century, the voyage to the moon.

When in May 1961 President Kennedy announced to Congress that a lunar mission was to be carried out within a decade, there was no other rocket team in America comparable to the von Braun team with its expertise in the design, instrumentation, fabrication, and testing of large rockets, such as the A-4, Redstone, Jupiter and Pershing. The continuing failure of earlier American efforts to loft a small satellite into space gives evidence of this fact.

The space history of this country reveals that during the 1950s, the von Braun team had developed a multi-stage rocket by adding solid propellant rocket stages to a Redstone rocket as boosters. In 1956, such a rocket with two solid stages made successful high-speed rocket re-entry tests with model warheads covered with ablative heat protection. With three solid stages, such a rocket could have placed a satellite into orbit, more than a year before the U.S. was defeated by Sputnik. However, and almost unbelievably, the von Braun team was given direct orders from Washington to stop further development. The team was restricted to the development of rockets whose range was less than 200 nm. It was only after President Kennedy announced the lunar mission in 1961 that the German rocket team was finally released from antagonistic bureaucratic blunders from Washington, and was given a free hand, and orders, to accomplish von Braun's lifelong goal to travel into space.

It is my contention that had it not been for the dedicated efforts of the von Braun rocket team, there would be no American footprint on the moon today.

William E. Winterstein, Sr.
Lt Col, Army (Ret)

Acknowledgments

In writing this book, the thought has often come to me that I have led a very eventful life. God Almighty had placed me into positions where I have been blessed to see important history made throughout my life span of 90 years in this year of the Lord 2005. In short, I was at the right place, at the right time.

In addition, I deeply appreciate the assistance of Dr. Friedwardt Winterberg, Professor of Theoretical Physics, University of Nevada. Dr. Winterberg, through his intensive investigation into the Rudolph case while on sabbatical leave in Germany after Rudolph was exiled in 1984, has furnished me with an abundance of firm, legitimate, documentary evidence revealed in the book.

In addition, my heartfelt thanks go to two of the surviving members of the German rocket team, which, in the U.S., was led by Dr. Wernher von Braun, from 1945 to after the moon landing in 1969. Dr. Walter Haeussermann has furnished me with much documentation and other information concerning both the Arthur Rudolph case, and the advancements made in space exploration. I also want to give my appreciation and thanks to Dr. Ernst Stuhlinger for his assistance.

I am also deeply appreciative of the two in-depth outstanding articles published in the Los Angeles Times, by Washington correspondent Robert Gillette, Times staff writer, in the Sunday, April 27, and the Monday, April 28, 1986, issues. These articles, with evident exhaustive research, clearly presented the situation involving the newly created Office of Special Investigations, Department of Justice, along with the Russian KGB, concerning the prosecution of suspected Nazi war criminals living in the U.S.

In addition, I am deeply appreciative to The Huntsville (Alabama) Times for the extensive news coverage in the Sunday, June 18, 2000, edition, by The Times Staff writer Washington correspondent Brett Davis, concerning the OSI (Office of Special Investigations), with the front page banner headlines reading: "OSI FOREVER?" Also for the other articles concerning members of the German rocket team led by former Huntsville resident, and enthusiastic civic booster, Dr. Wernher von Braun.

I am thankful for the support and encouragement of my family during the many years I was engaged in attempting to restore truth and get justice for the Arthur Rudolph case. My wife of fifty-nine years, Elizabeth, before she passed away in September 1999, my son William Jr., and daughter Constance Winterstein-Good. Also I deeply appreciate the active assistance of my nephew David Winterstein in helping me produce this book.

In closing, I wish to thank two local individuals in assisting me concerning the preparation of this book. Joseph P. Kern, my lawyer, gave me support in my appeal to the U.S. District Court, District of Columbia. Curtis French provided computer support in arranging the various aspects of the book.

Author's Credentials

I have written legal authority from Arthur Rudolph (and family) to pursue the clearing of his name. This includes access to all pertinent records and representing the family in regard to restoring Arthur Rudolph's United States citizenship.

Dr. Stuhlinger, when he first met my daughter at a reception in Huntsville, Alabama, in May 2000, told her: "had it not been for your father, we would not have made it to the moon." (See endorsement letter referring to this and page 48.) The members of the German rocket team, who stayed together as a single unit until the lunar mission was accomplished, plainly exhibited their dedication, loyalty, and outstanding patriotism, to the United States government, by staying together as a unit during very trying times. Immediately after the war, at Fort Bliss, Texas, the scientists realized that Russia would soon pose a threat to the United States, due to the gross diplomatic blunder when the U.S. gave the entire V-2 facility at Nordhausen, Germany, to the Soviets. They were eager to help the U.S., but were ignored by Congress. They sacrificed financially by remaining as Civil Service employees instead of going to private industry at much higher pay. All members of the team cherished, and held dear, their U.S. citizenship, which they obtained in the mid-'50s. The team showed their patriotism for the U.S. by trusting that eventually their talent would be needed.

I am proud and honored to have served my country and thank God for allowing me to be part of the United States Apollo rocket team who placed U.S. astronauts on the moon.

Author's Short Biography

1915—Born in Albany, Oregon, the 6th of 12 in the family.

1925—Made muzzle loading pistol and black gunpowder from reading the Encyclopedia, with ingredients purchased from a local pharmacy. Second favorite reading was funny papers. Once drying the gunpowder after lunch in the oven Mom closed the oven door and as I smelt singeing paper and remembered the gunpowder drying. Quickly rescuing the gunpowder, I luckily saved the woodburning stove from blowing up and burning the house down. Normally I dried gunpowder outside as I mixed it wet to give it an even mixture of the ingredients. Since it had been raining, I decided to dry the ingredients in the woodburning stove. This was the first and last time that I tried to dry gunpowder in an oven. [Photo of pistol later in book.]

As already noted some of my childhood reading materials were from the comics in the newspapers and the encyclopedia. One of my favorite hero stories came from the encyclopedia, involving the legendary Dutch boy who poked his finger in the leaking dike, thereby saving Holland. After eighty some years, I still recall the boy's name, it was Tiki Tiki Rimbo. So, not only did the encyclopedia teach me how to make black powder for my homemade pistol, but also gave me interesting information about ancient and later history, plus a myriad of other subjects.

1926—In a field a bull charged me and as I jumped over the fence, I grabbed a rock and threw it in one swift action hitting the bull right between the eyes, which caused the bull to immediately stop, dazed.

1927-29—Made rocket boats propelled by gun powder diluted with flour from Mom's flour bin and launched them in a small reservoir at the back of the property. Later I learned von Braun was well known by the local police for firing store bought rockets attached to toy cars in his hometown during his youth.

1934—Enlisted in Army: My first involvement with items of historical interest occurred in 1935 at Fort Stevens, Oregon. I enlisted in the Regular Army at Fort Stevens on July 6, 1934. During 1935, Major William Stewart, the Harbor Defense Commander, ordered that all of the Civil War cannon balls, which were ornamentally stacked on most street corners, be removed and dumped into the Columbia River. My regular job was to keep the rust off the machined parts of the big coast defense guns. Also in my 'spare time,' I along with another soldier had the job of loading up the cannon balls on an old antiquated WWI hard-rubber tired Liberty truck, and dumping them into the Columbia River off the mine planting dock (see 1993).

1942—My next involvement in history occurred in June 1942, when the Japanese submarine, the I-25, shelled Fort Stevens. I was still a member of the garrison there when the attack came near midnight hours. The garrison at that time had been greatly expanded by the Oregon National Guard, with all gun batteries being fully manned. It is my observation that the submarine commander was fully cognizant of the traverse of each particular gun battery and therefore remained out of the field of fire of Fort Stevens guns. Due to the handful of troops prior to WWII, security was very lax at the fort, with local civilian inhabitants, including the local Japanese cannery workers, openly visiting the installation on Saturdays and Sundays. This was the first time in U.S. history that an enemy ship fired on a continental military installation since the War of 1812.

1943—Selected as Ordnance Technical Intelligence Officer in February upon graduation from the Ordnance School at Aberdeen Proving Ground, Maryland. The Chief of Ordnance, Washington, D.C., selected me to be among the few of a new breed of officer for the Army. Here, as an Ordnance Technical Intelligence Officer, my headquarters were in the Pentagon, but I was never assigned a desk there. The job assignment of a technical intelligence officer was unique in that he was sent to the combat fronts to give prompt reports via Teletype or courier pouch directly to the Pentagon. These reports covered technical evaluation concerning of what arms and ammunition, or other equipment, such as tanks, the enemy was using against our troops. Also, of which items of captured enemy equipment were selected for shipment to the Aberdeen Proving Ground for further evaluation. An important part of the job was to report on the success, or the failure, of our own equipment. In cases of failures, immediate action would be taken at the source of manufacture to correct malfunctions from reaching the field, and also alert other commands of possible malfunctions. Another very unique aspect of an Ordnance Technical Intelligence Officer, was upon assignment to a combat front, he was 'on his own,' as his next senior military officer, or CO, could be many hundreds of miles away for extended periods. There were only two Ordnance Technical Intelligence officers assigned to cover the Aleutian Campaign.

My first assignment as an Ordnance Technical Intelligence Officer was to cover the Aleutian Campaign. We recovered the Alaskan islands of Attu and Kiska, which had been occupied by Japanese troops. After a debriefing in Washington, I was immediately ordered to proceed to the South Pacific Theater of operations with headquarters in Noumea, New

Caledonia, under Admiral Halsey. My next combat operations were in the Northern Solomon Islands in the Bougainville Campaign.

1944 early 1945—I was transferred to General McArthur's staff in Brisbane, Australia, and participated in the West New Guinea Campaign at Aitapi. After New Guinea, I was involved in the landing at Morotai, Dutch Netherlands East Indies. After Morotai, I returned to Finschhafen, New Guinea, in preparation for the Luzon Campaign in the Philippines. It was during the battle of Manila that our troops captured large Japanese rockets. They came in two sizes and were designed for field artillery use, one had a 1000-pound warhead, and the other had a 100-pound warhead. The launcher for the smaller rocket resembled a very large mortar; however, there were no launchers for the large rocket. Evidently, these larger rockets had never been used by the Japanese forces before and being of a new design, and spun stabilized, did not have the launchers available. In order to make a comprehensive report to the Chief of Ordnance in Washington, I designed and built four launchers for the larger rockets. I then fired a number of both types of the rockets back at the Japanese, using a U.S. observation plane to determine the results, such as range, dispersion, etc. I received a Bronze Star, from the Ohio 37th Infantry Division, for this effort.

General McArthur was so concerned about this Japanese development with rockets that he ordered me back to Aberdeen Proving Ground with four of the 1000-pound and eight of the 100-pound warhead rockets for further analysis on a high priority basis. McArthur was then preparing for the invasion of Okinawa. After assisting technicians at Aberdeen in the analysis of the Japanese rockets, I was assigned as Proof Officer on our own rockets. I was rather amazed at the lack of effectiveness of our own rockets at that time due to poor design.

1945—President Truman invited the 118 German rocket scientists led by Dr. Wernher von Braun to the United States shortly after the war with Germany. Since they had designed and manufactured the V-2, Truman evidently thought that they would be valuable in aiding the U.S. in future defense efforts for this country.

In September of 1945, I was selected to be the custodian of the 118 German rocket scientists, who were to be housed at Fort Bliss, Texas. I was the first Commanding Officer of the 9330th Ordnance Technical Service Unit, Sub-Office (Rocket). Since it was immediately after the war, the question arises; what do you do with 118 German rocket scientists who were responsible for the V-2, and house them in an army fort populated by a large number of veterans from Europe? Commanding General of Fort Bliss issued orders to place our barracks area OFF LIMITS to all other military personnel, except maintenance people, or persons specifically invited by me, or my boss, Major Jim Hamill. The Germans jokingly called themselves "Prisoners of Peace" (PoPs).

Fully recognizing the huge potential that the 'rocket team' held for the United States, my wife Elizabeth and I invited Wernher von Braun, and several of the other scientists, to our family quarters for impromptu dinners once and sometimes twice a week. This was to relieve the boredom of barracks confinement. To keep within budget, the menus were very plain, like spaghetti, or stew, with an occasional barbecue. I had a bar built and placed it in a former bedroom. We had a highball before dinner, and later after dinner drinks. We later joked about the Moon and Mars missions that we launched from that bar. I still have that historical bar. During one of these sessions, in 1946, I casually asked Wernher; "If we could give you all of the money you wanted, how long, and how much would you need to get man to the moon, and bring him back?" Wernher replied; "Bill, give me some time to think it over." It was at this time that we referred to the 'dark days' when Congress was very reluctant to give us any money for rocket research. I believe that it was about several weeks later that Wernher gave me his answer. "Give us three billion dollars, and ten years, and we will go to the moon and back." At the time, I merely observed the statement as an interesting observation. However, the next time that I heard the words mentioned concerning a lunar mission of 'ten years' was in May, 1961 (see 1961).

1957—Military Advisor to South Vietnam: After an interesting military career I retired from the Army in January 1957. In October of 1957, I was employed, as a civilian, to be a military advisor to the newly founded democratic government of South Vietnam in Saigon. I held this job for about 3 years when I voluntarily resigned and returned to the U.S. in June of 1960.

1960—Participated in construction of ICBM bases: I received a Certificate of Achievement for this job, which I left in January 1963, to accept employment by NASA, under Dr. Wernher von Braun, to join the Apollo Team to put U.S. astronauts on the Moon.

1963—Selected as Member of Apollo Team Moon Mission: first person to hold the position of Administrative Officer for Bay St. Louis, Mississippi, test site of Saturn V rockets for the moon mission.

1968—Logistics Manager for second stage Saturn V Rocket: Responsible for the 2nd stage Saturn V Rocket from Seal Beach, California, manufacturing facility to testing grounds Bay Saint Louis, MS, and then to Cape Canaveral, FL. Responsible for coordinating all parts needed to be delivered when and where needed during this process. The 2nd stage was transported from Seal Beach via Panama Canal, then up the Mississippi River into the Pearl River to Bay Saint Louis test site. After testing, it was transported to Cape Canaveral for a Moon launching.

1983—In April 1983 my wife Elizabeth and I were both honored by the City of Huntsville, Alabama. Mayor Joe Davis presented us with certificates making us Honorary Citizens of the City of Huntsville. These certificates bore the signatures of the City Council.

1993—My first attempt to start action on the recovery of the Ft. Stevens civil war cannon balls was in a letter to then Oregon Governor Barbara Roberts in August 1993. The response to this recovery effort would be put on hold indefinitely, due to cost of the equipment for the operation, and other factors. 1995—My second attempt was in a letter to Governor John Kitzhaber in September 1995.

2000—Early in the year 2000 the president of the University of Alabama, Huntsville, invited my family to participate in the dedication of the Dr. Wernher von Braun Research Hall on the campus. In May 2000, Dr. Ernst Stuhlinger, recognized leader of the remaining 118 Old Timers from Fort Bliss days, had an interesting talk with my daughter Constance. The very first words he uttered to her when he first met her at a reception in Huntsville, Alabama, were "Had it not been for your father, we would not have made it to the moon."

2001—Wrote book on early U.S. rocket history and injustice to Arthur Rudolph: *Gestapo USA—When Justice Was Blindfolded.*

2004—Dr. Carol Rosin, President of the Institute for Cooperation in Space, appointed me to be on the Advisory Board for the Institute for Cooperation in Space. It is an organization working on an international treaty for the peaceful use of space. The Director of this Board is Edgar Mitchell, the Lunar Command Pilot for Apollo 14.

This year, 36 years after the event, there has been no nationally designated location of where Man's first flight to the Moon originated. That is, where did the plans and designs of the Moon mission take place, and who were the primary persons responsible for the event? We know that the vehicles departed from the Kennedy Space Center, and that the astronauts rode them to the Moon, but without the vehicles there would be no footprints of the astronauts on the Moon today.

Contents

Figures

Part I

Sacrifices and Struggles to Get to the Moon

Foreword

This story is about my association with the German rocket team under the leadership of Dr. Wernher von Braun. This began at Fort Bliss, Texas, in October 1945, and would culminate in the year 2005 as I publish this book.

It was because of the current trend of the vilification of our space heroes in the public news media, without one shred of legitimate evidence to do so, that I decided to write this book. This is my attempt to present to the American public a true story of their glorious heritage of the accomplishment of the greatest technological achievement of all humankind, Man's first voyage to the Moon. The average patriotic American does not want the history of this country's entrance into the space age contaminated with literary rubbish. The book contains various aspects such as the very early history of this nation's emergence as a world leader in the exploration of space, the prosecution and persecution of distinguished American citizens who were instrumental in placing U.S. astronauts on the Moon, and the distortion of facts which deals with the betrayal of U.S. space heroes.

My involvement with the German rocket team began with a very close relationship at Fort Bliss. After I left the team due to military transfer in 1947, I kept occasional contact with Dr. Wernher von Braun during the years leading up to employment by NASA for the Apollo Program in January 1963. I was then assigned to the Marshall Space Flight Center, Huntsville, Alabama, which was under the direction of Dr. Wernher von Braun. As the story evolves, you will note that much of this book is about the circumstances regarding the Dr. Arthur Rudolph case. In the Fort Bliss days, Rudolph was only a casual acquaintance. It was not until 1985 that I became actively involved in his case.

At this point, I wish to go into some detail about the conduct of a small investigative unit within our Department of Justice. By Act of Congress the Office of Special Investigations (OSI) enjoys a total cloak of protection from disclosing any information concerning their activities! The involvement of the OSI in the Rudolph case began in 1982 about 13 years after he retired from NASA in late 1969.

As the book evolves, the flagrant and gross prosecutorial misconduct of officials in the OSI progresses to the point of being unbelievable except for the firm documentary evidence which has surfaced to support such as fact.

What also alarms me as an American citizen is the behavior of senior officials in the Department of Justice, and members of Congress who have participated in the obvious cover-up of the OSI, and their refusal to take positive action to get truth and justice resolved in this case. This will be revealed in detail as the story progresses.

My appeal to the U.S. District Court was based on my request, under the provisions of the Freedom of Information Act, to the Department of Justice for a copy of the Prosecution Memorandum of the Rudolph case. The result was another decision confirming the refusal of access to the memorandum, but this time on entirely different grounds. The court relied not on the exception provisions of the Freedom of Information Act, but rather on a most peculiar clause added to the Nazi War Crimes Disclosure Act in November, 1997, well after my attempts to get at the truth had begun. That Act, as originally adopted, provided for the dissemination of all kinds of information pertaining to war crimes committed or possibly committed in the Nazi cause. The amendment vitiated the purpose of the Act in the following language: "This (Act) shall not apply to records (A) related to or supporting any active or inactive investigation, inquiries, or prosecution by the Office of Special Investigations of the Department of Justice; or (B) solely in the possession, custody, or control of that office." The meaning is clear: no matter what, the OSI cannot be made to give up any information it possesses. That is the meaning the District Court found when it refused my application for relief (they applied this recent change retroactively).

It is difficult to suppose that Congress entertained that intention as it enacted the amendment. The result is that the OSI, among the smallest of federal law enforcement organizations with about 50 total government personnel, is and has been free to engage in gross prosecutorial misconduct. The OSI, without accountability, may blast reputations by falsely claiming possession of incriminating evidence but never divulging what that may be. As this is revealed later on, this false inclination on part of the OSI was put to the test when the West German war crimes prosecutor requested a copy of the Rudolph file from the Department of Justice. This request was made due to a possible prosecution of Rudolph as a war criminal by the West German government.

After much delay, the response from the OSI revealed that they did not offer one shred of legitimate evidence, either in documentation, or in witnesses to support their allegations. This was a gross and most embarrassing slap on the face of American justice. Thus, this unit, the OSI, chartered to hunt down Nazi war criminals, was borrowing the same operational tactics enjoyed by the Gestapo under Hitler—complete freedom of operation without accountability.

Nor is the issue here solely the concern of the surviving family of Arthur Rudolph. Eli Rosenbaum is an intrepid prosecutor who led the celebrated prosecution of John Demjanjuk and claimed it as one of his most successful efforts at tracing down and bringing to justice a brutal concentration camp guard. Upon closer examination of the case by the Israel Supreme Court, the man's sentence of death was overturned on the grounds of mistaken identity. Exculpatory evidence had been deliberately withheld by the OSI. Rosenbaum's attitude toward the exoneration was caught in his reply to the press: "You have to live with that."

The behavior of the OSI in the Rudolph case hints strongly that the facts denied here would expose the oppressive program of the OSI in the forced deportation of Rudolph, followed by later attempts to deprive him of the NASA Distinguished Service Medal awarded him in 1969. In addition, the campaign attempted to blacken his reputation and standing as a distinguished former American citizen by introducing two falsely procured Congressional Resolutions. These resolutions were evidently the source of deceptive information being infused into publications, one copyrighted by the Smithsonian Institution, and other presentations to the American public by television or other news media outlets. A more detailed explanation of the extent of the contamination of the early phases of this country's history as the leader in the exploration of space is revealed in a later chapter.

William E. Winterstein, Sr.

1

America's Voyage to the Moon

The story of mankind's greatest technological achievement of the 20th century—Man's voyage to the Moon—and how America secured for itself this distinctive heritage when it planted the stars and stripes in the Sea of Tranquility, includes not only the familiar facts of the fledgling U.S. space program, but also the untold story of unsung genius. Yet it was not, as we might conclude from the textbook version of the Apollo program, exclusively American genius. The story begins not in Houston, Texas, wrestled from a neighboring nation by American might; or even in the chain of launch complexes anchored in the Florida wetlands, subdued by persistence of the American will. Rather, the story begins in Germany, whose flag, but for a different fate, might have risen from the unstirring dust of *Die Lune*, the moon.

The rocket team that eventually placed U.S. astronauts on the Moon in 1969 first emerged in Germany in the late 1920s. Influenced in part by the German film *Woman in the Moon (Die Frau im Mond)* based on a Victor Hugo novel, a number of young German scientists and engineers were inspired to rocket research as the only viable way of sending man into space. Among them was Wernher von Braun, recognized universally as a pioneer of space flight.

If necessity is the mother of invention, war is arguably its father. War often supplies the expedient to technological breakthrough that is lacking in times of peace. It was the A-4 rocket, developed by von Braun and his team and known to the world as the V-2, which first promised to throw off the mantle of gravity. Pressed desperately into service as a weapon at the end of World War II, the A-4—46 feet long and 14 tons at liftoff—was designed by von Braun not to destroy, but rather to realize the destiny of manned space flight. Upon its first successful launch at Peenemünde, the far-sighted observation "There goes the world's first space vehicle" was heard.

The V-2, after a successful test launch, was still considered experimental by its creators. It was a masterpiece of precision requiring highly skilled labor in the fabrication of its many parts. At the time, it far exceeded the design capabilities of the best rocket engineers the U.S. or its allies possessed. Nothing on the American drawing boards approached the V-2 design. As sophisticated as it was however, the V-2 required many modifications before final acceptance as a standard production item whether for war or peacetime use. A clue to the intention of the rocket engineers at this point is suggested by an unusual action on the part of von Braun. When queried about the future use of the rocket, von Braun responded by publishing an article in a German scientific journal. He indicated that with careful development, such a rocket could be used for international mail delivery—specifically between Germany and the U.S.—*after the war.* The article, suggesting as it did a state of international relations unforeseen by the Reich, infuriated German Gestapo chief Heinrich Himmler so much that he jailed von Braun, charging him with 'lack of attention' to promoting the German war effort. Von Braun's vision of impending change would prove to be correct. Himmler's hope of a victorious war effort, regardless of the attention given to it, would not.

Under an iron winter sky at Yalta in February 1945, the allied partitioning of post-war Germany was planned. Borders were drawn roughly, without full knowledge of what lay within them. President Roosevelt, seemingly without consideration of the long-term effect of his actions, surrendered to the Soviets the area of Germany which contained the complete V-2 manufacturing facility at Nordhausen. American troops captured the facility intact, with no evidence of sabotage by the departing German forces, only to yield it to the Russians. Later at Potsdam, President Truman confirmed the U.S. commitment to post-war German boundaries. After five years of war, the world with the stroke of a pen would endure 45 years of ideological tug-of-war between East and West. **The threat to the West from ballistic missile attack was directly attributable to the Soviet possession of German rocket technology inherited at Yalta and Potsdam.** The V-2 factory once gutted and transported to the remote and closely guarded Ural Mountains of the Soviet Union, gave that country many years' advantage in the race for space, and the development of ballistic missile system technology.

A remarkably clear perspective of the U.S. concession to Russia of this technological bonanza is described in the newspaper clipping that follows. It was extracted from the only English newspaper printed in Saigon, South Viet Nam, where the author was advisor to the government from 1957 to 1960. The headline was eye-catching:

"Vital Missile Secrets Handed By Americans to Russians At The End Of World War II, A Former Red Colonel Claims New York, Jan. 21 (AP) A former lieutenant Colonel in Russia's Red Army claimed Monday that the Americans handed over to the Russians some of Hitler's vital missile secrets at the end of World War II."

Vital Missile Secrets Handed by Americans to Russians at the End of World War II, a Former Red Colonel Claims

New York, Jan 21 (AP) A former Lieutenant Colonel in Russia's Red Army claimed Monday that the American's handed over to the Russians some of Hitler's vital missile secrets at the end of World War II.

Backing up this claim, an American officer quotes high level orders he received in writing indicating at the same time that the U.S. held the Nazi V-2 rocket facility in Nordhausen, Germany, "all plans and equipment were to be left for the Soviets."

These statements are made in two articles in Look magazine in a series titled, "We gave the Russians the key to Sputnik." The assertion is made that "for 10 weeks, the American army had in its hands the rocket plans that gave the Russians their head start in the missile race."

Telling one story is Vladimir Shabinsky, the former Russian officer who, late in the war, worked on a special committee headed by Georgi Malenkov, later to rise and fall as premier. It had the job of removing plants, laboratories, and scientists into the Soviet Union.

The American account, by Look writer Peter Van Slingerland, quotes Major James P. Hamill of the U.S. Army Ordnance technical intelligence as saying that while he had orders "originated at a very high level" to leave the Nazi rocket plant and equipment for the Russians, "unofficially and off the record, I was told to remove as much material as I could, without making it obvious that we had looted the place."

As it turned out, Hamill was said by van Slingerland to have "managed to have picked up 100 nearly complete V-2s together with a large collection of plans, manuals, and other documents," and, in late May 1945 to have shipped 300 carloads of material from Nordhausen to Antwerp." From there, he accompanied his booty back to the U.S."

But, he said, what was left behind for the Russians "was enough to contribute perhaps 15 to 20% to the launching of their sputniks." He called the incident "American's costly blunder," and fixed the blame upon what he called "a series of fuzzy directives."

Shabinsky, once electrical superintendent of a Leningrad shipyard, fled across the iron curtain in 1947, and now, as an American citizen, is an editor-writer for radio liberation, which broadcast to the communist countries. He relates how, just after the Americans left, he stumbled upon the V-2 laboratory-arsenal in a deep cave near Nordhausen, "two to three stories high in places":

"I counted more than 1,000 machine tools for rocket production," he said in his story, related through Ellsworth Raymond, Russian expert for New York University.

"Everything was in complete order, as if the plant had shut down for the night. Storehouses were filled with spare rocket parts, alloy steel, copper sheets, and the most intricate radio-directional equipment.

"Contrary to my fear, nothing had been mined by either Americans or Germans." A Soviet colonel laughed and said: "The Americans gave us this. But in five or ten years, they will cry. Imagine when our rockets fly across the ocean." Shabinsky said he, himself, saw "the V-2 plant depart for Russia. Every spare scrap of raw material, every rocket (complete

or incomplete) was carefully packed in boxes labeled, USSR to the NKVD of the Volga-Dom."

The Russians also said that while the Americans left all of this V-2 equipment, plus an almost complete set of V-2 blueprints and designs for later rockets, including the intercontinental A-9/A10, they did blow up a hunting rifle factory in Suhl.

He told them how, by combing East Germany, and "by bribery, blackmail, threats, or outright kidnapping getting some out of West Germany, the Russians were able to obtain German rocket scientists." He said a chief scientist in Russia was able to get "a private automobile and the ruble equivalent of 2,500 dollars a month."

Later at a Russian military party in Berlin, said Shabinsky, a lieutenant colonel named Tarakanov shouted: "What fools these Americans are."

Van Slingerland wrote that the Americans, in leaving Nordhausen a few hours before the Russians arrived, "debated blowing up the plant, but since they lacked the authority, they felt forced to leave it to be captured by the Russians."

He placed the blame on the directive that filtered down from the Yalta conference to be put into decrees by General Dwight D. Eisenhower and acted upon by lesser commanders.

Members of the von Braun rocket team were also fully aware of the implications of the U.S. surrender of the V-2 manufacturing facility. Upon their arrival in the U.S., their chosen nation of residence, they were very eager to resume meaningful rocket research on behalf of their new home to protect it from future enemies, mindful that the Soviets now posed the most serious threat. One can imagine their chagrin when the U.S. Congress failed to appropriate meaningful funding for rocket research, or to provide adequate research facilities. Despite this alarming setback, the rocket team, so recently removed from the hectic pace of wartime Germany, did not sit idly by, but plunged in once more to recover lost technology, and lost time.

The original organization overseeing operation of the German rocket team at Fort Bliss, Texas, was a satellite of the Office Chief of Ordnance, Washington, DC. As such, they were effectively guests of the commanding general of Fort Bliss. Major James P. Hamill was commanding officer of the Sub-Office (Rocket), and the author was commanding officer of the 9330th Technical Service Unit, directly under the Sub-Office. The main contingent of the German team was stationed at Fort Bliss, with a small unit detached to the White Sands Proving Ground 40 miles to the northeast near Las Cruces, New Mexico. White Sands Proving Ground and was now home to 100 captured V-2 rockets removed from Germany by Major Hamill under the noses of the Red Army prior to their take-over of the V-2 plant.

The housing and work facilities at Fort Bliss were primitive at best. The rocket team was billeted in a remote corner of the base, near the cemetery. The barracks were unfinished on the inside and deteriorating badly on the outside. U.S. Army support troops, most of them veterans of the European theater, were housed in the same area of the base as the German rocket team, but in separate barracks.

The combined team soon acquired additional workspace in the annex of the William Beaumont Hospital adjacent to the area. The Annex was of temporary wooden construction built during the war to house overflow patients from the main hospital. For the purposes of research, assembly of sensitive electronics, and precision manufacturing, the work facilities at Fort Bliss were wholly inadequate. Workspaces were impossible to seal against the frequent area sandstorms, and nothing approaching today's high technology 'clean' rooms was made available.

The detachment of scientists at White Sands Proving Ground had marginally better working conditions. Their task was to refurbish the 100 V-2s acquired by Major Hamill, and to launch them over the New Mexico desert with experiment payloads onboard developed by the Fort Bliss team. Refurbishing of the V-2s was accomplished under the supervision of Arthur Rudolph. Launch activities were conducted by Dr. Kurt Debus, later to become the first launch director at Cape Canaveral. The initial launches were performed using captured equipment from the German Wehrmacht. The first launch platform consisted of a single concrete pad. The launch control 'facility,' some distance away, was simply an oversized foxhole dug into the desert sand, reinforced with sand bags. Such were the humble beginnings of America's entry into the Space Age.

In spite of congressional unwillingness to provide appreciable funding for research, the German rocket team made do with equipment and materials on hand. The Bumper Program, as it was known, advanced rocket technology literally to a second stage. By adding a smaller solid-fueled U.S. Army WAC Corporal missile to the nose cone of the V-2, a rudimentary two-stage vehicle was effectively created. By adding instrumentation to the second stage, which was recovered by parachute following each flight, experiments were conducted to study high altitude environments.[1] Among the sources of makeshift materials available at Fort Bliss, and adjacent Air Force Biggs Field, was the extensive salvage yards located at the bases. The resourceful rocket teams were able to fashion primitive but usable laboratory equipment from cast-off military parts. Still technically enemies, these dedicated men displayed a vigorous patriotism for their adopted homeland that was moving to behold. No longer puppets and virtual prisoners of the Gestapo, America's newest and brightest scientific minds set about creating from the ruin of war what they had intended at the beginning: the peaceful application of technology to the challenges of space flight.

---

[1]During one of these flights, a camera mounted in the WAC Corporal revealed the unmistakable curvature of the horizon, confirming to humankind for the first time that the earth was truly round.

2

V-2—How It Affected Getting to the Moon

In order to grasp the magnitude of the moon landing, it is important to understand the events that made it possible. The lunar mission could not have been achieved without the development of an accurate, instrument-guided rocket. The development of the original A-4, or V-2 rocket as wartime Europe and America knew it, made it possible for the trip to the moon. In addition, the same core team developed the V-2 rocket in wartime Germany that also placed U.S. astronauts on the Moon in 1969. A V-2 rocket, on display at Fort Bliss, Texas, is shown in a following figure. The Saturn V rocket that evolved from the V-2 is shown later in the book.

The first successful launch of the V-2 occurred at Peenemünde, Germany, on October 3, 1942. The following is the eyewitness account given by the former commander at Peenemünde, General Walter Dornberger (translation courtesy of Martin Hollmann):

The command for lift off, cleared for launch, was given at Test Stand VII as I laid my microphone down. It was a beautiful clear sky today at Peenemünde in northern Germany. I could see the plush evergreen forest and the isle of Greifswalder Oie in the distance.

The A-4 rocket stood erect on its launch pad and it was still connected to the cables leading to the launch bunker.

The motor, guidance and control engineers stood in the launch bunker and concentrated on the multitude of instrument readings from the manometer, frequency oscilloscope, volt and ammeter, red, white and green lights. Their hands were fixed to the switches that controlled the launch. In one corner, the Siemens engineers were adjusting the TV camera while the telephone was squawking. Over the loudspeaker, you could hear a conference call between the launch managers, instrumentation, and power supply and launch responsible engineers. Finally, the checkout of the electric system, stabilization and control system, all valves, pressure tanks and plumbing lines was complete.

My eyes gave a quick glance to the roof of the assembly and development complex. There stood military commanders, Commander Stegmaier, Dr. von Braun and Dr. Steinhoff, Chief of the onboard electronic packages, control, and instrumentation. A small distance from this group I recognized the personnel from the supersonic wind tunnel and Drs. Hermann and Kurzweg. It was their job to independently follow the rocket with 10-x magnification, precision binoculars. Hundreds of people who had worked so hard and diligently on the A-4 for the last 10 years were standing in the streets and eager to witness this launch.

The control and rate gyros in the rocket were spinning. Over the loudspeaker came 'X-3 and counting.' Still 3 minutes left before lift off. The TV screen showed the beautiful, glistening, long and slender shape of the rocket which had been aerodynamically optimized in every respect. I could sense the pressure rise in the oxygen tanks. 'X-1 and counting' came over the loudspeakers as the tension mounted.

A smoke flare whistled through the sky to show the wind profile. Only 10 seconds before lift off. Then came ignition.

The power plant engineer had switched the first of three levers on as smoke and sparks spewed out of the rocket. First stage.

Then a wonderful red-yellow flame shot out of the rocket nozzle producing 16,000 lbs of thrust. The thrust of the 1st stage was insufficient to lift the 29,700 lb rocket.

After 3 seconds, lift off. The power-plant engineer had switched the third lever and now more clouds of smoke and debris flew in all directions. The umbilical cables had been released and the rocket was self-sustained. At 4,000 rpm and 540 hp, the turbo-pump provides a pressure of 3 atmospheres and 33 gallons of fuel and oxygen a second to the rocket motor.

After one second, a thrust of 50,000 lb accelerated the rocket majestically and steadily skyward at acceleration equal to a falling rock. Smoke from the lifting rocket continued to fill the TV screen.

Through my binoculars, I looked north as I watched the rocket climb. The engine plume was sharp and confined in shape. The first critical moment had passed. The rocket was stable in all axes. It did not rotate about its longitudinal axis and the black and white pattern painted on its side was visibly unchanged.

Thunder filled the sky. Only now did the engine's full volume and thunder reach our ears. The sound was deafening and the earth shook beneath our feet.

The A-4 had reached an altitude of 5,000 feet. Exhaust gasses reach a velocity of 6,560 ft/sec and a temperature of 5,000 degrees F.

The rocket engine would develop over 650,000 hp before the end of its burn. After 4.5 seconds, the vertical trajectory changed as the nose of the A-4 began to gently pitch over. I watched breathlessly as the accelerating missile reached a pitch over angle of 45 degrees, which gave it its optimum-range-trajectory. Besides the thunder of the engine, I could hear the time count, 14—15—16 . . . And a steady, low monotone hum. It was the acoustic measure of the rocket's velocity. It grew from a dull sound to a steady whistle as the velocity increased.

A microwave station located 8 miles from the launch pad transmitted the exact location of the rocket. "19—20—21. . . . The time count continued.

With a steady roar, the rocket flew faster and faster. It had reached a speed of 671 mph. Within the next second, it would exceed the speed of sound. 'Speed of sound' was the next announcement over the loudspeaker. My heart missed several beats because little was known about the dangers of breaking the sound barrier.

On this day, the 3rd of October 1942, history was made. It was the first time that a liquid fueled rocket exceeded the speed of sound.

At an altitude of 33,000 feet, the A-4 reached a speed of Mach 2 according to the velocity signal. In the distance, I could see the steadily climbing, white, and black missile.

Suddenly, out of the clear blue sky came a shock. A white trail was spotted behind the rocket explosion. Then the loudspeaker announced 'Nonsense, those are contrails.' Then, 'She is falling!' Then, 'No, the oxygen valve just opened! 'But I just saw the fins fly off! The steady drone of the velocity meter assured us that everything was OK. She is flying on!

For the first time the world had witnessed the frozen Blitz or jagged contrails that a rocket traveling at over 2,240 mph exhibits. 49—50— 51 . . . Thrust termination was approaching. Several conditions had to be met for this to happen. First, the correct azimuth angle had to be obtained. Second, the desired velocity must have been reached. Finally, the tangential attitude of the desired trajectory must be achieved. The preprogrammed rate gyros and autopilot would assure that these conditions are met and would turn off the engine. A ground based microwave station also transmitted the exact position and attitude of the rocket.

Suddenly a thought came to my mind. Before the war, a number of magazines had predicted that the upper atmosphere contained large amounts of hydrogen. This meant that the rocket would explode at any moment. However, the explosion never happened.

With my strong binoculars and on this clear day, I could still see the small body of the missile at a distance of 19 miles. 54 . . . ! Someone shouted Engine shut off! However, I could still hear the increasing pitch of the velocity meter and smoke coming from the rocket nozzle.

57—58 . . .! Now the engine was shut down as all of the valves were remotely closed. The A-4 was traveling at 3,356 mph.

With a deep breath of relief, I put my glasses down. The test was a success. For the first time in the history of humankind, we had launched an automatically controlled, rocket propelled, projectile, on a predefined trajectory to the upper edges of the atmosphere and into the vacuum of space. For this day, we had worked for 10 years.

I am not ashamed to admit that I had tears of joy in my eye. I could not speak but I could see that Colonel Zanssen had the same feelings. I could see the tears in his eyes. He stuck his hand out, I grabbed it, and we shook. Then our feelings overwhelmed us. We yelled and hugged each other like small kids. As I looked around, I could see that everyone else was yelling, shaking hands, hugging and dancing. I am still surprised today that no one fell off the roof tops on which they were standing. I quickly went down to my car to drive to Test Stand VII to congratulate my loyal friends and co-workers who had worked so hard to make this launch a success. I could hear the steady whistle of the velocity meter and the monotone of the time counter. 89—90—91—92 . . . .!

As I stepped into the street, the technical team rushed me and we all shook hands. I grabbed von Braun and pushed him into my car as we sped at an illegal speed to Test Stand VII. As we approached the building, we could see that workers had formed a circle around Dr. Thiel. Everyone wanted to tell him what they had witnessed during the flight. Even today, I still see Dr. Thiel in front of me. Behind sharp eyeglasses his intelligent and scientific eyes sparkled. He had a pipe in his mouth. As we shook hands, he made numerous suggestions on how we could improve the rocket. I knew that even on this momentous evening he would sit at his table and write down his observations and the many suggestions that he had. He was a relentless worker/scientist that knew no bounds.

I had to ask for silence. The test was not over. Any second now the rocket, at a speed of 3,356 mph would reenter the earth atmosphere, which would slow the rocket to 1,800 mph. What would happen when the air-friction would increase the skin temperatures to 1,250 °F? We did not know if the rocket would survive. 295—296! Impact. The velocity meter produced no sound. We knew now that we had succeeded.

That evening I held a small party and I gave a small speech of praise to my friends: History of technology will show that, for the first time, a man made vehicle with a structural weight of 28,373 pounds at lift-off, traveled 120 miles with a lateral deviation of 2.5 miles. Your names, my friends, are associated with this feat. We achieved this feat with an automatic control system. A velocity of 3,356 mph and acceleration of 5gs was achieved. We have demonstrated that an unmanned or manned air vehicle can break the sound barrier. We achieved an altitude of 300,000 feet and have thus broken all altitude records. Our rocket was the first vehicle to enter space and return to earth. We have developed and demonstrated a rocket engine that can be used for space travel. This 3rd of October 1942 is the first day for the beginning of space travel!

However, as long as there is war, our efforts will be used to produce weapons. However, the day will hopefully come soon when we can use the rocket for the purpose of space travel and peace!

This version of the first launch, told by the commander of Peenemünde during WWII, clearly gives evidence of the primary goal of the team that developed the V-2—to achieve space flight. The development of the rocket had started in 1932, before Hitler came to power, and was not envisioned by the designers to ever be a weapon of war.

The important element that associates the successful first flight of the A-4, or the V-2, as we know it, and the triumph of Man's first flight to the Moon, is the basic design of the rocket engine of the V-2. The multiple engines that powered the Saturn V rocket were only vastly up-scaled, and improved, versions of the V-2 rocket engine. The primary design features of the rocket engines used for the lunar mission originated at Peenemünde, Germany, in 1942.

Vehicle	Height (ft)	Lift-off Weight (lb)	Engine Thrust at Lift-off (lb)
V-2	46	28,373	50,000
Saturn-V	363	6,423,000	7,650,000

Figure 1 **Comparison of the V-2 and Saturn V vehicle stats**

Figure 2 **A V-2 at Fort Bliss, Texas**

3

Before America

The early years of the German rocket team—from the Allied victory in 1945 and the creation of the team, to the desert country of Fort Bliss, Texas, to the rolling hills of Huntsville, Alabama—are remembered by team member Dr. Ernst Stuhlinger from his following selection of speeches titled *From Peenemünde to America*, and *The Rocket People Come to Huntsville.*

Around 1926, a 14-year old teenager in Germany, Wernher von Braun, decided that he would devote his life's work to the development of powerful rockets with precision guidance systems that would be able to travel into space, far enough to reach the moon, and even some of the planets. After several years of systematic work, he realized that all his efforts would be futile if he could not back them up by a powerful funding source. In 1932, he accepted a contract offered by the German Reichswehr that was interested in von Braun's rocket ideas because they could see long-range artillery weapons. The Rocket Development Center at Peenemünde was established, and in October 1942, in the middle of WWII, the guided missile A-4 (or V-2 as it would become known) achieved its first successful long-range test flight along the coastline of the Baltic Sea in northern Germany.

In spite of extreme efforts to keep the project secret, Peenemünde soon became the target of British and American air raids. The bombs indicated to the rocket people that the Allies knew what was happening on their little island in the Baltic Sea.

After six long years, the war finally came to its end. The mood of depression and hopelessness was overwhelming. Germany lay in ruins. Not only the buildings and installations, but also all the many infrastructures of a functioning communal system were destroyed. American, British, and French troops poured into the country from the west, Russian troops from the east. At a rare moment during that time, von Braun made a remark to some of his close co-workers: "I just cannot believe that all our work to develop rockets for the future should have been in vain. I have a hunch that at some time in the future, those of us who are fortunate to survive this ordeal will have a chance to continue our work, and to achieve some solid success perhaps, who knows, in America."

Well, it so happened, that at about the same time a similar thought came alive in the minds of some individuals who had the power to decide, and to act. Besides that power, they had the vision and the wisdom to realize that there was the opportunity for a productive cooperation between individuals of two nations that—it is true—were presently locked up in a bitter, relentless, and destructive war, but who had been on friendly terms during the most of the past 300 years. After all, no less than 55 million of today's American citizens derive their origin from German immigrants who came here during the previous three or four generations.

During the final weeks and days of the war, special units of the Allied Forces searched and found many of the scattered remains of the mysterious Peenemünde rocket project in Germany. The Chief of U.S. Army Ordnance Technical Intelligence, Colonel Holger N. Toftoy, had been ordered by his superiors in the Pentagon to organize a "Special Mission V-2" with the objective to locate parts and components for about 100 complete V-2 missiles, and to ship them from occupied Germany to the United States. Toftoy had several very efficient helpers, among them Major Robert Staver, Major James Hamill, and Dr. Richard Porter, and he soon could also count on the cooperation of rocket people from Peenemünde who wanted to see the products of their work in the hands of the Americans rather than in the hands of the Russians.

At that time, an idea took hold and began to solidify in the minds of the special mission V-2 people, an idea that was vigorously spearheaded by Colonel Toftoy, who then broached it with his superiors in Washington. The idea was to transfer a number of the Peenemünde specialists, in person, to the United States, and to have them continue their rocket development work there. Surely, such a wholesale transfer at the end of the war of live men, who had worked on a specific weapons system, would be an absolute novum (new twist) in modern military history, but why not? Toftoy pointed out that this transfer could and should be done on a voluntary gentleman-like basis. A cable was then drafted for General Eisenhower's signature which contained the words "have in custody over 400 top research personnel of Peenemünde, developed V-2, thinking of the scientific directors of this group is 25 years ahead of U.S. recommend that 100 of very best men of this research organization be evacuated to U.S. immediately." President Truman approved the recommended action and Col. Toftoy was ordered to organize the roundup of former Peenemünde rocket men, who by that time were spread out over much of war-torn ruined Germany. A number of those men, many of them with their families, were taken to Witzenhausen, a small town near the geographical center of Germany. I was personally still at a town near Weimar where I was found by one of Toftoy's officers and told to stay put until further notice. Therefore, I met Toftoy for the first time only years later in the United States, but von Braun and others had told me of the exciting events of those days.

When Toftoy first saw the Peenemünde folks at Wittsenhausen, many of them with their wives and children, and all of them tired, hungry, and emaciated from six years of relentless war, he ordered milk from an Army depot for the children. That is how he introduced himself to the Germans. Then he started long discussions with von Braun about rockets and guided missiles; about test ranges, and proving grounds, and about human voyages to the moon, and rocket-driven spacecraft to some of the planets. Surely, Col Toftoy was primarily a soldier, a West Pointer, but he was also a very broad-minded citizen of the world and above all, he was a warm-hearted, caring human being. Col., later General, Toftoy continued for some years to be in charge of the rocket people from Peenemünde. More and more he became a father figure for us. In turn, he sometimes simply called us 'my children' that made us proud. The first list that Toftoy that and von Braun worked out at Witzenhausen as a potential nucleus for a new American-based rocket development team, contained about 350 names. "Absolutely no way" almighty Washington replied "not more than 100." Well the final list had 127 names. When asked to explain, Toftoy said, "Sorry I was never good at mathematics. In fact, I never could count real well."

[Author's note: Of interest to a later subject—why the Soviets beat us into space—is the fact that while America absorbed 127 members of the core German rocket design team into its fledgling space program, the Soviet Union conscripted 271! According to General Toftoy, this blunder in the appreciation of critical German human resources aggravated the existing 25-year gap that separated the U.S./Soviet, and German teams. Add to this the fact that the U.S. surrendered sophisticated German equipment and tools to the Soviets, and you will appreciate the level of concern for a potentially dangerous imbalance of power expressed by the German Rocket team.]

The people on the Toftoy/von Braun list were then contacted by American officers and they were invited to become members of Project Paperclip, to be transported to the U.S., and to work for the American Government on a preliminary contract for one-half year, with the Government's option to extend the contract at the end of the half-year. That was the minimum of the contractual arrangement offered to the Germans. It was voluntary with no pressure or compulsion exercised by the Americans upon the Germans.

In my own case, I was contacted by a U.S. captain in October 1945. At that time, I had moved to Tübingen, where my parents lived, and where I held a position as assistant professor at the University in 1936. When I returned to Tübingen, after the end of the war in 1945, the university's department of physics accepted me again in my old position. It was there and then when the captain visited me and offered me an invitation from the U.S. War Department to come to the United States. First I asked him what I would do in the U.S. "Build rockets," he said, "continue the work you did at Peenemünde, and whatever else the American Government deems appropriate. Your friend von Braun is already there and he is collecting former co-workers around him." I asked the captain to allow me some time to think it over. He readily agreed. "OK, I will be back in a week from now," he said. Therefore, I spent a week of intense thinking mixed with many talks with my parents, friends, relatives, and colleagues at the university. All the aspects of emigrating under those special circumstances were considered and discussed. Would it be right to leave the country at this time? Would we rather be needed at home where a gigantic task of reconstruction was waiting for every able-bodied young man? Could we hope that our move to America and our willingness to live and to work with our former enemies may help us to build a bridge, however tenuous at first, from people to people and to convince our new American colleagues that not every German was an ardent Nazi? Could we hope that Americans would accept us as co-workers and take us at our face values, in spite of all the war propaganda that had painted a very different picture of the Germans? Could we hope that we would work as colleagues in a joint program of developing modern rockets and promoting space flight? Could those of us who had families be joined by their wives and children soon? Could we hope to be permitted to send gift packages to our loved ones at home where hunger and deprivation were still rampant? There were questions with no end. Immigrating to any country other than America would have been a different prospect for us young German scientists and engineers in 1945. Compared with European nations, America was different. It was a young nation and land in which the idea of freedom together with the striving for progress and for equal rights for everybody had moved closer to reality than everywhere else. In this process of making democratic ideals work, a nation of remarkable economic strength and political stability had come into existence. The powerful flow of immigrants from Germany and other European countries during the past 300 years had certainly contributed its share to this development. Immigration of young Americans to America after WWII would not merely be a move from one country into another, it would be step in an ongoing natural demographic evolution, a reaching out from one nation into another one, to which that nation had been related for 300 years by strong ties of kinship in body and mind. When the American captain returned to my home later in October, I happily accepted his invitation, and signed up for the voyage across the Atlantic.

Von Braun and a handful of his co-workers had been shipped to the United States by airplane in September 1945. The rest of the team arrived on 5 military ships between late 1945 and mid-1946. Some of those who had been invited preferred to stay in Germany to pursue an academic career or to takeover their father's business, but a total of 118 young Germans were given a temporary home in the barracks of a former Army hospital annex in Fort Bliss, Texas.

The four years we spent at Fort Bliss and nearby White Sands, New Mexico, were in essence a disappointment. Besides launching a number of old V-2s that had been brought over from Germany (and whose empty warheads were filled with a remarkable assortment of scientific instruments for high altitude research) we were not given a development project commensurate with our work in Peenemünde during the previous eight years. Von Braun complained to our commander, Maj. Hamill, only to be told, "We put you fellows on ice for later use." That later use came in 1949 when the Korean War loomed on the horizon. An order arrived from Washington "Build us a guided missile similar to the V-2 but bigger and better, but be real quick." Together with this order came a decision to move our entire team (which at that time had been doubled in size by the advent of young American colleagues) to Huntsville in Alabama.

Our move to the city of Huntsville in the summer of 1950 was certainly the most significant and the most fortunate event in the history of the German rocket team in the United States. To us it was the definite proof that the American Government wanted us to stay here. A time of extreme activity began for us, coupled with a phenomenal growth of the city of Huntsville, far beyond what could be described in a brief luncheon talk. It was in Huntsville where we developed the Redstone, the Jupiter, and the Pershing and launched the first American satellite. Beginning in 1960, after the group had been transferred from the Army to NASA, we developed and launched the Saturn V rocket for the Apollo moon project, followed by the Skylab and the Hubble telescope and we contributed substantially to the shuttle and the international space station projects.

We former Germans were overjoyed and really touched when not only hundreds, but thousands of young American engineers and scientists joined us in our endeavor to develop rockets and spacecraft, first for the armed forces, and then for the exploration and utilization of the vast expanses of space. There was not only a spirit of solid cooperation and joint effort; there was the spontaneous growth of close and genuine friendships many of which are still strong and lively today after more than 50 years. In each of our many projects, American industries played very substantial roles. GE, Chrysler, Boeing, Pratt and Whitney, Lockheed, Martin, Convair, North American Rockwell, McDonnell Douglas, General Dynamics, Grumman, Fairchild, TRW, Honeywell, Ford Instrument, IBM—all of these companies and corporations and many more established their office, and even some manufacturing places, in Huntsville. Several new companies arose in our city, such as Spacecraft Incorporated, which has reached worldwide renown in a rocket-like business ascent. Along with Huntsville's industrial growth, many other branches of a healthy community sprouted. Our young university became a full-size academic establishment. The hospital grew into an impressive complex. A space and rocket center, combining a large museum with a space camp came into being. Huntsville's airport became a large and busy place for passenger as well as international freight traffic. The cityscape of Huntsville changed into that of a modern large city within a dozen years. Population grew from 14,000 to almost 180,000. With justified pride, Huntsvillian's called their city the space capital of the universe. Yet, in the middle of this fantastic growth, Huntsville kept its original charm as a beautiful southern city to the fullest extent. The impact of the modern age of technology did not change its innate character as a place where it simply is a pleasure to live and to work, and to raise children. Huntsville citizens, the original ones and the many newcomers, took the fabulous growth in stride and kept their city on a high level of health and prosperity. We original immigrants from Peenemünde received full-fledged American citizenship in the mid-'50s. Our center, named the George C. Marshall Spaceflight Center, in honor of one of the greatest Americans of all time, counted 8,000 members at the height of the Saturn-Apollo project. By that time, we really felt that the United States had become our place to live and to work, the land and the people to whom we wanted to offer our loyalty as good citizens, just as millions of Germans had done before us. The city of Huntsville would certainly be our beloved home from now on. The daring and courageous experiment to transfer a team of young experts from Germany to America at the end of WWII had proven to be a brilliant success.

4

Coming to America

History, as revealed in this book, will place the beginning of America's Space Age to the events which occurred to a small group of German rocket scientists who arrived at Fort Bliss, Texas, in late 1945. It was there, that the majority of the group determined to stay together, so that they could achieve their lifelong dream to conquer space for exploration into the realm of the unknown. The outlook at this time was most discouraging and seemed impossible to accomplish 'Mission Impossible.' Through the following years their dedication resulted in considerable individual financial sacrifice (as related in a future chapter), to accomplish this victory for their beloved adopted country, the United States of America, 24 years after their arrival in this country.

The humble beginnings at Fort Bliss should properly be regarded as the threshold of America's emergence in history as the leader among nations in the exploration of outer space. "Humble" is perhaps understated, considering the almost primitive conditions encountered by the team.

U.S. Army intelligence realized that the development of the V-2 (known in Germany as the A-4) rocket was far more advanced in design and performance than anything produced by the best of U.S. industry at the time. Consequently, President Truman prudently invited the German rocket scientists to the U.S. to assist this country in the field of rocket research following the war.

Administration of the German team was under the direct supervision of the Office Chief of Ordnance, Washington D.C. A sub-office was established in October 1945 at Fort Bliss, Texas. The first Army officers assigned to this organization were Major James P. Hamill, who was in charge of the Sub-Office (Rocket), and the author, who was the first Commanding Officer of the 9330 Ordnance Technical Service Unit, falling under the Sub-Office, Rocket. The 9330th was responsible for the housing, security, and general welfare of the German team. Very strict secrecy was exercised for a little over a year after the arrival of the Germans. In view of a general, prevailing anti-German sentiment so soon after the war, this secrecy was well advised.

The German team and the 9330th were housed in a remote corner of Fort Bliss, near the cemetery. The barracks at that time were in disrepair resulting from disuse. Military and German personnel were housed in the same barracks area, and ate at the same time in the same mess hall. General Homer, the commandant of Fort Bliss, issued orders that our area of the Fort was strictly "Off Limits" to all personnel, except those who were authorized to enter the area, such as service personnel for utilities, etc.

A veil of secrecy was closely pulled over all aspects concerning the presence of the Germans at Fort Bliss. All military personnel involved in the project were ordered not to discuss the operation with outsiders. The Germans were restricted to the barracks area, unless accompanied by military personnel. Family members of the 9330th were similarly prohibited from discussing the activities of their husbands. No photographs were to be taken of the German team members. This level of security remained in effect until December 1946, over a year after the German team had arrived at Fort Bliss. At that time a news release finally made public that, the U.S. had an ex-patriot German rocket team and that the team, rather than the Army, was responsible for test firing of captured V-2s at White Sands Proving Ground, New Mexico.

Dr. Wernher von Braun, leader of the rocket team, readily convinced me of his ambition to go to the moon. His team had already conquered the problem of producing a liquid fueled rocket engine that would not burn up after a few seconds' flight. An examination of the mighty Saturn V engine—the rocket that took our astronauts to the Moon—will reveal that it was an improved version of the V-2, on a much larger scale.

The original orders establishing the activities at Fort Bliss were sent by teletype from Office Chief of Ordnance, Washington D.C., to Colonel Eddy, Aberdeen Proving Ground, on 4 October 1945. This Teletype was rated Priority "A," which called for the immediate movement, within 24 hours, of the first contingent of personnel to support Project Fireball in the vicinity of Fort Bliss, Texas.

Project Fireball was eventually divided into two organizational elements, The Sub-Office, Rocket, Fort Bliss, and the 9330 Ordnance Technical Service Unit. The original orders activating Fireball are shown in Appendix Fireball Orders.

As Commanding Officer of the 9330th, one of the most serious problems I faced was also an urgent problem. Most of the enlisted men in the 9330th were veterans from Europe, and had been engaged in combat with German soldiers only months prior to their assignment at Fort Bliss. I gave a number of briefings to these troops urging them to cooperate with the German team. The briefings were successful, and one year later, the 9330th received a Meritorious Service Unit award citing *"accomplishment of difficult tasks."* A copy of the citation is located in Appendix Meritorious Service Unit Plague.

The arrival of 61 rocket team scientists coincided with the arrival of the 9330th support troops in early December 1945. This posed an interesting dilemma, since the move was to be made under tight security and with utmost secrecy. The movement was scheduled to take place by rail from Fort Strong, Massachusetts, to Fort Bliss, Texas. At that time rail was an accepted and economical mode of travel. Air travel was expensive, and no transport planes of sufficient number or size were available. To complicate matters, the influx of returning European veterans congested rail depot waiting rooms in the rush to be home for Christmas. See Appendix on Rail Movement of 61 Civilians.

I was ordered to the Office Chief of Ordnance Washington, D.C., for a briefing on the plan for the move. Selected railway officials were also briefed on the plan. Four Pullman cars were selected for movement of the rocket team. One of the cars was stripped of seats. This provided space for boxes containing drawings, and an assortment of gauges and tools. The other three cars provided passenger accommodation. The four cars were to be placed at the extreme rear of the train, with the dining car being placed immediately in front, separating the cars from those containing the unknowing U.S. veterans. The plan dictated that when all other passengers on the train had eaten, the Germans were to be ushered in for their meals. At no time in the journey were other cars to be added to rear of the train. Two Ordnance Office captains were assigned to me to assist in the move.

A serious incident occurred on the first day out, following the train's 9:00 p.m. departure from Boston. During the night, several cars loaded with returning European veterans were switched to the rear of the train. The next morning, GIs passing through cars occupied by the rocket team on their way to the dining car encountered the Germans. Some of these veterans had been delayed in their travels as the result of competition for transportation resources, and were in less than civil moods. In the near riot condition that ensued, I appealed to senior non-commissioned and officers for help, explaining what the move was about, adding that it was in the best interest of the U.S. The situation was calmed, and at the next rail station, the cars containing the veterans were promptly switched to a position ahead of the dining car. The rest of the trip was accomplished without any further serious incident.

A humorous account with two older women is mentioned in Chapter 7.

Upon arrival at Fort Bliss, the scientists were promptly settled into their barracks area. Because the 9330th troops and the Germans ate at the same time in the same mess hall, the issue of American GIs serving on KP—already an onerous task—arose. This matter was solved by importing German prisoners from a nearby Prisoner of War Camp, so that Germans were served by other Germans. It is easy, in the enlightened 21st century, to forget the patriotic—or merely nationalist—tensions in America embodied in attitudes toward persons of German or Japanese descent. Especially among members of the military, these sentiments affected the routine administrative duties associated with housing and transporting the German rocket team in the otherwise insulated American southwest.

At first, shared-mealtime logistics issues were solved by voluntary segregation of German team members and American GIs into separate areas of the mess hall. The need for this separation abruptly changed on Christmas Day, 1945, when Jim Hamill and I managed to provide some beer to supplement the Christmas dinner. These extra-official 'rations,' combined with the fact that this was the first Christmas Day in recent memory that the world was not at war, served to dissolve pre-existing tensions quickly, and permanently. After that dinner, an ever-increasing camaraderie developed between the GIs and the Germans.

The starting pay for the German rocket scientists was a per diem of $6.00. Of this, $1.20 was deducted for food and lodging, leaving $4.80 per day, or $144.00 per month. This was all that was authorized under the terms of a "Short Term Contract" until the early part of 1947, when a regular contract with appropriate pay schedules was affected.

Life at Fort Bliss for the scientists was predictably regulated. They were strictly forbidden to leave the barracks area unless escorted by one or more military personnel. The standing orders for both military and scientific personnel on their shopping visits to El Paso required that they move in very small groups, remain inconspicuous, avoid large crowds, and refrain from involvement in public disturbance. Restrictions designed to safeguard the fact of their presence remained in effect for over a year, until December 4, 1946, when the War Department made the news public.

While these security regulations were understandable given the circumstances, we did as much as possible to ensure appropriate freedoms and dignities. Military buses were obtained from the Fort

Bliss motor pool, driven by our own drivers, to take groups of the scientists to the countryside or places of scenic interest on weekends.

My wife Elizabeth and I hosted Dr. Wernher von Braun and several other scientists for informal family dinners once and sometimes twice a week. The dinners were very simple, intended largely to relieve them of the tedium of the barracks environment. In addition to hosting the dinners, we often took Wernher out for Sunday drives into the countryside. On one such occasion, we visited Carlsbad Caverns, New Mexico. We also let him drive our car during some portions of these trips so that he might enjoy a greater sense of normalcy and freedom. The friendship between Wernher and I became very close during those early years at Fort Bliss. We had numerous discussions on subjects both personal to scientific. We were very candid in these discussions, and soon discovered that our childhoods were very similar in that we were both inquisitive about rockets. Some of his first experiments involved toy cars propelled horizontally by small pyrotechnic rockets.

See Chapter 7 for additional youthful accounts.

Wernher spoke a lot about how much he loved America, particularly the freedoms enjoyed by its citizens, compared to the nightmare suffered by the Germans during World War II. He also was a victim of the Gestapo. He was imprisoned by Himmler for failure to be "attentive" to the war effort. Wernher was in prison several weeks until General Dornberger, von Braun's boss, pleaded with Hitler, correctly arguing that the continued imprisonment of von Braun jeopardized the further development of the V-2.

Among the many discussions I had with Wernher during those days was the theme of space exploration. The first step, naturally, was a voyage to the Moon. This was his lifelong ambition. At that time, the outlook for any rocket research for such a project was unfavorable. Development efforts for meaningful rocket research for U.S. national defense were minimal. Congress was very reticent about funding rocket research. It appeared that the attitude in Congress was "the war is over; rocket weapons research is unnecessary, send the Germans back."

In the summer of 1946, I asked Wernher "If we could give you all of the money you wanted, how much, and how long, would it take you to put Man on the Moon?" Several weeks later, he said "Give us three billion dollars, and ten years, and we will go to the moon and back." At the time, I thought it was merely very interesting information, never dreaming of their importance.

It was fifteen years later that similar words, concerning the time frame at least, were uttered by President Kennedy to a joint session of Congress on May 25th 1961. "Before this decade is out," described the time frame. Prior to President Kennedy's address to Congress, Dr. von Braun had convinced the President that the trip to the Moon was technologically possible. This further convinced me that Wernher must have done a lot of planning for a Moon mission, years before he gave me the same information concerning the time element in 1946.

It is probable that he did not have his mind entirely on the German war effort during development of the V-2. During our informal discussions, Wernher related problems that his team had with the V-2 in Germany. When the V-2 was deployed by the Wehrmacht, it was still under development. At that time, it was the most complex technological piece of rocket equipment in the world. The initial development of the V-2 was accomplished at Peenemünde, Germany on the Baltic Sea. After the British nearly leveled Peenemünde during bombing raids, the production of the missiles was conducted in the underground factory near Nordhausen, Germany. Most of the workers, about 5,000, provided by the German government, were concentration camp inmates. Arthur Rudolph, one of von Braun's chief engineers, was the production manager of the V-2 facility, which was only one of the three manufacturing facilities at the Mittelwerk, near Nordhausen. Rudolph would have preferred skilled German civilian technicians to meet the almost impossible production schedules. Skilled German labor, however, was diverted to other areas of the war effort.

Rudolph did have about 5000 civilian engineers and technicians at his disposal. The V-2 development schedule was very aggressive with work conducted around the clock (two 12-hour shifts), seven days a week. Rudolph attempted to reduce this to three overlapping 8-hour shifts per day, so that his workers could get adequate rest, but was flatly rejected by the SS, who strictly controlled all work schedules, and supervision of the prisoners. This presented a production problem since the V-2 was a highly complex missile, requiring expertise in a number of disciplines for its manufacture. Thus for an example a lathe operator, working to extreme tolerances, may find that precision is elusive after an exhausting day. Another difficulty, at first was the training of the camp inmates to perform precision work on the many parts of the V-2, which was 46 feet long, and weighed 14 tons at launch.

In 1946, Congress appropriated limited funds for basic rocket research. The project was a ramjet missile designated as the Hermes II. The missile was designed to be powered by a ramjet motor, and with its short wings, to have an approximate range of 1,500 miles. The focus of the research program was the design for the motor. To my knowledge, no previous American research had been conducted concerning the design of a ramjet motor. The ramjet principle required that the fuselage bearing the device must travel at a very high rate of speed in order to activate the engine. Air forced into a narrow intake valve created friction, and therefore heat, sufficient for combustion of the jet fuel. In this arrangement, one rocket was required to lift and accelerate a second rocket—technically the 'booster stage' concept. Enter the V-2.

The V-2 was the proposed launch vehicle for the Hermes II, which would be attached to the nose of the V-2. The development of the Hermes II, however posed a logistical problem; where was the 1,500-mile test range to be located? At that time, the U.S. did not have, nor were there any plans for, an extended sea range of the type existing today (the Western Test Range between Vandenberg Air force Base and Kwajalein Island). My first choice was the Gulf of Baja California, in Mexico. This narrow strip of water would have provided good land-based observation posts to observe flight characteristics of the missile, and would have minimized any danger in case of failure.

The U.S. Department of State contacted the government of Mexico. I was notified that Mexico refused to grant permission for the request. I then requested maps from the U.S. Army Corps of Engineers covering the states of New Mexico, Arizona, Nevada, and Utah. These maps were so detailed they included crossroads where few buildings were located. Areas of population were sparse. I plotted a course across the desert, 50 miles wide and 1,500 miles long. The launch site would be at White Sands Proving Ground, New Mexico. Ironically, this range was never used, since the U.S. had developed sea ranges by the time the Hermes II was finally developed to the extent that the missile was ready for testing.

Another problem facing the development of the Hermes II was the lack of a vacuum chamber in the U.S. where small-scale rocket motors could be tested for performance in a simulated high altitude environment. To compensate for this, it was decided to locate a site on a high mountain, at least 10,000 feet in altitude, and then extrapolate the results of the test. The location of the site would be chosen based on the presence of a suitable, existing road network and the availability of adequate facilities for the test and support crews. The site selected was near Parcher's Camp, a summer camp located in the Sierra Mountains near Bishop, California. The location of the test site was South Lake, several miles up the road from Parcher's Camp. No launch pad was required to be built, because the testing device was mounted on a flatbed trailer. The Army Corps of Engineers, however, had to improve the access road to the site. This was of benefit to the public after the area had been returned for public access after completion of the tests.

On May 29, 1947, while I was helping with preparations at Parcher's camp, came the news that a V-2, fired at White Sands, had reversed course and landed near a cemetery in Juarez, Mexico. The gyroscope guidance system had apparently been reversed, causing it to go south, instead of north. There was no personal injury or property damage involved, but the kinetic energy of the impact created a hole 30 feet deep and 50 feet in diameter. This event was well covered in the media, and the State Department apologized to the Mexican government. In view of their refusal to grant over flight rights for testing in Baja California, it is a wonder they were not more indignant at so convenient an engineering mistake. Nevertheless, the fact remains that this was the first ballistic missile fired by the U.S.— accidentally or otherwise—at a sovereign nation.

During the early days at Fort Bliss the families of the German scientists were housed and maintained in Landshut, Germany. Toward the end of 1946, preparations were made to have the dependents of the scientists brought to the U.S. Jim Hamill made arrangements with the Post Engineer at Fort Bliss to convert the empty wards of William Beaumont Hospital, not used for rocket research activities, into apartments for the families. In December of 1946, the first dependents began to arrive and settle in their new home in America.

In May 1947, I was alerted by the Army that I was due for routine reassignment for duty in Germany. I would have preferred to stay at Fort Bliss, to see how things would develop for the German Rocket team. Wernher had me convinced of the technical feasibility of going to the moon, but the notion was inconsistent with geopolitical (and economic) verities at that time. Indeed, those were the "dark days" concerning the realm of rocket research. Funding from Congress was sporadic at best. My main concern, at the time, was that von Braun would keep the team together. Here, collectively, was a close-knit group of rocket scientists who had the knowledge of the various disciplines necessary to design, fabricate, and control rockets of much larger dimensions than the V-2, provided they were afforded the necessary funds and facilities. They were to prove their value later when the U.S. launched its first satellite, and eventually placed men on the moon.

Late in 1946, Elizabeth and I invited von Braun to dinner at the La Hacienda restaurant, on the road between El Paso, Texas and Las Cruces, New Mexico. After dinner, Wernher invited me to go out on the patio for a discussion. At that time, Wernher 34 years old, was planning to get married, and had a very critical eye on the future. In our rather lengthy discussion he wanted an honest answer to what I thought was the future of the project at Fort Bliss, because at that time it was not very encouraging. He asked me whether it would be better for him to take a more promising job in private industry. A scientist of his experience could make much more in private industry than on civil service pay working for the Army. I agreed with him, but asked what the prospects were in private industry for obtaining the vast resources needed for a lunar mission? The lunar mission was his lifelong ambition to that point, and if he went to the private sector, he would probably nullify any possibility of achieving that goal. I reminded him that if he left the rocket 'team' would probably be disbanded to other assignments, and that it was crucial that the team remain intact. I was thoroughly convinced at that time that the team was the only viable group who had the ability, given resources and time, to engineer a Moon landing.

In July of 1947, I left Fort Bliss for overseas assignment. Prior to my departure, Wernher presented me with a large photograph of one of first V-2s fired at White Sands. On it, he had written:

> *"For thankful appreciation. For wonderful cooperation.*
> *To Capt. W.E. Winterstein. April 1947.*
> *Prof. Dr. Wernher von Braun."*

Also in small script was the signature of Dr. Kurt Debus. Dr. Debus was in charge of launching the V-2s at White Sands Proving Ground, and was later director of the launch site for U.S. missiles at Cape Canaveral, Florida.

On leaving Fort Bliss, I thanked Wernher for coming to America to assist this country in trying to establish a missile program for defense. We were fully cognizant that the Russians had taken over the manufacturing facilities of the V-2, and knew that some day the U.S. might have to confront a threat from the communist government. From my new post, I followed with interest the developments affecting the German rocket team. A logistical improvement occurred in 1950, when the group was moved to Huntsville, Alabama. The Army's Redstone Arsenal had been deactivated and Major Hamill and Colonel Toftoy, Hamill's boss, jumped at the chance for getting adequate facilities for a rocket research environment. This move helped preserve the unity of the rocket team (and coincidentally moved them closer to what would become the launch facilities in Florida). In spite of the efforts to keep them together, however, several of the original members left the team in pursuit of lucrative careers with private industry.

5

Gaining Acceptance

The following account is from Dr. Ernst Stuhlinger's collection of various papers and speeches remembering the time of moving to Huntsville.

At the time, the German rocket team moved to Huntsville, a small town of approximately 15,000. The main industry was the growing and processing of cotton. During World War II, the Redstone Arsenal was built, adding a measure of industry to the cotton economy. The presence of the German rocket team created a sensation among the local grocers who had little experience stocking tortillas, enchilada sauce, and other items of Texas cuisine to which the team had become accustomed.

The team settled in and was instrumental in bringing a sense of sophistication to the community. It was not long before Huntsville had a symphony orchestra, and an observatory on Monte Sano mountain. Because rocket research was accelerated due to the Korean War, high technology support industries began operation in Huntsville, and soon the small town atmosphere changed to that of a growing city. At this same time, the rocket team also acquired the sea test range facilities at Cape Canaveral in Florida.

The German rocket team, while at Huntsville, was involved in two historical events which contributed to the leading position this country was soon to enjoy in the field of space exploration. After overcoming much Government opposition, they launched America's first satellite in 1958. A little over ten years later, in 1969, they were instrumental in landing U.S. astronauts on the moon.

The year 1957 was designated internationally as the Geophysical Year. As a corollary of this scientific milestone, able nations of the world began attempts to launch a satellite into earth orbit for the purposes of terrestrial and space study. President Eisenhower ignored the German rocket team as the logical candidates to pursue such a program, selecting the Navy for the task. The Navy chose the Vanguard program and the best U.S. scientists to design the satellite launch vehicle. Prior to the Soviet launch of Sputnik, the German rocket team had already launched a missile in November 1956, which reached an altitude of 682 miles, and flew 3,335 miles. This achievement made the German team the obvious candidate to place a satellite into earth orbit. On hearing of this success, Washington issued immediate orders to halt further experimentation. President Eisenhower was insistent that U.S. engineers have the honor of launching the first U.S. satellite, notwithstanding the newly acquired U.S. citizenship of the German rocket team.

The order from Washington D.C. specified that the Army restrict its experimentation to vehicles limited to a 200-mile range. This order slammed the door shut for any further research by the team concerning a vehicle capable of 3,000 miles travel. Because the team at that time was under the supervision of the Army, disobedience of the presidential edict was impolite to say the least. Work on the Vanguard program, however, encountered technical problems. Readers may be familiar with film footage of launch vehicles rising a few meters before exploding on the launch pad. This sequence of repeated Vanguard failure continued through the successful launch of Sputnik by the Soviets in October 1957. The Russian technological victory over the U.S. was devastating to the national psyche. When the Soviets placed a dog into orbit in late 1957 aboard Sputnik 2, the emotional obstacles posed by the possibility that a German rocket team might salvage the American reputation began to dissolve. Following public pressure on Washington for an accounting of its decisions, the German rocket team was finally given the go-ahead in early November of 1957. Most of the launch delays by this time were the result of efforts to assemble a meaningful instrumentation package to be carried aloft by the satellite. A number of scientists at the Jet Propulsion Laboratory in Pasadena, California, were busily engaged in this task. Finally, almost 90 days later, Explorer I, America's first satellite, was placed into orbit on January 31, 1958. What took over two years by American engineers to fail at was accomplished within 90 days by Naturalized Americans of German descent using a Redstone rocket, which was modeled after the A-4 (V-2).

The Russian head start in the "space race" provoked the U.S. into taking prompt action in establishing an organization whose dedicated mission was space exploration. The year 1958 marked the birth of the National Aeronautics and Space Administration (NASA).

In September of 1960, the George C. Marshall Space Flight Center, Huntsville, Alabama, was dedicated by President Dwight D. Eisenhower. Present at the ceremony was Dr. Wernher von Braun, who became its first Director. Truly, the "better days" I had predicted to Wernher 14 years before in Fort Bliss, had finally arrived, and his team was still intact.

When John F. Kennedy became President in 1961, he inherited a nation technologically cowed by the Soviets who now, at the height of the Cold War, had assumed the status of national enemy. The President sensed that he must do something to overcome the prevailing national mood of defeat. He had been following von Braun's career, particularly after the satellite launch, was convinced that Wernher and his team were fully capable and had the expertise to conduct a mission to the Moon. The President apparently wasted no time. On May 25, just four months after inauguration, he addressed a joint session of Congress with the announcement that the U.S. should embark on a lunar mission "within the decade," which were words quite familiar to me. [See information about talks with von Braun at Fort Bliss.]

During the years after I left Fort Bliss, I had kept in touch with Wernher through an occasional letter. At the time of President Kennedy's announcement, I was assigned to the Army Corps of Engineers who were constructing three ICBM bases for the Titan II intercontinental ballistic missile. This construction program was nearing completion in 1962. I wrote Wernher that he was finally on the way to achieving his lifelong ambition, and asked whether he had a job for me. In October 1962, I received a letter from Wernher in response to my request. The full text of the letter is located in Appendix Letter from von Braun. Note that in it, he refers to Jim Shepherd, a member of his staff who was in charge of hiring for the Saturn Program. The Saturn Program involved the design and development of the first three rocket boosters that would ultimately take U.S. astronauts to the Moon.

***Figure 3* Dr. Wernher von Braun presenting William E. Winterstein with a Certificate of Achievement**

I was employed by Marshall Space Flight Center in January 1963. The Center was responsible for building test stands for the first two stages of the Saturn V rocket. I was the first Administrative Officer of the associated test site, designated Mississippi Test Facility, which was managed by Navy Captain William Fortune.

Figure 4 **William E. Winterstein as the Administration Officer of the
Mississippi Test Facility**

In 1968, I was transferred to the Marshall Space Flight Center in Huntsville, Alabama as a logistical manager for the Saturn II stage. The Saturn II stage was manufactured at Seal Beach, California. It was then transported by sea, through the Panama Canal to the test site bay at Bay Saint Louis, Mississippi. Following a successful test phase, the Saturn II was transported, again by sea, to Cape Canaveral, Florida to be readied for launch. My responsibilities included support of the stage throughout its journey from Seal Beach to the Cape. I was also responsible for the availability of all subassemblies and parts for the Saturn II's throughout their manufacture and transportation.

Arthur Rudolph was appointed manager of the Saturn V program. He had complete responsibility for the design and fabrication. This involved a tremendous undertaking involving numerous contractors and thousands of employees.

The Apollo program, of which the Saturn V development program formed a major part, was, according to some historians, one of the greatest undertakings in the history of humankind. It gave Americans a new sense of national pride and international prestige at a time that both were sorely needed. This program provided an opportunity for the von Braun rocket team to pursue their lunar ambition. True, the original team had surrounded themselves with hundreds of talented and dedicated American scientists and engineers, but throughout the eight years from May of 1961 to the moon landing in July of 1969, it was the personal experience, expertise and guidance of the German rocket team that carried the program to success.

One has only to look at the development of rockets in the U.S.—and the rest of the world—at that time, to draw the conclusion that the German rocket team deserves most of the credit for a successful lunar mission. It was only four years prior to 1961 that the best in U.S. engineering had miserably failed to place a satellite in low earth orbit, much less trying to master the technology required for travel to the moon. A lunar mission required the development of enormous launch vehicles capable of many hundreds of times the thrust required to reach low earth orbit. It is my firm belief that had it not been for the President Kennedy/von Braun discussions, U.S. astronauts would not have set foot on the Moon in 1969, or in any year since then. Russia, with all of its engineering expertise, managed to land instruments only on the moon, but could never execute a manned lunar mission.

Thus the rocket team, finally given robust Government funding, accomplished the lunar landing in only eight years, instead of the 10 years total time forecast by von Braun to me in 1946. Because of the delay caused by Government resistance to an earlier start, inflation took its toll, and the cost was roughly 24 billion dollars—a substantial increase over the 3 billion projected in 1946. At the time of the lunar landings, and for some time afterward, there was a measure of public criticism regarding the allocation of funds for the space program at a time of perceived domestic need. I believe that a very great number of Americans fail to realize the benefits they have acquired as the result of the program. Much of the research that was expended on the program resulted in spin-off benefits for all of humankind in many areas including medical, manufacturing, micro-miniature communications, new materials, etc. [see chapter on benefits of the Apollo Program].

An easily recognizable example of this is the personal computer, now considered indispensable in our daily lives. When I first began work for NASA, the 'mainframe' computer that was used to design the miniature computers for the space capsule occupied a building several stories high.

In May of 2000, the President of the University of Alabama, Huntsville, invited me, and members of my family, to participate in the dedication of the Dr. Wernher von Braun Research Hall on that campus. Since my wife had passed away, I invited my daughter Constance and her husband to accompany me. At one of the receptions, while I was visiting with some of the other members of the rocket team, my daughter introduced herself to Dr. Ernst Stuhlinger, the recognized leader of the surviving members of the rocket team Old Timers. When Dr. Stuhlinger recognized my daughter, he grasped her extended hand with both of his, and exclaimed, "Had it not been for your father we would not have made it to the moon." What he meant was that there would have been no dedication of a Dr. Wernher von Braun Research Hall. A photo of Dr. Stuhlinger is shown later in the book.

Two letters from Dr. Stuhlinger to Constance recall the details of that day, and of the rocket program that began in Fort Bliss.

June 16, 2001
Ernst Stuhlinger

Dear Constance,

It was nice to hear from you again. We enjoyed so much seeing your father, and meeting you, at the Von Braun ceremonies in Huntsville last summer. I am happy to know that your father is writing a book on the Fort Bliss and White Sands times, and I am glad to contribute some of my own memories of those times, particularly about events in which Bill Winterstein was so decisively involved. Much of what I am going to write about had been known to me only superficially and in fragments while it happened. I learned about the details much later after a close friendship between von Braun and me had developed, and when I learned more about the thoughts and concerns that occupied von Braun's mind during the Fort Bliss days, and when, again later, Fred Ordway and I wrote a biographical memoir about von Braun. At that time, Fred conducted a series of interviews with our Oldtimer friends and colleagues, among them your father. On April 18, 1986, Colonel Winterstein and Fred Ordway had a long conversation in Huntsville, backed up by numerous letters and phone conversations during that year.

More details about the events described in this letter can be found in the Stuhlinger-Ordway book. In order to present here a complete story, I repeat the essence of the book text, but I am adding some thoughts that have crystallized in my mind since the book-writing times.

Von Braun's original America Team of 118 former Peenemünde had settled in the Beaumont Hospital Annex buildings at Fort Bliss between the fall of 1945 and the summer of 1946. Major (later Colonel) James P. Hamill was the commander of the "Paperclip People," Captain (later Colonel) William E. Winterstein was in charge of housing, maintenance, and support services for the group.

Working and living conditions for the PoPs ("prisoners of peace" as somebody had called us) were primitive, as Winterstein recalled;

however, after six years of a devastating war, we savored the peaceful life, and the plentiful food. The nature of our activities was defined by Washington.: We were to train military, industrial, and university personnel in the art and technology of rockets and guided missiles; to help refurbish, assemble, and launch a number of V-2 rockets (we continued to call them A-4.) They had been shipped from Germany to White Sands Proving Ground in New Mexico; and we were to make some paper studies of the potential of rockets for military and research applications.

While this work program provided a certain framework, and a modest substance for our workdays, it marked a decisive departure from the intense, fast-moving pace of work to which we from Peenemünde had been accustomed. Very soon, the Team became restless. They missed the fast pace of a well-defined development project that would have absorbed their ability and their willingness to work hard. It was not only the absence of a technical project; they also felt that such work would justify the Army's effort in bringing them to the United States, as well as their own personal decisions to leave their home country and to start a new rocket development program in America. Their eagerness to continue rocket development work became even more urgent when it became known that those of their former colleagues, who had fallen into Russian hands and were transported to Russian factories, were busily working on the improvement of V-2 missiles, and on advanced rocket systems.

More details about our life in the Fort Bliss barracks, about our daily hopes and frustrations, and about the very slow pace at which the prospects for our fate during the forthcoming years evolved, are described in Ordway's and my biographical von Braun book. The absence of a demanding development project for the group led to nervousness and even some quarreling between team members. "Lack of a real project to work on," Von Braun remarked to some of his associates, "has a severe impact on the mood and morale of our men. If they have no scientific or technical problem to sink their teeth into, they create human problems." He often found himself in the role of a counselor and pacifier; he had to present himself as an optimist, to recommend patience, and to express his belief that things will soon get better-although he was by no means convinced that his optimism was justified. His team members began to observe a growing nervousness and tension in his otherwise well-balanced, easy-going, joyous, and optimistic behavior.

There were bright moments, too, in our daily routine of low-level activities that Major Hamill characterized with the words: "We put you fellows on ice for later use," but von Braun really had his gloomy days. "The lack of resources," Winterstein said in 1986," was one of the uppermost problems confronting the group at Fort Bliss, and particularly von Braun. At that time, any large-scale operational research facility for conducting basic research on improved rockets for national defense or space ventures was still a far distant dream during the early times at Fort Bliss."

Von Braun made numerous attempts to obtain at least some very basic support. He talked to his boss, Major Hamill, and he wrote Urgent memoranda to him asking for laboratory facilities, tools, access to a library, and contacts with other groups engaged in rocket development work. He pointed out that his present situation meant a terrific waste for the government that had brought to the United States this group that offered a remarkable experience, knowledge, cooperative spirit, and will to work for the development of a very promising novel technology, but under present conditions is left to waste away in a little desert camp.

Hamill never responded to von Braun's pleas. Twenty years later, when the von Braun team worked on the Saturn V rocket for the Apollo Moon project in Huntsville, Hamill told his former wards during an Oldtimer reunion: "Von Braun was so impatient. He wrote me notes, threatening that he would leave the organization if I did not do this or that. I always ignored what he said, and what he wrote I threw into the waste paper basket."

Von Braun meant what he said and wrote, but he did not leave the organization. However, a breakup of the team was not averted by Hamill's wisdom or leadership prowess, nor by a sudden change of Congressional policy, but by a gentle, almost invisible, but immensely effective action on the part of Winterstein. A warm and genuine friendship had developed between the two men during the past months. Winterstein had his hand on von Braun's pulse and felt the danger signals. Forty years later, he shared this story with his old friends from Fort Bliss: "The lack of resources for any extensive rocket research concerned von Braun quite a bit. One evening, my wife and I took Wernher and several other Germans out for dinner at the Hacienda restaurant on the road from El Paso to Las Cruces, New Mexico. After dinner, Wernher and I briefly went out on the patio where we were quite alone.

It appeared that he was on the verge of deciding to leave the organization and go to private industry. "—Wernher, don't do that!" Winterstein told von Braun and he argued that no private industrial corporation had the resources to sponsor substantial rocket and space work. If von Braun joined an industrial corporation, Winterstein said, he would become a spokesperson for the company, and he would lose his persuasive power as a promoter of space flight and space exploration.—These arguments made sense to von Braun. "I see the purpose of my life is in the promotion of space flight," he had told some of his co-workers at another occasion, and he certainly would not have made the switch to industry unless it would have taken him closer to that goal.

During that night on the Hacienda patio, Winterstein spoke the decisive words. "I advised him to 'hang in there,' and I predicted that someday Congress would ease up and grant funds for space research. I also told him at that time that someday he would be known as the greatest rocket scientist in the United States, and probably in the world."

Von Braun did "hang in there." much of his nervousness subsided. He accepted the congressional indifference toward rockets and space flight. He created some low-cost, but still meaningful in-house projects that could be conducted on the meager financial means available to us, and he immersed himself in paper studies of future rocket systems, Earth-orbiting satellites, and manned expeditions to the Moon and to the planet Mars. His optimism, and his unbending belief and faith in a great future of space flight and space exploration returned.

During the fall of 1949, storm clouds accumulated over the skies of Korea.

Von Braun received an urgent call from Washington: "Develop and build a guided missile for a 250 mile range on the basis of your Peenemünde experience, but quick!" In 1950, the von Braun team moved from Fort Bliss to Huntsville in Alabama. In 1953, the Redstone Missile-made in Huntsville-was ready for military use. In 1957, the intermediate-range Jupiter missile was ready for deployment. In 1958, Explorer I, the first satellite of the free world, reached its orbit being launched by a Redstone rocket. In 1961, Alan Shepard, the first American astronaut, traveled into space on a Redstone rocket. In the same year, President Kennedy initiated the Apollo lunar landing project, and in 1969 von Braun's Saturn V rockets began launching American astronauts on their voyages to the Moon. In 1973, Skylab, a by-product of the Saturn V program, became America's first manned space station. **Bill Winterstein's early predictions, made on the Hacienda patio in 1946, became impressive historical facts.**

What would have been the course of history without that fateful Hacienda talk? Sometime in the future, when the true history of the birth of the space age is being written, the name of Colonel William E. Winterstein will be listed among the early space heroes that have helped bring this exciting phase in humankind's history to life.

Constance, I hope this will be of some use to your father. My very best wishes to both of you!

Cordially,
(Signed) Ernst

Below are the contents of the second letter that followed the first by two weeks:

June 30, 2001
Ernst Stuhlinger

Dear Constance,

Thank you for your very nice reply to my letter of June 16. I am happy to know that my writings were useful to your father. You asked me for some more memories of events in Fort Bliss in which your father played an important role. Here is another story in which I was not involved personally; however, von Braun told me about it much later, and your father mentioned it in his interview with Fred Ordway. It is reported briefly in the Stuhlinger-Ordway book about von Braun (pages 70-84).

In the summer of 1946 when we "prisoners of peace" led a lonely life in the Beaumont barracks at Fort Bliss, your father obtained a special permission from Major Hamill, our commander, to invite some of the Germans to a barbecue dinner at his officers quarters. It was a first introduction for von Braun and a few members of his "inner circle" to the delightful American habit of a steak fry, barbecue style, and the PoP's enjoyed the evening with Colonel and Mrs. Winterstein thoroughly, particularly Wernher von Braun. Your father had built a simple bar where the men could enjoy a highball and talk business, which was, of course, about the future of rocketry. That subject had been on von Braun's mind ever since he was a fourteen-year-old teenager. During the Peenemünde years in Nazi Germany, 1937 until 1945, any talk about that subject was strictly forbidden; but now, in America, von Braun had the freedom to talk about it, and he did! Your father recalls the colorful descriptions, with many details, of rocket voyages to the Moon and even to the planet Mars. Von Braun was overflowing with ideas, with detailed knowledge of the technical problems, and with optimism that one day, human travelers will walk on the Moon, and even on Mars, and will return home safely to tell all about their adventures. "Wernher, how much will an expedition to the Moon cost?" he was asked. He did some quick mental figuring, and then said: "With an all-out effort, we may be able to do it for about 3 billion dollars."—That was in 1946. Twenty-six years later, 12 American astronauts had walked on the Moon. Mr. Webb, NASA's Administrator, tallied the total cost of the Saturn-Apollo Project: 23.5 billion 1972-dollars.

That barbecue evening at the Winterstein home was not only a most delightful and enjoyable interruption of the monotonous life for some of the Paperclip Germans; for von Braun, who was in his real element when he told his spell-bound listeners of the wonders of outer space, and about possibilities for humans to travel to the Moon and the planets, it was far more. It was a first recognition of the fact that here, in this country, he may find a broad audience that will share his enthusiasm for space exploration, and that can be stimulated to provide the foundation for a national effort to develop man's space faring capability. Shortly after the Winterstein barbecue, on January 16, 1947, von Braun gave his first speech to a public audience in the United States, the El Paso Rotary Club. His subject: "The Future Development of the Rocket" around the same time, he started writing his book: "The Mars Project," an all-time classic of space literature. By the end of his life, he had written several hundred papers, essays, articles, and speeches.

Constance, you may realize again what an important role your father played in the evolution of the space age—just by doing the right thing at the right time!

Sincerest wishes

(Signed) Ernst.

6

Unknown Sacrifices Made by the Rocket Team

One of the most amazing elements concerning the early history of the entry of the United States of America into becoming the world leader in the exploration of space was the total dedication of the scientists who successfully engineered the lunar mission. They were the guiding nucleus of the tremendous organization that participated in this 'Mission Impossible.'

The words *total dedication* indeed should not be taken lightly. History reveals that their dedication exceeded the bounds of personal financial gain in order to achieve the dream of a lifelong ambition of exploring outer space. How many average Americans, in normal peacetime activity, would give up a financial fortune in order to fulfill a dream?

As related in the book, I had full confidence in the ability of the von Braun team, that if they remained essentially intact, gaining a few more like-minded members along the way, that they were the only hope in the foreseeable future for America to achieve space exploration. Knowing that sacrifices had to be made, I finally asked Dr. Walter Haeussermann for some details. His response, which in my opinion would apply in general to all of the scientists on the von Braun team, is quoted in its entirety below:

Dear Bill:

Between 1950 and 1954, the following top scientists left the Army Ballistic Missile Agency (ABMA) of Dr. Wernher von Braun's Team:

Mr. John Klien (guidance and control scientist)

Dr. Erich Manteuffel (field: electrical/electronics, magnetic amplifiers, servomotors etc.)

Dr. Joachim Muehlner (scientist in electronics)

Dr. Hans Friedrich (physicist, guidance, & control specialist)

Dr. Helmuth Schlitt (guidance & control system and instrumentation)

All left to accept higher paid positions in industry.

A great loss was in 1954 Prof. Dr. Theodor Buchhold, he accepted a challenging position in industry, because it seemed hopeless to get a GS 15 position as director of ABMA's guidance and control laboratory.

In 1959 the two top designers for inertial instruments Mr. Heinrich Rothe and Mr. Wilhelm Rothe together with my deputy in the guidance and control laboratory, Dr. Fritz Mueller accepted leading positions in industry, here in Huntsville. I was offered too a position in the same company with a salary of $100,000 (about 2 1/2 times my compensation in Civil Service.)—Several very good engineers (U.S. born) joined the group.—I rejected the offer because I considered it unfair to leave the von Braun Team and its loss, especially by losing additional specialists who would have joined me.

The loss of specialists and scientists mentioned above were all in the field of guidance/control and instrumentation. The following are only a few regrettable losses in other fields:

Dr. Martin Schilling
Dr. Wilhelm Raithel
Mr. Dieter Huzel

They all accepted leading positions in industry.

Signed: Walter Haeussermann

This letter, dated January 11, 2004, clearly indicates the financial pressures and temptations that the von Braun team scientists had to endure from soon after they arrived in this country in 1945 until July of 1969. It took a dedicated hero to the American and humankind cause to accomplish this feat of human endurance. To forego a 250% increase in salary in order to accomplish a goal for the benefit of all humankind is truly honorable dedication.

Figure 5 **Dr. Walter Haeussermann**

Embarrassment Trying to Establish a Home

When we began to realize, around 1951 and '52 that we will stay in Huntsville for a long time to come we wanted to build our own houses. At that time, obtaining a FHA loan at very favorable conditions was relatively easy, but Mr. Spraggins' bank wished that customers for a loan had an account of at least $5000 dollars of their own. This amount was far beyond our means; we arrived in this country empty handed, and we lived on modest civil service contracts $5000 dollars was far beyond everyone's means. So some of us pooled our savings, put them all together on the account of one of the group, who then showed the $5000 dollars to Mr. Spraggins and promptly received his FHA loan. Then the money was transferred from his account to the account of another member, and he got his loan. In this way, a number of new houses were built, and soon there were many happy house owners among the newcomers. Years later, when we had come to know Mr. Spraggins well, we confessed to him what we had done. "You dummies," he replied. "Do you really believe that I did not know exactly what you were doing? But I trusted you, and I did not regret it for one moment!" That made us quite proud indeed.

The previous account is from one of Dr. Ernst Stuhlinger's speeches to a local group of citizens in Huntsville. It has some humor to it. It is here to emphasize that the group came from Germany with none of the resources they had gained during their working in their younger years; and that for a professional person of honor to stoop to an action they felt was deceitful was embarrassing and hard for them to do. Also, for the reader to understand the full impact of how little these men were being paid for numerous years; especially when compared to their contributions to U.S. security and their actual skills had they been paid by the private sector. It is the author's belief that few men would have been so dedicated to their country and willingly sacrificed financially as much as the German rocket team did with pride and patience.

7

Humor on the Way to the Moon

W hen President Kennedy announced to the world in May of 1961, that America was going to the moon "in this decade," American citizens were galvanized into a patriotic fervor. It was in the midst of the Cold War, and this country was still smarting from being technologically defeated by the Russians with Sputnik. This monumental challenge of breaching the space frontier almost immediately elicited helpful hints on how to overcome the many problems facing such a mission. Letters poured into NASA Headquarters from old and young alike, proposed solutions or other comments. Also appropriate to mention are anecdotes about prior events in the lives of personnel involved in the moon mission. In crossing the frontier into outer space, humankind was entering into a region never before explored by a living person. We did have knowledge that the environment was fatal unless properly engineered protection was provided. Throughout all the planning and completion of the mission, the tension lifting quality of humor presented itself. Here are a few of the events garnered from a number of sources:

One might ask, "who decided to put a man into space for the first time"?

Prior to putting Man into space, NASA was experimenting with sending small monkeys in capsules into near earth space to study the physiological effects on living subjects. These capsules were recovered by parachute. From small capsules NASA went into the larger Mercury capsule which could accommodate one man. NASA then selected chimpanzees, evidently with a higher IQ than monkeys.

Ham, the chimpanzee was specially trained to perform certain functions while in flight, and which he did successfully. However Ham's patience evidently wore very thin, so on his last scheduled flight, on the launch pad, Ham made up his mind that he was definitely **not going to get into that capsule again—no way!** The mission manager and Alan Shepard were both present, so without much comment the mission manager pointed to Shepard and said, "you're next." So the chimp essentially said "no more monkey business," which made Shepard the first American in space. This was related by Alan Shepard at a Fort Bliss Old Timer's reunion which I attended in Huntsville, Alabama

The Author's Youth

I made my own muzzle loading pistol and gunpowder from reading the Encyclopedia and I purchased the ingredients from the local pharmacy. Once drying the gunpowder in the oven Mom closed the oven door and as I smelt singeing paper remembered the gunpowder drying. Quickly rescuing the gunpowder, I luckily saved the wood-burning stove from blowing up and burning the house down. Normally I dried gunpowder outside as I mixed it wet to give it an even mixture of the ingredients. Since it had been raining, I decided to dry the ingredients in the wood burning stove. This was first and last time that I tried to dry gunpowder in an oven.

Wernher von Braun's Youth

I learned von Braun was well known by the local police for firing store bought rockets attached to toy cars in his hometown during his youth. After firing the rocket, the car would race down the streets of town, which was fun to watch, but when the car concluded its run or reached a wall or other obstacle, at the end of the store bought rocket's life the fireball that came out of the rocket is what the police feared the most. The potential of something catching on fire in the center of town prompted many talks from the police to von Braun and his parents.

Safe European Sport of Mountain Climbing

At Fort Bliss, after some restrictions had been lifted regarding the movement of the Rocket Team, one of the members decided to go mountain climbing. One of Arthur Rudolph's V-2 launch crew from White Sands decided to go climbing in the adjacent Organ Mountains. This is a common sport for Europeans and while the Rocket Team had been informed about the dangers in the Desert, the full impact of that was not realized yet. While climbing and placing his hand up on the next ledge, a rattlesnake bit him. realizing what it was he took the proper action to get the venom out so he luckily suffered no harm. Arriving back at the base he informed the others that you needed to be careful where you placed your hands when mountain climbing in the United States.

Needing to Establish a Sense of Home

As previously mentioned, security was very tight in the barracks compound during the first year at Fort Bliss. So it did not take very long for them to improve the situation of staring at four unpainted barrack walls. From bits and pieces of lumber from the Fort Bliss salvage yard, they erected a makeshift bar and lounge, or club house, at the edge of the parade ground. To make things easier to look at, they planted a flower garden around the structure.

I noticed a sign on the wall behind the bar. It was a formula of at what potency the drinks would be served. Their favorite drink was Scotch and soda—that is when available! To my recollection the formula ran something like this:

First drink	1-1/2 oz. Scotch	6 oz. Soda
Second drink	1 oz. Scotch	6 oz. Soda
Third drink	3/4 oz. Scotch	6 oz. Soda
Fourth drink	1/2 oz. Scotch	6 oz. Soda
Fifth drink	SODA PURE	

The next two accounts are from speeches given by Ernst Stuhlinger.

What Happens When You Write Your Numbers Differently?

When I think back of our first years in Huntsville, a few impressions stand out very distinctly in my memory. The people in Huntsville were of an overwhelming friendliness. Our neighbors offered their help wherever they could; they called us by our first names and tried to make us feel at home in this town in every way possible. So did the people in the stores and offices; they accepted our problems with the new language with humor and patience. In Germany, we write the '1' with a little extra line, as shown here, it looks almost like a '7.' One morning, my wife wanted to have one cup of whipping cream from the milkman, she wrote '1 whipping cream' on a note for him, but he left 7 whipping creams, so for a whole week we lived practically on whipping cream!

"Crazy" Speeding People Are Needed

I remember a day in 1952 when I went to Tullahoma in Tennessee to visit the Air Force Research Center. Driving through Fayetteville, I slowed down to 30 miles per hour as the road sign demanded, but I was soon stopped by a police officer. "You are speeding," he said. "Well, I drove at 30 miles per hour," I replied. "Yes," he answered, "but the speed here is 15 miles per hour. There is a sign over there—I admit that it is hard to see because it is hidden behind a shrub, but it is the law, and I'll give you a ticket." While he was writing, his eyes fell on a little sticker on my windshield with the words 'Redstone Arsenal.' The officer stopped writing, and said, "Are you one of those crazy guys in Huntsville who want to go to the Moon?"—"Yes, Sir," I replied, "that's correct."—"Well," he said, "then I figure you have to travel fast, haven't you? I wish you good luck, and drive carefully! We need guys like you badly!"—Ever since that time, the city of Fayetteville has occupied a warm place in my memory.

The "Playboy" Redstone

In the early 1950s when the Army began test-firing its Redstone missiles from Cape Canaveral, someone suggested that each one be decorated with a huge cheesecake painting for good luck.

It was difficult for illustrators in Gerd deBeek's office to paint directly on the missile skins, so the figures were drawn on huge posters and then taped onto the sides of the missiles a day or two before the firings.

Decorating the fourth Redstone was a gigantic painting of an unusually voluptuous blonde described by those present as "really a masterpiece."

When the missile was launched, the wind peeled off the painting, and it fell away from the speeding bird. The tracking radar automatically locked onto the "blonde" and lost contact completely with the missile which fluttered down into the Atlantic.

"That," recalled a project official years later, "was the last Playboy Redstone."

It seemed the Radar was more interested in the blonde then in the missile it was supposed to track.

The radar probably had a better target with the lead paint on the poster then the actual metal of the rocket.

Almost Discovered in Transport

This incident occurred when the author was transporting 61 rocket scientists by rail from Fort Strong, Massachusetts, to Fort Bliss, Texas, in late 1945. In accordance with the agreement with the rail company, the Germans would only be allowed in the dining car when all other passengers had left. One day, however, two elderly women dawdled over their lunches. Since I did not consider the presence of the women a security threat, I allowed the Germans into the dining car. One of the women, perhaps curious about the foreign language she could not help but hear being spoken, asked me about the mysterious strangers dining nearby. With a straight face I immediately responded, having anticipated such a question, "These are Polish agricultural students here to learn advanced production methods." This apparently satisfied the women's curiosity.

Bob Ward, who received an endorsement from von Braun, compiled anecdotes from a large number of sources, authored a paperback in 1969, published by Fawcett Publications Inc. titled *A Funny Thing Happened On The Way To The Moon*. Here are some of these anecdotes:

The divine plan

Dr. Wernher von Braun recalled that that an intense woman of the If-God-Had-Meant-For-Us-To-Fly-He'd-Have-Given-Us-Wings school of thought once up-braided him for advocating the exploration of space by man.

"We should not tamper with the universe," she declared, "We should stay at home, mind our own business, and watch TV as God intended!"

Heap Good Advice

A gruff, wrinkled, old Cheyenne Indian from Montana by the name of John Wooden Legs was attending a session of the National Advisory Committee on Rural Poverty. The subject of space exploration came up. Mr. Wooden Legs interrupted the discussion and growled: "If they find Indians on the moon, tell them not to make a treaty."

Here are some of the letters sent to Cape Kennedy by youngsters:

"To the Director and Boss at Cape Kennedy:

"I would like to volunteer to ride on your first space ship to Mars, I weigh only sixty pounds and am an observant boy. I would not marry any of the women up there because I am not fond of girls, any kind, or shape."

"P.S. I think you are depending on men with baldheads who are old like my dad. I have lots of hair and am young. My brain will stay warm and function better up there where it is cold."

And from a boy in Arizona:

My boyfriend and I think you should send kids to Mars, because if there is something dangerous there you wouldn't have to waste spacemen. Besides, I always wanted to be great.

A Pennsylvania girl wrote:

"I am nine years old and would like to go to the moon. Please put me on your list of volunteers, but would liken to be fairly near the bottom, because I don't want to go just yet."

This request topped all others:

From a boy in Washington:

"Would you please send me the John F. Kennedy Space Center?"

An Illinois boy advised "What you should use for rocket fuel is Bufferin. It works twice as fast."

From a California boy. "I think the blast-off of your Gemini rocket was very good. But I think you should send a woman to the moon, because my dad said that a woman driver can hit anything."

Liquids vs. Solids

German-born missile man Arthur Rudolph, who was the director of NASA's Saturn 5 rocket program until his retirement in 1969, remained a dyed-in-the-wool advocate of liquid fueled rockets over solids throughout his career. In the 1950s when the Army's solid fueled Pershing was having its troubles, he attended a dinner meeting at which the featured speaker dwelled on the glories and advantages of solid propellants. Afterwards, with martini in hand, Rudolph approached the speaker and said:

"That was a very interesting speech, but I must tell you that I am by birth a liquid propellant man. This" said the outspoken Rudolph, pointing to the olive in his drink, "represents the ratio of my confidence in solids versus liquids!"

Moments later, Rudolph began to feel twinges of remorse over his biting comment. He returned to the bar, dropped five more olives into his martini, and again buttonholed the speaker. "My friend, you see that my confidence in solids has increased, and the more I drink of this liquid propellant, the higher my level of confidence in solids rises!"

Confused Chris

In the same vein, Dr. Wernher von Braun said in a 1961 speech to the Texas Municipal League:

"A classic example of exploring the unknown is Christopher Columbus. He didn't know where he was going when he left, he didn't know where he was when he got there, and he didn't know where he had been when he got back."

8

Why the Soviets Beat America into Space

Because the passion of the German rocket team members was to use rocket technology for the peaceful and scientific exploration of space, it was with no small disappointment that their efforts were constantly directed toward weapons applications by two Governments—the Nazi and American Governments. An irony of this singular focus on weapons actually contributed to the delays in launching U.S. satellites that allowed the Soviet Union to be first in space with Sputnik. The following account is the recollection of Ernst Stuhlinger, and sheds some light on the events behind this rarely mentioned series of bureaucratic decisions.

Washington's answer to our satellite proposal, instead of an assignment to build a satellite, was the nomination of a series of evaluation committees who recommended more studies. In addition, President Eisenhower did not wish to have a purely scientific, peaceful satellite launched by a military rocket; at that time, he was proposing an "open sky" policy among the nations. Therefore, the assignment to build and launch a satellite was given to the Naval Research Laboratory in response to its proposal to build a new three-stage rocket, the Vanguard. In spite of great and dedicated efforts of a very capable project team, Vanguard experienced a string of delays and failures. The project was too ambitious to be accomplished within the permitted time and budget.

As the years 1955 and 1956 went by, Russian experts under the leadership of Sergei Korolev were busily at work to build a satellite and launch it, hopefully before an American satellite would appear in orbit. During 1956 and '57, several announcements by Russian scientists, and even by the Moscow Tass newspaper, gave hints that a Russian satellite was imminent, but none of the American officials in Washington took these indications seriously, although U.S. satellites were discussed quite frequently by people involved in rocket work. At a congress of the International Astronautical Federation in Copenhagen, Denmark in 1955, some of the American attendees asked professor Sedov, chief scientist of the Russian space program, whether the first traveler in space would be Russian or American. "Neither one," he replied, "the first satellite traveler will be a dog. A Russian dog, of course."

Von Braun and his superiors, among them General Toftoy in Washington and General Medaris in Huntsville who had been named Commander of the Army Ballistic Missile Agency in 1956, had the strict order from the Secretary of Defense not to prepare a satellite launching—only continued paper studies were permitted.

However, it so happened that a military project that had been assigned to the Huntsville team in 1953, the 1500 mile IRBM Jupiter, had to be equipped with an efficient heat shield for its warhead to survive atmospheric reentry. Von Braun proposed a protective layer of a material that would melt under the impact of the atmospheric heating, but would have such a low heat conductivity that the molten surface material would be blown away before the heat could penetrate into the lower layers of the protective mantle. This scheme had to be tested on a scaled-down warhead model on a trajectory similar to the long-range Jupiter trajectories. It so happened that the best way to do this was to use a Redstone rocket with two upper stages of solid propellant rockets, similar to the proposed satellite-launching rocket, the only difference being the number of stages, two for the warhead test, and three for a satellite launch.

On September 20, 1956, a modified Redstone with two upper stages, called Jupiter C and designed for nosecone test flights, achieved a 682 mile altitude with a range of 3,355 miles. The same launcher, with a third upper stage, could have orbited a satellite in 1956, if the Huntsville group had been given permission.

In the same year 1956, the Ordnance Missile Command in Huntsville became the Army Ballistic Missile Agency (ABMA) with General Medaris as Commander and von Braun as Technical Director of the Guided Missile Development Division.

In the fall of 1957, those few who tried to keep their hands on the pulse of our Russian competitors became more and more convinced that a Soviet satellite launch was imminent. By the end of September, in a conversation with General Medaris, I tried to suggest that he should make another attempt to obtain permission from the Secretary of the Army for a Huntsville satellite launch. The shock for our country would be immense, I argued, if the Russians did it first, but the general was not moved. "They won't be able to do it," he said, "you know for yourself how difficult it is to launch a satellite." Go back to your laboratory and relax. I guarantee you that we will be the first.

One week later, Sputnik was in orbit. The news was broken in Huntsville by Gordon Harris, our Public Relations Director, at the cocktail hour after a meeting with Secretary of Defense designate McElroy, Secretary of the Army Brucker, several high-ranking generals from Washington, and the ABMA leadership. Everybody was shocked. "We could have done it two years ago," von Braun could not help but exclaim. Then he said to Secretary McElroy "Give us the green light, and we will have an American satellite in orbit in 60 days." General Medaris chimed in "Wernher, make it 90 days."

A few days later, von Braun, who knew about my earlier conversation with General Medaris, asked me "Did the general talk to you since it happened? I think he owes you an apology." "Yes," I answered, "but all he said was 'those damn bastards!'"

In October 1957, after Sputnik, but before Explorer I, there was another congress of the IAF in Barcelona, Spain. In a friendly conversation with Professor Sedov from Russia, some of the delegates from Huntsville asked him whether Sputnik was a military satellite or a civilian satellite. "Neither one," he said, "it is a Soviet satellite. We do not recognize a difference." Von Braun had recently been heard to say something similar—"we should not try to build an Army satellite or a Navy satellite or an Air Force satellite," he said, "we should build an American satellite."

It took another Soviet launch with a dog onboard, another Vanguard rocket failure, and another letter from Medaris with the threat of his resignation, before ABMA in Huntsville received the go-ahead from Washington. By that time, the 'silent coordination' that von Braun and his team had maintained with the JPL and with Van Allen had borne fruit. JPL was ready with the Sergeant rockets, the Microlock transmitter, and the design and fabrication of the satellite that had been started in Huntsville and completed at JPL. Van Allen had his Geiger counters ready with which he discovered the famous Van Allen radiation belts, the modifications for the Redstone rocket as well as the apex predictor happened to be ready for the launching. In essence, only the final assembly and a very thorough testing had to be carried out. Eighty-nine days after Huntsville received the order, Explorer I was in orbit.

The launching of America's first satellite was a great event not only for the people of Huntsville, but also for all Americans who are impressed by technical and scientific accomplishments.

9

Benefits of the Apollo Moon Mission

The Blessings That America Gave Unselfishly to Humankind

America's determination to be the first pioneer in man's exploration of outer space presented a multitude of problems. First of all, it was a new dimension of the universe, and Man was never there before. We did know enough that the environment would be lethal to man in an unprotected position. We also knew that there would be extremes of temperature in the airless void. Also of very important consideration was what the prolonged effect of the strong cosmic rays emitted by the sun would have on both man and manmade materials in space. Man was about to enter the unknown and he must ensure, through his engineering expertise, to take man to the moon and safely return him to the earth, in a never before designed vehicle was going to be a monumental task! It was said at the time, that it was like a golfer expecting to make 18 holes-in-one on his attempt at the golf course.

Needless to say, research proceeded in numerous avenues of manufacturing techniques to obtain the optimum quality materials required for the vehicles of the lunar mission. Primary objectives were light-weight, strength, durability and ease of manufacture. Research was extensive in developing new alloys, improved methods of machining difficult parts requiring precision tolerances, improved casting methods etc. In short, a general revolution was conducted of how we produce a product requiring precision work, with rugged strength, and the lowest possible weight. This was just the research that was done in the development of the hardware required for the Moon mission.

Research oriented to maintaining the health of the astronauts on their round trip journey to the Moon also resulted in a multitude of benefits for the average person. Medical doctors on earth were in constant touch with the vital signs of each of the three astronauts on their round-trip journey to the Moon.

This vast amount of research directed to a successful voyage to the moon surfaced in a multitude of benefits for all humankind. Much of this research never ended up in products or techniques associated with the hardware that landed on the Moon. However the most outstanding examples of the items that did land on the Moon and were of immediate benefit to man on earth as spin-off benefits were the miniature computer, and the microminiaturizing of communication and navigation guidance components.

NASA soon realized that much of this research would not end up in direct benefit to the lunar mission but that the spin-off benefits would be useful to all humankind. Therefore NASA set up an Office of Technology Utilization which would be the focal point for the public, or any industry to gain information which could lead to the solving of manufacturing or technological problems.

All of the funding and cost of this huge amount of research associated with the lunar mission was paid for by the American taxpayer. However the spin-off benefits, which amounted to thousands of items, were made available for use by all humankind world-wide. There has been considerable criticism, evidently from uninformed individuals, of the cost of the lunar mission. It has been calculated by well informed individuals that for every dollar that we spent for the journey to the moon, that industry and personal benefits have amounted to seven dollars in return. Now I will itemize just a few of the blessings which America gave to all of mankind due to our research concerning this country's entry into space.

This cost of $30 dollars per year for each taxpayer with a net benefit per taxpayer of $2,100.00 per year (even dot coms were hard pressed to return such results during the internet boom).

The Computer

The research on the miniaturization of the computer in my opinion was the most earth shaking business event that emerged from the spin-off benefits generated by the lunar mission. It completely revolutionized how the world does business today. This ranges across activities from private homes to the largest, financial, industrial, manufacturing, transportation, marketing, communication and entertainment industries of today.

Eye surgery

A device was developed using a hypersonic sound technique whereby eye surgery for cataracts was performed by homogenizing the cataract by sound and drawing off the residue by needle. Thus producing non-invasive eye surgery.

Vital signs monitor

Intensive care units at hospitals are using the vital signs monitoring technique whereby one nurse can monitor many patents from a central station. Thus reducing the number of nurses required for this phase of activity in the Intensive Care Units of hospitals.

Pacemaker

The pacemaker for heart patients is another life giving support item that was generated as a spin-off benefit of the space program.

Medical Imaging

NASA developed ways to process signals from spacecraft to produce clearer images. This technology also makes possible these photo-like images of our insides, CT and MRI scans.

TV Satellite Dish

NASA developed ways to correct errors in the signals coming from the spacecraft. This technology is used to reduce noise (that is, messed up picture or sound) in TV signals coming from satellites.

Bar Coding

Originally developed to help NASA keep track of millions of spacecraft parts. Bar-coding is now used by almost everybody who sells things to keep track of how much of what is sold and how much of what is left. Just imagine how long the lines would be in grocery stores if now the clerks would have to individually punch out the prices of items on an old fashioned cash register.

Vision Screening Systems

Uses techniques developed for processing space pictures to examine eyes of children and find out quickly if they have any vision problems. The child does not have to say a word!

Ear Thermometer

Instead of measuring temperature using a column of mercury (which expands as it heats up), this thermometer has a lens like a camera and detects infrared energy, which we feel as heat. The warmer something is (like your body), the more infrared energy is put out. This technology was originally developed to detect the birth of stars.

Fire Fighter Equipment

Fire fighters wear suits made of fire resistant fabric developed for use in space suits.

Smoke Detector

First used in the Earth orbiting space station Skylab (launched back in 1973) to help detect any toxic vapors. Now used in most homes and other buildings to warn people of fire as well as toxic vapors.

Sun Tiger Glasses

From research done on materials to protect the eyes of welders working on spacecraft. Protective lenses were developed that block almost all the wavelengths of radiation that might harm the eyes, while letting through all the useful wavelengths that let us see.

Automobile Design Tools

A computer program developed by NASA to analyze a spacecraft or airplane design and predict how parts will perform is now used to help design automobiles. This kind of software can save car makers a lot of money by letting them see how well a design will work even before they build a prototype.

Cordless Tools

Portable, self-contained power tools were originally developed to help Apollo astronauts drill for moon samples. This technology has led to the development of such tools as the cordless vacuum cleaner, power drill, shrub trimmers, and grass shears.

Aerodynamic Bicycle Wheel

A special bike wheel uses NASA research in airfoils (wings) and design software developed for the space program. The three spokes on the wheel act like wings, making the bicycle very efficient for racing.

Thermal Gloves and Boots

These gloves and boots have heating elements that run on rechargeable batteries worn on the inside wrist of the gloves or embedded in the sole of the ski boot. This technology was adapted from a space suit design for the Apollo astronauts.

Space Pens

The Fisher Space pen was developed for use in space. Most pens depend on gravity to make the ink to flow to the ball point. For this space pen, the ink cartridge contains pressured gas to push the ink to the ball point. This means, that you can lie in bed and write upside down with this pen! Also, it uses a special ink that works in very hot and very cold environments.

Shock Absorbing Helmets

These special football helmets use a padding of Temper Foam, a shock absorbing material first developed for use in aircraft seats. These helmets have three times the shock absorbing ability of previous types.

Ski Boots

These ski boots use accordion-like folds, similar to the design of space suits, to allow the boot to flex without distortion, yet still give support and control for precision skiing.

Failsafe Flashlight

This flashlight uses NASA's concept of system redundancy, which is always having a backup for the parts of the spacecraft with the most important jobs. This flashlight has a extra-bright primary bulb and an independent backup system that has its own separate lithium battery (also a NASA developed technology) and its own bulb.

Invisible Braces

These teeth-straightening braces use brackets that are made of nearly invisible translucent (almost see-through) ceramic material. This material is a spinoff of NASA's advanced ceramic research to develop new, tough materials for spacecraft and aircraft.

Edible Toothpaste

This is a special foamless toothpaste developed for the astronauts to use in space (where spitting is not a very good idea). Although this would be a great first toothpaste for small children, it is no longer available.

Joystick Controllers

Electrical Joystick controllers are used for lots of things now, including computer games and vehicles for people with disabilities. These devices evolved from research to develop a controller for the Apollo Lunar Rover, and from NASA research into humans actually operate (called "human factors").

New Man-made Materials

In the realm of man-made compounds, great progress was made in epoxies, phenolic and graphite compound research. Spacecraft and other electronics needed very special materials as a base for print circuits like those inside your computer. Some of these "liquid crystal polymers" have turned out to be very good low-cost materials for making containers for foods and beverages. Other research produced super strong, light weight and stiff materials appearing in a large number of products, such as sporting equipment, fishing rods, golf clubs, tennis rackets, boats and many other items. Also such materials saw extensive applications in airplanes, cars, furniture and other household items. Our kitchens were introduced to items such as non-stick pots and pans, and most importantly, the non-stick frying pan.

WD-40

Also much research was expended in the development of new lubricants as lubrication of moving parts of spacecraft in the harsh environment of space was a key element for research. The now common household lubricant WD-40 is a spin-off product.

These are but a few of the many thousands of the spin-off benefits that the United States of America has given to humankind to enhance living conditions for everyone on the earth today.

Part II

The Aftermath: What Happened after Lunar Mission, Intrigue and United States Space Heroes Betrayed

Author's note: In that the nature of my pursuing justice required me to interface with many people, I needed to repeat my story to each. So be forewarned that the letters following will be repetitive with the same information although each has a different focus for the person being contacted.

Foreword

An American citizen can go to their government to get justice done. I am one of those citizens. For twenty years, since May 1985, I have gone through all of the accepted legal channels, first the Department of Justice, then individual contact with my congressional person, then to the House Judiciary Committee, then to the Senate Judiciary Committee, then to the President of the United States. My goal was to see that justice was done concerning one of this nation's top space pioneers and heroes, Dr. Arthur Rudolph. So far my attempts, backed by incontrovertible documentary evidence have failed, in this land where **justice American style** (innocent until proven guilty) is held to be almost sacred.

In the revelation of my story this part of the book will contain statements that will appear to be repetitious, however bear in mind that my approaches to the various levels of our government to gain justice in my quest necessitated the use of the same, or related, information at each level of endeavor.

It was, at the time, the greatest technological achievement in the history of Man. The foot set down upon the surface of the moon by Neil Armstrong in July 1969 left an historical imprint on the face of the earth. How epic were the words "One small step for Man, one giant leap for Mankind." That leap far exceeded the linear distance from earth to the Moon.

This event occurred at the height of the Cold War between the U.S. and the Soviet Union. Both nations were on the very precipice of nuclear annihilation. The weak signal from the Soviet satellite Sputnik little more than a decade earlier was a loud proclamation of Soviet technological superiority over the U.S. in the Cold War. Imagine, then, the resounding—and timely—victory the lunar landing represented for the U.S. America's journey to the moon, sailed, as it were, under the flag of the American Republic, was a voyage that tipped the balance of power in the world.

The attitude of the rocket team upon their arrival at Fort Bliss, Texas was phenomenal, though they were yet technically enemy aliens, according to international law, their endeavor to assist in the defense of the United States against enemies in the emerging space age was most remarkable. Though they had engineered, in 1943 wartime Germany, a successful first launch of the V-2—a vehicle commandeered by the Nazi government and pressed into service as a weapon—evidence reveals that the scientists led by Wernher von Braun had their sights, and their hearts, set on the peaceful exploration of space. They collectively foreswore lucrative opportunities to enter the private sector as eminently employable individuals. They remained humble civil servants of the American people throughout their useful careers with the dream that some day, they would be called upon to mount a lunar expedition.

The author has been compelled to document the events leading up to America's lunar program in order to obtain a perspective of the historical facts already known and familiar. As detailed in this book, important elements of our space history have been contaminated—innocently or otherwise—by respected and normally reliable sources. The author had the honor of serving as custodian of the German rocket team for the first crucial year that they were in the U.S. After he left the team in 1947, he later, in 1963, again reunited with them for the Apollo program.

This story also reveals to what extent governmental and bureaucratic intrigue touched (and in one infamous case, destroyed) the lives of these space heroes and pioneers. These events occurred in the aftermath of America's journey to the moon. One of the leading German engineers was exiled from his adopted—but beloved—country, the United States, without one shred of legitimate evidence to justify such a shameless betrayal. The telling of this part of the story is so bizarre as to be unbelievable, except that the evidence clearly reveals that it did happen, in a corner, behind doors, in a political darkness so thick, not even the torch of liberty for which this man gave his life and career, could reach him.

William E. Winterstein, Sr., Lt. Col.,
U.S. Army, Retired   January 1, 2005

10

The End of the Rocket Team
By Act of NASA

The story of the brilliant team of German rocket engineers would not be complete without the rendition of what occurred to them after the lunar mission. As custodian of the team upon their arrival in this country in 1945, at Fort Bliss, Texas, I soon was convinced that this unique group, by remaining intact, offered our country a tremendous new advance in the field of rocket research. My job just prior to taking custodianship of the team was Proof Officer conducting tests on the latest U.S. rockets at Aberdeen Proving Ground, Maryland. This revealed, positively to me, that American industry was far behind in rocket research at the time.

What impressed me most about the team was their desire to get into immediate and comprehensive rocket research for the defense of the U.S. However, very early in my frequent discussions with von Braun, I soon discovered that he had an intense desire to be able to go beyond the boundaries of this earth and explore the universe. His first target would be the moon.

It was in 1946 that it became an obsession with me that the team remain intact for its most effective use as an asset to this country. I had full faith in Wernher von Braun's personality in accomplishing this difficult mission. Because it involved personal financial sacrifice on their part. I could see on the horizon that private industry would be anxious to recruit various members of the team for their advanced experience in the disciplines of rocket research, and offer them very lucrative salaries. However I did have one thing in my favor, in my daily contacts with von

Braun, and others of the team, was the underlying talk concerning a possible moon mission, after some more meaningful rocket research was accomplished.

At that time, the future appeared almost hopeless that Congress would approve sufficient funds for substantial rocket research. The turning point on the future of the existence of the von Braun rocket team occurred one evening in late summer of 1946. After dinner on the patio of the La Hacienda restaurant on the road between El Paso, Texas, and Las Cruces, New Mexico, Wernher approached me for an honest opinion. What did the future hold for rocket research at Fort Bliss? He was planning to get married in Spring, and he was concerned about his financial future. He talked about going to private industry. I had to agree with him on his logic, however I argued, like a Dutch uncle, that his team without his leadership would vanish. Private industry could never offer the opportunity to engage in a future lunar mission, so there his boyhood dream would also vanish. I pleaded with him to 'hang in there' and that times would get better. I remember my parting words, which were to the effect, *"Wernher, someday you will be known as the greatest rocket scientist that the U.S. ever had."*

My dream about the team became fulfilled in July 1969 when Neil Armstrong made U.S. footprints on the Moon. He had piloted the vehicle that the team had provided for him to make the journey. The ability of the United States of America to place man on the moon and return him safely to earth caused a profound change in world history. The balance of world power had swung in favor of this country. This event occurred in the midst of the Cold War and Wernher von Braun was acclaimed the world's greatest space hero and rocket scientist by world leaders outside the Soviet sphere of influence. He was welcomed worldwide by heads of state. Thus, the members of the von Braun rocket team were true heroes for this country in the fight against the Soviet Union during the Cold War.

When I heard that Wernher was being transferred to NASA space headquarters, I had mixed feelings. Was it truly a promotion? Through the years from 1961 on, ever since President Kennedy stated that we were going to the moon, I had noticed that it was von Braun who was appearing before Congress or its sub-committees whenever funds for the lunar mission were required. Needless to say, it would take many billions of dollars. This was much more than the three billion that he quoted to me in 1946 at Fort Bliss. Wernher von Braun was constantly in the national limelight with NASA headquarters personnel in the background. The country was infused with the exciting prospects of being involved in the moon mission. It appeared that von Braun was running his own show, thus not requiring any assistance or support from headquarters. His objective was plain: *"...to the Moon we go, and I know every step of the way. I planned this for many years."*

One of von Braun's greatest assets was the personality that he projected. He was profoundly honest in his approach and the air about him exuded this quality of a gentleman without guile. Thus he could approach Congress and essentially say; "After a careful study we need another 10 billion to complete this phase of the lunar program." Moreover, after possibly very little or no debate, was promptly granted the funds. The presentation of his logical approach to the many difficult problems on getting Man to the Moon was almost magical in essence. As you will note, NASA headquarters forever lost the voice of this great engineer when they transferred him to their headquarters on the eve of his magnificent triumph.

Initially von Braun was very excited when he heard that NASA was going to transfer him to headquarters. He thought that this was going to be the place on planet Earth where he and his friends could create the most magnificent space exploration program anyone could envision. Knowing his personality, I could imagine how elated he must have been. Normally this being advanced to a prominent post in Headquarters would appear, on the surface, to be a promotion. His lifelong dream of going to the moon had just been accomplished, and now the avenue to the planets seemed to have been opened to him.

It was in February 1970, just eight months after Eagle had landed on the moon, that Wernher von Braun left Marshall Space Flight Center for his new job as Deputy Associate for Planning at NASA Headquarters (truly an appropriate spot for his ambition of further exploration of the universe, with the Mars mission in mind). However, it was almost immediately that von Braun sensed the feeling of defeat. He later confided to a close friend; "I felt like a mushroom, they kept me in the dark, once in a while the door would open for some fertilizer to be shoveled in, and then the door would shut again."

After a short stay at NASA headquarters, due to his frustration of not being offered a challenging assignment, von Braun resigned from NASA in July 1972. Upon his resignation, Wernher accepted a job as Vice-President at Fairchild Industries. Evidence now emerges that suggests the transfer to NASA headquarters was definitely not a promotion. Was this an act of vengeance or censure? Was this done because von Braun 'ran his own show' by getting U.S. astronauts to the Moon? For one thing, it did break up his beloved rocket team. The irony of this strikes me. Here it is in history that the von Braun team, by lofting the first American satellite into space in 1958, was the very basis for our government to activate NASA in the first place. Thus, Dr. Wernher von Braun was actually the very founder of NASA!

It has now become evident that bureaucratic intrigue has stepped in to demobilize the Wernher von Braun rocket team.

When von Braun was assigned to NASA headquarters, Dr. Eberhard Rees, von Braun's former Deputy at Marshall, was appointed director of the Space Center. However, Rees did not hold that position for very long. In January 1973, NASA appointed Rocco Petrone as director of Marshall Space Flight Center. He was the third MSFC director and the first that had not been part of the original Rocket Team. Petrone had spent much of his career at Kennedy Space Center and had established his reputation as a ruthless in-fighter as he worked his way up to NASA headquarters.

Petrone did not waste any time in letting Marshall Employees know where they stood with him. He took every opportunity that he could to belittle, demean, and humiliate everyone from working level engineers to the highest levels of management. During a NASA-wide reduction in force, the German Rocket Team members were targeted for removal. They were forced out of their management positions at all levels on short notice. Most retired from Marshall in a matter of weeks after Rocco Petrone's purge got underway. For the most part, the Germans left quietly and retired to their homes in Huntsville.

This managerial blunder by NASA headquarters was a blow to the method of management that Marshall Space Flight Center had adopted under von Braun. This type of management that insured a successful lunar mission was scuttled by the Petrone purge. Some of the Germans may have been past their prime or more technical than managerial, but as a group, they were competent, effective, and respected by their employees. They made things happen with a phone call rather than sitting in a meeting all day. Ripping this organization apart was not in the interest of Marshall, NASA or the American space program. It only served the interests of those who were motivated by personal ambition, jealousy, or vengeance against the Germans.

When the German managers were thrown out, the unique communication chain between engineering was broken. Engineering rapidly lost control to the project managers, accountants and administrators, the engineering and technical culture that once set the goals and policy at Marshall went into a decline that truly was never recovered. The evidence for this was the failure of maintaining Sky-Lab as a viable U.S. space station in orbit, another defeat by the Russians after Sputnik. Again, with no von Braun team at the helm, the Russian MIR space station remained in orbit for many years, and the U.S. had none. Recalling the Challenger disaster, where the very poorly designed 'O' rings on the solid rocket boosters caused the destruction of the shuttle and its crew. Typical German team engineering logic was evidently missing in the recent Columbia disaster. Why wasn't an inspection ordered of Columbia after it reached the space station, after it was previously observed that a sizable piece of insulation had broken off the main tank and collided with the shuttle's wing? This was obvious poor management on the part of Marshall Space Flight Center. It was too bad that the very tight management/engineering methods adopted by the von Braun rocket team had been dismantled.

This is what NASA, and America, lost when von Braun was transferred to NASA headquarters. This effectively broke up the finely tuned team of experts in the design, manufacture and testing of large guided missile components. History reveals that von Braun, during over fifty years in the hazardous business of rocket research, had NOT ONE FATAL accident associated with any program that was under his responsibility. It is indeed sad to say that he was not involved in the design, manufacture or testing of the capsule which sat atop the complete Saturn V vehicle. (In that incident we lost three astronauts.) Wernher von Braun was a meticulous taskmaster in every detail in the production of a viable product, as history proves.

This loss of the finely tuned research philosophy concerning the very intimate relations between management and engineering, which von

Braun had integrated into the way Marshall Space Flight Center operated its business, was lost and never regained as history has revealed. I retired from Marshall in 1971 after the lunar mission was a success. I receive weekly bulletins informing me of space developments not normally revealed in the news media. In one article was the design of the "O" ring that was to be used on the newly developed solid rocket booster for use on the upcoming space shuttle. Something struck me that there was a serious flaw. I mentioned to my wife Elizabeth several days later, "there it is, an accident that's going to happen." History proved me right; when the Challenger disintegrated, America lost the crew and a billion dollar shuttle. I am familiar with the construction of the huge central tank used in shuttle launchings and the insulation on the tank as well as the comparatively fragile nature of heat insulation tiles protecting the shuttle on reentry into earth's atmosphere. So it was with heart rending dismay that I watched the shuttle Columbia with its crew destroyed on its return to earth. To me, as a member of the Apollo team, and a member of the NASA Alumni League, I behold this event as inexcusable due to gross mismanagement that would not have been tolerated under von Braun's concept of operation. Logic would have dictated that an inspection for damage at the space station would have revealed that Columbia was unfit for the return flight to earth before temporary repairs were made. Thus, in my opinion, America lost two shuttle crews, and two billion dollar spacecraft because of poor management. That leaves America with only three shuttles for space exploration. Currently not viable.

It was indeed very fortunate for me to have recently, in early 2004, to have met Dr. Carol Rosin, President of the Institute for Cooperation in Space. Dr. Rosin was von Braun's representative during the last three years of his life, when he was slowly dying of cancer. Carol Rosin at that time was a manager at Fairchild Industries. When von Braun's illness interfered with his appearance at scheduled public meetings, she would deliver his speech. Thus, she was able to get firsthand knowledge of the true feelings that were on his mind. The very first presentation Carol delivered of a von Braun speech was in 1974 at the National Educator's Association Convention in Chicago before eighteen thousand participants. Von Braun was a most strong advocate that space should be only used for peaceful purposes. Those words are firmly entrenched in the charter establishing NASA; however, things have gone astray, which caused deep concerns with Wernher in the closing days of his life.

Now, Carol Rosin in her own words shares history with the world of today.

*"By the time I met him in early '74; he was dying and waiting for someone he could trust to deliver his message and share at least as much of his vision as that person could absorb. That person turned out to be me... which was fortunate and unfortunate for me. Fortunate because he filled my heart and my life with mission and purpose, with vision and a knowing of what is possible. Unfortunate because he also filled me with the truth that was not being officially acknowledged, and with vision that was not going to be fulfilled because the intention, he learned, was to 'weaponize' space instead of to create a space program that would excite and benefit all on earth. Further, because I learned of his pain over what had happened to him—the way his efforts and vision was being squashed, and the way people saw him as a Nazi and the hurt from the ridicule he felt. What was worse was the fact that he knew he was dying, that there was a slim chance in all of history to get his vision produced in full, that if the military, industrial laboratory, NASA, and governmental complex continued to limit the space program in exchange for a continued war program—**just as he had experienced under Hitler**—that it would be proven that the U.S.A was not the home of truth and freedom, or of peace, well, he was crushed to the end of his life.*

In addition, picking up where he left off was at first the most exciting notion imaginable. Such an expansive vision, a feasible plan of action I could present for educators, for children, for the suffering people and polluted environment, for all together around—his vision was realistic, feasible, and possible. Learning gradually and with some hard knocks from people I, like him, thought there would have been many friends who would support me after he died. There were some, but there were also too many good intentioned people who were, still are actually, misinformed, at best, and dishonest, selfish self-absorbed betrayers who function under the guise of doing something good. It has been almost unbearable to me, at times, to know even the little I knew of what he knew, to see what he saw and to have so few hear what he was saying. Moreover, I have felt, and continue to feel, almost the depth of hurt that he felt from the time he entered NASA and could not proceed with a bigger vision after Apollo.

He told me how he escaped—how he had no choice but to do his 'job' and that he had planned the escape so he and the rocket scientists could come to the U.S.—thinking this was the land on which he could live in peace and share his vision and create it. Nevertheless, that was not what happened. Sure Apollo, lots of other projects and great people entered his life—but in the end, a little school teacher who pretended her classroom of students was in space, got the job. Of trying to continue his work, to share his message and vision—to create a path for achieving real peace on earth and by maintaining it in space.

In fact, he knew that we would never be able to achieve peace on earth if we did not maintain it in space. And he knew the formulas for how the U.S. spins the truth to make the public and decision makers believe there are enemies against whom people need to build more weapons, soon to be in space unless a Treaty gets signed and fast—all for self interests. There are still people who actually believe more weapons and more war will make us more secure and able to live in peace. In addition, he told me that he was staying alive longer than the doctors predicted, because he wanted to teach me all that he could. And he added, one day before he died, he was so desperate that he felt he had only one choice and that was to find a "woman" whom he hoped nobody would close the door on if only to be polite to her—who "they" might listen to. He felt he was not heard—and that peace, our lives, the whole space program, was at stake. Though he also knew there could be a space program that would emerge based on escalating weapons into space, he wanted no part of this and wanted it stopped.

All he wished for was peace on earth and in space so the human species could explore space with our pooled resources and brains not to come together to fight more wars. But to come together to apply Space Age technology to solutions to urgent problems on this planet and to find out the truth about who we really are in the universes-- who and what is out there. Of all people, after of all he had been through, he knew the magnitude of the potential---good and horrific. He just wanted a space program, not more of a war program."

Dr. Rosin's remarks clearly reveal the fact that one of Wernher von Braun's greater ambitions, after Apollo, was that space remain free of weapons whether placed there in the configuration of a satellite, or under the false premise of providing some kind of security or defense—which he knew was based on lies. This indicates, no, it proves that he was truly dedicated to work for a peaceful world.

Dr. Rosin's remarks also reveal a very interesting insight to the true character of America's No. 1 space pioneer and hero, Dr. Wernher von

Braun. It puts to abysmal shame those who in our society who, without legitimate and truthful information, try to label him a war criminal. This lack of common sense logic is totally ludicrous. In addition, her remarks indicate Wernher's gigantic stature as a great philosopher who understands man's intricate nature in relation to the universe. Truly, the world, as we behold it from space, and as our own eyes behold it, is the most beautiful crown jewel in the universe in all its gorgeous colors. What von Braun was trying to say, as he so desperately tried to get the message out to humankind, was quite simply put, and was most vitally important for his future survival and for the existence in an undamaged world. I believe that Wernher's message could be summed up as this: "Man, God gave you the intellect to destroy yourself through nuclear warfare or through any one of a number of disasters caused by yet more weapons of any kind. Any intensive warfare, anywhere on this planet, in space, aimed into space or from space to earth, will affect the life of all humankind. Let us all get together and ensure that our evil instincts do not overwhelm this beautiful planet of ours." Thus, Dr. Wernher von Braun has truly become not only this country's greatest space pioneer and hero, but also humankind's greatest friend, a great philosopher unequalled.

11

Sinister Activity by the OSI

The Dr. Arthur Rudolph case had gained considerable attention before I became involved in 1985. Dr. Friedwardt Winterberg, professor of theoretical physics at the University of Nevada, was on sabbatical leave in West Germany in 1984 when the press release revealed that Rudolph had returned to Germany and the reason why. Dr. Winterberg had never met Rudolph; however, he sensed that something was definitely wrong concerning the circumstances. He immediately began his own investigation, searching for witnesses who had worked on the V-2 production line under Rudolph. Dr. Winterberg met with both the West German and East German prosecutors for war crimes. In his efforts, Dr. Winterberg produced firm documentary evidence that completely refuted the allegations of the OSI (Office of Special Investigations) of the Department of Justice, which prosecuted the case.

It was not until the Fort Bliss Old Timers Reunion in May of 1985, in Huntsville, Alabama, that I developed a strong personal contact with Dr. Walter Haeussermann, the German rocket scientist in charge of the instrumentation and guidance of the Saturn V rocket boosters, which carried man to the moon. He was also responsible for the instrumentation and guidance on Explorer I our first satellite. Dr. Haeussermann was in possession of some of the documentary evidence accumulated by Dr. Winterberg. I had made known at the reunion that I intended to do something about the Rudolph case. My plan was to approach the DOJ (Department of Justice) for a reconsideration of the case. Dr. Haeussermann provided me the documents with which I went to Attorney General Edwin Meese on May 30, 1985, requesting a reconsideration of the case. It was my impression at that time that the majority of the Old Timers—most of whom were retired—were hesitant to become entangled with the DOJ, and who could blame them? After all, Rudolph was a recent victim of the chicanery of the OSI, and who would want to come to the 'special attention' of such an organization by way of even an orderly protest?

The Arthur Rudolph case began in October 1982 when officials of the OSI began interviewing Rudolph about his wartime role in Germany. Arthur Rudolph retired from NASA in late 1969 and several years later moved to San Jose, California. In October 1982, the OSI requested that he appear for an interview concerning his immigration and naturalization status, and his activities in Germany between 1939 and 1945.

He was told he could bring a lawyer, but was not told of his right to deny answering questions. Rudolph evidently did not consider that the meeting could pose a threat to him, after all these officials were from the Department of *Justice*. Further, at the time he arrived in this country in 1945, he had been interrogated by U.S. Intelligence officers concerning his wartime role in Germany. He had fully related his wartime activities to the intelligence officers at that time, and again to the FBI when he was investigated because he had received a TOP SECRET security clearance for his work in the design and construction of ballistic missiles.

During this interview with the OSI, he answered all questions openly and without reservation, and offered more than 80 pages of his own personal documents, which became government exhibits to the interviewers. These covered his work, first at Peenemünde and then at Mittelwerk, which was the underground plant near Nordhausen.

Rudolph was shown a staffing plan by the OSI that showed him as the director of V-2 production. Also during the discussions, it was revealed by the OSI that a Mr. Sawatzki was in charge and controlled the underground operations in the complex, which included tunnel digging, and several manufacturing facilities, only one of which was dedicated to the V-2 production line.

***Figure 6* Arthur Rudolph**

In addition, Sawatzki was the only one authorized to requisition prisoners from the nearby concentration camp known as 'Dora.' This was noted in comments repeatedly made (to OSI, Army, and FBI) by Rudolph "For V-2 production the prisoners were allotted to me by Sawatzki. They were a precious part of my workforce. I did everything in my limited power to improve their condition. Together with the head of the Prisoner Assignment

Office of the Camp, a sergeant Simon, we established a bonus system for the prisoners working in production. Further we worked together for improvement maintaining footwear and clothing; allotment for coffee or tea besides the normal rations; separation and treatment of prisoners falling sick; relieving the conditions for the prisoners going to and from work; prevention of additional work of the prisoners when off-duty."

Rudolph was interviewed again by the OSI on February 4, 1983, at a location in San Jose, California. On this occasion, the atmosphere was not as 'neutral' as the first visit. He was shown a copy of his application for the Nazi Party of 1931. In 1931, there were two main parties in Germany. The Nazi, (or National Socialist Party), and the Communist Party. Rudolph had a deep dislike for the Communists, so his choice was the Nazi party at that time. Hitler became Chancellor in 1933 and Rudolph's 1931 application predated Hitler's assumption of power. Rudolph stated that he had mentioned that fact in numerous questionnaires that he had to fill out beginning in 1947.

In addition, he was shown copies of his immigration and naturalization applications. The question was raised by the OSI about whether he was ever involved in the beating of prisoners. Rudolph stated to the officials "I stopped production for a whole shift to allow an interchange of shifts, so that the prisoners during their off-duty hours in camp could see daylight. The spies of Sawatzki reported that to him, so he called me on the carpet and threatened to put me in the concentration camp if I ever dared to do that again. So while I did my best to improve the lot of the prisoners, Sawatzki was opposed to it." Rudolph also stated that it was the understanding of his German civilian workforce that the way to improve production was to treat the prisoners well.

Rudolph received a letter from the OSI on July 25, 1983, informing him that the investigation was continuing, and that important preliminary decisions had been made. He was told that he should be prepared to discuss these decisions, as well as the evidence assembled to date, with an attorney present.

Rudolph, in poor health following a recent cardiac bypass, hired attorney George H. Main of San Jose; they met in his office, September 2, 1983, with Mr. Neal Sher and Eli Rosenbaum of the OSI. Here the atmosphere drastically changed; the OSI requested that Rudolph not be present at any of the meetings, and declared that they would not have further personal contact with him. From that point forward, Rudolph did not know what transpired during the meetings, but could rely only on what his attorney told him after the fact. As Rudolph would later learn, the OSI was building a case against him on the grounds of mistreatment of prison labor. The OSI intended to deport him in disgrace after 24 years diligent and honorable service to the U.S. space and defense sectors!

When Attorney Main inquired of the OSI representatives concerning the identities of witnesses against his client, he was told that the OSI could not reveal the information. Attorney Main asked about the nature of evidence the Government intended to introduce. The OSI responded that there would be two forms of evidence, documentary, and personal testimony. They believed that the primary evidence against Rudolph were *his own depositions* obtained in previous interviews, with government exhibits attached (Government 'exhibits' were Rudolph's personal documents brought to OSI interviews cited above), and living personal witnesses and documents from depositories in Germany, Great Britain, and the United States. Some of the main allegations against Rudolph would be:

- That Rudolph was linked to reports charging prisoners with sabotage attempts. (A sabotage report against a prisoner would result in the death of that prisoner.)

- That Rudolph was involved in a structured organization of persecution and system of abuse of labor.

- That Rudolph had a blind drive to meet production quotas and to further his career at all costs.

- That Rudolph had long-standing anti-Semitic feelings and was an ardent Nazi and his drive at Mittelbau project was the synthesis of his blind hatred for 'inferior races' and drive for personal ambition.

Rudolph's reply to these allegations was that he had stated in his deposition that he did not believe in an Aryan race and did not consider the prisoners inferior because of race or anything else.

He further stated that he joined the Nazi Party to prevent a takeover of the Government by opposition members of the Communist party. Also in his deposition, Rudolph had related how, far from degrading, he had actually *improved* the conditions of the prisoner workforce at Mittelwerk. Rudolph indicated at this point that the hounding by the OSI with the allegation that he had persecuted prisoners had placed him under extreme duress, at best a personal, and at worst a calculated attack for someone recovering from heart surgery.

During the period September to November 28, 1983, the date of the signing of the final agreement, there were numerous visits by Rudolph to Attorney Main's office, with many phone calls between visits. Finally the OSI offered Rudolph a 'settlement,' the terms of which stipulating that if he departed the U.S., never to return or seek an appeal of his case, and that he relinquish his U.S. citizenship, the Government would permit him to retain his Civil Service annuity and Social Security benefits. Further, the Government would not seek litigation concerning the U.S. citizenship status of his wife and daughter, which had been obtained based on Rudolph's citizenship.

The first draft of The Agreement on October 24, 1983, shocked Rudolph since the compromise effectively required that he admit to acts of wrongdoing he had never committed. Rudolph was vehemently opposed to the allegation in The Agreement that he participated in the "persecution" of forced laborers. The OSI was adamant that the allegations remain. Rudolph at this point stated that he was under duress, and had been for several months. Attorney Main, at this point, advised Rudolph not to press for changes in the terms of the settlement, because he felt that the OSI would become more aggressive in their prosecution, and perhaps rescind all agreements. At this time, after 40 years, Rudolph did not know of any witnesses who might still be alive to support him in defending his innocence.

Thus, in poor health, physically and financially unable for an extended court fight against the resources of the United States Department of Justice, Rudolph was coerced into signing an agreement, drafted by the OSI and containing contemptible lies, on November 28, 1983. As a result, this is how Arthur Rudolph lost his U.S. citizenship, from the country he loved. The country, which he had helped place preeminent in the exploration of space. Arthur Rudolph was forcibly exiled from the U.S. in March 1984 when he departed for West Germany.

In Rudolph's Synopsis, which he compiled after the discussions between Attorney Main and the OSI, he revealed that during the discussions between Main, Sher, and Rosenbaum, the OSI stated that the Government did not desire publicity about the case and would honor an adamant statement from Rudolph concerning his feelings against publicity. Rudolph never gave such a statement in writing, because if he did, the OSI would have an excuse not to release any information about the case, which would have been a violation of personal privacy.

Throughout all of the discussions Rudolph was not shown any direct evidence implicating him as a participant in any war crime. As indicated previously the OSI was hesitant in revealing any evidence, only implying that they possessed enough legitimate evidence to mount a formidable case. The text of The Agreement is located in the Appendix titled Agreement by OSI for Arthur Rudolph.

12

West German Prosecutor Proves Rudolph Innocent

On Rudolph's arrival in West Germany, the West German Government protested to the United States, contending that Rudolph illegally emigrated there under pressure from the U.S. DOJ and wanted the U.S. to readmit the scientist. The German Government objected to the manner in which Rudolph became their responsibility, by first entering the country and then after both events happening promptly renouncing his U.S. citizenship, both under pressure from the U.S. DOJ. John Russell from the Justice Department's Public Affairs Office said the agency would not comment concerning the protest. The representative of the West German embassy in Washington, Mr. Peter Mende, stated that Rudolph was admitted to Germany as a U.S. citizen with a U.S. passport but without a visa, and noted that only tourists were allowed entry without visas. Mende further stated; "We objected to his being sent to the Federal Republic of Germany under an agreement to give back his U.S. citizenship there. That is not the way cases like this should be handled between Governments. It means, for us, he illegally entered Germany."

Coincident with Rudolph's return under improper circumstances, the West German war crimes prosecutor promptly requested a copy of the Rudolph file from the DOJ because of OSI allegations that he was a war criminal. It was apparently the intent of the German Government to proceed with an investigation that Rudolph was 'spared' in the United States.

As a result of delays caused by the OSI in failing to submit a prompt reply to the first request of the German prosecutor (who had to make several requests for the Rudolph file) the question arose, why the delays? The original request by the German prosecutor should have been honored immediately had the OSI compiled a firmly documented case, as was implied in their discussions with Rudolph. The answer for the delays surfaced when the OSI, in the meantime, had been advertising in newspapers for witnesses against Rudolph. This tactic suggests that they did not have a case against Rudolph when they pressured him into leaving the U.S. The following is from a newspaper clipping taken from the Las Vegas Israelite, dated January 11, 1985, a year after Rudolph had left the U.S.:

> *The Department of Justice has asked the assistance of the World Jewish Congress in locating survivors among laborers at the underground V-2 rocket factory attached to the Dora/Nordhausen concentration camp. The Justice Department request comes in the aftermath of the disclosure that Arthur Rudolph, the German-born space official who developed the rocket that carried Americans to the moon, surrendered his American citizenship earlier this year and left the country rather than face charges that he had brutalized slave laborers at the Nazi rocket factory during World War II.*

> *According to the Justice Department's Office of Special Investigations —the agency responsible for prosecuting Nazi war criminals presently living in the United States—Rudolph "participated in the persecution of forced laborers, including concentration camp inmates, who were employed there under inhumane conditions." A third to one half of Dora's sixty thousand prisoners died.* [Author's note: Alleged by OSI, not fact]

> *The Office of Special Investigations, in seeking to locate survivors of the Dora/Nordhausen concentration camp, has advised the WJC that it particularly wishes to contact persons who worked in the main rocket production facility (Mittelwerk underground plant) prior to January 1, 1945.*

> *Individuals who can be of any assistance in this investigation are asked to contact: MS. BESSY PUPKO, WORLD JEWISH CONGRESS, ONE PARK AVENUE, New York, New York, 10016, (212) 679-0600.*

The full text of the news clipping is located in Appendix titled Las Vegas Newspaper ad by OSI/World Jewish Congress.

On April 26, 1985, Neal Sher responded to the request of the German prosecutor for a copy of the Rudolph file. The response consisted of a three-page letter naming nine witnesses and a selected list of 35 documents.

Mr. Sher failed to include in this evidence two documents containing exculpatory material concerning Rudolph.

One was the statement of Mr. Frank Barwacz, an American citizen held prisoner by the Nazis and who had worked in the Mittelwerk V-2 production line under Rudolph. Mr. Barwacz had responded to the newspaper ad placed by the OSI. He had emphatically defended all German civilians who had worked on the V-2 production line. In addition, Sher failed to include information obtained from the East German prosecutor of 1945 that revealed Rudolph's name could not be found in any of the files concerning war crimes.

It seems impossible that in a case personally prosecuted by Sher—a case involving an eminent scientist whose whole work in the United States was indispensable to our space program—Sher could have overlooked those two documents. This omission runs contrary to the principles of fairness bearing on every prosecution in American law. The opinion is inescapable that Sher's selective response was purposeful and meant to induce the West German prosecutor to proceed against Rudolph and the West German tribunal to convict him. This alone suggests OSI subversion of the practices of American law. [Author's note: See appendix on Neil Sher disbarred which shows the true character of Sher.]

Because of the unusual circumstances of the case (a prominent American space scientist accused of war crimes, and the objections from the German Government over the manner of Rudolph's repatriation) the West German prosecutor began a very thorough and intensive investigation into the matter.

This investigation took more than two years, and covered more than 2,300 pages of transcript testimony. The testimony of 65 witnesses or depositions was evaluated. The witnesses consisted of former camp inmates who worked on the V-2 production line under Rudolph: civilian coworkers with Rudolph in the Mittelwerk facility, and former members of the SS who participated in the operations at the Dora/Nordhausen complex.

After a careful and thorough investigation, the West German war crimes prosecutor came to a finding that completely refuted the allegations made by the OSI. As part of a short summary of witness evaluation Attorney General Duhn made this comment "Questioning of the defendant (Rudolph) by the American Government officials have not yielded a sufficient basis for a criminal investigation."

A copy of the short summary by the German prosecutor is located in Appendix titled Summary by German Prosecutor.

A review of the 'evidence' submitted by the OSI revealed that of the nine witnesses presented, four did not know Rudolph, one testified for Rudolph, two contradicted themselves, and two were mentally incompetent! The documentation submitted did not contain any direct evidence implicating Rudolph in any war crime. The OSI failed to produce one shred of legitimate, to say nothing of incontrovertible, evidence to support their allegations against Rudolph. So besides withholding evidence that would have cleared Rudolph the OSI provided *no* witnesses against Rudolph, and in fact provided Germany with false witnesses!

Thus the OSI, falsely, under pretense that they had a solid mass of evidence against him, coerced one of the greatest of America's space pioneers to surrender one of his most treasured possessions, his American citizenship. This story is virtually unbelievable in that such an action emanated from the halls of our very own Department of Justice, the guardian of our system of justice, were it not for the evidence to support it.

Rudolph was a man without a country during the two-year period that he was being investigated by the German prosecutor. After the investigation and acquittal, Rudolph was granted citizenship in West Germany. When this was announced by the news media, Neal Sher, Director of the OSI, promptly issued a news release, which was titled in the March 19, 1987, issue of the *San Jose Mercury News*, "Rocket scientist Rudolph is still a war criminal, U.S. says."

The full text of the Mercury news clip is located in Appendix titled Mercury News Article.

Furthermore, Mr. Sher issued a false statement in his news release. He is quoted as saying that Rudolph "ran the whole program." This implies that Rudolph was involved in all of the operations concerning the Mittelwerk concentration camp complex where "at least 25,000 died." [An allegation by World Jewish Congress ad in Las Vegas]

There were at least four operations running concurrently in the complex, including tunnel digging, where the use of non-skilled labor virtually guaranteed a high volume of deaths, and in any event, tunnel digging was not Rudolph's responsibility. There were production lines for the manufacture of the V-1, production lines for the V-2, and the aircraft jet engine. These lines required highly trained and skilled workers. Rudolph supervised only the production activities on the V-2 line. The V-2 was a very highly complex rocket used as a guided missile (originally designed for space exploration NOT as a weapon), requiring considerable expertise in its manufacture as workers had to maintain extremely close tolerances on many parts. This involved welders, sheet metal workers, machinists, electricians, and others.

What glares back at us when we evaluate the tactics of the U.S. Government in dealing with Arthur is the obvious lack of common sense by prosecutors. The V-2 production required trained and skilled workers. In the latter days of the war, skilled workers were scarce in Germany. If a production manager, particularly of a high priority weapon system deemed critical to the war effort, had willfully eliminated, or otherwise injured his workforce so that production suffered, he would have been guilty of high treason!

13

Justice Department Injustice

After the lunar landing on July 20, 1969, the Fort Bliss rocket team held occasional reunions of the "The Fort Bliss Old Timers." This group consisted of the German scientists, and associated Army and civilian contractor personnel who participated in the activities at Fort Bliss and White Sands.

One such reunion occurred at Huntsville, Alabama, in the spring of 1985. Arthur Rudolph, the Saturn V program manager, did not attend that reunion. I soon found out why he was not present. He had left the U.S. about a year before as the result of threats of deportation by the OSI. Needless to say, this disclosure about one of the key personalities of the Old Timers was of very great concern to the group. Members who had been close to Rudolph were very angry about the circumstances under which Rudolph was forced to leave this country and, above all, were angry that he had been forced to surrender his U.S. citizenship.

Before my return home, Dr. Walter Haeussermann gave me sufficient documentary evidence to support a request to the DOJ for a reconsideration of the Rudolph case. Dr. Haeussermann was responsible for instrumentation and control of the rocket that placed Explorer I into orbit. Later he was responsible for the instrumentation and control of the Saturn V stages.

Having full confidence in the evidence presented to me by members of the Old Timers, I was the first to endorse a letter written to President Reagan by retired Major General John B. Medaris. There were an additional 107 endorsements to that letter. To my knowledge, General Medaris never received a response to his letter.

I believe that the President was never shown that letter, which is here reproduced in its entirety.

The Venerable
John Bruce Medaris
MAJOR GENERAL U.S. ARMY (RETIRED) *May 24, 1985*

The President of the United States
The White House
Washington, D.C. 20500

Dear Mr. President:

Your resolute dedication to protecting American citizens against will-full excesses by their government prompts me to invite your attention to an outrageous violation of the most rudimentary of human rights and of due process perpetrated by The Office of Special Investigations of the DOJ.

Following procedures reminiscent of immoral, unjust tyranny, officials of the Office of Special Investigation intimidated and harassed Mr. Arthur Rudolph, a naturalized citizen for nearly 40 years, until he was persuaded to relinquish his United States Citizenship and return to his former country. For 23 of those years, he and his colleagues served their adopted nation with great dedication, talent, and skill. They helped create three ballistic missile systems for our defense and that of the North Atlantic Treaty Organization as well as the mighty Saturn rocket that propelled American astronauts to the moon. Mr. Rudolph received the nation's highest civilian awards.

As Commanding General, I directed the endeavors of this group during their most productive period. Their joint achievements were of incalculable value to our nation's security and progress. They were and are loyal, patriotic, and trustworthy citizens.

I urge you to review the secretive, deceptive, and totally unjust process by which Mr. Rudolph was literally forced to abandon his friends and deny his oath. He deserves nothing less than immediate restoration of citizenship and invitation to return in honor to his country of choice.

Sincerely, (Signed) John B. Medaris Major General U.S. Army (Ret.)

Attachments:

1) Petition signed by 108 native and foreign-born citizens

2) Letter of Dr. Eberhard Rees, dated April 26, 1983

3) Open letter of Dr. Ernst Stuhlinger dated Feb. 18, 1983 (not included) with documented references (copy)

Next picture shows the first page of the petition cited in Attachment 1 above. My signature is the first listed on the petition.

Old Timers of the U. S. Rocket and Space Program in Huntsville
Tranquility Base
Huntsville, Alabama 35807

The undersigned fully endorse and support the letter of the Rev. Canon
John Bruce Medaris, Maj. Gen. USA (Ret.) to: The President, The White House
Washington, D. C. 20500

On May 30, 1985, I wrote a letter to Attorney General Edwin Meese. Attached to the letter were 10 enclosures containing evidence to justify a reconsideration of the case. See Appendix titled Letter to Edwin Meese.

Two enclosures were letters from Colonel Milton Hochmuth, who was the first U.S. Army Ordinance Intelligence Officer on the scene when U.S. Army troops captured the V-2 manufacturing facility at Dora/Nordhausen, Germany. The first letter, to Mr. Ordway, was dated

November 19, 1984. The second letter, to Senator Sam Nunn, was dated April 25, 1985. In both of these letters, Colonel Hochmuth stated emphatically that Arthur Rudolph was innocent of any war crime.

In the third enclosure was a letter from Dr. F. Winterberg to Senator Laxalt concerning the testimony of Mr. Francis J. Barwacz. Mr. Barwacz was an American citizen who had gone with his parents back to Poland in the early 1930s. When Germany invaded Poland, Mr. Barwacz was a very young man. He was captured by the Gestapo and was held prisoner in a number of concentration camps. Finally, he was selected by the Gestapo to be transferred to the Dora/Nordhausen camp, there to work in the manufacturing of the V-2s.

In 1983, the DOJ sent a five-page questionnaire to Mr. Barwacz concerning his imprisonment in Germany. This questionnaire was issued by the OSI. On page five of the questionnaire, Mr. Barwacz indicated that Arthur Rudolph, the manager of the V-2 line, was completely innocent.

We were housed at Sangerhausen-Dora. Our commando was called flying commando, because working in many places, so we heard and saw allot. (sic)

If Justice Dep. will find that SS or that Kapo who torture me so much, I will be glad to testify against them, but not against on any German civilian.

There were two groups of German civilians. One, they were our supervisors and they work with us every day. The other group, did wear light clothing, like white shirts, they were called engineers. Some of them did walk(sic) farther out from us, had boards, or pencils or pens, in deep thinking many times only talking to each other but never to us prisoners. We knew that they were the brains. In addition, I saw about 8 or 10 of them by the rocket V2, only talking to each other. The others were our bosses. Now let me make myself clear once and for all. All the German civilians (Engineer-Scientist) and German Civilians our supervisors were very kind to us prisoners, never holding, yelling, or hitting any prisoner. They were extremely polite to us; never any one of them hurt, or harms us prisoners, that are a fact.

Thank you, F.B.

PS—They never told us their names, and prisoners were numbers. I remember one German Civilian called me Franz; he knew I was an American. He was kind too, but extremely kind to me.

All of the enclosures in my letter to Mr. Meese contained firm evidence to support my request for a reconsideration of the Rudolph case. I am not disclosing the contents of all of the enclosures, but enclosure 6, written to Chairman of the Senate Judiciary Committee Senator Thurmond by Dr. F. Winterberg and dated August 2, 1985, is reproduced in its entirety below. Dr. Winterberg clearly defines the connection between the OSI and the Russian KGB. His letter is as follows:

Dear Senator Thurmond:

I am an American scientist on a sabbatical leave from the University of Nevada. My letter is directed to you, the Chairman of the Senate Judicial Committee, because of a grave concern I have regarding the U.S. Dept. of Justice.

As reported in the press, the highly decorated U.S. rocket engineer, space flight pioneer and close associate of the late Wernher von Braun, Dr. A. Rudolph, was stripped of his citizenship by a controversial organization of the U.S. Dept. of Justice, the Office of Special Investigation (OSI). I say controversial, because not only has this organization been accused by U.S. war veteran organizations and in the Swiss Media to collaborate with the KGB, but it's first director, a Mr. A. Ryan, has according to a story which was printed in the Wall Street Journal brazenly admitted to have the full cooperation of the Soviet Union, which as every intelligent person knows, means the full cooperation of the KGB!

In order to weaken the U.S. space program and the NATO Alliance, an attempt by the communists was made in the early sixties to equate the German scientists and engineers under Wernher von Braun, the father of the U.S. space program, with Nazi war criminals. For that purpose, a book was published in communist East Germany by a Soviet agent with the name Mader. Because it was reported that Mader had received the material for his book from such U.S. organizations as "Women strike for peace," which is believed to be a communist's front, the FBI at that time conducted a probe. The charges contained in this book are the same kind of lies which have now 20 years later again been raised, this time however, by a U.S Govt. organization. That in the Rudolph case the OSI was in collusion with the communists appears to be also independently confirmed by a radio interview over German radio with Robert Kempner the chief U.S. prosecutor in the Nuremberg war crimes trial. In this interview, it was stated that in the Rudolph case the OSI had collaborated with the STASI, the East German arm of the KGB.

In order to follow up on the charges by the OSI, I have written to the West German special prosecutor for Nazi war crimes, Attorney General Streim. Mr. Streim, in answering my letter (copy attached) states that his office had conducted extensive investigations about the surroundings of the V2 factory where Rudolph had worked, but that the name of Rudolph had never come up. In his letter Mr. Streim adds, that he had not received any information from the OSI since (exactly since last June) the material against Rudolph by a bilateral legal assistance treaty between the Federal Republic of Germany and the U.S. is obligated to turn over to the W. German prosecutor. **Furthermore, I was still able to locate after 40 years witnesses who state that the charges made by the OSI against Rudolph are outright lies; I may add well-known communist lies!**

The OSI has charged Rudolph and hidden the fact that concentration camp inmates from a nearby camp worked in the V-2 factory where he held an executive position, and that he therefore had illegally obtained his citizenship. This however, is completely untrue and false, because I can report to you that I am in the possession of an official U.S. Govt. interrogation of Mr. Rudolph, conducted in 1947 by Major Eugene Smith, Lt. R.B. Payne and 1st Lt. Gordon A. Mc Gannon. The interrogation was conducted for a U.S. military court prosecuting the concentration camp commanders, that the German scientists never had jurisdiction over the camps or the inmates.

In this transcript, Dr. Rudolph had given a full account about the circumstances of the V2 factory. I may add, that in practically all German armament factories concentration camp inmates worked in helping German specialist workers." Sincerely (signed) F. Winterberg

This was the last of the enclosures in my letter to Attorney General Meese. A copy of the letter is located in Appendix so titled. Attorney General Meese ignored my letter.

Concerning the letter referred to above as enclosure No. 6, Dr. Winterberg wrote another letter to Senator Thurmond:

*Dear Senator Thurmond, the OSI has been congressionally mandated to expel from the U.S. Nazi war criminals, but not German scientists who were never accused of any such crimes. I therefore would like to urge you to initiate an investigation of the OSI, in particular the aspect that it collaborates with the communists and advances communist goals. I learned with amazement that Mr. Ryan, and now Mr. Sher the present OSI director, are not even attorneys. How is it possible that such unqualified persons can assume a high position in the Justice Dept.? Moreover, what is Mr. Ryan's political background considering his public bragging to have the full cooperation of the Soviets? I may finally add that the handling of the Rudolph case is hardly in the best interest of the U.S. This can perhaps best be understood by **the fact that already more than 10,000 signatures have been collected in one state in W. Germany alone, for a referendum against the stationing of Pershing II missiles. The many friends the U.S. has in W. Germany may sit out such a referendum in disinterest if the Rudolph case is not resolved in an honorable way.***

Sincerely (signed) F. Winterberg

In late 1986, I requested assistance from California Senator Pete Wilson, informing him of my failure to receive a response from the DOJ. In February 1987, Senator Wilson sent me a copy of a letter he had received from Assistant Attorney General John R. Bolton. In this letter, dated January 29, 1987, Mr. Bolton invited me to present any new legitimate evidence concerning the Rudolph case.

Dear Senator Wilson:

This is in further response to your letter of December 1, 1986, on behalf of W. E. Winterstein of Fillmore, California, who is of the opinion that Arthur L.H. Rudolph was unjustly expelled from the United States for his work in Nazi Germany during World War II. I regret that Mr. Winterstein disagrees with the disposition of the Rudolph case. The fact is, however, that Mr. Rudolph left the United States freely and voluntarily rather than face charges that he participated in the persecution, of slave laborers and concentration camp inmates while serving as Operations Director of the Nazis' underground V-2 rocket facility in central Germany, where prisoners died in large numbers from overwork, disease, malnutrition and brutalities inflicted, by the Nazis.
[Author's note that this is hearsay NOT proven fact.]

I want to emphasize that Mr. Rudolph was represented by competent counsel and when faced with incontrovertible documentary evidence, he freely and voluntarily entered into an agreement to leave this country and renounce his citizenship and he did so.

Let me assure you that before proceeding in cases such as the Rudolph matter, we at the DOJ carefully review the evidence and weigh its credibility. We proceed only after we are convinced that the evidence supports the allegations.

Mr. Rudolph was not unjustly expelled from this country as Mr. Winterstein suggests and I am not aware of any procedures, which might be undertaken to initiate a new investigation of this case. If Mr. Winterstein is in possession of any new legitimate evidence which indicates a problem with the way the case was handled, have him bring it to our attention and we will look into it.

I trust that the foregoing adequately provides sufficient information to respond to the concerns of your constituent. Please do not hesitate to write if I can be of further assistance to you."

Sincerely, (signed) John. R Bolton   Assistant Attorney General

On March 1, 1987, I replied to Mr. Bolton's invitation. Because of the importance of Mr. Bolton's later response, I am including the entire contents of the letter, consisting of 5 pages, with 10 enclosures.

Dear Mr. Bolton:

Your kind invitation to me, as expressed by you in your letter to Senator Pete Wilson, dated 29 January 1987, for me to bring to your attention any new legitimate evidence in the Arthur Rudolph case which indicates a problem with the way this case was handled, is sincerely appreciated.

I wish to make one thing very clear at this point. I do not condone war crimes that were committed by the Nazis during World War II. Such criminals should be prosecuted on legitimate evidence. In view of the information contained in the following comments, it is my opinion that Arthur Rudolph is innocent of unjustified charges and was improperly expelled from the United States.

At the time the case was apparently closed by the Office of Special Investigation in 1984, Rudolph did not personally know of one witness alive, after 40 years, who could refute the allegations presented by the Office of Special Investigation. In addition, at that time he was in poor health and financially unable to mount a court defense against the resources of the Office of Special Investigation. Since then, after the case received publicity, a number of witnesses appeared giving information in defense of Dr. Rudolph. These witnesses, some of whom are former prisoners who worked on the V-2 production line where the Office of Special Investigation alleges they (prisoners) were persecuted by Rudolph, and others, have either stated that Rudolph is innocent of any war crimes, or give strong evidence confirming that fact. Contrary to allegations by the Office of Special Investigation, some of the former prisoners have stated that Dr. Rudolph was responsible for improving the living conditions of the prisoners. In this respect, he went a little too far at one time, in the opinion of his (Rudolph's) supervisor. The plant manager, a Mr. Sawatzki, threatened Rudolph with imprisonment for improving the conditions of the prisoners too much. Rudolph, however, was allowed to help establish a bonus system for prisoners working in production. This provided an improvement of footwear and clothing, allotment of coffee or tea besides normal rations, and for the separation and treatment of prisoners becoming sick. See enclosure (1) for copy of Bonus coupons used.

Some of the witnesses referred to previously are:

–Colonel Milton Hochmuth–

U.S. Army Intelligence Officer, on the scene after U.S. troops captured the V-2 plant. See enclosures (2) and (3), letters from Hochmuth to Mr. Ordway and Senator Sam Nunn.

–Mr. Francis J. Barwacz–

U.S. citizen, former prisoner-laborer in V-2 plant. See enclosure (4) which is page 5 of a five-page questionnaire (undated) sent to Mr. Barwacz by the Office of Special Investigation.

–Mr. Gerhard Schramm–

West German, former prisoner-laborer in V-2 plant. See enclosure (5), deposition.

–Mr. Rudi Koenig–

West German, former prisoner-laborer in V-2 plant. See enclosure (6), statement.

–Mr. Theodore Webers–

West German, former clerk on working assignment at Sawatzki Facility and Camp Dora. See enclosure (7), letter to Dr. Winterberg.

–Mr. Heinz Hilgenbocker–

West German, former quality and acceptance engineer at the V-2 plant. See enclosure (8), letter to Dr. Winterberg.

–Mr. Roman Drung–

Former political prisoner in Camp Dora. See enclosure (9), excerpts of interrogation.

–Mr. Streim–

West German Prosecutor of Nazi war crimes. See enclosure (10), letter to Dr. Winterberg.

It appears that the investigators of the Office of Special Investigation involved in this case have not taken into full account the exact role of Dr. Rudolph as the production engineer for the V-2 line, particularly in the scope of his authority over the prisoner-laborers. It also appears from comments by the Office of Special Investigation and action taken; that Rudolph was accused of being responsible for the death of thousands of prisoners because he (Rudolph) happened to be production manager of the V-2 line and., therefore, was responsible for all deaths that occurred in the general vicinity of the nearby concentration camps. The role of the SS in wartime Germany was the control of all concentration camps.

They maintained strict control over all phases of prisoner activities, both on or off work assignments. Prisoners from these camps formed a substantial workforce in the German industrial complex. Rudolph was not a member of the SS. He was a civilian, working for a private German company, which had a contract with the German government to produce V-2s. The government provided the labor and the facilities and the labor were furnished under the direct supervision of the SS.

Colonel Hochmuth supports the fact that there were "murder" camps nearby. However, he states that the laborers that came from the camp that worked in the V-2 plant were well fed, in good health, and were obviously not mistreated. The V-2 production line occupied only a portion of the Mittelwerk or tunnel complex.

There was also the V-1 line along with the jet fighter engine operations going on. In addition, during this time it is understood that considerable activity was going on in expanding the tunnel complex to house more defense operations so as to be protected from Allied bombing raids. It would appear, as a logical deduction, that many deaths could have resulted from tunnel construction where unskilled labor was probably used.

It is inconceivable that a production manager or engineer, even in such a place as Germany was in those days, would deliberately sabotage his efforts in trying to meet the almost impossible production quotas set by the German government. Anyone with a bit of mechanical knowledge would know that a rocket, as complex as the V-2, requires highly skilled workmanship to fabricate the parts, some with extremely fine tolerances, and to assemble these parts. Skilled labor to accomplish this type of work was scarce in Germany in those days. To willfully mistreat, persecute or murder personnel in such a workforce would have been highly illogical and unproductive.

Another insight into the operations of the SS is provided in the book "Inside the Third Reich," by Albert Speer, who was a convicted Nazi war criminal. As former Armaments Minister under Hitler, Speer explains in quite some detail the working of the SS at the V-2 factory site. This is found in pages 369 through 374 of the Macmillan 1970 edition. Speer also describes in this section the arrest of the top rocket engineer in Germany at that time when SS Chief Himmler jailed Dr. von Braun. It happened when von Braun and some of his associates had their minds on other civil type projects rather than giving full attention on the war production effort.

The Office of Special Investigation has furnished information to Congress, which has resulted in the formulation of Congressional Resolution, 99th Congress H. RES. 68, dated Feb. 1985. The purpose of this resolution was to rescind the NASA Distinguished Service Medal awarded to Arthur Rudolph in 1969. As of 17 March 1986, a total of 27 Congressmen endorsed this resolution. Some of the wording in the resolution is unbelievable to me in light of the evidence revealed by witnesses referred to above. Words such as; "Whereas under Rudolph's supervision 60,000 slave laborers worked in subhuman conditions, resulting in the death of an estimated 20,000 to 30,000 workers." There have been reports from other sources that indicate there was not one death on the V-2 production line under Rudolph due to any mistreatment of a prisoner by an engineer. Other documentation available to me stated that Dr. Rudolph's first two interviews with the Office of Special Investigation were without counsel; however, he was informed of his right to have one. He evidently thought that these interviews were like the many he had had before and he gave the same type of information. He was never informed of his rights under the Miranda Act. At the third and subsequent interview, Rudolph was represented by counsel but he, Rudolph, was excluded from being present by the specific request of the Office of Special Investigation. He was told that witnesses would testify against him; however, the Office of Special Investigation refused to identify the witnesses.

The recurring comments from the Office of Special Investigation to persons interested in the disposition of the case would be misleading, in my opinion, in light of new evidence since the case was closed. The fact that witnesses have come forth in defense of Rudolph contradicts such key statements from the Office of Special Investigation as, "Rudolph's role in the exploitation of slave labor is not open to question." Also such statements as, "I want to reemphasize that Mr. Rudolph was represented by competent counsel and, when faced with incontrovertible documentary evidence, he freely and voluntarily entered into an agreement to leave this country and renounce his citizenship and he did so." A review of the case should bring up the question of competent counsel. Why did his attorney apparently refuse to demand that his client be present at all interviews? Why did his attorney fail to have his client afford the right to see and review all the documentary evidence submitted by the Office of Special Investigation against him? Finally, Rudolph's attorney did not succeed in having changes made in The Agreement, dictated by the Office of Special Investigation, at the request of his client. The Office of Special Investigation's comment that he "freely and. voluntarily entered into an agreement to leave this country" is partially nullified by the fact that Rudolph, over many objections, finally signed an agreement to leave the country.

He had steadfastly maintained that he was innocent of any war crime. It was definitely not done in a spontaneous manner nor with any degree of alacrity on his part; he apparently was under duress at the time.

I have been informed that the Office of Special Investigation contacted witnesses in the United States and Israel and forwarded a list of these witnesses to the Federal Republic of Germany.

It has been learned from all witnesses who cared to reply, and most did so, that they did not know A. Rudolph and did not work in the V-2 underground facility. Extensive and thorough trials about the Dora-Nordhausen concentration camp took place in West Germany, such as in Essen 1967 and 1969. Not a single complaint against any one of the Mittelwerk civilian engineers and technical supervisors was brought up during the several hundred interrogations of witnesses. See enclosure (10). The Office of Special Investigation apparently did not contact the Federal Republic of Germany about the specifics uncovered in these trials. However, the Office of Special Investigation requested after a first contact in 1981, again with its note No. 433, dated July 15, 1985, specific information about A. Rudolph from communist East Germany. Copies of this correspondence, including the last German reply, have now been obtained. The reply does not incriminate Dr. Rudolph in any way.

The current status of Dr. Rudolph is that he is a stateless person, a man without a country, living in exile in Hamburg, West Germany. He is 80 years old. He has devoted much of that lifetime as a dedicated and patriotic citizen of the United States. He was in the forefront of establishing the United States as a leader in space.

In view of the fact that reliable witnesses in defense of Dr. Rudolph have been showing up since his exile or deportation, a prompt reconsideration of this case is justified at this time. I hope that the foregoing evidence and information will assist you in the re-evaluation of this case.

Sincerely, (signed) W. E. Winterstein LTC, Army Ret.

Copy to: Honorable Pete Wilson (w/encl.), Honorable Howell Heflin (w/encl.)

The following is the list of enclosures

Encl No. 1 is the Bonus System for prisoners at Camp Dora, Figure 7.

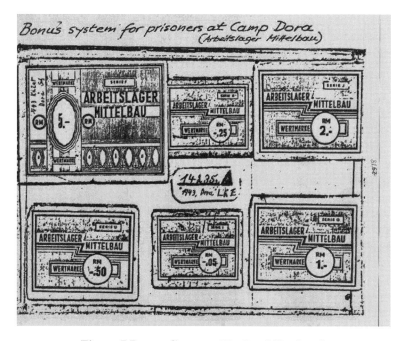

Figure 7 **Bonus Coupons Used at Mittelwerk**

Encl. No. 2 letter from Col. Hochmuth to Mr. Ordway

Dear Mr. Ordway,

On my return to Paris on the 16th, I got your letter dated November 6. I was rather shocked about Rudolph and immediately wrote a letter to the Int. Herald Tribune, a copy of which I sent to Walt Wiesman in Huntsville. My computer/word processor is out of order, hence this letter.

To save time I am enclosing a (copy) letter I wrote to Senator Sam Nunn.

I was the first U.S. Army officer tracking V-2s and other missile developments to get to Nordhausen and Mittelwerk. Because I was part of Ordnance Technical Intelligence Team #1. Attached to the first U.S. Army, I was informed that it was an intelligence target and arrived a few hours after an infantry regiment (I have forgotten its identity) overran the area.

I am not sure who the von Braun group member was who we arranged to help pick out parts for 100 V-2s, was it Rudolph? Was it Günther Hintze? I do not remember.

I continued to search out other members of the von Braun group scattered throughout the wide area in farms, small factories, etc., always being the first to get to them, because it was my job. Meanwhile (then) Col. Toftoy arranged to have an Ordnance Heavy Automotive Maintenance Company sent to Nordhausen to actually pack and ship the parts.

I visited this company and its efforts several times to make sure they picked all the right parts. They were aided by some Germans, but I do not remember whom. I could go into greater detail but I want to get this letter off.

Mittelwerk was devoted to the assembly of V-2s, V-1s and aircraft jet engines (Junkers as I recall, but I may be wrong). Our infantry had identified Director Sawatzki as the civilian in charge. There were also SS in overall charge (I am sure of this) who had fled before being overrun. When I talked to Sawatzki he admitted being in charge and I forgot the details of a 30 to 40 minute session I had with him, though I believe I wrote a report up for forwarding to Col. Toftoy.

We were so excited about getting the V-2 plant and parts that I hurried back to make my report and told the sergeant (infantry? or division civil affairs? or what) who was holding Sawatzki as a prisoner that I would return the next morning to interview/question him in depth. When I got back the next morning Sawatzki "could not be found." Moreover, the infantry had moved on.

*Rudolph had nothing to do with V-1s or jet engines. Prisoners from the camp were apparently assigned to work by a central labor administration. As I mentioned in the letter to Sen. Nunn I was so shocked to see the dead and dying ELSEWHERE in the Nordhausen area that I did take the trouble to find a "haftling" (slave laborer) who happened to be a lathe operator. I remember being surprised at how well fed he looked and in good health. Obviously, they were not mistreating those who worked in the plant. Of course, I do not know about those who built the plant. **It would have been stupid to mistreat workers assigned to skilled jobs. That there were at least two camps I know, and I remember concluding that the camp where the workers came from were not ill-treated as were those in what were apparently near-by camps.***

If Rudolph is guilty, so are millions of other Germans who were spectators or who found themselves near the scenes of forced labor and we might well send back to Germany? All Germans who have come to the U.S. since World War II who were over 18 in 1945 we might also break diplomatic relations, It would be just as logical as forcing Rudolph to go back. I have one or two vignettes bearing my Nordhausen experiences but I hope this in enough.

Sincerely, (Signed Hochmuth)

P.S.—You can quote me.

Encl. No. 3 Letter from Professor (Col.) Milton Hochmuth to Senator Sam Nunn

Dear Sam,

Last September or October when as now I was temporarily staying at our home in southern France I saw an article where one of the Von Braun rocket team members, Arthur Rudolph, had been forced to renounce his citizenship and returned to Germany. At that time, I wrote you a hand-written letter explaining my unique connection and knowledge of his case. My files with a copy of that letter together with your reply enclosing the DOJ's letter to your assistant are unfortunately in my Paris apartment so I cannot give you the specific dates. Hopefully your office staff can lay their hands on the correspondence.

I was disappointed with the DOJ's response for a number of reasons. First and foremost I was at that time fairly certain of Rudolph's innocence of the charges brought against him; Second, because of the categorizing of my effort to see justice done was "specious";-hardly the language to use when a disinterested retired regular Army officer tries to prevent a injustice by presenting new, personal evidence; and three, because part of the letter contains a quote from a Washington Post editorial on the quote "foolish and ill-advised nature" of the Army's bringing Von Braun and his team over as an argument for expelling Rudolph! (The quote is not exact because I cannot have the letter here in St. Jean de Luz). Never the less, I decided to dig deeper, write Rudolph, and see exactly what the facts were before taking any further action. A copy of that letter is enclosed. Meanwhile articles appeared in the International Herald Tribune stating that Rudolph was a member of the SS and that even von Braun was a member of the SS. Now, I could not know of course whether these accusations were true or false but I would be willing to bet a substantial sum that they are false for a vast number of reasons, too lengthy to go into here. I did, however point-

blankly ask Rudolph to let me know the facts from his side. His reply is enclosed.

I am now firmly convinced a grave, serious injustice has been done to Rudolph and I would ask you to use your influence to have the Justice Department review this case. We all make mistakes, and I think that in an era where countless guilty go free that it behooves us to take the trouble to undo this wrong.

You may recall that I wrote you that I was the first intelligence officer to get to Mittelwerk (V-2 assembly plant) and I interviewed the head of V-2 assembly—a man named Sawatzki- and that Rudolph was the engineer in charge, and of V-2s only, not the entire plant which also manufactured V-1s and aircraft jet-engines. I also mentioned that I was surprised at seeing numbers of apparently well-fed, healthy "haftlinge" (slave laborers) and even took the time to talk to one at some length. I did not mention that the next day I went to a small village where there was a large ammunition plant where V-2 warheads were loaded with high explosive. The labor in this plant was also forced labor and I was the first American in the village- troops of neither side had been through. These people were quite healthy, robust enough to start looting and strong enough to carry sewing machines etc., which they were liberating.

This confirms the fact that you do not use horrible methods to exact work that requires care and precision. There were of course several concentration camps around the Mittelwerk. At least one was a horror camp as I wrote you. Indeed I was so furious that I took it out on one of the two German scientists who was helping me round up others as well as V-2 laboratory equipment. The Russians could never accept the fact that the von Braun team offered themselves to the U.S. and refused their very generous offer. It is well within the realm of probability that the Russians are amusing themselves while at the same time punishing a member of the "Paperclip" exodus by planting false information that cannot be substantiated or easily refuted.

While I knew Rudolph fairly well for a period in 1946 when he worked for me, I have seen him once or twice, briefly after the Germans were transferred to NASA. We have no personal relationship or even a friendship.

My motivation is to correct a manifest and serious miscarriage of justice. I do know that he and the rest of the von Braun team made it possible to catch up with the Russians who made much better use of the far fewer Germans they managed to get (they were unencumbered with inter-service rivalry which cost the space effort five years at least) and to enable us to ultimately put men on the moon etc.

Sincerely yours, (signed) Milton

Encl. No. 4 Statement by Mr. Frank Barwacz to questionnaire from OSI.

[see Appendix titled letter from Frank Barwacz to President Reagan for another statement]

All the German civilians (Engineer-Scientist) and German Civilians our supervisors, wear very kind to us prisoners, never holding, yelling, or hitting any prisoner. They were extremely polite to us; never any one of them hurt, or harms us prisoners, that are a fact."

Thank you, F.B.

PS—They never told us their names, and prisoners were numbers. I remember one German Civilian called me Franz; he knew I was an American. He was kind too, but extremely kind to me.

Encl. No. 5 Statement by Gerhard Schramm.

TRANSLATION

DEPOSITION

"I, the undersigned Gerhard Schramm, give the deposition that I was a concentration camp inmate with the No. 14235 in the camp Dora-Nordhausen and that I worked for Mr. Rudolph on electrical cables in the V-2 manufacturing tunnels therefore I knew him very well. Mr. Rudolph stood up very well for us prisoners and got us additional rations. He treated us concentration camp inmates always well and I know of no case, where Mr. Rudolph was rough, or where he would have even mistreated prisoners. I can state further that we prisoners had esteem and respect for Mr. Rudolph and I heard never a complaint about him from another prisoner.

I give these statements to the best of my knowledge and conscience and I am aware of the meaning of a deposition. Also I am ready to repeat my statements before a court and to answer questions."

(Signed) Gerhard Schramm.

Encl. No. 6 Statement by Rudi Koenig.

STATEMENT

I worked from 1941 until August 17, 1943 in Peenemünde as a former member of the VKN (Versuchs-Kommando-Nord / Test Command North) and thereafter in the Mittelwerk GMBH in Niedersachsenwerfefl. At both places, Mr. Arthur Rudolph was technical director and factory manager. Concentration camp prisoners under the authority of the Security Division Subcommand Nordhausen were employed too. Board and lodging, medical attention and also custody during working hours were assigned to the GESTAPO. Mr. Rudolph had no influence or any authority over this group of persons. For several months in 1944, I was put into the concentration camp Dora because of an alleged political offense and had to work in the factory as a prisoner.

According to my knowledge, no Jews were working in the factory. *Mr. Rudolph was a well-liked supervisor by everybody, including the prisoners; he obtained for quite some prisoners special rations and alleviation.*

(signed) Rudi Koenig

Encl. No. 7 Letter to Dr. Winterberg from Mr. Webers

Dear Prof. Winterberg,

In reply to your letter mentioned above I inform you as follows, The information in the Süddeutsche Zeitunq, October 22, 1984 is not true with respect to the statement that Dr. A. Rudolph as Technical Director of the V2 rocket production in the Mittelwerk and concentration camp Dora worked to death thousands of Jewish slave laborers. ***From 1943 until the termination of the concentration camp Dora in early April 1945, never any Jewish prisoners were employed.***

Why? Because there were never Jews in Dora.

I myself worked only for about 3/4 of a year in the tunnel of the Sawatzki facility as a clerk in a working assignment. Later I was engaged outside the tunnel and the electrically charged fence of the concentration camp in a group as clerk. ***During my long stay in the concentration camp Dora, I did not learn of a single case of prisoners beaten or flayed by civilians, no matter what assignment they had.***

The civilian employees and blue-collar workers had no direct influence on the pace and the working lapse. This was assigned to the Kapos and work leaders of the individual working groups and last not least to the SS supervisors.

I knew from hearsay the name of Dr. Rudolph as the director of the total production. Consciously I have never seen him.

I assure you that I am willing to give this information under oath at a trial. With friendly greetings"

(signed Webers)

Encl. No. 8 Letter from Heinz Hilgenbocker to Dr. Winterberg.

Dear Dr. Winterberg,

I am referring to your letter of 12/ 7/ 85 and would like to introduce myself first.

I had been working first at Peenemünde, being employed as quality and acceptance engineer by the Office for Armament of the Army, Department of Acceptance.

My office got transferred to the Mittelwerk (near) Nordhausen after the production of rockets was started. My assignment comprised testing of the rocket motor and acceptance of the rockets after manufacturing in the big workshop 42.

To the content of your letter:

The total assembly was carried out by the prisoners of camp Dora under the supervision of the SS. First Lieutenant Förschner was in charge of the camp. The work was carried out around the clock in 12-hour shifts, one week on daylight, and the other week at night. In your letter you inform me that the former director of the plant is said to have worked to death thousands of Jewish prisoners despite the fact that every coworker in the plant can verify, that the guards of camp Dora were responsible for every prisoner. If the accusation would be correct Mr. Rudolph would have been accused in court with others at the Federal Court, Essen, where the Nordhausen trial took place in 1969. Four SS soldiers from camp Dora were accused in this court for serious crimes on prisoners. The prosecutor was Attorney General Dr. Rosier. I was a witness under oath at this trial.

When I was interrogated in Herford Dr. Rosler told me, that he had also interrogated Mr. Wernher von Braun in the U.S.A.

The former minister of armament Albert Speer was interrogated at this trial too. Acts of sabotage by prisoners were discussed too; they had clogged up fuel pipes with rags. This was detected when a rocket did not obtain the (necessary) thrust at start and exploded on ground. After this was recognized, all rockets were withdrawn. To discourage (prisoners) to commit such and possibly other acts of sabotage a number of prisoners were executed by hanging by the camp-SS by order of Himmler; the execution was carried out with lift-cranes in the workshop 42.

Hoping that I have given you the desired information I remain with best regards. "

Yours Heinz Hilgenbocker (signed)

Encl. No 9 Statement by Mr. Drung

TRANSLATION

Protocol taken on March 11. 1985.

Excerpts of interrogation protocol of former political (non-communist) prisoner and camp eldest of camp Dora, Mr. Roman Drung; criminal police of the Fed. Rep, of Germany carried out the investigation.

As camp eldest the prisoner-police had to report to him, (all concentration camps had their internal police staffed by prisoners). Mr. Drung was all the time in camp Dora. Mr. Roman Drung was born August 6, 1908 in Kotschanowitz (Upper Silesia).

Mr. Drung stated:

"At no time did I learn that, as a result of complaints or denunciations from members of the technical management, prisoners were called to account by the SS." *Roman Drung (signature)*

Encl. No. 10 Letter from Mr. Streim, West German Prosecutor, to Dr. Winterberg

Central Office of State Judicial Administration Ludwigsburg, West Germany
January 15, 1985
To: Prof. Dr. F. Winterberg
Konstanz University Konstanz, West Germany

Dear Professor Winterberg,

In reply to your letter of January 9 of this year, I inform you, in accordance with your request that at the central office there is no incriminating evidence against Mr. Rudolph. I may add that because of the Nazi crimes at Dora-Mittelbau—in particular, because of the hanging of prisoners in the underground factorie—intensive investigations have been conducted. The name Rudolph never came up.

By the way, the documents that I had requested several months ago from the Office of Special Investigations of the U.S. DOJ have not yet arrived. After receiving these documents, I will determine whether, on the basis of the information drawn from these, I have to initiate (legal) proceedings.

Sincerely yours, (signed) Streim Attorney General

This completes the full text of my letter to Mr. Bolton with enclosures.

Dr. Winterberg also located former concentration camp prisoners who worked on the V-2 line, and obtained their affidavits, in which they stated that Rudolph was innocent.

On July 6, 1987, I received a response from Assistant Attorney General John R. Bolton. His response denies that I had given him new evidence. From my perspective, this constituted an outright lie.

During my career in the Army as an officer, I had to go under intensive training in the administration of military law. I was a member of numerous court-martials, participating as simple board member, and as prosecutor and defense counsel. I had, and have, clear knowledge about the rules of evidence. For evidence to be

**admissible in any court, civilian or military, it must be material
and relevant.**

Letter from Assistant Attorney General John R. Bolton.

U.S. DOJ
Office of Legislative and Intergovernmental Affairs   July 6, 1987
W.E. Winterstein LTC, Army Ret.

Dear Mr. Winterstein:

*This is in further response to your letters of March 1 and March 9, 1987,
forwarding information regarding the Arthur Rudolph case.*

*We have reviewed and analyzed the contents of your letters and find no
new legitimate information that would serve to justify or cause a
reevaluation of the Rudolph case.*

*Rudolph entered into an agreement with this Department that resulted
in his permanent departure from this country in March of 1984 and
renunciation of his United States citizenship. This matter has been
terminated and Mr. Rudolph will not be allowed to enter the United
States again.*

*We can add nothing further to our previous response to you through
Senator Pete Wilson, which clearly states this Department's position
toward the disposition of the Arthur Rudolph case. This position is
likewise well articulated in the many detailed responses sent by this
Department over the past several years to Dr. Friedwardt Winterberg
whose "investigative report" on the handling of the Rudolph case was
enclosed with your letter of March 9, 1987.*

Sincerely, (signed John R. Bolton)   Assistant Attorney General

**[2001 to now Mr. Bolton is employed as Under Secretary, Arms
Control and International Security]**

This rather direct rebuff from a senior official of the DOJ was quite a
shock. I had forwarded copies of my letter, dated March 1, 1987, to
Assistant Attorney General John R. Bolton, to both Senators Pete Wilson,
and Howell Heflin. The reason for going to Senator Heflin was that
Arthur Rudolph was a resident of Huntsville, Alabama, at the time he was

Program Manager of the Saturn V. At this time, I had not requested any response from either of the Senators; the copies of the letters were for the purpose of information only.

However, since being rebuffed by Mr. Bolton in his response to me in July, I wrote letters, dated 4 September 1985, to both Senator Pete Wilson and my Congresswoman Bobbi Fiedler, requesting that action be initiated for a congressional hearing into the Rudolph matter, and that the hearing should determine whether the tactics employed by the OSI in this case were consonant with the congressional mandate establishing the OSI. There were seven enclosures to these letters. They contained legitimate documentary evidence to fully support a congressional hearing.

I did not receive a response to my request for a congressional hearing from either Senator Wilson or Congresswoman Bobbi Fiedler.

The DOJ was adamant in its refusal to reconsider the case, so Congressional action appeared to be the only remaining avenue for obtaining justice in the case. My last letter to Senator Wilson was dated December 27, 1989. This letter was about a complaint that I had with the DOJ concerning their reluctance to provide me with information I had requested under the Freedom of Information Act. In this request, I had asked for a copy of the document that was the source of information contained in the fourth paragraph of Congressional Resolution House Resolution 68, dated February 21, 1985. This paragraph reads:

> *Whereas under Rudolph's supervision 60,000 slave laborers worked in subhuman conditions, resulting in the death of an estimated 20,000 to 30,000 workers this resolution was introduced to Congress for the purpose of taking away the NASA Distinguished Service Medal presented to Rudolph for his participation in placing U.S. astronauts on the moon.*

In October of 1989, the DOJ informed me that the Criminal Division did not furnish that information to Congress.

This was indeed shocking news to me that such a statement would come from the DOJ, because there, in plain English, in the third paragraph of the resolution are the words:

Whereas Arthur Rudolph has renounced his American citizenship and returned to West Germany rather than face deportation charges stemming from allegations brought by the Office of Special Investigations, DOJ...

The OSI is in the Criminal Division of the DOJ. Prior to this, I had furnished legitimate documentary evidence that completely refuted this allegation against Rudolph. This evidence revealed that the total workforce of camp inmates who worked on the V-2 line, under Rudolph, was about 5,000. It also suggested that Rudolph was very concerned about the welfare of his workers. In the course of fabricating the very highly complex guided missile, Rudolph, with much difficulty, had arranged that his skilled workers would receive supplemental rations and better than average medical attention and clothing.

I also informed Senator Wilson that the situation concerning H.RES.68 was compounded two years later with the reintroduction of an identical text Congressional Resolution, H.RES.164, dated May 11, 1987. This was accompanied by derogatory remarks against Arthur Rudolph in another public document by Congressman Bill Green of New York, in the Congressional Record, page E 1841, dated May 11, 1987. In his remarks, Mr. Green quoted the DOJ as his source of information.

My request in this letter was for Senator Wilson to find out the truth of who furnished the information about the allegations in H.RES.68 to Congress, and to request a copy of the document. I never received a response. In fact, of the several brief responses from Senator Wilson concerning the case, there was no specific information given which indicated a forthcoming resolution to any of the problems presented.

I sent a copy of my letter to Mr. Bolton, and also to Senator Howell Heflin of Alabama, since I had sent him a copy of my original letter to Mr. Meese. I received a very prompt response from Senator Heflin. On March 6, 1987, I received his first reply:

I am writing to acknowledge, with thanks, receipt if your communication dated March 1, 1987.

It goes without saying that I appreciate your thoughtfulness in sending me a copy of your letter to Mr. John Bolton. U.S. DOJ, relative to the Dr. Arthur Rudolph case. I shall make this additional information a part of my file.

I was quite elated by the response that I received from Senator Heflin; however, on July 17, 1987; he informed me that he could not spend much time on the Rudolph case due to his position on the Senate Select Committee, which, at that time, was deeply involved in the Iran-Contra affair. He wrote:

Dear Bill:

Thank you for your letter of July 6, 1987, which has been brought to my personal attention.

I appreciate your furnishing me with a copy of your letter of July 4, 1987 to Mr. John B. Bolton about Dr. Arthur Rudolph. I am glad to have your correspondence for my file. Because of the full Senate agenda and intensive work on the Select Committee on Secret Military Assistance to the Iran and Nicaraguan Opposition, I have not been able to spend as much time reviewing the case as I would like. I do not foresee any immediate action on my part because of my hectic schedule. However, I do retain an interest in Dr. Rudolph's case, and I shall continue to study all aspects of his case.

With kindest regards, I am

Sincerely yours, (signed) Howell

In conjunction with this correspondence between Senator Heflin and myself, I wish to compare the manner in which a venerable scientific organization viewed the Rudolph case, about a year later, with the letter from Senator Heflin to me. On June 10, 1988, Senator Heflin received a letter from James J. Harford, Executive Director of the American Institute of Aeronautics and Astronautics. This is the narrative account of the letter:

Dear Senator Heflin:

Enclosed is a commentary on the Arthur Rudolph case, written by AIAA Associate Fellow Frederick I. Ordway, III, which will appear in the Institute's magazine Aerospace America in August. A copy of which is enclosed, goes to 71000 aerospace engineers, scientists, libraries and others throughout the world.

Dr. Rudolph was elected a Fellow of the Institute by his peers for his many contributions to the U.S. defense and space programs.

How appropriate it would be if his case were reopened, and he were cleared of the accusations against him (which seem to be based on no more evidence than existed when he first was investigated after World War II) in time to return his citizenship before we celebrate the 20th anniversary of the Apollo landing, to which he contributed so substantively. That celebration occurs on July 20, 1989.

The commentary indicates that Rudolph's friends are seeking ways to reopen the case. We urge you to support such an effort.

Sincerely yours, (signed)   James J. Harford

My next approach in seeking congressional help was to contact my Congressman, Elton Gallegly, in July of 1987. He had just been elected in November of 1986, and had defeated Bobbi Fiedler. Since Elton was a freshman, I did not make any requests at first, but furnished him with background information so he could evaluate various aspects of the Rudolph case. In my first letter, I had enclosed a copy of my letter to Mr. Bolton, with the enclosures. I received a response in October thanking me for the information.

After furnishing Representative Gallegly with a considerable amount of evidence, I received a very favorable response in November 1987, advising me that he had contacted the DOJ to respond to the evidence I had submitted.

He also stated that based upon my documentation and presentation, he agreed that House Resolution 164, designed to take away the NASA Distinguished Service Medal from Rudolph, had nothing to do with the charges against him.

As this had been the position of NASA concerning the case, and based on this, he assured me that he would not be a co-sponsor to H.RES.164. He also stated that he would be in touch with me as soon as he had a response from the DOJ. At first, Rep. Gallegly responded quite favorably to my requests for assistance. After Mr. Bolton rejected my request for a reconsideration of the case in July 1987, Rep. Gallegly sent a strongly worded letter to him coinciding with my request that Dr. Rudolph be admitted to the U.S. to attend the celebration of the 20th anniversary of the lunar landing.

In the letter, Rep. Gallegly raised the issue of my discovery of new evidence countering the arguments of the DOJ. He also asked Mr. Bolton what conditions would have to be met to allow Dr. Rudolph to attend an anniversary honoring the space program.

Rep. Gallegly received a response to his letter to Mr. Bolton, from Thomas M. Boyd, in November 1988. The bottom line was a restatement of the DOJ's adamant position that no new legitimate information existed to justify a re-evaluation.

The letter restated the DOJ's position that Dr. Rudolph had voluntarily left the U.S due to the OSI "investigation" and had become a (West) German citizen. As part of his agreement to avoid U.S. prosecution, Dr. Rudolph had agreed never to return to the U.S. It was the opinion of the DOJ that Dr. Rudolph could never set foot on U.S. soil again "for any purpose" and Assistant Attorney General Boyd's letter to Rep. Gallegly was a denial, forbidding Arthur Rudolph to visit the U.S. to attend the 20th anniversary celebration of the lunar landing.

During the period 1985 to 1990, Dr. Haeussermann, Dr. Winterberg, and I were aggressively engaged in seeking a resolution of the Rudolph case. We exchanged information among ourselves in order to present a united front. We made our approaches to officials in the DOJ, to members of Congress, and others, in our own individual ways. The principal officials we contacted in the DOJ were: Attorney General Edwin Meese (he ignored my request), Assistant Attorney General John R. Bolton, Assistant Attorney General Thomas M. Boyd, and Deputy Assistant Attorney General Mark M. Richard.

It appears that the mindset of DOJ officials concerning their approach in the many requests for a resolution of the case is reflected in the response dated April 21, 1988, received by Dr. Haeussermann, from Mark Richard.

> *Dear Dr. Haeussermann:*
>
> *Your letter of September 30, 1987, addressed to Mr. Frank Carlucci has been referred to this office for a response. We have had previous exchanges of correspondence with you and other supporters of Dr. Rudolph regarding the* **Rudolph** *case and officials of this Department certainly are aware of your views. In earlier correspondence, we advised you of our position. please be advised that I am aware of no one in this Department who has seen or received any new or additional information from any source whatsoever that would provide a basis for reopening this matter.*
>
> *Thank you for your interest in this matter.*
>
> *Sincerely, (signed)   Mark M Richard*

This is the same Mark Richard mentioned earlier in this book, of whom I requested, under the Freedom of Information Act, a copy of the Rudolph prosecution memorandum from the DOJ.

You will also note that the prosecution memorandum was presented to Mark Richard by Neal Sher, the same director of the OSI who failed to submit exculpatory evidence to the West German prosecutor, thus involving himself in two counts of obstruction of justice.

There was considerable publicity about the Rudolph case in the news media beginning in 1985 after Arthur Rudolph had left the U.S. A news article that appeared in the *Huntsville* (Alabama) *Times* by the API dated July 1, 1985, reveals a very interesting difference of opinion among important public officials concerning the case. The person quoted as being against Rudolph was Jeremiah Denton, the Republican Senator from Alabama. According to the quotes, Senator Denton had based his opinion on information received from the DOJ.

The text of the story follows.

The Huntsville Times Monday, July 1, 1985

Rudolph Merits Try at Defense, Heflin Asserts

By the Associated Press

Arthur Rudolph, a German scientist who helped launch America's space program, deserves a chance to defend himself against the charge that he used slave laborer in a Nazi V-2 missile factory in World War II, Sen. Howell Heflin, D-Ala says:

"If he brings charges that there was hounding by the DOJ of him in this instance and indicates he is willing to testify as to that, I would certainly do what I could do and see that he had an opportunity to testify," Heflin said.

The 78-year-old Rudolph who directed the development of the Saturn V moon rocket at the Marshall Space Flight Center, renounced his U.S. citizenship and returned to Germany after being threatened with deportation by Justice Department agents. Heflin said Rudolph might be able to get his case examined by a congressional committee, but that the former member of Huntsville's "old team" of German rocket scientists would have to request such a hearing himself.

Alabama's Democratic senator made his remarks at an American Legion convention where Jeremiah Denton, Alabama's Republican Senator earlier called Rudolph "a war criminal."

"History is such that there is no question that he is a war criminal and that he was by any reasonable standard not a savory person," Denton said Friday.

Retired Army Major General John B. Medaris responding to Denton's characterization of Rudolph as "an unsavory person," said Denton would not denounce the former NASA scientist if Rudolph's true role in Nazi Germany was known.

Denton said Justice Department evidence he has seen indicates that Rudolph knowingly used slave labor at a V-2 rocket plant in Germany during World War II.

However, Medaris said Rudolph has been "deprived of his citizenship" without facing a judge or jury, "I hope he (Denton,) was misquoted because I don't want to believe that Sen. Denton would make that kind of remark without being aware of the facts," Medaris said at the convention.

Medaris said Rudolph had told colleagues, in the United States that he knew about slave labor at the V-2 factory, but that "the evidence we have from all sorts of sources has proven that he had absolutely no control over the program."

Rudolph lived in Huntsville from 1950 until 1969 and also headed the Army's Redstone and Pershing missile programs. He was awarded NASA's highest honor, the Distinguished Service Medal, for his work on the Saturn project.

On January 23, 1989, I gave Rep. Gallegly a response to the letter he received from Mr. Boyd in November 1987. I reminded Gallegly that Mr. Boyd's letter positively confirmed my past statements to him of the adamant stand that the DOJ had taken in not reconsidering or reopening the case. Moreover, this is an apparent total disregard of the considerable amount of evidence in defense of Rudolph since the OSI closed the case and Rudolph returned to Germany.

I referred to a bit of history that contradicted statements made by Mr. Boyd in his letter. I also reminded Rep. Gallegly's that Mr. Boyd failed (in his letter) to address the issue raised in the 65-page report by the National Legal Research Group. This issue concerned fraud by the U.S. Government in obtaining The Agreement under which Rudolph lost his citizenship rights. The following are a few of the quotes contained in the report.

"The fraud was committed by the doctoring of the evidence which the government had available to use against Dr. Rudolph. The doctoring of the evidence, rather than the threat of legal proceedings, also serves as the primary basis of the duress claim."

"In short, the OSI did more than merely overstate the evidence supporting its case, it mislead Dr. Rudolph and Mr. Main as to the nature of that evidence."

"The wrongfulness of the government's conduct in misrepresenting the state of the evidence can be demonstrated in two ways. The first arises from the doctrine of fraud-in-the-inducement. In considering whether to execute The Agreement, the state of the evidence against him must have

been a material factor in the minds of Dr. Rudolph and Mr. Main. As previously indicated, had they known that the statement of Bannach, a person they thought might exonerate Dr. Rudolph, they might well have taken a different course. In any event, Dr. Rudolph would have been able to exercise his free will in deciding whether to execute The Agreement. The same can be said of the other puffing, inaccurate, and misleading statements made by the government regarding the state of the evidence."

Besides the above, I gave Rep. Gallegly additional documentary evidence to support my request that congressional action be initiated to bring about a just resolution.

Some of the additional documentary evidence that I submitted, which had come into my possession, disclosed very important key information. It was a news item from the *Baltimore Sun*, dated November 17, 1984. Please note that this was eight months after Rudolph left the U.S. and five months after the news release by the OSI in June. The author of the article was Mr. Milton Crook who was a member of the U.S. legal staff and who participated in the original Nordhausen war crimes trial at Dachau, Germany, in 1947. This was the trial that determined who was guilty of the war crimes committed at the Camp Dora/Nordhausen complex.

Copy from the *Baltimore Sun*, November 17, 1984.

War Crimes

By Milton Crook

Editor: Recent articles concerning the alleged participation of Arthur L.H. Rudolph, former American and German scientist, in atrocities committed during 1943-45 at the Dora-Nordhausen Concentration Camp in Germany, were of much interest to me as I was a member of the U.S. legal staff and participated in the original Nordhausen War crimes trial at Dachau, Germany in 1947. From all reports, Mr. Rudolph was an eminent scientist in the field of rockets and space missiles and at wars end was recruited by the United States to help develop its own space program. However, later managed the Saturn V project leading to the Apollo moon shot.

Other colleagues of Rudolph were likewise recruited by our government and performed well in similar projects here. War crimes investigations were commenced in 1945 involving slave labor at Dora-Nordhausen, and upon completion, some of the scientists so recruited by us and working in U.S. installations were formally accused of such crimes and returned to Germany for trial at Dachau. Likewise accused and joined in the trial were various camp officials, guards and other personnel. After a long thorough trial, the war crimes court considered the evidence and testimony introduced by the parties and adjudged the scientists not guilty of all charges. The other defendants were all found guilty as charged and duly sentenced. In view of recent development in the Rudolph incident and his earlier Dora association with his fellow scientists, long since tried and acquitted, the allegation of similar charges against him almost 40 years after the fact gives rise to certain questions:

In the interim, where was the evidence of Rudolph complicity? Moreover, where were the persons knowledgeable of such evidence? Why did they not speak up during the 1947 trial or since then? This trial was an international event known to anyone interested. Rudolph's whereabouts were no secret and he was evidently available at all times. Moreover before making its decision to oust Rudolph from the country and to induce forfeiture of his citizenship, did the DOJ consider the 1947 precedent of the Dachau War Crimes Tribunal in its judgment concerning the question of the liability of Nordhausen scientists for alleged war crimes?

The V-2 line was one of the major production activities at the underground complex. The reason Rudolph was not even a defendant at this trial has been previously explained in this chapter, in that he was very much concerned about the welfare of his camp inmate workforce, and was therefore not guilty of any war crime. The significance of the outcome of this trial is that the OSI had full cognizance of the results prior to launching the vendetta against Rudolph.

I consider the above news item as one of the very important documents in this book. As will be revealed, the OSI was fully aware of the outcome of this trial prior to their interrogation of Rudolph in 1982 and 1983.

In collecting evidence and information over the past 20 years, I have amassed a collection of hundreds of pages of newspaper and magazine articles. I have previously referred to several of the items in the book;

however, the following Washington Times item by Pat Buchanan, dated July 17, 1989, brings the Rudolph story into another perspective.

Hero or Noxious Nazi?

By Pat Buchanan

Twenty years ago, President Nixon gathered his White House staff, and we all headed, before dawn, down to Cape Canaveral. The historic occasion: The launching of Apollo 11.

When the mighty Saturn V rocket thundered off its pad, with Neal Armstrong, Col. Edwin Eugene "Buzz" Aldrin, Jr., and Lt. Col. Michael Collins aboard, the earth shook for miles. It was a marvelous moment. The huge rocket, flames blazing half a mile from its tail, roared to the world a clear message: Russia may have been first in space, but America is No. 1.

Few can claim more credit for man's journey to the moon than Arthur Rudolph can, the brilliant German scientist and production manager of the Saturn V. His life's dream fulfilled, Mr. Rudolph retired that year, full of honors, to live out his days in California, near his only daughter, Marianne. Today, Mr. Rudolph, 82, is a man disgraced, stripped of citizenship, living in Hamburg, forever branded a Nazi war criminal by the nation that once exalted him and pinned medals on his chest.

What a story!

About his early career, there is no disagreement. Fired by the dream of space travel, Mr. Rudolph hooked up with the young Prussian aristocrat, Wernher von Braun, to co-lead the Luftwaffe team sent to Peenemünde to build Hitler's "Vengeance Weapon," the V-2, which rained upon London in the closing days of the war.

In August 1943, Bomber Command paid a visit to Peenemünde, killing in one night 1000 men, women, and children, almost wiping out Mr. Rudolph's own family, and forcing transfer of V-2 production to the mile long tunnels at Mittelwerk in the Harz Mountains.

Here, Arthur Rudolph's character was tested. For the hard labor at Mittelwerk was done by slave labor, prisoners from Buchenwald, housed in the nearby concentration camp of Dora-Nordhausen. One day, in January 1945, the SS called the workforce together in the tunnel

*to witness a hanging of six workers for an attempted uprising. Mr.
Rudolph was there.*

*At war's end, hoping to be captured by the Americans, Mr. Rudolph
made his way westward. Interned at Garmisch, Bavaria he was
interrogated on his wartime service, brought to the United States under
President Truman's "Project Paperclip," interrogated again, and then
sent to Fort Bliss, Texas, where he taught the Army to fire the V-2s the
Yanks had captured. After a third transcribed interrogation, Mr.
Rudolph was offered citizenship. Sent across the border to Juarez,
Mexico, he obtained a visa, re-entered the United States legally, and in
1954, became a naturalized American citizen.*

*Thirteen years after he retired, Mr. Rudolph got a letter from the Office of
Special Investigations of the Justice Department. Could they meet?
Twice, he did so. without a lawyer, telling OSI's Neal Sher and Eli
Rosenbaum what he had told his captors decades before, that, and yes, he
had been a nominal member of the Nazi Party, and of the SA until 1934.*

*Following the interview. Mr. Rudolph was informed that the OSI now
considered him a Nazi war criminal, that he was in danger of being
prosecuted, stripped of pensions and citizenship, bankrupted and
expelled. So, too, were his wife and daughter.*

*Horrified, fearing he would not survive a trial, Mr. Rudolph, a heart
attack victim, capitulated, lied, signing a paper saying that he had
persecuted unarmed civilians because of race, religion, national origin,
or political opinion. Then, heart broken, he flew to Germany and
renounced his U.S. citizenship. In return, the OSI promised not to go
after his daughter.*

*A stunned Bonn, Germany, an alleged war criminal dropped in its
midst, began an investigation. After extracting from the OSI all its
"evidence" (basically. the transcripts of Mr. Rudolph's interviews, and
the names of nine witnesses), the West Germans gathered the testimony
of 26 forced laborers, 23 of Mr. Rudolph's coworkers, and 15 members
of the SS, producing 15 volumes of files. After two years, Bonn,
Germany found the OSI's case to be a cruel joke. (Four of the OSI's nine
knew nothing of Mr. Rudolph—two were mentally unfit to testify; one
defended Mr. Rudolph's innocence, the remaining two accusers were
judged non-credible).*

Others came forward. A former Nordhausen prisoner who had worked on the V-2 testified: "Mr. Rudolph stood up very well for us prisoners and got us additional rations. He treated us concentration camp always well I know of no case, where Mr. Rudolph was rough, or where he would have mistreated prisoners."

This was echoed by the first American officer in Nordhausen. At the '47 Dachau trial of SS collaborators at Mittelwerk, Mr. Rudolph's name never came up. Where were his accusers then? Ex-colleagues at Fort Bliss and Huntsville, AL, journalists who studied the case, came to his assistance. Not only is Rudolph innocent. Writes author Thomas Franklin in "American in Exile." Messrs. Sher and Rosenbaum behaved like "vigilantes riding hell for leather to a necktie party, determined to see to it that their own kind of justice was dished out." Gen. John Medaris, Mr. Rudolph's superior in Huntsville, now an Anglican bishop, denounced the OSI's action as "unjust, immoral, and illegal."

What do friends of this 82-year-old man ask? Only this; that considering his service to this country, America give him the public hearing, the fair trial, that he was denied.

All that is needed is for one congressional representative of courage to propose that Mr. Rudolph's citizenship be restored. Then, let us have public hearings, under oath, so the American people can decide whether Mr. Rudolph was a Nazi victimizer of slave labor, or himself a victim of an American political atrocity.

In the beginning of his article, Pat Buchanan gives quite an impressive description of the launch of the Apollo 11, which culminated with the first lunar landing. My wife, Elizabeth, and I were also there to view this launch. It was indeed a very impressive event. Pat only remarked that the earth shook for miles, I wish to add that the air also shook with the shock waves radiating out from the launch site. The shock waves were so intense that they were visible. Normally shock waves are only visible at the site of a large explosion.

There is a photo displaying the exhaust ends of the five mighty F-1 engines of the first stage of the Saturn V rocket. This combination consumed **fifteen tons of fuel per second**. It was the rapid consumption of this huge volume of fuel that produced the shock waves, essentially a controlled explosion. The V-2, the forerunner of the Saturn V by about 26 years was basically the same engine design.

Since Assistant Attorney General John Bolton's response to my letter in July 1987, I began to accumulate evidence that other Assistant Attorney Generals were quoting similar phrases as contained in Mr. Bolton's letter to Senator Pete Wilson, in reference to my complaint, when answering inquiries from other members of Congress, or others, in reference to the Rudolph case.

The paragraphs, which caught my eye in Mr. Bolton's letter to Senator Pete Wilson, numbered three and four:

> *I want to emphasize that Mr. Rudolph was represented by competent counsel, when faced with incontrovertible documentary evidence, he freely and voluntarily entered into an agreement to leave this country and renounce his citizenship, and he did so.*

> *Let me assure you that before proceeding in cases such as the Rudolph matter, we at the DOJ carefully review the evidence and weigh its credibility. We proceed only after we are convinced that the evidence supports the allegations.*

Finally, on December 7, 1995, I made a request to the DOJ, under the Freedom of Information Act, for a copy of the documents, which reveal the incontrovertible documentary evidence referred to in paragraph three of Assistant Attorney General John R. Bolton's letter dated 29 January 1987 to Senator Pete Wilson.

On July 22, 1996, I received the response, which was a full 3-inch thick stack of documentation, consisting of 704 pages. About half of this documentation consisted of the sworn, verbatim, testimony taken from Rudolph by OSI officials in the two interviews of 1982 and 1983, at San Jose, California. Much of this testimony revealed evidence in favor of Rudolph, such as helping the prisoners get supplemental rations, better medical attention, and alleviating working conditions of the prisoners to the point where he himself was threatened with imprisonment. In addition, Rudolph emphasized his hate and distrust of the SS, indicating that near the war's end, with defeat for Germany in sight, he feared he would be murdered by the SS.

Also included with the documentation were 49 Government Exhibits, the majority of which were composed of Rudolph's own personal files, which he voluntarily had given the OSI.

Among the Government exhibits was a 62-page reproduction of the book; *The Dora Nordhausen War Crimes Trial.*

The book contained a detailed description of the complex, including a number of photos of accumulation of corpses. There were 19 defendants at the trial, including Georg Rickhey, Rudolph's immediate supervisor, but Rudolph was not one of the defendants.

After a careful search of this documentation, I could not find a shred of the "incontrovertible documentary evidence," referred to in the letter from Mr. Bolton to Senator Pete Wilson that Arthur Rudolph was a criminal. Therefore, I contend that Mr. Bolton, in plain language, lied to Senator Pete Wilson. This is further borne out by the fact that the OSI advertised for witnesses against Rudolph shortly after he left the U.S., indicating that they did not have any legitimate evidence to even begin, or justify, their prosecution in the first place. **They simply went fishing, using Rudolph as bait.**

14

The Appeal to the U.S. District Court

The first action concerning this appeal occurred on October 14, 1997, when, under the provisions of the Freedom Of information Act (FOIA), I submitted my request to the Department of Justice (DOJ) for the Prosecution Memorandum. This memo was from Neal Sher to Mark Richard. It was dated April 21, 1983, and consisted of 51 pages concerning the Arthur Rudolph case.

Neal Sher at that time was the director of the Office of Special Investigations (OSI) for the DOJ. Mark Richard was an Assistant Attorney General. The OSI was a very small Government entity within the DOJ, whose origin and function will be discussed in detail in a later chapter.

I realized that there might be some portions of the memorandum that would be restricted to public disclosure. I stated in my request that of particular interest to me was the portion that contained the specific allegations against Arthur Rudolph, and any evidence that would be presented to support the allegations. Simply put, I wanted the information that would have been presented in open court, had there been a trial.

On February 17, 1998, the DOJ denied my request, with the schedule of the document withheld in full. The reply indicated that nothing would be released—not even that which would be revealed in open court. This proved to me that the Government must not have had anything substantial in their files to back up a prosecution. Though I was denied, the letter stated that I had a right to an administrative appeal, which had to be filed within 30 days.

On March 2, 1998, I filed an administrative appeal. I had received information that the current director of the OSI was Eli Rosenbaum. Since the OSI had custody of the prosecution memorandum, it became apparent to me that the denial of the document involved a potential conflict of interest, since Mr. Rosenbaum had been involved in the prosecution of Rudolph in 1983.

I enclosed documentary evidence citing false information Mr. Rosenbaum had given to a member of Congress in 1985. I called the DOJ's attention to the last paragraph of enclosure No. 1, to a letter dated July 23, 1985, from Mr. Rosenbaum to a member of the Senate. In this letter, Mr. Rosenbaum states, "I am particularly looking forward to refuting the ludicrous charge made by Rudolph's supporters that there was East Bloc involvement in the initiation or development of the Rudolph case."

Substantiating my allegation that Congress had been lied to is information contained in Diplomatic Note No. 433, dated July 15, 1983, from the U.S. Embassy in Berlin, to the East German Government, which was marked as enclosure No.2. This note explicitly mentions the OSI as requesting information concerning Arthur Rudolph that would be of a derogatory nature. This was during the Cold War when East Germany was part of the Soviet bloc. The East German response, far from being derogatory, was exculpatory in nature. This information further supported my request that a copy of the Prosecution Memorandum, dated 4-21-83, be furnished to me, as originally requested.

I was fully aware of the provisions of the FOIA that explicitly forbids the request for personal information concerning an individual unless specific written permission from that person was granted. I enclosed a notarized letter from Arthur Rudolph wherein he granted written consent to the DOJ to release any documentation concerning his case to me.

On February 17, 1998, I received a response from the DOJ concerning my request for the prosecution memorandum. Their denial of my request was based on four exemptions associated with the FOIA. I clearly understood the first exemption, which permits the withholding of interagency or intra-agency memoranda or letters reflecting the pre-decisional deliberative processes of the Department, and/or which consist of attorney work prepared in anticipation of specific litigation. I did not see how that exemption could be applied to the denial of my request because I could not see any "anticipation of specific litigation." The Arthur Rudolph case had been closed in 1984 following his departure from the U.S. Furthermore, Arthur Rudolph died in January 1996.

The next three exemptions refer to the invasion of personal privacy. These exemptions were unwarranted because Arthur Rudolph gave specific written permission for me to have full access to any information concerning his case.

On October 28, 1998, I received notification from the DOJ that my appeal had been denied. I was also informed that the judicial review of the action by the DOJ was available to me either in the U.S. District Court for the judicial district in which I resided, or the District of Columbia, the location of the records I sought.

On March 8, 1999, I filed a complaint to the U.S. District Court for the District of Columbia for an injunction prohibiting withholding of agency records, and requesting an order to produce records improperly withheld from complainant. I was the Plaintiff, and the defendants were the Office of Information and Privacy, the DOJ, the U.S. Attorney General (Janet Reno), and the U.S. Attorney.

On June 4, 1999, I offered supplemental evidence to the court to support statements made in my complaint concerning the reason for the FOIA appeal. Legitimate evidence that had evolved since Arthur Rudolph left the U.S. in early 1984 suggests mishandling of the case by officials in the DOJ and the OSI.

A letter dated May 30, 1985, to Attorney General Edwin Meese requesting reconsideration of the Arthur Rudolph case, had been ignored. Consequently, I sought assistance from Senator Pete Wilson to help me in getting the attention of the DOJ.

The court issued its final decision on the case on March 21, 2000. This decision was not based on the provisions of the FOIA, under which I filed my complaint, but under the provisions of the Nazi War Crimes Disclosure Act which was introduced on November 5, 1997, in an amendment which specifically states; "This (Act) shall not apply to records—(A) related to or supporting any active or inactive investigation inquiries, or prosecution by the Office of Special Investigations of the Department of Justice; or (B) solely in the possession, custody, or control of that office."

This action by the court effectively denied the right to appeal to a higher court. This is not in keeping with the best traditions—to say nothing of precedents—of recourse to justice in the U.S.. Indeed this action by the court puzzled me because I gave the presiding judge (Judge Friedman) information that implicated the OSI in criminal activities, and the judge in his deliberations failed to refer this information to proper authority for further investigation or prosecution. The decision was based on law put into effect after the case was submitted. (Law is not retroactive. Much less circumvent the intent of FOIA.)

As it stands, this amendment to the Nazi War Crimes Disclosure Act prohibits any American citizen from even submitting a request under the provisions of the FOIA, which concerns any document solely in the possession of, or control of, the OSI.

It may be supposed that Congress has oversight authority over the OSI, and Congress is bound to uphold and defend the right of the people to pursue and receive justice. The oath of office notwithstanding, Congress felt no such duty in this case. I submitted a number of requests for oversight investigations of the OSI to both the Senate, and the House, which included incontrovertible evidence of gross persecution on the part of the OSI to no avail, and with negative results. It had become evident to me that the members of Congress contacted were, by ignoring my requests, protecting the OSI.

Thus the OSI, a very small organization consisting of about 50 total government personnel chartered to prosecute Nazi war criminals, has evidently been engaged, under the protection of Congress, in the same tactics employed by the Gestapo. These tactics include knowingly making false statements in general and to Congress in particular, obstruction of justice, violation of human rights, and persecution of innocents. In the John Demjanjuk case, claimed by the OSI as among their most successful, the OSI had extradited Demjanjuk to Israel under false charges, and was instrumental in having him sentenced to death. The Israeli Supreme Court, however, evidently obedient to higher standards of justice than those guiding the OSI, overturned the Demjanjuk sentence when persuaded of the illegitimacy of the charges.

When Rosenbaum was questioned about the Demjanjuk verdict, his reply was "you have to live with that" as though some are won, and some lost. This callous remark by Eli Rosenbaum, the director of the OSI, clearly revealed his mindset concerning this very serious case wherein a man was sentenced to death by false information given to the Israeli court by the OSI.

To the international community, this evident gross prosecutorial blunder by the OSI in the Demjanjuk case resulted in a black eye on the face of American justice. In a matter of this gravity, it would be proper for Congress to immediately assume an oversight role, to investigate the circumstances, and to preclude such violations in the future. To my knowledge, Congress ignored the matter entirely. OSI officials recognized this, and Eli Rosenbaum issued the disgraceful remark cited above, with impunity, as though it were an accepted norm in OSI operations. **In fact, the OSI continues to present a case against Demjanjuk saying he is a different person and still evil notwithstanding his statement of innocence.**

[**Author's note**: See articles written by Alfred de Zayas former UN Secretary for Human Rights titled "Human Rights of the Unpopular." Published in the journal "Human Rights" of the Section of Individual Rights & Responsibilities of the American Bar Association, Winter 1994, Vol. 21, Issue 1, p.28, under the misleading title "Demjanjuk: Examining his Human Rights Violations," which was not Dr. de Zayas' title. You would think that the article focused on war crimes and crimes against humanity by Demjanjuk, whereas the articles is about the human rights of the unpopular—i.e., of Demjanjuk himself.

Also published an op-ed piece in the Chicago Daily Law Bulletin, on 23 November 1993, under the title "Demjanjuk and human rights guarantees" and a longer piece in The Globe, January 1994, Vol. 31, No. 5, pp.3-7, Journal of the Illinois Bar Center, Springfield, Illinois, under the title "Human Rights Implications of the Demjanjuk Case." This latter article was read in its entirety into the United States Congressional Record in May 1994. [See the following web site http://www.alfreddezayas.com.]

One might think that OSI officials would, in accordance with their oaths of office, conduct their operations with a high degree of honesty and integrity. In the pursuit of genuine war criminals, they should strictly submit to the rules of evidence, the principles of fairness, and consideration of human rights. Nevertheless, the OSI in both the Rudolph and Demjanjuk cases failed miserably in what was supposed to be their mission.

What concerned me most about my appeal to the U.S. District Court were the circumstances surrounding the basis for the denial of my appeal. It was my belief that no Government agency was utterly exempt from complying with the letter of the FOIA, to say nothing of the spirit. Surely, the White House would have welcomed such an exemption during the latter days of the Nixon administration! The Court denied my appeal, not in accordance with the FOIA under which I filed my appeal, but under the provisions of an amendment to the Nazi War Crimes Disclosure Act, which had gone into effect some two years later in October of 1998. So the case was decided retroactively by a seemingly unrelated law contrary to the intent of the Freedom of Information Act!

The timing of this amendment also aroused my suspicions. Senator DeWine sponsored the bill on November 5, 1997, a few weeks after I had submitted my request to the DOJ for a copy of the Prosecution Memorandum on the Rudolph case. It seemed no mere coincidence, but a direct attempt to cover up gross prosecutorial misconduct by the OSI. Now this bit of governmental intrigue becomes more interesting because Senator DeWine had introduced the revision of the Nazi War Crimes Disclosure Act about three weeks **after** I had requested the Rudolph file from the Department of Justice in 1997. The District Court denied my appeal based on the language in this revision. Therefore, this amendment should have no effect as it was enacted AFTER my request. The revision to the Nazi War Crimes Disclosure Act as sponsored by Senator DeWine is located in Appendix titled Revision to Nazi War Crimes Act.

Because of this amendment, Congress erected a shield around a small Government organization, effectively forbidding the examination of their operations or conduct. This is the same type of environment and protection that the Gestapo enjoyed under the Third Reich.

A very disturbing question that has entered my mind since I was rebutted by the U.S. District Court, District of Columbia, in my appeal for a copy of the Prosecution Memorandum of the Rudolph case, held by the Department of Justice. Why did Congress completely protect a very small organizational element within the Department of Justice, The Office of Special Investigations (OSI), from the Freedom of Information Act? The District Court denied my appeal based on the language in this revision. This action by the Congress brings up the question of why the OSI should be the only unit within the government not involved in sensitive matters of national security to be totally exempt from the provisions of the Freedom of Information Act? The mission of the OSI concerned civil matters only such as the legal investigation, prosecution, and deportation of alleged Nazi war criminals. The mission of the OSI did **NOT** involve matters of a sensitive nature such as vital security matters therefore this protection is completely unjustified. Thus, the OSI is completely protected, by act of Congress, from disclosing any information concerning how they operate, legally or illegally. In the Rudolph case, this book contains incontrovertible legitimate evidence that the OSI acted in an illegal manner. The fact is that the OSI methods of operations were evidently given the same protection as the Gestapo enjoyed under the Hitler government.

Hard evidence to support my allegations will unfold in the following chapters. Since this story concerns the Arthur Rudolph case—the man, as stated by von Braun, most instrumental in placing U.S. astronauts on the moon—I believe that what is revealed here justly claims a fitting place in our early space history. Since Rudolph was an important part of the German rocket team led by Dr. Wernher von Braun, the story of America's voyage to the moon must include the impact of the rocket team, felt from 1945, and extending to 2005 and **ending?**

15

Congress Shelters Its Own

In my attempts to obtain a reconsideration of the Rudolph case, I relied heavily on the support of my Congressman, the Hon. Rep. Elton Gallegly. The DOJ had taken an adamant stand against any such reconsideration, so the only recourse, outside of a very expensive court battle, was through the ordinary administrative channels of Congress available to all citizens. The issue appeared to be clear that incontrovertible evidence the OSI was directly involved in gross prosecutorial misconduct existed. Thus it should have been an appropriate matter, and within the scope of congressional responsibility, to conduct an oversight hearing. Rep. Gallegly's initial response was rather encouraging; however, after several years, and numerous letters from me, I observed that no positive action had been taken. At this point, I felt ignored by Rep. Gallegly, a member of the House Judiciary Committee, which had the responsibility to conduct oversight hearings concerning misconduct of Government officials.

In the meanwhile, the equally intensive efforts of both Drs. Haeussermann and Winterberg also met with negative responses. The next logical approach to the problem was to obtain direct congressional action and abandon any further attempts to resolve the case through DOJ channels.

When I first became involved with the Arthur Rudolph case in May 1985, I was quite confident that with the solid documentary evidence I had in hand, a prompt resolution to the case would be forthcoming by simply making a request to our DOJ for a reconsideration of the case. As I have shown, my first request was completely ignored by Attorney General Edwin Meese. My second attempt, directed to Assistant Attorney General John Bolton and including additional, updated evidence, was rebuffed in a manner that was almost insulting. The denial asserted that I had not offered any new evidence to justify a reconsideration of the case. This refusal nearly caused me to give up. Rather, I was galvanized in my quest. I decided that the issues—the concern for the preservation of truth in the American system—should not be casually abandoned. As a professional soldier, I had survived four major campaigns in the Pacific Theater in World War II, and I did not take my oath as an officer lightly. **(To protect the U.S. from enemies whether they are without or within its borders.)**

On September 30, 1991, I wrote a letter to Chairman Joseph Biden, Jr., of the Senate Judiciary Committee. My introduction to the letter referred to a news release by Senator Howell Heflin, from Washington, dated July 12, 1991.

> *Earlier this year, Senator Howell Heflin, D-Ala., had filed a petition, prepared by Dr. Rudolph's attorney, requesting the committee to conduct a hearing into the Rudolph matter*

A copy of this news release was furnished to me by Senator Heflin by letter dated August 23, 1991. The subject of the news release was "Judiciary Committee Turns Down Request For Rudolph Hearing." The news release stated that the Chairman of the Senate Judiciary Committee had rejected a request to hold a hearing regarding the deportation of Arthur Rudolph.

The news release quoted Senator Joseph Biden, D-Del.:

> *Dr. Rudolph voluntarily entered into an agreement with the United States Government in which he relinquished his citizenship and agreed to leave the country in return for a commitment by the U.S. not to press charges, which could have resulted in his losing retirement benefits. In light of this agreement, as well as the policy of the Judiciary Committee not to intervene in individual cases, particularly when there is a possibility of federal court litigation involving the underlying matter, I do not believe that it would be appropriate for the committee to investigate this matter farther," Senator Biden said.*

In my letter to Chairman Biden, I objected to his identification of the Rudolph case as an "individual case," indicating that this perspective was

concerned only with the guilt or innocence of one individual, conveniently sidestepping related events including misconduct by the OSI
and DOJ.

In the introduction of my letter, I quoted the efforts of Senator Heflin to
get a congressional hearing into the Rudolph case, which had resulted in
articles about the case appearing in various newspapers around the
country. Of great concern to me as an American citizen was that, some of
the information quoted in the articles was false and misleading, and this
information was emanating from the DOJ.

In my letter to Chairman Biden, I enclosed a copy of an article published
in the *San Francisco Chronicle*, whose sources included the *New York
Times*. I also included an article from the *San Jose Mercury News*, the city
in which Rudolph lived for 10 years prior to his return to Germany.

I indicated that in my reply to the editor of the Chronicle, I had
mentioned issues involved which went far beyond the issue of the
innocence or guilt of Arthur Rudolph. I referred to facts unknown to
Chairman Biden at the time of his decision not to hold hearings—a
matter that should have been of concern to the Senate Judiciary
Committee. He was evidently unaware of some of the issues that grew
up around the case. I then briefed Chairman Biden about my attempts to
get the DOJ to reconsider the case, citing the amount of documented
evidence available to support reconsideration efforts. I mentioned the
rebuff from the DOJ in which it denied that new evidence existed or had
been submitted.

I also briefed Chairman Biden on the problem I had with the DOJ in
attempting to get information under the Freedom of Information Act,
specifically a copy of the document, which was the source of information
contained in the texts of two identically worded Congressional
Resolutions, H.RES.68 of 1985; and H.RES.164 of 1987. The resolutions
directly implicated the DOJ and the OSI as the sources of the information,
but the DOJ informed me that they had no such document.

Chairman Biden was also informed that Rudolph was investigated by the
Governments of both West Germany and Canada based on the OSI
allegations of "persecution" of laborers in the V-2 complex during the
war. I pointed out to the Chairman that the OSI failed to provide evidence

to support their allegations of war crimes, and that both Canada and West Germany had found Rudolph to be innocent of the OSI charges.

I also enclosed a copy of a letter that I had received from Mr. Robert S. Smith, Rudolph's lawyer in Huntsville, Alabama, in 1991, stating that the DOJ had failed to provide (after two years), under the Freedom of Information Act, any document incriminating Rudolph.

I informed Chairman Biden that the evidence that I had submitted fully justified a hearing by the Senate Judiciary Committee. I closed my letter to Chairman Biden with the following statement:

> *As an American citizen, I hereby request that the Senate Judiciary Committee conduct an inquiry into the operational tactics employed by officials of the Office of Special Investigation into their investigation of the Arthur Rudolph case.*

Prior to receiving a response from Mr. Biden, I submitted additional information in March 1992. I provided detail about my submissions to Assistant Attorney General John Bolton in 1987.

In my four-page letter to Chairman Biden, I emphatically stated that OSI officials were involved in gross prosecutorial misconduct in pursuing the case, and that the prime issue was not whether Rudolph was innocent or guilty, but **the conduct of the Government officials involved in the case.**

I also informed him that there was a new turn in the bizarre conduct of OSI officials, which involved the character assassination of Rudolph in the news media. This involved both Neal Sher and Eli Rosenbaum, who appeared on ABC Television on the program "Inside Edition," on September 9, 1990. A 15-minute segment of the program was titled: "Arthur Rudolph, Hero or Nazi War Criminal."

In this program, which was strongly biased against Rudolph, Mr. Sher calls Rudolph a liar several times, and Mr. Rosenbaum refers to him as a "beast."

I also informed Chairman Biden that the program was linked to Rudolph's vacation trip to Canada in July of 1990. Prior to Rudolph's trip to Canada, the OSI had notified Canadian authorities that Rudolph was on an excluded list for entry into the U.S. As a result, Canadian authorities detained him for questioning upon his arrival. Following an investigation, Canadian authorities found that Rudolph was not guilty of "persecution" as alleged by the OSI. Thus, two countries—Canada and West Germany—had found that the OSI allegations were not substantiated by credible evidence.

The TV program manager appears to have had knowledge of the outcome of the West German and Canadian investigations of Rudolph. Why were Sher and Rosenbaum not confronted on the program for furnishing false information to German and Canadian authorities? This act alone had the potential for creating an embarrassing, public incident with international scope.

Continuing my written brief to Chairman Biden I stated:

> *Available evidence fully justifies an inquiry by the Senate Judiciary Committee to determine whether misconduct by some officials has occurred in the administration of justice. It is suggested that the following items be considered:*

> • *New, legitimate, and exculpatory evidence was offered to the Department of Justice about the Rudolph case. The Department denied that such evidence was offered, and did not use that evidence to reconsider the case.*

> • *The removal or withholding of exculpatory evidence from the file that was received from the East German prosecutor. This, and item No. 1 above, appears to constitute obstruction of justice.*

> • *Denial by Department officials to members of Congress that evidence was solicited from East Germany, when such a request was in fact made.*

> • *Obvious bias against Rudolph is made manifest on the part of OSI prosecutors by their placing an advertisement in the news media for witnesses against Rudolph after the case was closed in 1984.*

> • *Denial by Department officials that there was not a supporting document in the file to substantiate the gross criminal allegations against Rudolph contained in paragraph four of H.RES.68 of 1985*

and H.RES.164 of 1987, both of which directly implicate the Department and OSI as being the source.

- *Failure by the OSI to provide credible evidence to the governments of Germany and Canada to substantiate their allegations against Arthur Rudolph.*

- *Failure to provide timely information to Mr. Smith, Rudolph's attorney, according to FOIA rules. Failure to provide credible evidence to Mr. Smith to support OSI allegations against Rudolph.*

- *OSI officials making insulting and derogatory statements about Rudolph in the public media, which is evidently not supported by actual evidence in the file.*

I have documentation to support the information revealed above in this letter, and will be happy to release it to responsible officials upon request. Your cooperation to bring about justice in this matter will be appreciated.

Eight months after my September 1991 letter to Chairman Biden, I finally received a response on May 12, 1992.

Dear Colonel Winterstein:

Thank you for your letter regarding the case of Arthur Rudolph and the Office of Special Investigations. I appreciate your sharing your concerns with me. As legislation related to the points you have raised comes before the committee or the Senate, I will keep your views in mind. In the meantime, I hope you will continue to stay in touch on issues of concern to you.

Again, thank you for contacting me.

Sincerely, (signed) Joe Biden   Joseph R. Biden Jr. .Chairman

After patiently waiting and having presented conclusive evidence to fully support a Judiciary hearing, this response was quite disappointing. In effect, it said that no action would be taken unless legislation directly relating to the issues was brought before the Committee. What were the chances of that happening without action of the very kind I was specifically requesting from the Chairman?!

I did not have to wait long for the second and last letter from Chairman Biden on the topic. About two weeks later, on June 2 1992, I received his response on whether my request for a hearing would be granted. Here is his reply:

Dear Mr. Winterstein:

Thank you for your letter regarding the Office of Special Investigation of the Department of Justice. I appreciate hearing from you.

It is a general policy of the Judiciary Committee not to intervene or investigate individual matters. Congressional intervention in situations such as this risks violating the constitutional separation between the legislative and executive branches of government. Unfortunately, after having examined the facts, I believe that the Judiciary Committee can be of no further help to you. I wish you a swift and satisfactory resolution of this matter.

Thank you again for your letter.

Sincerely, (signed) Joe Biden   Joseph R. Biden Jr. Chairman

From my perspective, this letter was a slap in the face because I had stressed the point that the case **did not solely involve** an individual matter, but was rather an issue of far greater concern—the evident malfeasance of office by public officials. **A felony!** Thus in my opinion, Chairman Biden was himself guilty of, at best, passive misuse of office for failing to consider a matter directly related to the function—indeed, the purpose—of his committee. It is the duty of the Judicial Committees, whether of the House or the Senate, to take oversight action and intervene when wrongdoing on the part of Government officials is suspected or has taken place.

Though I met resistance in my quest, I did not give up on trying to get Chairman Biden to change his mind and take some positive action to resolve the OSI/Rudolph case. Approximately two months after he denied my request for a hearing, I sent him another letter on August 28, 1992, stating that events had occurred which would further justify my request for an investigation of the OSI of the DOJ.

On June 6, 1992, a news item surfaced relating to a Federal Appeals Court in Cincinnati, which was investigating whether John Demjanjuk was improperly extradited to Israel in 1985 to face charges that he was "Ivan the Terrible"—the sadistic SS guard at Treblinka. Following the trial, the court found Demjanjuk guilty and sentenced him to hang, this with the full cooperation of the OSI. The OSI had hailed the Demjanjuk case as one of their outstanding accomplishments.

On June 8, 1992, a related item appeared on CNN. The Israeli Supreme Court, on their review of the case, ruled that the Israeli prosecutor failed to provide solid evidence to support his allegations. Based on this ruling, the Supreme Court freed Demjanjuk from jail.

On June 9, 1992, there were two items about the Demjanjuk case on the NBC TV channel. In the morning, on the "Today Show," was a brief item, which indicated that misconduct by OSI officials had occurred concerning the case. Later in the evening, on the "Nightline" show, there was a short presentation going into more detail about the case. Among the principal items indicating misconduct by the OSI were the withholding of exculpatory evidence from the defense, the attempted destruction of exculpatory evidence, and the withholding of evidence from the defense upon their request for such evidence.

On August 12, 1992, a news article appeared in the Los Angeles Times about the Federal Appeals Court in Cincinnati, Ohio, severely criticizing the DOJ for withholding evidence in the Demjanjuk case in 1985, when the same three judges were considering evidence presented to the court for the extradition of Demjanjuk to Israel. The key issue in the hearing was why the DOJ did not disclose Soviet statements from two former Treblinka guards who implicated a man named Marchenko as "Ivan the Terrible." The Department also withheld a Polish document that listed Marchenko as a Treblinka guard.

I also informed Chairman Biden of another instance of gross prosecutorial misconduct on the part of the OSI in another case. This also indicated participation in an event where a death sentence was involved, similar to the Demjanjuk case. A news media report at the time revealed that the evidence used to extradite 88-year old Andrija Artukovic from the U.S. to Yugoslavia was false **(notice a pattern of sick old men being chased by the OSI?),** and that the U.S. prosecutors were aware of it. An article in the Washington Times claimed that perjury and other offenses were committed by the OSI officials in the case. Artukovic died in 1988 of natural causes in a Yugoslav prison while awaiting execution by a firing squad.

In my letter I summarized the information I had accumulated about the improper conduct of the OSI, and that the evidence fell into two categories. In the Rudolph case, of which I had personal knowledge and documented evidence, the misconduct included obstruction of justice, fraud, application of interrogation tactics resulting in duress, mistake of law and other acts of injustice by the OSI.

In the Demjanjuk and Artukovic cases, my knowledge was based on various news media reports. Here the evidence appears to be credible, but with a more shocking impact than that of the Rudolph case. Both of these men were extradited from the U.S. when exculpatory evidence was withheld from the defense, and the courts, by the OSI prior to extradition. Trials were conducted in foreign countries with the full cooperation of the OSI. Both men were sentenced to be executed. Had the executions taken place, the OSI officials who knowingly and willfully withheld exculpatory evidence (which would most probably have resulted in a different verdict, or acquittal in the U.S. courts prior to extradition) **would, in my opinion, have been guilty of accessory to murder** of innocent men as well as the duress and mental anguish that the families endured.

Consider for a moment that a solitary news media report of the Watergate break-in brought prompt and immediate congressional action, and created a national uproar. The political nature of the Watergate case brought down an entire presidential administration, yet egregious abuses of power, cumulatively amounting to what would have been conspiracy to murder, brought not the slightest censure of the OSI from Congress.

I closed my letter to Chairman Biden by urging that prompt congressional oversight action is taken to correct the pattern of prosecutorial misconduct engaged in by the OSI.

I never received a response to this letter from Chairman Biden. This silence, in the face of facts that cried out for justice for Rudolph, indicated to me that I was being ignored by the Senate Judiciary Committee and that any further efforts to provoke action on the case would be futile. Worse still, the silence clearly suggested either that the Committee considered the OSI guiltless, or that it was exempt from investigation into its actions. In addition, this, from the Senator who cited "separation of powers" in his letter to me as he excused himself from fairly evaluating the matter. In this case, separation of powers appears to mean that one branch will turn a blind eye to offenses committed by the other.

After giving up hope that the Senate Judiciary Committee would conduct a hearing, I approached the House Judiciary Committee. Though I did not get any positive results from Rep. Gallegly the first time around, I contacted him again in February 1994, with a request for House Judiciary Committee action. The reason for this was two fold; first, he was a member of the Committee, and second, Arthur Rudolph was a California resident prior to his exile in 1984, and Gallegly was a California congressional representative.

By this time, Rep. Gallegly had numerous letters from me whose enclosures contained sufficient documentary evidence to justify a House Judiciary oversight hearing. He brought the matter to the attention of House Judiciary Committee Chairman Jack Brooks. I was quite surprised, and frankly elated, when Rep. Gallegly received a prompt response from Chairman Brooks on March 11, 1994.

Dear Elton:

Thank you for your recent letter forwarding correspondence from your constituent, William E. Winterstein, LTC Army (Ret.). Colonel Winterstein has requested an investigation into the Office of Special Investigation, Department of Justice, in the Arthur Rudolph case.

As oversight of the Office of Special Investigation, Department of Justice, falls within the jurisdiction of the Subcommittee on International Law, Immigration, and Refugees, I am forwarding the correspondence to the Chairman of that Subcommittee, Congressman Romano L. Mazzoli, for further consideration.

Meanwhile, with best wishes, I am

Sincerely, (signed) Jack   Jack Brooks, Chairman

To further substantiate my request for a House Judiciary hearing, on August 24, 1994, I sent Chairman Brooks a four-page letter, with eight enclosures, containing documentary evidence in support of the case. Essentially, it was the same information that I had earlier submitted to Chairman Biden of the Senate Judiciary Committee. The response was prompt.

Dear Colonel Winterstein:

Thank you for your correspondence and additional documentation requesting an investigation by the Department of Justice's Office of Special Investigation in the Arthur Rudolph case. I appreciate having your views on this important matter.

As you know, oversight of the Department of Justice's Office of Special Investigation falls within the jurisdiction of the Subcommittee on International Law, Immigration, and Refugees, I am forwarding your letter and documentation to Congressman Romano L. Mazzoli, Chairman of that Subcommittee, for further consideration.

Meanwhile, with best wishes, I am

Sincerely, (signed) Jack   Jack Brooks, Chairman

My association with Chairman Brooks was short lived. Though he was the first congressional leader to refer to the Rudolph case as an "important matter," he was voted out of office only a few weeks later. During this election, the House majority changed hands, resulting in a clean sweep of committee members who were at all familiar with the Rudolph case. It was time to start over. Fortunately, Rep. Gallegly was a Republican, and remained a member of the House Judiciary Committee.

Since I had lost the support of Chairman Brooks, I was hopeful that Rep. Gallegly would be industrious in pursuing the Rudolph case. In beginning again, I wrote Rep. Gallegly a letter on December 30, 1992, several months after the election.

In the past, I had recognized the administrative difficulties and pitfalls that he probably experienced in trying to get any recognition for my requests concerning the Rudolph case. I reminded Rep. Gallegly that now, since the elections, the jurisdiction and control of this matter was under the responsibility of the Republican Party. Prior to this, I had sent Gallegly numerous letters and considerable documentary evidence, which should have fully convinced him of the pattern of gross prosecutorial misconduct undertaken by the OSI in their pursuit of the case. "As you are aware," I told him, "I have been attempting to have this case reconsidered by going through various appropriate governmental channels for about nine years, but to no avail."

I briefly recapped the Rudolph case, adding additional information concerning the operations of the OSI, which had become known since last, we corresponded on the subject. Since Rep. Gallegly was now a member of the party in control of the activities in the House, I made the following request:

> *"I am again appealing to you as my Representative, and as a member of the House Judiciary Committee, that prompt and positive action be initiated to investigate the aberrational conduct of officials in the Office of Special Investigation of the Department of Justice in their conduct of operations in the Dr. Arthur Rudolph case. And, if the allegations of fraud, duress, undue influence, misrepresentation, obstruction of justice are substantiated, or other gross misconduct is uncovered, that Arthur Rudolph's U.S. citizenship is rightfully restored to him."*

I never received a response to my letter of December 30, 1994, and I felt ignored by my own Congressman concerning an issue of urgent importance. I sent a number of other letters containing additional information in an attempt to spark a sense of responsibility and attention to duty, but to no effect. Finally, on May 8, 1995, after being ignored for five months, I wrote Gallegly a letter requesting an answer concerning my request. I expected a reply, at least, as to whether I had presented a legitimate request or not.

I did not receive a response to this, or to a number of other letters I wrote to Gallegly in 1995, most of them requesting a statement of intention regarding my many requests. Again, from a different member of a different political party, silence. Again, I was stonewalled, without the courtesy even of a response.

This did not seem like the same Elton Gallegly that my wife Elizabeth and I helped to elect in 1986. As with most politicians, election victories selectively cloud the memory. By his actions—and failures to act—Rep. Gallegly was at least passively participating in efforts by Congress to draw a tighter cloak of secrecy and protection around the OSI so that their conduct would not be revealed to the public.

Since the Senate Judiciary and my own congressional representative had shut me out, my next course was to go to the Chairman of the House Judiciary Committee, Henry Hyde. On July 1, 1996, I sent a request for action, supplemented by evidence that justified an oversight hearing in the Rudolph case. I referred to the two House Resolutions (H.RES.68 of 1985 and H.RES.164 of 1987) which had been introduced into Congress. (Subsequent evidence however, revealed that they contained a gross lie concerning Arthur Rudolph: that he was responsible for thousands of deaths at Dora/Nordhausen.)

I pointed out to Rep. Hyde that Rudolph's V-2 production work force was composed of about 5000 camp inmates. Many of these were highly trained technicians, doing precision work on the highly complex missile. For a production manager to deliberately sabotage his workforce, while trying to meet impossible production schedules, would have been sheer folly. (This bit of logic was overlooked by the OSI.) In addition to the evidence I presented, I suggested that the OSI had no basis for initiating prosecution against Rudolph in the first place. A competent war crimes court had been convened in Dachau, Germany, in 1947, to determine who was guilty of atrocities committed at Dora/Nordhausen and other facilities. All scientists were found not guilty of all charges. Many of those scientists wound up in the U.S. working on defense programs. When Rudolph was a civilian employee of the U.S. Army, the FBI, after conducting thorough background investigations, had given him a clean bill of health and cleared him for access to TOP SECRET materials. How is it possible that the 'closet' of this man, so thoroughly investigated, should suddenly yield skeletons at the convenience of the OSI?

I also referred Rep. Hyde to the statement of the former Chairman of the House Judiciary, Jack Brooks, in which he stated that the issue of an oversight hearing was an important element. I mentioned that Rudolph had died of a massive heart attack, six months before, on January 1, 1996, in Hamburg, Germany. I suggested that available evidence implicates DOJ officials in having deprived Rudolph of his U.S. citizenship through fraudulent means. Finally, I appealed for a public apology to his widow and daughter, to be given in the interest of truth, fairness, and compassion, though given far too late to help Rudolph. I also requested the posthumous restoration of Rudolph's U.S. citizenship, a small thing to ask for a distinguished, loyal, and brilliant servant of the American good. So ended my first letter to Chairman Hyde.

On November 19, 1996, Rudolph's widow, Martha, wrote an appeal to Chairman Hyde requesting that the House Resolutions No.68 of 1985, and No.164 of 1987, be refuted and annulled.

She referred to three letters of mine, of which I had furnished her copies, and which previously I had sent to Chairman Hyde, and concerning the contents of which she concurred completely. She did, however, wish to add her views concerning the case.

> *"In 1983, after coercion and duress by officials from the Office of Special Investigations (OSI), of the Department of Justice, my husband signed an "Agreement" drafted by the OSI. This agreement alleged that Arthur Rudolph had participated in the "persecution" of unarmed civilians in wartime Germany. He strenuously objected to the word persecution, but to no avail. I clearly remember his anguish at the time; he did not wish to sign anything that was false. My husband was an honorable man, and from the beginning, I was firmly convinced that he was absolutely innocent of any OSI allegations of persecution or any other crime. Being in very poor health with a heart condition, he did not have the physical stamina or the financial resources for a court battle with the OSI. The 'Agreement' resulted in the loss of his U.S. citizenship. It did, however, provide for future financial stability in granting continuing Civil Service pension and Social Security benefits. In early 1984, at which time he was a retired resident of San Jose, California, he left the U.S. to begin exile in Germany.*
>
> *In 1985 came another devastating blow perpetrated against my husband by certain officials of the U.S. government. It was the introduction into Congress of House Resolution 68 of 1985. This resolution contained the allegation that Arthur Rudolph had been responsible for the deaths of 20,000 to 30,000 slave laborers in wartime Germany. This resolution directly and implicitly implicates the Department of Justice, and the Office of Special Investigations as the source of the information. The Department of Justice has failed to provide a single thread of legitimate evidence to support this allegation, therefore making it a malicious, gross, and deliberate lie.*

Investigations by three countries, the United States in the early post war years, Germany in the 1980's, and Canada in 1990, have found no evidence to substantiate any of the charges.

Two years later, to further insult and harass my husband, House Resolution 164, of 1987, was added to the public documents. The wording is identical to the text of the previous mentioned resolution. The prime purpose of both resolutions was to strip him of the NASA Distinguished Service Medal. He was awarded this medal for his immense contribution as Program Director of the Saturn V rocket which made the moon voyages possible.

I have further proof that the resolutions are based on lies. My husband had a TOP SECRET security clearance, which was granted by the FBI during the many years he was employed by the Army in work vital to the defense of this country, and later on at NASA. The FBI made thorough and intensive background checks of his participation in the German war effort. Had he been guilty of any of the OSI allegations he most surely would not have received a TOP SECRET clearance.

It has been thirteen years since my husband, and I, began exile. These last years, which should have been the happiest in his life, were instead spent in trying to clear his name. This consequently put him under much stress, mental anguish, and despondency, which ultimately shortened his life. We have attempted to clear his name through proper channels, which so far has been to no avail. The continued existence of House Resolutions 68 and 164, as public documents, have been a source of deep embarrassment, distress, misery, and unhappiness to my husband and surviving members of his family, and should therefore be abolished. Since these resolutions originated in the House, it is self evident that the House should take action to have justice restored. Therefore, I am requesting as a citizen of the United States, that the House Judiciary Committee to take appropriate action to have House Resolutions No. 68 of 1985 and No. 164 of 1987, refuted and annulled. Also, that the public be notified that the resolutions should not be accepted as historical documents concerning this countries early history in the conquest of space, and the reason therefore."

Much has been said about House Resolutions 68 of 1985, and 164 of 1987. Both of these were not adopted by Congress, Thus nullifying any official action. However, by congressional rules, even though containing horrendous demeaning lies, they remain in the public record for exhibition forever. Thus, the OSI and the Department of Justice have labeled Rudolph a war criminal through their influence over a congressional representative, Bill Green of New York, in inducing him to introduce the two identically worded resolutions. Thus, Arthur Rudolph was branded a criminal, not only once but twice, not by a court of law, but by act of Congress, with no appeal. What a terrorist act to place upon one of our greatest national heroes and members of his family!!! Now, as related in this book, individuals and other sources intent on vilifying our national space heroes, have evidently referred to the resolutions as historical records to be used as reference material.

The full text of Martha Rudolph's letter, with enclosures, is located in Appendix titled Letter from Mrs. Rudolph to Mr. Hyde.

To my knowledge, Chairman Hyde ignored the appeal for action by Martha Rudolph, and she received no response.

At this point I wish to bring into perspective the **truth** of what the House Resolutions 68 and 164 has done to Arthur Rudolph, with reflections on his family, forever!!! They have, **under current congressional rules**, branded him a national war crimes criminal, and destroyed his good reputation. This was perpetrated without one shred of legitimate evidence to substantiate the allegations. The reputation of a law abiding American citizen is normally held as something almost sacred. Thus in this day that terrorist activities are held in utmost contempt by most of our citizens, we have a venerated, and distinguished former American citizen falling victim to an act implicating terror! The life of one of our space heroes, by act of Congress, and not through a court of law has been destroyed. It truly would be most interesting of what the verdict would be if the evidence would be presented to a jury convened by a court of law. I submitted my fourth and final letter to Chairman Hyde for action on February 3, 1997.

In addition to brief reviews of the information covered in previous correspondence, I added the following information, which in my opinion, should have motivated a Chairman of an important committee in our Congress, and was he honorable enough to fulfill the letter and spirit of his oath of office:

> *The introduction of House Resolution 164, two years after House Resolution 68, is evidence of the persistent and apparent efforts of OSI officials in attempting character assassination against Rudolph with false allegations. Since Rudolph left the U.S., OSI officials have been involved in*

planting a number of news items containing false and derogatory statements about him.

The continued existence of the House resolutions referred to above is a shameful reflection on our system of justice. Being totally false in their allegations, they have become instruments of persecution to the Rudolph family, and stumbling blocks for historians interested in space exploration history. Therefore, I am requesting that you take appropriate action that these resolutions be refuted, annulled, or eliminated, and that the public be notified that they do not represent a valid source for historical reference, and the reason therefore. This matter should no longer be ignored.

As expected, I was ignored again, and the courtesy of a reply was not forthcoming. It would seem that a situation involving the degradation of the American system of justice, and the apparent gross violation of the human rights of a former distinguished American citizen would, at least elicit some kind of a of reply from a public official sworn into office to support and defend the Constitution.

The following section contains various pictures of interest about the Space program or places in which the Rocket Team stayed.

[Author's note: To understand why Arthur Rudolph is innocent bear in mind the following. After World War II, the victorious allies held a series of war crimes trials. The most famous of these were the Nuremberg trials. The Dachau trials were held specifically for the Nordhausen/Dora facility at which Arthur Rudolph worked. These trials took place at a time immediately after the conclusion of the war. The memories of witnesses were far fresher and the zealousness of prosecutors unchecked. Arthur Rudolph was not even charged. His superior, who did stand trial, was found innocent!

There was a later set of trials in the 1969 time period known as the Essen trials and again focusing on the Nordhausen/Dora facility. Again, Arthur Rudolph was not charged, because there was no indication or evidence of any wrongdoing on his part.

A thorough Army and FBI background investigation cleared Rudolph of any inimical behavior.

Upon return to Germany, Rudolph was investigated, cleared, and his German citizenship was restored. After Rudolph's forced expulsion from the United States a Canadian court cleared him of any culpability in 1990.

A more important fact is that Mr. Rickey (Arthur Rudolph's immediate supervisor) was a defendant at the Dachau trials and was found innocent. Which would make Arthur Rudolph innocent by the nature of how the trials were conducted in that superiors were held responsible for those that worked under them.]

Figure 8 Preparing to launch a V-2 at White Sands using the German captured equipment. Dr. Kurt Debus used a sandbag reinforced foxhole as launch control.

Figure 9 Entrance to the Space and Rocket Center in Huntsville, Alabama.
The Saturn V is in the background.

Figure 10 **One of two airplanes built to hold some of the components of the Saturn V stages. It was affectionately called the "Guppy."**

Figure 11 **Other missiles and rockets built by the Rocket Team.
The Saturn V is on its side in the background.**

Figure 12 **The Lunar Lander, foreground, with three of the stages of the Saturn V in the background.**

Figure 13 **Seeing just two stages, and part of the third stage, gives one an idea of how large the Saturn V is.**

Figure 14 **The author with the muzzle loading pistol he made when he was 11 years old**

Figure 15 Titan II ICBM. The author worked as monitor of construction supply contractors at three missile areas in Arizona, Arkansas, and Nebraska for the Army Corps of Engineers.

Figure 16 **The mighty Saturn V fully assembled is 364 feet tall and 33 feet in diameter.**

Figure 17 **Dr. Ernst Stuhlinger. Timeless man whose dream it has been since his youth to have an ion propulsion system.**

Figure 18 Now in the home of the author, this bar was used by the German Rocket Team at Fort Bliss to discuss the Moon and Mars missions in 1946/1947.

Figure 19 **Arthur Rudolph proudly standing next
to the Saturn V**

Figure 20 Stand back, please. 7.5 million pounds of thrust, or 3,500 tons, is a lot of power from five engines.

Figure 21 **Ed Buckbee, left, Konrad Dannenberg, and wife Jackie, at a luncheon with Old Timers. They still are being sought out for information on how to go to Mars. Ed Buckbee was the first Director of the Huntsville Space and Rocket Center.**

16

Presidential Dismissal of Significant
Human Rights Issue

As events evolved, I came into possession of documents produced by private citizens and civic groups who became involved in a campaign to attract Presidential attention to the Rudolph case.

From my perspective, the most remarkable document was a letter dated May 20, 1985, from a Mr. Frank Barwacz, and addressed to President Reagan. Mr. Barwacz, previously mentioned in this book, was an American citizen who had accompanied his parents to Poland in the 1930s. When the war began, SS troops captured him, resulting in his internment in four concentration camps, one of which was the Dora/Nordhausen complex, site of the V-2 production line. In his 1985 letter to President Reagan, he refers to his experience and identifies those responsible for the persecution of prisoners. His letter begins:

"For the last few weeks in the news media, press, TV, radio, there was so much confusion about your trip to Germany. I saw on TV when Mr. Wiesel did receive from you Mr. President the Congressional Medal of Honor in commemorating the Holocaust. Mr. President I was in that suffering Holocaust too, I did suffer there plenty, and many times I was near death. My blood was spilled there in Germany. I was in four concentration camps, Auschwitz, Birkenau, then Buchenwald, then Dora where we inmates were forced to work on those V-2 rockets, then Bergen-Belsen. I was liberated with others by the British Army. Many times before, and lately they were showing on TV the horrors in Bergen-Belsen. They were showing the corpses of the dead and still alive inmates. I was there and I was near death too, but thanks be to God, I

survived, and Mr. President I was there as a prisoner, flesh and bones American, born in Chicago. Mr. President I did write to you before, but you did not answer me. Maybe your aides were holding back my letters but I do hope Mr. President that you will answer me this time."

On page 2 of his letter, he continues:

*"Now Mr. President, I also did ask you for justice. I did ask you Mr. President to bring justice to Mr. Dr. Arthur Rudolph. I did mention before to you Mr. President that Mr. Dr. Rudolph is 100% innocent, and my testimony proves it, because I was in Dora and the V-2 rocket plant, and I am repeating, again and again, and again, what I saw in Dora, what I heard from other prisoners, and what I experience on my own flesh, I am stating wholeheartedly, that no German civilian high or low group or any scientist-engineers hurt or harmed me or any other prisoners in Dora, and that is the truth. Nobody can give any better proof for that than me because **I was the only American prisoner.***

When I was forced to work with other inmates on the secret production of the V-2 rocket, inside and outside the tunnels, I was beaten there by a Kapo, and a SS guard sent a dog on me and that dog was ripping my body's right leg and right arm, but one German civilian with one arm saved my life. When I was laying on the ground in blood and the SS man did pull the gun to shoot me and finish me off, this German civilian grabbed his arm and asked the SS man not to shoot me. In doing so, he not only endangered himself, but also saved my life.

On another occasion, which I forgot to say before in my testimony given already to our Justice Department, I once was told by a German civilian to do a certain job, to separate metal parts and put them in certain places. I made a mistake, a big mistake because I was putting things wrongly. When this German civilian came over to me and saw it that I did wrong, he very kindly and quietly told me that I did wrong. He did not raise his voice, but again showed me kindly. He could have called the SS from nearby, and accused me for sabotage and I would be shot or hanged; he therefore too saved my life.

I never heard, or saw that any German civilian, from the top to the bottom, any German civilians hurt us prisoners, that is the reason my heart is crying out loudly to you Mr. President to help me that I could prove that Mr. Dr. Arthur Rudolph is innocent. If only one German civilian would hurt us inmates, I would not fight so hard for Mr. Rudolph. Those German civilians from the top to the bottom were told *to do their jobs, or else, the prisoners were told to do their jobs, or else. We were victims, and those **German** civilians were victims in the hands of the oppressive hands of the SS even though not all SS men were mean, some were treating us prisoners fairly.*

Once a reporter in a large newspaper here in Chicago asked me these words. Mr. Barwacz were there also Jews in Dora? I said: I did not see any Jewish prisoners in our Kommando, as a matter of fact, nowhere. Then he asked me why I am doing this for Mr. Rudolph. I said: God was good to me there, I am repaying now for my neighbor, because I know that Mr. Rudolph is innocent. Mr. President I am not doing this because what Mr. Rudolph with Mr. von Braun did for America, American people already know, I am doing this because Mr. Rudolph is suffering injustice and I know what it is to suffer injustice, therefore Mr. President please help to bring and restore honor and dignity to Dr. Arthur Rudolph because he is innocent.

Also, Mr. President, I want to say this. When I was in Buchenwald, I know that in Buchenwald were German communists as prisoners, also some, I heard, in Dora. If some of them as hard core communists went to serve communism, and if some of them brought accusations, then Mr. President, who are you going to believe me as a truly American or are you going to believe someone who does not (sic) belong to our country, who has maybe some selfish aspirations or to hurt our beautiful America."

The Barwacz letter in its entirety is located in Appendix so titled. To my knowledge, Mr. Barwacz did not receive a reply to this letter, which along with the others that he mentioned had been ignored. In my opinion, I believe that his letter vanished after it arrived at the White House mailroom, so that it could not be delivered to the Oval Office. I firmly believe that had President Reagan read that impassioned appeal from Barwacz, that some type of action would have resulted. Here, in plain English, was unquestionable eyewitness testimony exonerating Arthur Rudolph from the war crimes charges fabricated by the DOJ. **Again the thought arises in my mind on what evil influence is behind this vendetta on the vilification of one of our greatest national heroes?**

Among the documentation that I have in my possession, concerning appeals through presidential channels is one of two appeals from the City Council of the city of Huntsville, Alabama. The title of the document is Resolution No. 85-587, dated 19 September 1985. It is included here in its entirety.

"WHEREAS, at the invitation of our Government, there came to this community after World War II a group of eminent German scientists who worked long, hard and faithfully in the service of our country; and

WHEREAS, these scientists became citizens of the United States and of this community and distinguished themselves as leaders in the forefront of, first our defense missile developments, and later in our moon landing program; and

WHEREAS, Arthur Rudolph was a member of this group of German scientists and became an American citizen and a citizen of this community, and made notable patriotic contributions, especially as the leader who developed the Saturn V Rocket, without which, the United States of America could not have taken our giant leap for mankind; and

WHEREAS, Arthur Rudolph has heretofore relinquished his citizenship in this great republic, the United States of America, under circumstances which indicate that his constitutional rights were not respected, and which indicate in fact such rights were in essence violated by representatives of the United States of America in that he was confronted with accusations concerning matters which allegedly happened more than thirty (30) years ago of an outrageous and stigmatizing nature, without formal charges, and without said charges ever having been reviewed by a detached and impartial Magistrate or by a Grand Jury; and

WHEREAS, Arthur Rudolph and all citizens of these United States, whether natural born, or naturalized, are entitled to all the rights, privileges and immunities secured to them under the constitution and laws of the country; and

*WHEREAS, the procedure followed with respect to the accusations against Dr. Rudolph, in substance, has the effect of establishing in the eyes of uninformed citizens, **his guilt by association, and not by legal evidence** establishing his guilt beyond the shadow of a doubt and to a moral certainty, **a standard of proof to which he was, as a citizen, constitutionally entitled;** and*

WHEREAS, the Mayor and the City Council of Huntsville believes that the United States of America should take all appropriate steps to promptly rectify the grievous wrong done to Arthur Rudolph, and thereafter reconsiders any allegations against him in a manner which actually secures to him all his rights as a citizen, and secures these rights to him both in form and in substance.

NOW, THEREFORE BE IT RESOLVED by the City Council of the City of Huntsville, Alabama, as follows:

First, the United States of America is hereby respectfully urged to restore Arthur Rudolph to full citizenship as recognition of the substantial wrong inflicted upon him.

Second, The United States of America, and specifically the President of the United States, Honorable Ronald Reagan, and the Attorney General of the United States, Honorable Edwin Meese, are hereby respectfully urged to take all appropriate steps to see that allegations against Arthur Rudolph are considered by all elements of our government in a manner calculated to secure to him, in both form and substance, all the rights of any native born or naturalized citizen.

BE IT FURTHER RESOLVED that copies of this resolution be forwarded to the President of the United States, and to the Attorney General of the United States, with a sincere request that the position of the governing body of the City of Huntsville be considered by them with respect to Arthur Rudolph.

ADOPTED this 19th day of September, 1985.

Signed Ernest C. Kaufmann II

President of the City Council of the City of Huntsville, Alabama

APPROVED this the 19th day of September, 1985.

Signed Joe W. Davis   Mayor of the City of Huntsville, Alabama

I have been informed by a very reliable source that this resolution by the City of Huntsville was ignored by President Reagan, as evidenced by the fact that they did not receive a response from the White House.

At this time, I wish to refresh your memory by referring to the appeal of Retired General John B. Medaris to President Reagan, the sum of which is encapsulated in his words:

"I urge you to review the secretive, deceptive, and totally unjust process by which Mr. Rudolph was literally forced to abandon his friends and deny his oath. He deserves nothing less that immediate restoration of citizenship and invitation to return in honor to his country of choice."

The following is another request for presidential assistance concerning the Rudolph case. It was made in the form of a petition to President Bush by seven of the leading citizens of Huntsville, Alabama, which was dated June 20, 1990

A PETITION TO THE HONORABLE GEORGE BUSH PRESIDENT OF THE UNITED STATES

Mr. President, in 1950 Wernher von Braun and his team of rocket scientists came to our city and began the brilliant exploration that led to our landing on the moon. Arthur Rudolph was a leading member of that team. He was the master designer of the Saturn V, the giant, unbelievable, rocket atop which Neil Armstrong and crew lifted off from Cape Canaveral.

But 13 years after Dr. Rudolph retired with high honors from NASA the government he had served so well accused him of having committed war crimes four decades earlier and pressured him into leaving the country and renouncing his much-prized American citizenship. Arthur Rudolph is a stringently honest man, Mr. President, and the so-called "investigation" that led to his expulsion revealed nothing that he had not disclosed at the end of the war. Further, an extensive investigation in Germany found that the accusations against him were without foundation.

Congressman James Traficant of Ohio has introduced a bill (H. Res. 404) designed to give Dr. Rudolph the fair hearing he has never received here in our country.

Mr. President, we do not ask you for a judgment regarding the guilt or innocence of Arthur Rudolph, but we do have a much smaller thing to ask. It is necessary for Dr. Rudolph to enter the country to see to his affairs, including discussions with members of Congress that could lead to support for the Traficant bill. Although Dr. Rudolph is even now, as an American exile, paying U.S. taxes, representatives in the Justice Department insist that he will never be permitted to set foot on our soil. We would respectfully request, Mr. President that you ask the Attorney General to reconsider the position of this Department and allow Dr. Rudolph in the country at least for a specified period.

Numerous petitions addressed to the Justice Department have been summarily turned aside without substantive comment, and it is clear that this one would suffer a similar fate if it should simply be forwarded there as a matter of conventional government business.

This is not a conventional matter, Mr. President, but one, which involves fundamental issues of American fairness, and we ask you to give it your personal attention.

Huntsville, Alabama

June 20, 1990 signed by below

Steve Whetting Mayor City of Huntsville; Luis Padul University President; Thomas J. Lee Marshall Space Flight Center

Edward O. Buckbee Director Alabama Space & Rocket Center,

Charles W. Eifler LtGen (U.S.A.-Ret), Former Redstone Arsenal CG;

John G. Zierdt MajGen (U.S.A.-Ret)), Former Redstone Arsenal CG;

Joseph C. Moquin Retired CEO Teledyne-Brown Engineering

I have been informed by Mr. Moquin, one of the signatories to this petition, that there was no response from President Bush concerning the matter. Again, an appeal for presidential help had been ignored.

Not withstanding the course of prior events concerning the requests for presidential assistance concerning the Rudolph case, I promptly made an appeal to President Bill Clinton shortly after his inauguration. In a three-page letter dated February 19, 1993, I gave a briefing of the history of the case, with particular attention paid to the gross prosecutorial misconduct of the OSI in their prosecution of the case.

To sum up my appeal I will quote the last three paragraphs of my letter (referring here to the second appeal by Huntsville):

Since I have exhausted my efforts in going through Department of Justice, and Congressional channels, to no avail, I now appeal to you Mr. President, to resolve truth and justice in this matter. That appropriate action be taken to investigate the operational conduct of the OSI in the Rudolph case, and in the other two cases referred to above, and that U.S. citizenship be restored to those who have been victims of unconstitutional acts perpetrated upon them by U.S. officials.

Your promise that special interest groups should not have the same influence over our government, as in the past, is most encouraging. It has become increasingly evident that there has been some strong action by special interest to suppress truth and justice in the Rudolph case. The City of, Alabama, sent a City Resolution, dated June 20, 1990, to President Bush, requesting an investigation be conducted concerning the Rudolph case. This request was ignored.

I have acted on a voluntary basis, as a U.S. citizen, in my attempt to get truth and justice resolved in this case, and have not received, or expect to receive, any monetary remuneration for my almost eight years of effort.

The full text of the letter to President Clinton is located in Appendix so titled.

The following is the response from the White House to my letter of February 19, 1993:

THE WHITE HOUSE WASHINGTON
April 8, 1993
Mr. William E. Winterstein

"Dear Mr. Winterstein:

Thank you so much for your letter, President Clinton greatly appreciates the trust and confidence you have expressed in him by writing.

To give your concerns the special attention they deserve, the President has asked me to forward your letter to the Department of Justice. I have asked them to provide you with a prompt reply, but please bear in mind that it may take several weeks to look thoroughly into the concerns you have raised. Should you have any questions after reviewing their response to you, you may write: Department of Justice, 10th and Pennsylvania Avenue, NW, Washington, D.C. 20530.

Many thanks for your patience."
Sincerely, (signed) Marsha Scott Deputy Assistant to the President and Director of Presidential Correspondence

I was very much surprised by the very prompt reply from the White House, in fewer than three weeks! However, the news that it was being forwarded to the DOJ for further action was a blow to me in a sense, because in my letter to the President I went into detail about the problems that I had encountered with the DOJ. The matter, in effect, was referred to the fox in charge of guarding the henhouse.

With a new administration in place, though, I was hoping that a new opportunity for truth and justice to prevail had arrived.

I patiently awaited a response from the DOJ and since none was received, I wrote President Clinton a letter dated August 16, 1993.

August 16, 1993

Dear President Clinton;

This letter is in reference to the Arthur Rudolph case, which was prosecuted by the Office of Special Investigation of the Department of Justice. I wrote a letter to you dated February 19th indicating that the OSI was involved in prosecutorial misconduct concerning the case.

In response to this, I received a reply from the White House dated April 8th, indicating that my concern was forwarded to the Department of Justice for a prompt response, however that I must realize that it may take several weeks for a reply.

As of this date, a period of over four months, I have not received a response from the Department of Justice in answer to the White House request.

I surmise that the reason that this request from the White House has evidently been ignored is that the request may have been referred to the same OSI officials who were present in the Reagan and Bush administrations. During that period, the Department of Justice stand was adamant in their refusal to consider new and legitimate evidence, which surfaced after Rudolph left the U.S. for a reconsideration of the case.

As you will note, the enclosure to my letter to Attorney General Reno is a review of the Rudolph case. This refers to incidents of misconduct by the OSI in their conduct of operations concern-the case. As a result of this misconduct, the U.S. has been put in an embarrassing situation. As a result of OSI allegations, Rudolph has been investigated by both West Germany and Canada. Because of these hearings or investigations, both countries found that the allegations of the OSI were not substantiated by legitimate evidence. In addition to this the OSI failed to provide Rudolph's lawyer legitimate evidence to support any criminal violations.

It is almost unbelievable to me that a small segment of our Department of Justice has been engaged in such operational misconduct. To me it is reminiscent of the operations of the Gestapo and the KGB in their hay day. That was when an accusation by one of those organizations was tantamount to being guilty.

A review of available evidence should indicate that a reconsideration of the Rudolph case is fully justified. Your kind consideration to resolve truth and justice in this case will be deeply appreciated."

Sincerely,
(signed) William E. Winterstein LTC Army (Ret.)

Since the 25th anniversary of the lunar landing was going to be celebrated the following year in 1994, I wrote the President a letter, dated November 1993, requesting that action be taken to restore Rudolph's citizenship so that he could return to the U.S. The following is the full text of the letter.

November 1, 1993
Dear President Clinton:

Next year, on July 20, 1994, will mark the 25th anniversary of U.S. astronauts landing on the moon. This, the greatest of man's technological achievements in recorded history, was made within the decade that President John Kennedy, in his State of the Union message, on May 25, 1961, challenged the American scientific community to accomplish this mission.

In 1963, Dr. Arthur Rudolph was appointed manager of the Saturn V Program, the mission of which was to develop and fabricate the booster vehicles for the lunar (Apollo) landing program. He was one of the key individuals most responsible in sending U.S. astronauts on the voyage to the moon in 1969.

As referred to in my letters, dated February 19, and August 16, 1993, to you, that Arthur Rudolph lost his U.S. citizenship through gross prosecutorial misconduct on part of officials in the Office of Special Investigation of our Department of Justice. This evidently is the same Office, which engineered the embarrassing and humiliating situation, and causing a dark blot on the face of American justice in the recent outcome of the John Demjanjuk case. As in the Rudolph case, the allegations of the OSI against Demjanjuk were not supported by legitimate evidence in a foreign court.

As also indicated in my letters to you, during the past eight years I have attempted to get the Rudolph case reconsidered by the Department of Justice. I have presented new and legitimate evidence to fully support such reconsideration, but to no avail. In addition, I, as an American citizen, have attempted to pursue my search for truth and justice, American style, through Congressional channel, also without any positive results.

Therefore, Mr. President, I appeal to you, that in the name of an American sense of fairness, justice, and compassion that you issue an Executive Order, if necessary, to restore Arthur Rudolph's U.S. citizenship to him so that he may return to the country of his choice. The restoration of his U.S. citizenship would be most appropriate at this time in expressing this country's appreciation for his dedicated efforts in placing the United States of America at the forefront among nations in the peaceful exploration of space.

I hereby respectfully request that I receive a reply from the White House as to what decision is made concerning the above request."

Sincerely,
(signed) William E. Winterstein LTC Army (Ret.)

I received no response to this letter, which indicated to me that the occupants of the White House at that time had no interest in truth or justice, or in resolving any other aspect of the Rudolph case.

The initial response that I received from the White House in April of 1993 cautioned me to "please bear in mind that it may take several weeks to look thoroughly into the concerns you have raised." I in fact did wait. I waited for a full year! The DOJ finally, on February 16, 1994, sent me their response, which to me was ludicrous in nature. They had completely ignored the fact that the OSI was guilty of gross prosecutorial misconduct, and had diverted my communication to the Immigration and

Naturalization Service as a matter of immigration concern. The full text of the response from the DOJ is as follows:

Dear Mr. Winterstein:

Thank you for your communication to the President. While the President would like to personally assist all persons with situations such as those described in your communication. Because of the tremendous volume of inquiries that he receives from people all over the world seeking his special attention, he is not able to address them all. Therefore, your communication and those cases with Immigration concerns have been forwarded to the Headquarters Office of the Immigration and Naturalization Service (INS) in order that we may be able to address them with the best possible information.

The concerns expressed in your communication will be personally reviewed by a member of this staff. After our review, if it is determined that your request is within the Jurisdiction of the INS Headquarters office, a thorough response to your inquiry will be sent to you as soon as possible. However, if it is determined upon review that your case falls within the jurisdiction of another office we will notify you of the referral and provide you with an address and telephone number for future contact."

Sincerely,
(Signed) Duane J. Tate Acting Chief Information Operations Unit

This transparent effort by the DOJ to stonewall the movement for restoration of citizenship to Arthur Rudolph is noted with sadness, but is by no means the last word on the matter.

17

The Canadian Episode

Arthur Rudolph had made plans to visit Canada in July of 1990. The OSI evidently got word of this and promptly notified Canadian authorities that he was on a list of persons barred from entry into the United States because of war crimes allegations. As a result, Rudolph was forcibly detained when he arrived in Toronto, Canada on July 1, 1990. He was kept in a small room for interrogation for eight and one-half hours prior to release contingent on the posting of a Canadian bond.

The findings of a Canadian court into the OSI allegations are contained in a 20-page report issued by the presiding judge. They are included here.

The Decision In The Case Of Arthur Louis Hugo Rudolph

> *On the 1st of July 1990, Arthur Louis Hugo Rudolph arrived in Canada at Pearson International Airport seeking entry to Canada as a visitor. On examination by an immigration officer he was refused entry to Canada and the report which has been marked as exhibit B at this inquiry was made alleging that he is a member of the inadmissible class of persons described in paragraph 19 (i) (j) of the Immigration Act. This inquiry has taken place as a consequence of that report.*

> *At this inquiry, I have had to determine whether Mr. Rudolph should be allowed to come to Canada. Section 8(I) of the Immigration Act provides that where a person seeks to come into Canada the burden of proving that person has a right to come into Canada or that his admission would not be contrary to this Act or the Regulations rests on that person. A visitor is someone who does not have a right in law to come into Canada who is seeking entry for a temporary purpose.*

The officer's report alleged that his admission would be contrary to paragraph 19(i)(j) In that he is a person who there are reasonable grounds to believe has committed an act or omission outside Canada that constituted a war crime or a crime against humanity within the meaning of subsection 7 (3.76) of the Criminal Code and that If it had been committed in Canada would have constituted an offense against the laws of Canada in force at the time of the act or omission. Mr. Rudolph at this inquiry in fact continued to seek entry to Canada as a visitor. Section 32(4) of the Immigration Act provides that where an adjudicator decides that a person who is the subject of an inquiry is a person who at the time of his examination was seeking entry and that it would not be contrary to any provision of this Act or the Regulations to grant entry to that person the adjudicator may grant entry to that person and except in the case of a person who may be granted entry pursuant to subsection 19(3) impose terms and conditions of a prescribed nature and section 32.5 provides that where an adjudicator decides that a person who is the subject of an inquiry is a person who at the time of the person's examination was seeking admission and is a member of an inadmissible class the adjudicator shall, subject to subsection 32.1(3), make a removal order against that person. Therefore, at this inquiry the burden of proving that admission is not contrary to the Immigration Act has rested with Mr. Rudolph. If he were able, to meet that burden I might grant him entry as a visitor however, should the evidence show that his admission is contrary to the Immigration Act in any way, should issue an order for his removal from Canada.

Section 30(4) provides that an adjudicator may at an inquiry receive and base a decision on whether the person who is the subject of the inquiry should be permitted to come into Canada on evidence deduced at the inquiry and considered credible or trustworthy in the circumstances of the case.

The Commission alleged that there are reasonable grounds for me to form an opinion that Mr. Rudolph committed acts and an omission outside of Canada that would be a crime against humanity and a war crime that if committed in Canada would constitute, an offense, against the laws of Canada enforced at the time.

In the Criminal Code, of Canada a Crime against humanity means "murder, extermination, enslavement, deportation, persecution or any other inhumane act or omission that is committed against any civilian population or any identifiable group of persons whether or not it constitutes contravention of the law in force at the time and in the place of its commission and that at that time and in that place constitutes a contravention of customary international law or Conventional international law or is criminal according to the general principles of law recognized by the community of nations."

War crime means

"an act or omission that is committed during an international armed conflict whether or not it constitutes a contravention of the law in force at the time and in the place of its commission and that at that time and In that place constitutes a contravention of the customary international law or conventional International law applicable in international armed conflicts."

The Criminal Code goes on to say that in the definition of "crimes against humanity" and "war crime" an act or omission includes for "greater certainty attempting or conspiring to commit, counseling any person to commit, aiding or abetting any person in the commission of, or being an accessory after the fact in relation to an act or omission."

Specifically the Commission said that Mr. Rudolph's offense would be an offense contrary to paragraph 297 of the Criminal Code of Canada 1927. Exhibit C at this Inquiry was an extract from the Criminal Code of that time. The Commission relied on 297(a){iii) which reads, "everyone is guilty of an indictable offense and liable to 25 years imprisonment who, without lawful authority (a) kidnaps any person with intent (iii) to cause such other person to be sold or captured as a slave or in any way held to service against his will."

The Commission alleged that the acts and omission took place between 16 April 1943 and April 1945. The Commission stated that the principal allegation was forcible confinement. The Commission alleged Mr. Rudolph would be guilty as a principal and also that he would be guilty of aiding and abetting and counseling to commit the offenses set out in section 297 (a)(iii). The Commission alleged that Mr. Rudolph did something which either aided or abetted or did something directly which amounted to a violation or a war crime or a crime against humanity concerning internment of civilians under inhumane conditions, forced labor of civilians in accordance with the military operations of the enemy, ill-treatment of wounded prisoners and prisoners of war, employment of prisoners of war on unauthorized work, or counseling the commission of these offenses. The Commission alleged that he forced people to work in the production of the V-2 rocket and he assisted or aided and abetted and counseled, within the meaning of section 21 and 22 of the Criminal Code, people to force prisoners to work on the V-2.

There has been voluminous evidence presented at this inquiry for my consideration in documentary form and in the form of testimony of various witnesses. The primary evidence in this case came in the form of the direct testimony under oath at this inquiry of the subject, Arthur Louis Hugo Rudolph. The other important and relevant evidence was contained in: Exhibit D, an agreement between Arthur Louis Hugo Rudolph and (sic) the United States Department of Justice requested by the Office of Special Investigations: Exhibit E, the transcript of an examination under oath of Arthur Louis Hugo Rudolph from the Office of Special Investigations dated on 13 October 1982 plus the continuation of the examination of Mr. Rudolph dated 4 February 1983: also exhibit Y, the Duhn report, a report concerning the results of the criminal investigation into Arthur Rudolph by the Department of Public Prosecutions at the Hamburg District Court on 17 February 1987. None of the other evidence presented was essential either for the Commission's case or for Mr. Rudolph's case. I found that the best evidence and the really essential evidence came from the testimony of Mr. Rudolph at this inquiry. The other exhibits listed above either expanded on areas that he had given direct testimony about or corroborated evidence that he had given at the inquiry. Other evidence that was presented either supported the testimony that Mr. Rudolph gave or was not as good or weighty evidence as the testimony that he had given under oath. In my final consideration, other evidence did not mean as much as his testimony at his inquiry and in my opinion was not as credible or trustworthy as the evidence that Mr. Rudolph gave.

Mr. Rudolph testified at the inquiry that he did not control the hours of work of the forced laborers. However, there was some evidence at the inquiry in a sworn statement of his superior, Albin Sawatzki, to the effect that Mr. Rudolph was one of the people that influenced the hours of work. On cross-examination at this inquiry, Mr. Rudolph's position was that Mr. Sawatzki was a liar and that his motive for lying would have been to save his own skin. The Commission attacked Mr. Rudolph's credibility by submitting that in the same way Mr. Rudolph would lie to save his own skin. There is no acceptable evidence to indicate that Mr. Rudolph has been lying at this inquiry. The Commission's position was that if I believed what Albin Sawatzki had said about the hours of work then Mr. Rudolph had lied when he was questioned about those hours by the Office of Special Investigations in the United States and at this inquiry. I could not, however, accept the evidence of Mr. Sawatzki over the testimony of Mr. Rudolph at this inquiry. Mr. Sawatzki is deceased. The evidence was in the form of a statement taken from a transcript of a previous proceeding. He had not been subject to cross-examination at this inquiry. It is not reasonable to give it as much weight as the testimony of Mr. Rudolph at this Inquiry.

At this Inquiry under oath Mr. Rudolph has stated that the food which the forced laborers received was about the same food that he received, Mr. MacIntosh characterized this as a preposterous contention. He said that no reasonable person would ever believe that and that it further showed that Mr. Rudolph was prepared to say anything at any time in order to advance his false claim that he did not do anything that was a war crime or a crime against humanity. However, I found no evidence to show that the statement Mr. Rudolph has made is untrue. **Mr. Rudolph has testified that he was not well fed during this time; that at Mittelwerk he himself lost 60 pounds.** No reasonable basis was presented to me to find Mr. Rudolph's statement incredible.

Exhibit P at this inquiry is an order concerning punishment of prisoners by civilian employees at Mittelwerk and concerning association of such employees with prisoners. It basically indicated that camp doctors had reported cases of mistreatment, beating or stabbing with sharp instruments by civilian employees or prisoners. It went on to warn employees and to reaffirm the rules and the policies concerning association with prisoners. It basically prohibited all association. Mr. Rudolph was questioned concerning this document because he had testified that he had seen no mistreatment of any of the workers or, on his V-2 assembly lines by any of his civilian employees and that he had never had to warn them or to order them to not treat prisoners in any such way. Mr. Rudolph has stated in his evidence that this did not happen on his line or in his part of the plant although in retrospect he believed that it could possibly have happened in other parts of the plant. In terms of credibility Mr. MacIntosh characterized this as yet another indication of Mr. Rudolph's tendency to try to minimize anything that was horrific or anything that was horrendous that happened and to suggest that somehow he played no part in it and that he was not responsible. I find Mr. Rudolph's statements in this regard plausible, given the testimony about his specific duties, the area that he was in charge of, the type of work that was done there, and the type of conditions that he said existed there. No evidence has been presented to show that Mr. Rudolph's statements in this regard are not truthful.

The Commission also believed another area of Mr. Rudolph's testimony impeached his general credibility. Mr. Rudolph's evidence has been that the SS was running things and that the SS was solely in control of all of the forced laborers.

The Commission pointed out that in some cases Mr. Rudolph could take actions to improve conditions. For example, he arranged ration stamps to be used as a reward for workers working faster in his department.

It was contended that this was an indication that while Mr. Rudolph said that the SS were running things that he actually was in a position of control. I could not however draw that same conclusion from the evidence. The fact that Mr. Rudolph could see to it that extra rations were given did not mean that he was untruthful about his explanation about the control that the SS exerted over the labor force or about the limitations he maintained he had on his control over the workers.

When examined by the Office of Special Investigations in the United States Mr. Rudolph had stated that he would walk through the tunnels "once a day, twice a day." However, on cross-examination at this inquiry he maintained that he only walked through once a day. When the difference was pointed out to him from the OSI material, he acknowledged the difference, that he had not amended the OSI record earlier. He stated that now at this inquiry he was amending it to say that he only walked through once a day. This was cited as on example of how the witness would say anything that would advance his cause. In the context of the total evidence surrounding the point I do not find here any lack of credibility.

He also testified that he thought his lawyer, Mr. Main, should not have taken his case in the U.S.A. at that time because the case was too deep and contentious for his experience and abilities. The Case Presenting Officer said that the fact that he claimed that Exhibit D was signed under duress indicated that he was lying because, simply, the document says that it wasn't signed under duress and because he could have at any time obtained another lawyer and because he hadn't obtained any action since signing the document to refute, appeal or contest it. Considering Mr. Rudolph's total testimony concerning the circumstances surrounding his signing of Exhibit D, I find in this no basis to doubt his credibility at this inquiry I decided to accept the testimony of Mr. Rudolph given at the inquiry as credible and as the best evidence presented. I find him credible because the evidence that he gave is not implausible, it is not unlikely, and it is consistent with the facts that were not disputed.

The evidence I believe is also consistent within itself. Mr. Rudolph has displayed in his demeanor and manner of testifying certain believability. He listened carefully to questions. He answered carefully and precisely. He noticed errors in questions that were put to him in numbers and figures that were repeated or mentioned. In short, it appeared to me that this whole matter was very important to him and that he has been diligent in attempting to provide the required answers. He displayed intelligence and a remarkable memory. He has not obviously lied under oath at this inquiry. His answers were not inconsistent. He did not contradict himself. What it was alleged that he did or aided, abetted, or counseled is horrendous. There was evidence, those crimes against humanity or war crimes of the very sort alleged by the Commission did take place in the concentration camp and in or around Mittelwerk. The nature of the allegations, however, is not grounds for doubting the credibility of Mr. Rudolph.

The following is a summary of the relevant facts as I have found them. Louis Arthur Hugo Rudolph is a citizen of Germany. Born there on 9th of November 1906. He arrived in Canada on 1 July 1990 at Pearson International Airport seeking entry as a visitor. He said that he came to Canada to visit with his daughter, with friends from Huntsville, Alabama and to talk to the Congressman James Traficant from the United States of America.

Mr. Rudolph's education and early job history is relevant to this decision. He stated that he grew up in a small farming village. He lost his father in World War I. His was not a wealthy family but he managed to finance graduation from the college of Berlin by selling part of the family farm he had inherited from his father.

He graduated with a Bachelor of Science degree in Mechanical Engineering and Industrial Engineering.

His first job after graduation was at the Heylandt plant; a company that he said produced and transported liquid oxygen. There he met a Max Valier, when, he said was a pioneer for space flight experimenting with rockets. Mr. Rudolph had testified that he himself had an early and abiding interest in space flight.

He volunteered and was accepted as an unpaid assistant to Valier. Max Valier died during an experimental test of a rocket engine that exploded. The company forbade continued rocket experiments but Mr. Rudolph continued on his own. He lost his employment during the depression. He

*and another unemployed colleague continued with rocket experiments
and eventually received some financing from the German Ordnance
Department. They dealt with a Captain Walter Dornberger. Who later
rose to the rank of Major General and was prominent in the German
rocket program. Through his work, he also came to know Wernher Von
Braun, who also later became prominent in the German rocket program
and who later came to work for the U.S.A. along with Mr. Rudolph. He
testified that at the time he wished to continue as a freelance inventor of
rocket engines. He sought further financing through Dornberger whose
counter offer made him a civilian employee of the German Army.*

*Eventually he came to work on the rocket he and his colleagues called the
A-4 but which was renamed by German officials, the V-2. Which Mr.
Rudolph testified meant vengeance weapon and was useful in propaganda.
Mr. Rudolph testified here that the original purpose of the A-4 or V-2 was
to establish a research vehicle to test rocket engines, however Dornberger
told him that the V-2 now was to be used as a weapon. He was told that he
should plan to equip a pilot production plant for the V-2 and that he would
be in charge of production. He said he did not want the job because he was
a research engineer not a production engineer.*

*Despite his protests, he was ordered to the job. The original production
works were set up in a place called Peenemünde in May of 1937. The
British forces bombed the works at Peenemünde on 17 August 1943.
Dornberger instructed Rudolph that the facility was to be moved to a
new safer facility called the Mittelwerk. He was sent there with one
Albin Sawatzki, an employee of the Armament Ministry who had been at
Peenemünde to learn about production. The site was a series of tunnels
in the Harz Mountains. Several factories were to be set up there, and the
V-2 line was to be one of them. The tunnels had originally been dug as
a gypsum mine shortly after World War I. There Sawatzki showed him
the underground area to be used for the V-2 production and informed
him that the work force used to build the V-2 would be political
prisoners. Mr. Rudolph testified that was the first time he knew that
forced labor was to be used in the V-2 plant. He testified that he was
shocked at the information. He said his opinion in the matter had not
been, sought and that he could not have overruled the decision which
he thought was a decision of the SS. Mr. Rudolph then returned to
Peenemünde and organized the movement of the machinery to
Nordhausen, the name of the overall underground factory.*

*The first V-2 got off the production line on 31 December 1943 and
production continued there, until March 1945. Mr. Rudolph reported*

that there were problems at the outset. The atmosphere was bad because of dust from excavation and condensation because of the cold tunnel walls. There were no real sanitary facilities. Oil barrels were cut in half and used as toilets. The forced laborers and the German civilians there worked in unhealthy conditions. He said he knew some of the German civilians had died as a result of the bad conditions and assumed that forced laborers died as well. He said the conditions improved as time went on. They installed a ventilation and heating system and succeeded in diminishing the dust. The sanitary facilities were improved and eventually they had normal toilet facilities. Mr. Rudolph maintained that he thought that the prisoners were adequately fed. He also stated that he himself lost 60 pounds in weight while working there. The working hours for German civilians and for the forced laborers were 12 hours a shift, seven days per week. He said his hours were the same, maybe longer. He said the people who worked on the V-2 did precision work not hard manual labor and that the prisoners and civilians on the line performed the same kind of work. He was the Operations Director for the V-2. Albin Sawatzki was his superior in the factory and he set manpower requirements which he submitted to the SS. Mr. Rudolph said the SS provided the manpower which they got from Camp Dora, a concentration camp outside the production facility. The SS ran and guarded the camp and transported the prisoners to the camp and back. They were also responsible for feeding and discipline of the forced laborers. Mr. Rudolph testified that he did not have authority or capability to arrest anyone and put them in the camp and that he did not guard the prisoners in any way.

He also testified that he could not have released any prisoners.

Mr. Rudolph testified that there were several factories in the underground cavern. There was the V-2 and another facility where aircraft engines were produced, the V-1 rocket production area, a jet engine factory, and an area for the production of solid propellant rockets; He was associated only with the V-2 plant. A contracting company called Wifo also continued with the excavation of the tunnels. All got workers from the prisoners of the SS and the main work force was for the tunnel excavation. He said there was 40 plus tunnels with a total of one million square meters of floor space.

Five percent of the area or 50,000 square meters was devoted to the V-2 production. Mr. Rudolph testified that once at the behest of his superior, a Mr. Kettler, he accompanied him to meet the Camp Commandant. They had a general conversation and drank schnapps.

The meeting took about half an hour and Mr. Rudolph did not see any more of the camp than the office that they were in. Mr. Rudolph said the prisoners used on the V-2 line were Russians. Poles, Czechs, Frenchmen, from Holland and probably from other countries too. He said he had no knowledge that any Jews were used on the V-2 production. He said he never asked for prisoners of any particular race, religion, nationality, or political belief. These things did not matter. He was only concerned with the production end and was interested in treating the workers well so that they could work. He said his purpose was to produce the V-2 rockets and nothing else.

Mr. Rudolph indicated in his evidence that as Production Manager he sometimes would ask for more workers so that his workers would not be overworked or to accommodate the workload but that sometimes he received more workers and sometimes he did not. He did not have control over whether he would be given more forced laborers. This was a decision made by SS authorities.

Mr. Rudolph maintained that he only witnessed one hanging himself and that he only really knew about conditions on the V-2 line. He stated that he only had knowledge of the V-2 plant and not other areas. He maintained that he only had a general idea that people were dying for various reasons in other places because of disease, starvation, and overwork or any other reasons. He testified that he had requested additional work force only to produce the V-2 not to persecute prisoners or for any other purpose.

Mr. Rudolph also testified that for about one month while Albin Sawatzki was sick he took over his responsibilities. However, he made no major changes at the plant at that time, as he did not believe it was reasonable to do so.

The productions eventually shut down because of lack of supplies caused by the advancing allied forces. Mr. Rudolph said that he was ordered by the SS to leave Nordhausen and go to Bavaria. He was released from service. He and colleagues hid out in the countryside fearing SS action and finally surrendered to American forces.

He was interviewed about his wartime activities at a U.S. camp in Garmisch, Bavaria, but no record of that interview was presented. He was next sent to the U.S.A. and interviewed at Fort Strong in Boston but no record of that interview was presented. In June 1947, Mr. Rudolph underwent an Army Interrogation at Fort Bliss in El Paso Texas. A record of that interrogation was included in the evidence presented at this inquiry. He went on to become an alien resident and then a citizen of the U.S.A. He was the subject of various ongoing investigations, stemming from his war time activities, by the Federal Bureau of Investigations in the U.S.A. Reports of some of those were presented as evidence here and generally showed a positive view of him.

Mr. Rudolph had a successful and distinguished career with the U.S. space program. He directed the building of the rocket, which took the astronauts to the moon and was the director for the development of the Pershing missile. He retired in 1969.

Then in 1982 and 1983, he was interviewed by the Office of Special investigations of the United States Department of Justice. The transcripts of these interviews were presented at this inquiry and entered here as Exhibit E and attachments. The Office of Special Investigations then required him to obtain a lawyer and indicated an intention to prosecute him alleging that he participated under the direction of and on behalf of the Nazi government of Germany, in the persecution of unarmed civilians because of their race, religion, national origin or political opinion.

His lawyer, G. Main, met with O.S.I. officials on 2 September 1983 at San Jose. California and he prepared a summary of that interview which was presented as evidence here and entered as Exhibit U. The O.S.I. officials indicated that they intended to prove their case with two forms of evidence, documentary and personal testimony. Their primary evidence was to be the personal testimony of Mr. Rudolph.

On 28 November 1983, Mr. Rudolph signed an agreement with the United States Department of Justice to leave the country, renounce his citizenship, and thus avoid prosecution. That agreement was entered as Exhibit D at this inquiry. He left for Germany in March of 1984 and shortly thereafter renounced his United States citizenship.

The German government then began a criminal investigation conducted by Oberstaatsanwalt Duhn of the Department of Public Prosecutions at the Hamburg District Court. In 1984, Germany requested the evidence that the United States of America had against Arthur Rudolph. The investigation considered the testimony of 64 witnesses and much documentary evidence and included the O.S.I. transcripts entered at this inquiry and the evidence of the witnesses the O.S.I. said would be used against Rudolph if prosecuted in the U.S.A. Duhn finished the investigation on the 17th of February 1987 and found that there was no basis for prosecuting him in Germany. Arthur Rudolph was then granted German citizenship in 1987.

I considered all of this evidence and in particular the transcripts of the interviews in 1947, 1982 and 1983 and it appears to me that in all areas Arthur Rudolph's testimony there was consistent with the evidence given at this inquiry even considering the opinions and allegations evident in the latter two that resulted in the actions taken by the Office of Special Investigations in the U.S.A.

The immigration Commission alleged That Arthur Rudolph committed acts and an omission that constituted crimes against humanity and war crimes that if committed in Canada would constitute an offense contrary to paragraph 297 (a) (iii) of the Criminal Code of Canada 1927 (Exhibit C at this inquiry). The Commission alleged that he would have been guilty as a principal and that he would also have been guilty of aiding and abetting and counseling to commit the offenses set out in section 297(a)(iii). The Commission alleged that he forced people to work in the production of the V-2 rocket and that he assisted or aided and abetted and counseled, within the meaning of sections 21 and 22 of the Criminal Code, people to force prisoners to work on the V-2.

The allegations more specifically were1 that he would have been guilty as a principal offender and as an aid and abettor of acts which amounted to internment of civilians under inhumane conditions, ill treatment of wounded and prisoners of war, forced labor of civilians in connection with the military operations of the enemy and employment of prisoners of war in unauthorized work. It was also alleged that he would have been guilty of counseling the above listed offenses. It was further alleged that he would have been guilty of committing to do something; that he had a positive duty in law to do when he failed to attempt to make conditions more humane and when he failed to ensure that forced laborers were not working on weapons that were going to be used against their own country and that this omission would have been contrary to section 241 of the Criminal Code of Canada 1927.

What I have had to decide was whether there were reasonable grounds to believe that he committed these acts or omissions and if these were crimes against humanity or war crimes and if they would have constituted offenses against section 297(a)(iii) of the Criminal Code of Canada 1927.

Judges Summary:

I find no reasonable grounds to believe the he committed any acts or of omissions as a principal offender. The evidence is that he never seized, confined, or detained anyone personally nor did he order the detention of anyone. The evidence shows that he never threatened or used force against a prisoner. He did not have the authority to release prisoners or to order detention, confinement, or punishment of prisoners. He was just one of the operations directors at Mittelwerk and his testimony and evidence from the Duhn report showed that his duties were not those of a typical personnel director. He was responsible for setting up the machinery and supervision of the assembly and production of the V-2 rockets. He requested more prisoners from the SS from time to time, but his requests were not always met.

He wore no uniform, held no rank, and was himself under surveillance of the SS. He was ordered to the job by General Dornberger and believed that he had no option but to continue with the work. The evidence from testimony and other sources such as the Duhn report is that the prisoners were seized and confined by the SS. The evidence indicates that the power of disposition over the prisoners was exclusively in the hands of the concentration camp commander. Mr. Rudolph like all the other civilians was officially forbidden to communicate with the prisoners who were exclusively subordinated to the supervision of the SS, guarded by the SS and lived in the SS camps.

It was submitted to me that Exhibit D, **The Agreement** *with the U.S. Department of Justice was in effect a confession and that clause two showed that he had violated The Hague Convention and the London Agreement.* **I was told that were this a criminal case The Agreement would constitute a confession. At this Administrative Tribunal this agreement means no more than it says in English and being operations director of a plant that used forced laborers including concentration camp inmates, as clause two says, doesn't necessarily make one guilty of the above mentioned violations of international law.** *The rest of* **The Agreement** *only indicates an understanding of the allegations, an agreement not to contest, to do certain things and certain concessions in Clause five which were not confessions to what had been alleged at this inquiry.*

It is also clear from testimony and other evidence that now and at the time of The Agreement Mr. Rudolph denied the allegations made by the

*O.S.I. despite having entered into **The Agreement**. Exhibit D does not provide reasonable grounds for me to conclude that he was a principal offender as alleged at this hearing.*

I find that there are not reasonable grounds to believe that Mr. Rudolph counseled any of the alleged offenses.

His direct testimony was that he had not. In particular I do not accept Exhibit 2-P as proof that he had counseled use of forced labor at Peenemünde as it is not as good evidence as his testimony. I also find that there are not reasonable grounds to believe that he would have violated section 241 of the Criminal Code 1927 by omitting to perform a legally required duty. That section lists duties and responsibilities of everyone who has charge of other persons and the evidence satisfies me that Mr. Rudolph was not in such a position.

I am satisfied from the evidence that the prisoners who were used for forced labor at Mittelwerk were during the course of their detention ill-treated and subjected to inhumane conditions. Mr. Rudolph gave general testimony to that effect and other evidence presented such as the Duhn report gave details that are more specific. I am satisfied from the evidence that Arthur Rudolph was not directly or personally responsible for such treatment or conditions. He was however the operations director for production of the V-2 and was successful in that function.

I find that there are not reasonable grounds to believe that he aided and abetted any offenses that involved internment under inhumane conditions or ill treatment of prisoners, as he had no interest in so doing and no intention of assisting such purposes. His purpose was not to ill treat or persecute the prisoners, in the V-2 facility the German civilians worked under the same conditions and did the same type of work, but it was to get production out of them. The evidence shows that he had little awareness of which these people were; he only knew some of their nationalities and that they were not criminals but political prisoners.

He needed workers to meet his production quotas and his purpose and intent in asking for more forced laborers was only to meet those quotas."

It is evident that the OSI failed in their attempt to offer legitimate documentary evidence to the Canadian court to support their allegation of "persecution" against Rudolph, as referred to in "The Agreement" signed by Rudolph, which resulted in the loss of his U.S. citizenship. The findings of the Canadian court are an indictment of our Department of Justice, under whose umbrella of protection the OSI engaged in gross prosecutorial misconduct.

On August 27, 1990, Rudolph issued a memorandum concerning his treatment by Canadian authorities on his arrival in Canada. The real culprits in this case were those officials in the OSI who were intent on persecuting Arthur Rudolph during his vacation trip to Canada. The following is a memorandum from Arthur Rudolph (who by now had wisely begun to document a record of his experiences) concerning a violation of his fundamental human rights.

August 27, 1990

To Whom It May Concern:

On July 1, 1990, my wife Martha and I arrived at Pearson International Airport in Toronto, Canada, from the Federal Republic of Germany. I had a valid passport from the Federal Republic of Germany, whereas my wife had a U.S. passport.

After arrival at approximately 15:30 hours I was detained with my wife, by Mr. Daniel Snow, an immigration official. For the next 8-1/2 hours I was kept in a small room for interrogation. I was released shortly after 24:00 hours, and only after a bond of $500 Canadian was paid by my daughter. I was wheeled out of the airport in a wheel chair.

The interrogation covered many areas, such as:

1) What is the purpose of my visit to Canada?

2) Whom am I meeting in Canada?

3) Am I planning to enter the U.S.A. from Canada?

4) My involvement and membership with Nazi organizations. When I was finally released, Mr. Snow retained my German passport.

During my detainment my daughter was allowed to see me twice only for approximately 1/2 hour each time. The first time was after two hours into my detention and after several requests to be allowed to see her friends, who were at the airport to greet me, and did not contact the German Consulate in Toronto or the German Embassy in Ottawa, on the day of arrival and detention, as it was a Sunday.

After bond was paid, I was allowed to stay in Canada for a hearing set on Friday, July 6, 1990 in Toronto. For technical reasons (e.g., the hearing room was too small to accommodate the news media) the hearing was postponed to the following Wednesday, July 11.

On July 9, Mr. Hugh McInnish and other friends visited Consul von Hessel at the German Consulate in Toronto. Thereupon the Consulate obtained copies of a report by State Attorney General Duhn, Hamburg, on his evaluation of my investigation by the Federal Republic of Germany. A phone call to the German Ambassador in Ottawa was without success. The Embassy did not want to get involved and referred us to the Consulate in Toronto. The German Consulate could not follow up on the request, by my friends, to send an observer to the July 11th hearing.

The hearing on July 11 did not bring any results or conclusions. A continuation was set for August 1, 1990, so that the case could be studied further. My passport was not returned. Instead, I received only verbal permission, through my Canadian attorney that I was free to travel within Canada. I therefore, requested that my attorney write a statement asking for safe transit during my stay in Canada.

In view of the fact that I was in the possession of a valid German passport, had never been accused of any war crime or any other crime in Germany or in Canada, I consider my 8-hour long interrogation and detention in Canada a violation of human rights .sign Arthur Rudolph"

The results of the Canadian court has revealed the second indictment by a foreign judicial magistrate concerning the failure of the U.S. Department of Justice and the OSI to provide legitimate evidence to support their allegations against a distinguished national U.S. space hero and pioneer. These investigations, conducted by two U.S. allies, West Germany at the time, and Canada. Since Arthur Rudolph came under the jurisdictions of both these foreign countries, (because of exile to West Germany, and vacation to Canada), and due the serious accusations by the Department of Justice and the OSI, both countries were induced to open investigations. The Results of the Canadian Episode clearly reveals the fact that the OSI, operating under the banner of our Department of

Justice, had badly, and ineptly bungled its second case, involving a foreign court, concerning the Rudolph matter. This parody about justice indeed cast a dark shadow, on an international scale, on how justice concerning a national hero is administered in this country.

Indeed, because of both of the investigations, the evidence surfaced that the shoddiness of the OSI attempt in their illicit conduct of investigating Rudolph was clearly revealed. The clearest indication, which revealed that OSI officials did not evidently comprehend what Justice, American style, was all about, was their frantic search for witnesses against Rudolph, **after** West Germany requested the copy of the Rudolph file. This frantic news media search was negative for the OSI, but produced one infallible witness for Rudolph, whose testimony the OSI concealed from the courts, a felony! This indictment by both the West German and the Canadian courts on the evident total disregard for the basic rules of evidence in the interpretation of justice by officials in the Department of Justice concerning Arthur Rudolph must be a source of derisive remarks among international lawmakers.

The most unbelievable part of this episode is that the Chairmen of both the House and Senate Judiciary Committees, Representative Henry Hyde, and Senator Joseph Biden, sworn to conduct oversight hearings in matters of governmental misbehavior, failed in their duties to conduct an investigation in this matter.

A review of the evidence presented here cannot help but confirm that the OSI, by precipitating the Canadian incident, knowingly, willfully, and grossly violated the human rights of Arthur Rudolph. The Canadian judge severely criticized one of the principal documents submitted to him by the OSI—"The Agreement" under whose terms Rudolph surrendered his U.S. citizenship. The judge stated that it had been submitted to him as a confession. In his findings, the judge stated that "The Agreement" was not a confession, but merely a paper stating certain things, and which did not qualify as a confession. This evidence of gross prosecutorial misconduct of Rudolph—across international borders—is an example of the shameful and shabby treatment received by a distinguished American citizen and scientist at the hands of the OSI whose charter, at best, specifies domestic activity, and whose authority under no circumstances allows what amounted in this case to the conduct of foreign affairs by involving our neighbor to the north.

18

Office of Special Investigation

Creation of the Office of Special Investigations was sponsored by the efforts of New York Congresswoman Elizabeth Holtzman in 1979. The mission of the OSI was to hunt down Nazi war criminals who had gained entry into the United States, and see that they were deported. This procedure was the responsibility of the Civil Division; however, Holtzman maneuvered the situation so that the OSI was placed in the Criminal Division of the DOJ. A fairly amazing detail is the charter of the OSI, with an emphasis on hunting "Nazi war criminals." There was no mention of "Japanese war criminals," for example, or Korean War criminals, or even Viet Cong war criminals, whose conduct would at least have been fresh in the memories of a multitude of witnesses. The creation of the OSI was formalized as a matter of law by what has been called the Holtzman Amendment.

This is to briefly recall the dilemma that Arthur Rudolph faced when he signed The Agreement, drafted by the OSI, wherein he surrendered his U.S. Citizenship.

History now reveals the true story of what the situation was when the OSI started their vendetta against Arthur Rudolph in 1982. The OSI was fully aware of the outcome of the Dora/Nordhausen war crimes trial held at Dachau, Germany, in 1947, and that they evidently had positive evidence that Rudolph was innocent of any war crime. However with the backing of the venerated aura of the United States Department of Justice, the OSI individuals involved, deliberately planned the prosecution of an innocence distinguished American citizen. Thus they knowingly, and willingly and with aforethought they entered into a criminal act against a U.S. citizen.

Rudolph's situation on the other hand was that he was in very poor health with a recent by-pass heart operation and positively in no financial status to mount any defense against the array of lawyers and funds available to the OSI. He was simply a helpless disabled victim at the mercy of the merciless OSI prosecutors. What a terrible terror he faced in the latter days of his life! He had the solid conviction that he was completely innocent of the allegations of the OSI. He evidently had in his mind that in going back to Germany that his case would be thoroughly investigated by the West German war crimes prosecutor and that he would be declared innocent. But the heart rending result was that in the process that he would loose his cherished United States citizenship. The inaction of Attorney General Ashcroft in dismissing any action on his part concerning this hate/terror crime is totally unconscionable.

One of the best sources of information concerning the origin of the OSI is contained in a book written by the first director of the OSI, Allan A. Ryan Jr., copyrighted in 1984, with the title: *Quiet Neighbors Prosecuting Nazi War Criminals in America*. One of the most damaging pieces of information concerning the operational tactics of the OSI, which came to the attention of the American public, was contained in two very lengthy news clippings in the Los Angeles Times, running consecutively, from Sunday, April 27, to Monday April 28, 1986. These articles emphasized cooperation between the OSI and the Russian KGB during the height of the Cold War.

On 28 October 1987, I wrote a critique on "Quiet Neighbors," which I now quote in full:

28 October 1987

Notes on "Quiet Neighbors—Prosecuting Nazi War Criminals in America"

Author: Alan A. Ryan Jr.
To whom it may concern:

Alan A. Ryan Jr. was Director of the Office of Special Investigations, of the U.S. Justice Department, for three and a half years from 1980 to

1983. He was one of the interrogators of Dr. Arthur Rudolph prior to the deportation of Rudolph in the early part of 1984.

Recently it has been brought to my attention that Mr. Ryan had made a remark in his book about the location of the huge underground factory where the Germans manufactured the V-2 rockets. Dr. Rudolph was the production engineer or technical director of the V-2 line. The misstatement of fact in this remark caused me to review the entire book for statements or comments from this man who evidently was responsible for the unjust deportation of Dr. Rudolph from the U.S. The book does not mention Rudolph, however the gross misstatement of fact, as stated in his book on page 194, (hard copy) where he located the V-2 factory about a hundred miles from Budapest, Hungary, at Dora in Austria, would indicate that Mr. Ryan did not know the geographical location of the place he alleged that Rudolph participated in war crimes. The fact was that the V-2 factory was in another country, hundreds of miles away, in north-central Germany, near Camp Dora, which was located in the vicinity of Nordhausen. This led me to believe that he may have been careless in other facts concerning the Rudolph case.

The following are comments based on information revealed in the book. The words in quotation marks are extracted from the book, and the words in brackets are my personal comments:

Page 32. The Immigration and Naturalization Service, INS, "administering a law that was festooned with obscure and often contradictory preferences, conditions, and exclusions." "INS was one of the most ingrown agencies in Washington. Where deportation was involved, INS was investigator, prosecutor, judge, and appeals court. (It appears to me that the OSI handled the Rudolph case in this manner.)

Page 45. Mr. Ryan has a statement on policy of INS investigations.

"Promotions, assignments, and raises were given out on the basis of what was produced, not on the moral rightness of the cases." (From available evidence, it appears that the OSI may have adopted this policy in the Rudolph case.)

Page 61. "Formulation of the OSI: initiated by Congresswoman Elizabeth Holtzman of New York." As the new chairperson of the immigration subcommittee Holtzman wanted INS to have nothing to do with Nazis, ever. She brought intense pressure or the Justice Department to take on the job with a larger staff and budget. Justice was distinctly cool to the idea. The Nazi cases had become legal lepers, unwanted, incurable, and probably contagious. It did not want them in its house.

However, Holtzman was no longer just another congressional representative and she could no longer be ignored. The Immigration Subcommittee—which also had jurisdiction over refugee matters and international legal affairs—could make life difficult for the Justice Department in any number of areas, and no one doubted Holtzman's determination to do just that if she were thwarted on the Nazi issue."

(No comment.)

Page 62. "At Holtzman's insistence, the newly named Office of Special Investigations was put into the Criminal Division of the Justice Department."

(Although the OSI would be pursuing civil, not criminal cases, the Criminal Division had a reputation as Justice's most effective and rigorous branch, Was this a proper action?)

Page 67. Mr. Ryan takes over the OSI.

"What was needed was tough, fair, prosecution."

(Fairness was apparently absent in the Rudolph case.)

Page 68. "Winning the cooperation of the Soviet Union was a critical step in our plans for OSI."

(What a strange alliance of the OSI with the KGB! The KGB still operated concentration camps and in the past exhibited the same bloodthirsty techniques as the SS or Gestapo!)

Page 71. Deposition procedure; right of cross-examination.

"A deposition does not require the presence of a judge, but it does require the attorney for the other side to given the chance to attend and cross-examine the witness to the same extent he would if the witness were actually testifying at trial,"

(This procedure was not given to Rudolph during the interrogations or at any other time.)

Page 85. Mr. Ryan, in dealing with the Soviets, portrayed himself; "as a spokesman for a legal system that placed due process of law above every other consideration." (Why was not Rudolph given this consideration instead of duress or coercion?)

Page 92. "I was determined that the Department of Justice would have no part in any process that infringe on the rights of defendants." (Same comment as pg. 85 response.)

Page 107. "I never looked for "Nazi hunters" in hiring lawyers." (An investigation into the Rudolph case would probably disprove this statement.)

Page 248. "We also had to prove, of course, that the defendant entered the United States illegally, because the whole point of the prosecution was to revoke his citizenship and ultimately to deport him." (Rudolph was investigated before he left Germany, and was invited by the U.S. Government to come to the U.S.)

Page 249. "First I wanted no witch-hunts, prosecuting people whose actual guilt was uncertain."

"I had no desire to bog ourselves down in prosecuting people who had simply joined the Nazi party." (Prior to the OSI interrogation of Rudolph, the West German Prosecutor for Nazi war crimes did not uncover one shred of evidence implicating Rudolph in any war crime. This was during the intensive investigations leading to the Dora/Nordhausen trials. These trials dealt specifically with the conditions in the underground factory complex at Nordhausen, including the V-2 line where Rudolph was the production engineer. Why did the OSI apparently fail to check with the West German government prior to taking action against Rudolph?)

Page 252. "OSI depended heavily on the cooperation and goodwill of other governments." (My comment to pg. 249 applies to this statement also.)

Pages 253 and 254. Mr. Ryan relates how he and Neal Sher made a trip to East Germany.

(I wish to point out again that Dr. Rudolph is not mentioned in the book, however later on, Eli Rosenbaum, a prosecutor in the Rudolph case, denied in a letter to a U.S. Senator, that it was a "ludicrous

charge" that there was East Bloc involvement in the Rudolph case. Dr. Winterberg has copies of documents given by the East German prosecutor to the OSI in response to diplomatic note #433 of the U.S. embassy. One of these documents exonerates Rudolph, but was apparently covered up by the OSI, and was not released to the West German prosecutor.)

Page 324. Conclusions by Mr. Ryan.

"My conclusions are that we have never known how to deal with Nazi war criminals in this country, and so our actions have been marked by ambivalence, and equivocation. We have said one thing and let another happen."

(In my opinion, this is a very truthful statement. An impartial, and unbiased review of the Rudolph case, with the current evidence available being considered, would reveal that the OSI prosecutors in the case evidently failed to check into the veracity of some of their sources of information, accepting misinformation as fact.)

(That misstatement of facts were given to members of Congress.

That evidence in defense of Rudolph was either deliberately suppressed, or not considered for a reevaluation of the case.

That coercion or duress was apparently exercised in getting Rudolph to sign a "voluntary" agreement that the OSI failed to provide creditable witnesses to support their allegations against Rudolph to the West German prosecutor. In the interrogation of Rudolph, the OSI refused to identify the names of their witnesses. Later the OSI, on request of the West German prosecutor for his investigation, furnished the names of nine witnesses.

5 witnesses stated that they did not work in the underground factory, four did not know Arthur Rudolph, and one stated that Rudolph had no contact with the prisoners and was not involved in any killings. Two witnesses gave clearly wrong information; one had not worked in the underground facility.

2 witnesses could not be investigated for psychological reasons. One stated clearly in an earlier letter that he cannot give any information on Arthur Rudolph, nor can he identify him from a picture.)

Page 341. "Citizenship cannot be lost except in two ways; voluntary surrender or denaturalization by a federal court."

(Based on currently available information, in my opinion, Dr. Rudolph, in poor physical health, and with lack of sufficient financial resources to sustain a civil suit against the Justice Department, was put under duress by the OSI in order that he (Rudolph) would sign a "voluntary" surrender agreement. The OSI apparently lacked sufficient legitimate evidence to win the case in federal court. This opinion is based on the evidence presented by credible witnesses in defense of Rudolph after he was deported, and by the results of the very intensive investigation by the West German prosecutor, over 2300 pages of transcript, in which Arthur Rudolph was cleared of the allegations brought by the OSI.)

Page 343. "Once citizenship has been stripped, the ex-citizen is subject to deportation (although he must be accorded a hearing on this question as well) (Dr. Rudolph was not granted such a hearing.)

Concluding comment:

I believe that had the OSI followed the concepts, as expressed in the book; about such things as fairness, protection of rights of the accused, thoroughness of investigations, impartial consideration of evidence, veracity of sources of information, that no action would have been taken against Dr. Rudolph.

(Signed) W.E. Winterstein LTC. Army (Ret.)

I am in complete agreement with Mr. Ryan's philosophy about what the OSI **should have** been. He espouses the virtuous use of fairness, impartiality, legitimate evidence, integrity, observance of law, etc. Unfortunately, misconduct by the OSI in prosecuting the Rudolph case— while exculpatory evidence existed to exonerate Rudolph—shows a willingness to play loose with the facts in a way that falls far short of the OSI's charter to pursue a noble goal in a noble fashion.

Among the most informative items concerning the establishment of the OSI, and the mysterious Russian KGB connection, was highlighted in a lengthy article published by the *Los Angeles Times* in two parts on Sunday, April 27, and Monday, April 28, 1986.

Soviet Proof Key in U.S. Nazi Cases
Some Jurists Express Doubts on Witness Credibility

By ROBERT GILLETTE Times Staff Writer

WASHINGTON—In January 1980, when the United States was angrily imposing economic and diplomatic sanctions on the Soviet Union for the invasion of Afghanistan, representatives of the U.S. Justice Department were quietly negotiating an unprecedented agreement for cooperation with their counterparts in Moscow.

In three days of amicable talk, the Justice Department reached an agreement with Alexander M. Rekunkov, now the Soviet Union's highest legal officer. The agreement called for Moscow to assist the United States in prosecuting Soviet refugees who had fled at the end of World War II and were now, as naturalized Americans, suspected of murdering or persecuting civilians during the Nazi occupation.

Under terms set largely by the Soviet side, Soviet judicial authorities agreed to supply documents and eyewitnesses testimony to the Justice Department's newly created Office of Special Investigations. The office's mission was to ferret out suspected war criminals and persuade the Courts to revoke their citizenship and deport them. However, to accomplish this, the bulk of evidence would have to come from the Soviet Union.

"Winning the cooperation of the Soviet Union was a critical step in our plans for the OSI," its former director, Alan A. Ryan Jr., observed in his 1984 book, "Quiet Neighbors." Almost all the refugees now under suspicion of war crimes had come from the Soviet Union. Captured German documents bearing on their ties to the Nazi occupiers were held in Soviet archives.

"We also needed witnesses to atrocities: bystanders, colleagues, victims, neighbors," Ryan said, "some of these, particularly victims, we might find in America or Israel or Canada or elsewhere in the world. However, most of the neighbors and bystanders had never left home. If we were to have their testimony, we needed the permission of their government."

Nothing in Writing

To ensure a proper atmosphere for the talks, the Justice Department representatives ignored a State Department request to register

Washington's strong disapproval of the Afghan invasion. To the Justice Department's surprise, the Soviets asked nothing in return for supplying the evidence the Americans wanted. However, there was to be no formal written agreement, only an oral understanding, making this a unique arrangement between the superpowers at a time when relations in every other field were rapidly deteriorating.

It was to be, as Ryan observed, a "wildly improbable marriage" between the judicial authorities of a democracy and those of a "totalitarian regime," who evinced "no hint that they understood what we were talking about" when the Americans tried to explain the basic concepts of due process that Westerners consider essential to a fair trial.

Just how improbable the marriage—and how nettlesome the legal issues raised by the U.S-Soviet agreement—has become clear since. Six years later, the Office of Special Investigations has won broad public approval for its aggressive pursuit of alleged war criminals. According to the agency's figures, 19 naturalized Americans have been stripped of their citizenship and nine deported-one so far to the Soviet Union-while another 35 cases are currently in the courts and 300 investigations are under way.

Soviet evidence has played a major role in these cases, often with little corroborating evidence from other sources.

Bitter Protests

Ethnic organizations of Baltic and Ukrainian nationalities, joined by some conservative political groups, have bitterly protested the use of this evidence, condemning it as inherently untrustworthy. The Office of Special Investigations, strongly supported by the American Jewish community, dismisses such criticism as reflexive anti-communism tinged with anti-Semitism and motivated by a thinly veiled desire to protect war criminals.

"No American judge has concluded that any documentary evidence obtained from the Soviet Union was fabricated," the Anti-Defamation League of B'nai-B'rith said in a 40-page defense of the OSI published last June. "Nor has any witness made available by the Soviet Union been found to have lied in connection with his or her testimony."

Over the last three years however, largely without public notice, a number of federal court jurists and defense lawyers have voiced serious

*misgivings about the use of Soviet evidence, especially witness
testimony, in American courts.*

**Although in the majority of cases federal courts have accepted it as
valid, there are at least four cases in which judges have rejected Soviet
testimony entirely or in part as seemingly coerced or invented, or
for other reasons "not worthy of belief," as one appellate opinion
phrased it.**

**In addition, a committee of the American Bar Association. has
considered a recommendation to organize a formal study of the
problems raised by the use of Soviet evidence but so far has taken no
action on the proposal.**

Reliability Question

*As the critics in the legal community see it, the troubling feature of the
OSI's war crimes cases is not only that they center on events distant in
time and place, and deal with the highly emotional question of complicity
in the Holocaust, but that they rest to a major degree on the acceptance
by American courts of evidence compiled by the Soviet KGB security and
Intelligence agency and selectively supplied to the Justice Department.*

*They question whether the U.S. Government, and, more important, the
courts, can reasonably expect to use such evidence to tell the guilty from
the innocent. As a memorandum circulated in recent months in the
American Bar Assn's committee on law and national security said, "Is
the evidence made available by the Soviet Union reliable, and does the
getting and use of such evidence conform to due process standards?"*

*The American Bar Assn. memo drew no conclusions but recommended
that a blue-ribbon panel be convened to study these and related
questions.*

*Concerns expressed in a number of federal court opinions and by
individual lawyers in a series of interviews are both political and
procedural.*

*They note, for example, the Soviet Union's long history of bending
justice and inventing evidence to suit its political aims, from the
theatrical show trial of old Bolsheviks in the 1930s to the trials of the
recently freed Anatoly Shcharansky and other human rights activists in
the 1970s and 1980s.*

In the case of accused war criminals living in the United States, the critics believe, the Soviet aim is not only to bring a small number of bona fide murderers to justice but to tar traditionally anti-communist émigré communities in the United States as broadly as possible with the same brush. The Soviets, the critics say, want to stir dissension among émigré groups and to blacken them in the eyes of Soviet citizens.

In a strongly worded dissenting opinion in the case of Serge Kowalchuk, 65, a Ukrainian-born émigré stripped of his citizenship for working as a clerk in a Nazi-controlled police unit during World War II, Chief Judge Ruggero J. Aldisert of the 3rd Circuit Court of Appeals wrote last September:

"The government case is based on evidence procured by the KGB to effectuate its political ends. Congruence between that purpose and individual justice has yet to be established."

Few if any critics in the legal community suggest that all Soviet evidence is tainted. The problem, they say, is to distinguish between testimony that is genuine, embellished, or simply invented, and to recognize when documents have been selected from the archives, omitting those that might exonerate a defendant or mitigate the charges against him.

Denial of Access

Under the terms of the 1980 agreement, this has not been an easy task. The Soviets have refused to give prosecutors or defense attorneys from the Office of Special Investigations access to wartime archives to search for other evidence that might bear on a defendant's guilt or innocence. Lawyers, and some federal courts, have objected that these restrictions make it almost impossible to guarantee defendants due process right to meaningful defense. In addition, the Soviets strictly control the Americans access to witnesses.

Their testimony is videotaped for use in American courts, U.S. defense lawyers have the right to cross-examine the witness, and the OSI will even pay the lawyers' travel expenses to the Soviet Union. Nevertheless, in all cases, Soviet prosecutors supervise the taking of depositions, frequently seek to restrict cross-examinations, and often urge the witnesses to adhere to written summaries or "protocols" of their earlier interrogations by the KGB.

Despite the OSI's initial hopes in 1980, no Soviet witness in a war crimes case has yet appeared in an American court, although some have traveled to West Germany to testify in other cases.

By contrast, Poland, where most of the Nazi extermination camps were located, has imposed no such restrictions on access to official archives or witnesses.

However, the OSI's cases have led the agency to depend far more heavily on Soviet evidence than on Polish; it has taken testimony, for instance, from fewer than half a dozen Polish witnesses since 1980, but in the same period has interviewed more than 100 Soviet witnesses. In Canada, where a royal commission has spent more than a year determining whether, or how, to conduct an investigation of suspected war criminals, misgivings about the use of Soviet evidence are shared by some members of Parliament.

"The American approach is totally inadequate," Andrew Witer, the chairperson of a newly formed parliament committee on human rights, said in a recent interview. At a minimum Witer said, Soviet witnesses should be interviewed in a non-prejudicial setting such as an embassy, out from under the gaze of a Soviet prosecutor.

Despite the procedural controls imposed by the Soviets, the Office of Special Investigations dismisses fears of false or distorted evidence, or an abrogation of due process, as illogical and unfounded.

As a practical matter, it is difficult to conceive of even the KGB-or anyone else for that matter-fabricating document after document and suborning perjury from witnesses after witness in every one of OSI's cases," the agency's current director, Neil M. Sher, said.

Pending Appeal

The OSI put this viewpoint even more categorically in an appeal currently before the 3rd Circuit Court in the case of a naturalized Lithuanian named Jozas Kungys. A federal district court exonerated Kungys in 1983 of charges that he took part in killing Jews during the Nazi occupation, and rebuked the OSI for failing to ensure that Soviet witnesses in the case had not been coerced.

In its appeal, OSI accused U.S District Judge Dickinson R. Debevoise of injecting "political bias' into his decision and went on to assert:

"While the Soviet Union may act with impunity in legal proceedings confined to its own borders, it cannot do so in cases under the scrutiny of foreign judges, lawyers, and witnesses."

Successful fraud by the Soviet Union in these matters, the OSI argued in its appeal. "Is beyond its capabilities" and in any case would be "Inevitably doomed to exposure." Asked in an interview whether this was not, in effect, an assertion of infallibility on the part of the American judicial system, Sher said it was not. "It is just an assertion of complete faith in the ability of our courts to ascertain the truth," Sher said.

Illogical Premise

He added that it would be illogical for the Soviets to risk destroying the credibility of all the evidence they supplied by tampering with some of it for propaganda purposes.

The agency's critics, on the other hand, argue that it fails to recognize the ease (sic) with which Soviet witnesses can be manipulated, perhaps because excessive zeal has clouded its judgment.

"The Soviets have everything they need-the motive, the experience, the control-to create staged cases," John Rogers Carroll, a Philadelphia trial lawyer, said in a recent interview. Carroll defended Kowalchuk, a Philadelphia tailor who now faces deportation to the Soviet Union. While the role of eyewitness testimony varies among OSI's cases, it dominates the Kowalchuk case, where, as a district court noted, "there is not one scrap of documentary evidence relating to the pertinent events."

Carroll said his experience in two evidentiary hearings in the Soviet Union in 1981 and 1983 convinced him that cross-examination of witnesses under Soviet control "has little effect on someone who knows that all he has to do is stick to his story and he won't get into trouble."

"He (a witness) knows I can't go into his story, investigate the details," Carroll said. "He knows that none of the normal sanctions (against false or misleading testimony) apply here."

Between 1983 and last year, at least four federal district and appeals courts have rejected such testimony as seemingly coerced, as prejudiced by the remarks of Soviet prosecutors or for other reasons as untrustworthy. In other cases notably Kowalchuk's dissenting opinions have voiced grave concern that the use of unverifiable Soviet information jeopardizes a defendant's constitutional right to due process.

In May 1984, a federal court district court in New York cited concerns about coerced testimony in dismissing an OSI suit to revoke the citizenship of Elmars Sprogis, a former Latvian police officer the Soviets accused of having murdered and persecuted Jews during the German occupation. The accusation depended heavily on the videotaped testimony of two Soviet witnesses, whose behavior, according to Judge Frank X. Altimari, suggested coercion.

At one point, Altimari noted, a key witness, when offered an opportunity to rest during his testimony, inexplicably began to cry.

"Whether it be due to coercion, discomfort, fear, old age or other factors, (it) counsels in favor of cautious acceptance of his testimony," Altimari wrote in his decision.

In May 1985, the 2nd Circuit Court of Appeals upheld the dismissal of the case, noting that Altimari had acted properly in rejecting the Soviet testimony as "potentially coerced" and "unworthy of belief."

Four months later, on Sept. 6, Sprogis, 70, narrowly escaped injury when a bomb exploded at his home in Brentwood, N.Y. The Federal Bureau of Investigation has said that this, and a smaller bombing three weeks earlier in Paterson, N.J.—which killed a naturalized Ukrainian who had been cleared by the OSI, may have had been carried out by the militant Jewish Defense League.

The similar case of Edgars Laipenieks, a former professor of physical education at the University of Denver, illustrates the important role of a judge's subjective impression and instinct play in gauging the creditability of Soviet witnesses from a videotape. In Laipenieks case, these impressions varied greatly from one court to another.

A local police chief in Nazi-occupied Latvia, Laipenieks was accused not of complicity in the Holocaust but of beating communist prisoners in his jail. In 1981, the OSI sought to deport him to the Soviet Union.

The government's case turned on the testimony of nine Soviet witnesses. An immigration court judge rejected it as untrustworthy, citing what he called an intimidating atmosphere highlighted by a Soviet prosecutor who curtailed cross-examination of the witnesses and repeatedly described Laipenieks in front of them as "the Nazi war criminal."

The Board of Immigration Appeals, however, found the testimony sufficiently valid to reverse the decision and order Laipenieks deported. Then in January 1985, the 9th Circuit Court of Appeals reversed the appeals board's decision, saying it was troubled by the board's "tacit acceptance" of Soviet evidence that appeared untrustworthy.

Moreover the court said, the Latvian police had valid reasons for jailing some of the Communists, who were suspected of having collaborated with the Soviet Union in its annexation of independent Latvia in 1940 under a treaty with Moscow's ally from 1939-41, Nazi Germany.

A key witness who claimed that Laipenieks had beaten him, the court noted, had in fact been suspected in 1941 of helping Soviet occupation forces a year earlier draw up lists of thousands of Jews and other Latvian civilians for deportation to Siberia.

The sharpest rebuke the Office of Special Investigations has yet received from a federal court came in 1983 in the case of Jozas Kungys, the former Lithuanian police officer. In an acidly worded decision, Judge Debevoise dismissed the government's case with the observation that the Soviet authorities had a clear political interest in pinning the blame for wartime atrocities on American defendants—namely to discredit anti-Soviet émigré communities.

It was observed that the Soviet authorities had the advantage in coaching witnesses, if desired, that if they did not testify in a certain way that they could be fired from their jobs. Similarly, a former officer in the Latvian KGB who defected to the United States in 1978, Imants Lesinkis, said he found that witnesses in war crimes cases with which he dealt as a propaganda officer were totally compliant.

While these cases focused mainly on the trustworthiness of Soviet evidence, a dissenting opinion in the widely publicized Kowalchuk case stressed the issue of a defendant's right to due process in the face of Soviet controls on access to the evidence to support the allegations which resulted, in fact, a "compelling" violation of Kowalchuk's right to due process which lay at the heart of the case.

"For reasons I refuse to regard as altruistic, the Soviet KGB has singled out an American citizen Serge Kowalchuk for immediate attention by our government in a stream of extravagant accusations subsequently not proved in District Court," Aldisert wrote in an opinion joined wholly or in part by three other judges.

Soviet restrictions, he said, effectively "denied Kowalchuk the opportunity to conduct even a primitive preparation of a defense. The most basic of due process rights."

A third factor is that in civil cases, the government is not required to give the defense any material in its possession that might be beneficial to its case, in criminal cases, this is required by the so-called Brady rule.

Most important, some defense lawyers believe, in the overpowering emotional context of the Holocaust that pervades these cases, regardless of how strong or weak the linkage may be between defendants and atrocities.

"We are, in a way, the victims of hydraulic pressures, of a wave of public sentiment that causes us to lose sight of certain realities," Carroll said, in a reference to special difficulties of verifying Soviet evidence.

"We tend to overlook this because we see that a terrible crime has been committed—the Holocaust—and we perceive that the OSI is finding the guilty and punishing them."

"The typical judge is just as impressed as anyone by the implications of this (Soviet) testimony," Carroll said. "But it occurs to me that our judicial procedures are not made for this kind of case."

Next: Do the Soviets Manufacture Evidence?

The following is the Monday, April 28th article in the *Los Angeles Times*:

Soviet Aide Warned U.S. In War Crime Evidence

WASHINGTON—A Soviet official, in apparent act of conscience, warned the United States nearly three years ago that Moscow was trying to deceive the U.S. Justice Department through evidence that has been supplied against alleged Nazi war criminals now living in the U.S.. According to informed government sources, the official confided to an American diplomat that some Soviet witnesses were being coached in their testimony for days before being allowed to give depositions to U.S. prosecutors, apparently to make their testimony more credible and incriminating.

The sources, who asked not to be identified by name or agency, said this information was relayed immediately to the Justice Department's Office of Special Investigations in the summer of 1983.

However, the Office of Special Investigations, whose mission is to ferret out and deport suspected war criminals, dismissed the warnings as insignificant and without substance and suggested that the official was merely "disgruntled."

U.S. prosecutors have continued to accept Soviet and captured German documents as authentic evidence and to travel to the Soviet Union to collect eyewitness testimony.

In an interview, one government source with direct knowledge of the incident expressed dismay that the Justice Department had ignored the Soviet official's warning and failed even to disclose it to the defense lawyer involved in the specific case in which it arose.

The source said there was no reason to doubt the accuracy of the information or the sincerity of the Soviet official, who took a personal risk in passing it privately to a U.S. diplomat based in Moscow.

In doing so, the informant was said to have asked the diplomat in disbelief, "How could you Americans be taken in like this?"

Since 1980, the Office of Special Investigations has worked under a unique agreement with Soviet judicial authorities in its investigation of wartime refugees who are suspected of having persecuted Jews, Communist Party members and other civilians in Nazi occupied areas of the Soviet Union and Eastern Europe. In the process, Justice Department attorneys and U.S. courts have relied partly on the product of investigations in the Soviet Union by the KGB security and intelligence agency.

The Office of Special Investigations continues to assert its faith in the underlying trustworthiness of evidence the Soviets have supplied against hundreds of alleged war criminals who came to the United States among an estimated 400,000 "displaced persons," as they were formally designated, at the end of the war. Most of these refugees, who later became naturalized American citizens, fled from the Soviet Union in the closing months of the war. In nearly seven years of operation, the Office of Special Investigations has succeeded in revoking the citizenship of 19 émigrés from the Soviet-controlled Baltic States and the Ukraine. Fourteen have been ordered deported, and nine have actually been expelled from the United States, according to figures supplied by the Justice Department agency.

Returned to Soviets

One deportee, Feodor Fedorenko, who acknowledged having been a guard at the Treblinka extermination camp in Poland but claimed he was forced to work there, voluntarily returned to his family in the Soviet Union last year and has since lost contact with his American lawyer. Several other alleged war criminals currently face possible deportation to the Soviet Union.

Investigations of about 600 others have been dropped for insufficient evidence, or because of the deaths of witnesses or the suspects themselves. The Office of Special Investigations is currently investigating another 300 former refugees, most of them from the Soviet Union, while about 35 cases are currently in the courts, according to the agency's director, Neil M. Sher. Since 1980, agency attorneys have taken testimony from about 100 Soviet witnesses. The agency acknowledges, as one of its annual reports put it, that these video taped depositions along with copies of hundreds of wartime documents supplied by the Soviets, have played a "crucial" role in its pursuit of suspected war criminals. Often, captured German documents supplied by the Soviets show that defendants worked for a local, German-controlled police force, for example. However, fall short of showing that they actually look part in persecuting civilians. Witnesses are then produced to link them to atrocities. The importance of Soviet evidence stems from the fact that persecutions and atrocities at the core of these cases took place largely in occupied Soviet territory, and little or no corroborating evidence is available from any other source.

Some defendants have admitted serving as concentration camp guards but maintained that they were forced by the Germans to choose between being guards or prisoners others have admitted that they worked in local police units controlled by Nazi occupation forces usually as clerks but insist they took no part in persecuting or killing civilians. Despite the agency's repeated expressions of confidence in the reliability of Soviet evidence, its use against naturalized Americans has spawned a bitter controversy in recent years that has sharply divided American ethnic communities whose roots are in the Soviet Union.

On one side of the controversy Baltic, Ukrainian and some Polish groups have accused the Justice Department of naively lending itself to the political aims of the Soviet regime, which has long tried to sow dissension among traditionally anti Communist émigré groups in the West, and to discredit them in the eyes of Soviet citizens.

In turn, the American Jewish community, spearheaded by the Anti-Defamation League of B'nai B'rith and joined by some Polish American groups, has staunchly defended the Justice Department and accused its critics of anti-Semitic motivations. Similarly, Sher said in a recent interview that while some of his agency's critics seem driven by reflexive anti-communism, "there is something more to this: They want to close us down."

The controversy took a violent turn last year, with twin bomb attacks-one of them fatal-on two former Soviet refugees who had been cleared of war crimes charges. A representative for the FBI in Washington, Lane Bonner, said the Bureau is continuing an intensive investigation into the two bombings and believes that the militant Jewish Defense League may have been responsible. Last Aug.15, Tscherim Soobzokov, 67, whom the Office of Special Investigations had sought unsuccessfully to deport, was lured out of his home in Paterson, N.J., at 4:30 a.m. by a ruse-a fire set in his car-and suffered massive injuries to his lower body as a bomb exploded at his doorstep. His wife, daughter, 4-year-old grandson, and neighbor were also injured. Accused by the Office of Special Investigations of having served in the German Waffen SS, the combat arm of Hitler's elite security force, Soobzokov had been a target of protests by the Jewish Defense League after the Justice Department dropped its charges for lack of evidence. Friends of the Soobzokov family have explained that he belonged to a small, persecuted ethnic minority and accepted a Waffen SS uniform as a ploy to escape the Soviet Union with retreating German forces.

Another Bomb Blast

Then on Sept. 6, the day Soobzokov died, a similar bomb detonated at 4:30 a.m. in the Long Island community of Brentwood, N.Y., damaged the home of Elmars Sprogis, 70, a retired construction worker exonerated by a federal appeals court in 1984 of persecuting Jews in his native Latvia. Sprogis was not hurt, but a passer-by, who apparently was attracted by a fire set in Sprogis' car as a lure, was seriously injured. Shortly after the explosion, the Long Island newspaper "Newsday" received a telephone call in which an apparently recorded voice reportedly said: **"Listen carefully. Jewish Defense League. Nazi war criminal bomb. Never again." The FBI has since warned defense attorneys involved in war crimes cases to be alert to the possibility of further violence and to urge their clients to take precautions against reprisals.**

In public statements, both the Office of Special Investigations and Jewish organizations have stressed the lack of concrete proof that the evidence in war crimes Soviets have actually falsified evidence in war crimes cases. **(Note: saying evidence is okay because it has been proven false is not a proper legal argument. Especially when forced testimony seems to have been involved as seen in video taped testimony and by numerous legal professionals).**

In its report last June, for example, the Anti-Defamation League said, in a passage underlined for emphasis: "For all their claims and charges, the émigré activists have been unable to document a single instance, over the past 40 years, of forged evidence or perjured testimony being obtained from the Soviet Union for use in Western trials of accused Nazi war criminals."

The 40-page report did not mention that several U.S. district and appeals courts in the last three years have cited troubling indications that some Soviet testimony supplied to the government has been falsified. These courts have expressed concern that Soviet authorities may have engaged in a broad practice of tailoring evidence to suit OSI's needs.

In a May 1984, speech to the Anti-Defamation League that has become the OSI's standard reply to its critics, Sher said: "There is today a concerted and extremely vigorous campaign by segments of the Eastern European émigré community questioning the appropriateness of our methods. Their claim in a nutshell: OSI and the Justice Department have become the dupes of the KGB."

"The charge of knowing use of false evidence is the most serious allegation that can be leveled against a prosecutor. It accuses him of abuse of office and a perversion of the entire system of justice."

"These accusations are simply untrue," Sher said. "Our evidence is in fact legitimate and the charges against us are not valid."

Evidence Emerges

According to the government sources, however, direct evidence of manipulated testimony emerged in July. 1983, during a session in the Ukrainian city of Cherkassy in which OSI attorneys took depositions from five Soviet citizens.

The case concerned a retired, 75-year-old Ukrainian-born factory worker now living in the eastern United States whom the Soviets accused of taking part in a massacre of Jews in the Ukraine in 1942.

The defendant was not present at the hearing but, in keeping with a standard practice accepted by the Soviets, his attorney was present to cross-examine the witnesses. In addition, a Soviet prosecutor presided over the videotaped hearing.

The attorney, John Rogers Carroll of Philadelphia. Asked that his client not be identified by name in view of the two bomb attacks last year.

The sources said the two OSI attorneys at the Cherkassy hearing were delighted with what the prosecutors called the "high quality of the Soviet witnesses," whose recall of events seemed remarkably clear despite the passage of 40 years.

Carroll, however, said he remembered the witnesses-one in particular-as some of the least convincing, he had encountered in a long career of trial practice. The main witness, who claimed to have survived the massacre, as a child was a "joke," Carroll said in a telephone interview.

"He was as absurd a witness as I have ever heard testify. He was so bad, and the KGB guy sitting next to him was so embarrassed by his oratory-he sounded like someone at a Soviet Trade Union Congress-that he told the guy to pipe down and just answer the questions."

Carroll said that only one of the five witnesses asked to identify his client from photographs, producing an equivocal response.

"One has to wonder why," Carroll said. They were witness to atrocities by someone in that village, but they were never asked to establish whom. It left a substantial evidentiary gap.

Carroll said he left Cherkassy as soon as the depositions were completed, partly to escape what he called an "unbearable oppressive atmosphere."

"The Soviets kept referring to me as the private advocate of the Nazi murderer," he said. "Defense attorneys are not made to feel welcome."

The day after Carroll left, however, a Soviet official involved in the hearing approached an American diplomat who was serving as liaison between the team from the Office of Special Investigations and local authorities.

Speaking privately and with some emotion, one source said, the official disclosed that the five witnesses had not been brought to Cherkassy the day before the Americans had been told, but had been confined in the town for well over a week of intensive coaching and rehearsals of their testimony.

Tailoring the Testimony

This source, who was fully informed of the incident that summer, said the official was unable to specify to what extent their testimony was actually perjured-that is, false or misleading. Nevertheless, the official made it clear that the Soviet aim in drilling the witnesses on their stories was to tailor them to the needs of the American prosecutors making the testimony as incriminating as possible.

It was in this context that the official asked in disbelief how the Americans could allow themselves to be "taken in" by what was, in fact, a staged performance.

"Don't you people know that we remember what we are told to remember, that we say what we are told to say?" the informant was reported to have said. He reportedly went on to describe Moscow's purpose in essentially the same political terms used by OSI's critics in the United States.

"This is the way the (Soviet) regime tries to legitimize itself in the eyes of Ukrainians, by discrediting the émigrés," the official was quoted as saying.

The U.S. Embassy in Moscow promptly reported the incident to the Justice Department. Several weeks later, the American diplomat was flown to Finland, where representatives of the Office of Special Investigations among them the current director, Sher spent about 90 minutes debriefing him in the security of the U.S. Embassy in Helsinki.

In an interview with The Times in January in which this incident was not mentioned, Sher said there was no evidence that the Soviets have ever dictated how witnesses were to testify to OSI attorneys or in any similar war crimes cases.

"There is no indication that the Soviets have said (to witnesses), "You have to say this, or you have to say that," Sher said. He added that if at any time the KGB had "spoon-fed a witness," then this "would show up on cross-examination. . . Our system provides the means to detect it."

Asked in a more recent interview how he reconciled this with the Soviet official's statement in Cherkassy, Sher acknowledged that he had debriefed the American diplomat in whom the Soviet official had confided but said the OSI concluded the incident had no significance.

"We looked at it very carefully," Sher said. "It was clear to us that there was no hard evidence about anything, that these witnesses were not compromised.

He said that he did not recall any reference to the coaching of witnesses. "It was clear to us that what was said was an offhand remark. Nothing hard to it, a comment by someone who may have been disgruntled," he said.

However, a U.S. diplomat who served in Moscow and was familiar with the incident said this characterization was not correct. He said that although any Soviet official who would dare to make such a disclosure would be disgruntled almost by definition, this did not impugn the accuracy of remarks that seemed carefully considered, informed, and sincere.

The official's point, the diplomat said, and "was to let us know we were being misled."

Out of Court Settlement

Sher said the case was later settled out of court, not because of concern about compromised testimony but out of consideration for the defendant's poor health.

Carroll, the defense attorney in the ease, said he was never told about the incident, although it would have substantially affected his handling of the case. "As for telling me anything about the coaching of witnesses- never," Carroll said in a telephone conversation. 'Why would they? I was the other side. "

He said the case lay dormant on the docket of U.S. District Judge E. Mac Troutman of the Eastern District of Pennsylvania for more than two years, from 1983 until last October. Then Troutman, impatient with the Justice Department's lack of action, prodded the Office of Special Investigations to settle it out of court. To his amazement, Carroll said, the OSI agreed to settle without trial, but offered no plausible reason for its action.

I keep close track of these things, but this was one of only two cases I had ever heard of in which they agreed to settle," he said. "They said they did it out of consideration for the guy's health, but that's patently false. They never do anything for anyone's health. "

He noted that the Justice Department deported 86-year-old Andrija Artukovic to Yugoslavia last December on a stretcher to stand trial on charges of directing the execution of thousands of civilians during World War II.

Other attorneys have complained that OSI continued prosecuting two other suspected war criminals even though they were hospitalized with terminal cancer and closed the cases only on receipt of death certificates and photographs of the bodies.

Under the settlement offered by the Office of Special Investigations, Carroll said his client agreed to surrender his American citizenship in return for permission to continue living in the United States as a stateless person, in effect, a man without a country.

Carroll said the man maintains his innocence and wanted to clear his name in a trial, but his family persuaded him that his history of heart disease made it unlikely that he could withstand the stress.

The Soviet official's statement, apart from the implications of other cases, Carroll said it might have substantially changed the outcome of this one, had the Justice Department told him about it.

"I thought all along that they (OSI) were holding off because they

perceived some weakness. This might have been the straw that broke the camel's back," he said. At a minimum, he said, he would have obtained a deposition from the diplomat involved in the Cherkassy matter that "would have directly impeached the testimony."

In addition, he added. "I certainly would not have advised my client to hand over his certificate of naturalization."

As a matter of historical record, the OSI–KGB connection is a clear betrayal of first Director Ryan's noble vision for the organization. The extensive research reflected by the Los Angeles Times staff writer, Robert Gillette, in his revelation of the KGB connection, shows a distinct failure to observe: "fairness, protection of the rights of the accused, thoroughness of investigations, impartial consideration of evidence, veracity of sources of information," as proclaimed in Ryan's book. In the Rudolph and Artukovic cases particularly, the protection of the civil rights of the accused were ignored on a number of occasions.

Claire Palley, member of the United Nations Social and Economic Council, summarized the intense pressures applied to naturalized citizens, 'imported' after the war, whose judicial fates parallel the Rudolph case, and include Demjanjuk and others. Because of the illegal tactics employed by the OSI in its efforts to consolidate bureaucratic power, most members of the distinguished German rocket team have entered a phase of their American experiences characterized by dis-ease. In a report to the UN Economic and Social Council dated 6 October 1994, Ms. Palley summarized the plight of our space heroes as follows:

"A special unit within the criminal division of the U.S. Department of Justice, the Office of Special Investigation (OSI), and the U.S. Immigration and naturalization Service (INS), have been concerned to seek out, deprive of their citizenship and deport central Europeans who are alleged to have illegally obtained entry to the U.S.A. by concealing that they had assisted in persecuting civilians in Europe between 1933 an 1945.

[Author note: Keep in mind that the loose definition of 'persecuting' would include *any* involvement or interaction with prisoners of war; for example, the mere supervision of camp inmate labor supplied to von Braun and Rudolph, whose rocket research and development efforts during wartime were built, at risk to their own lives and well being, on a foundation of personal concern, and earnest efforts to secure their favorable treatment under harsh conditions.]

> *"Persons deported will be separated from their American wives, children, and grandchildren and sent, often as stateless persons, to States they left more than 40 years ago. Over 1,000 persons' cases, are being examined and over 70 persons have already been separated from their families. Nearly all are in the age group 70–90 years. Those who oppose deportation forfeit their social security benefits (earned by 40 years of contributions paid by themselves and their employers; benefits are NOT Government-funded). They exhaust their savings and are forced to sell their homes, because no legal aid is available, and challenging denaturalization costs about $50,000. The U.S. offers to let such persons keep their old age pensions if they agree to leave the U.S.A., to admit that they concealed facts about wartime service, and to sign that they have agreed without duress. Tempted by this inducement (not to say blackmail), some have agreed, including the deceased Martin Bartesch, whom the U.S. answer says admitted to misrepresentation. Only a few have chosen to leave the U.S. with a pension and savings. The great bulk are fighting for their honor in the American courts, despite the near certainty that at the end they will be bankrupted, denaturalized, and exiled."*

We allow our present Department of Homeland Security certain latitude in dealing with known and suspected terrorists, implementing policies whose ends are deemed commensurate with the threat posed by the detainees. Arthur Rudolph, among the targets of OSI persecution only 20 years ago, was by no means either a clear and present danger to the U.S., an enemy combatant, or a foreign national—any of the things that might have argued in favor of outrageous OSI tactics, were the Rudolph case a matter of urgent national security. What the OSI did to Arthur Rudolph, a distinguished scientist serving the American defense and space programs, and an American citizen entitled to rights of due process, has more in common with the legendary tactics of the Soviet KGB than with anything a free society has come to expect from its appointed officials. The betrayal of Rudolph was also a betrayal of the American public, for when our representatives and their appointees act in contravention of the principles of law and justice; it is we the people who share the blame.

The following area is about recent information concerning Neil Sher that shows some insight into his character and how some of the associations and connections between organizations has been maintained. Also see Appendix titled Neil Sher Articles with recent news articles about Neil Sher his disbarment, divorce, etc.

Short biography on Neal Sher

• Former top "Nazi hunter" and director of the Office of Special Investigations, Executive Director of the American Israel Public Affairs Committee, and a partner in the Washington law firm Schmeltzer, Aptaker and Shepard.

• Sher was a reporter for Jewish World Relief newspaper and has written such articles as *Judge Gilbert Merritt's Obsession With Jews* (excerpt from beginning of article: THE FIRST PART of this series laid out the unassailable and utterly convincing evidence—as established in American and Israeli courts—that Ivan Demjanjuk was part and parcel of the Nazi's campaign of mass murder and genocide stemming from his service as an SS auxiliary at the Trawniki training camp, the Sobibor death camp and the Flossenberg and Regensberg concentration camps.).

[Other articles 6/22/98: *Sweep the Holocaust Museum clean;* 5/20/98: *The Case of Dinko Sakic: A Whitewash In The Making?;* 4/5/98: *Judge Gilbert Merritt's Obsession With Jews (Demjanjuk, part II);* 3/22/98: *The Continuing Saga of Ivan Demjanjuk;* 3/1/98: *Shameful Scapegoating At The Holocaust Museum* can be found at the Jewish World Relief website]

• Sher was also the President of the American section of the International Association of Jewish Lawyers and Jurists.

• As a former Washington chief of staff for the International Commission of Holocaust Era Insurance Claims (ICHEIC), he has been disbarred by U.S. Superior Court for taking "unauthorized reimbursements" on his extravagant worldwide travel expenses for the ICHEIC. Recently divorced and caught having an affair in Canada.

• Currently he is a legal consultant to the Canadian Department of Justice.

• Notice that Eli Rosenbaum was first associated with the World Jewish Congress and then became Director of the OSI. The source and movement of people leading the organizations is consistent.

19

The Contamination of Early Space History

In my opinion, the source of most of the contamination of United States space history is Congress, specifically in the House of Representatives. Two identically worded House resolutions (H.RES.68 of 1985, and H.RES.164 of 1987) were introduced into Congress, the text of which contains gross and horrendous lies concerning Arthur Rudolph.

To acquaint you with the texts, I will quote the first four paragraphs:

> *"Expressing the sense of the House of Representatives that the NASA Distinguished Service Medal should be taken away from Arthur Rudolph.*
>
> *Whereas Arthur Rudolph designer of the Saturn V moon rocket, has been accused by the Department of Justice of working thousands of slave laborers to death while supervising the production of the V-2 missiles for the Nazis for World War II;*
>
> *Whereas Arthur Rudolph has renounced his American citizenship and returned to West Germany rather than face deportation charges stemming from allegations brought by the Office of Special Investigations, Department of Justice;*
>
> *Whereas under Rudolph's supervision 60,000 slave laborers worked in subhuman conditions, resulting in death of an estimated 20,000 to 30,000 workers;"*

This information originated in the Department of Justice, more specifically the OSI. It is useful to remember that these resolutions are still active public documents, and information cited from these resolutions as historical fact has been appearing in books, magazines, newspaper articles, and TV programs. Thus, the existence of the resolutions is presumably because Representative Green, relying on the honesty and integrity of the information furnished by the Department of Justice, inadvertently lied by introducing the resolutions to Congress. **Thus allowing incorrect information to be available for the American public to misinterpret and possibly misuse.**

The House resolutions reflect the most current problem concerning history. However the background of the Rudolph case, wherein firm legitimate documentary evidence reveals gross and evidently criminal conduct on the part of certain Department of Justice officials involved in the case, evolves into an almost unbelievable story, were it not for the evidence, which has surfaced. The question is; how could this possibly happen in the United States of America, wherein a devoted and patriotic citizen, who contributed so much in the defense effort of this country during the Cold War and later to the exploration of space, be exiled from the U.S. by duress and coercion on false charges? This again, is painfully reminiscent of the tactics employed by the Gestapo and the KGB.

In my twenty year involvement in the Rudolph case, it has evolved from a very simple issue: whether the Department of Justice would reconsider the case based on new and legitimate evidence substantiating reconsideration. Now the public interest of this nation, in a truthful rendition of a glorious event in the history of humankind, is involved.

House Resolution, H.RES.68 of 1985, except for endorsements, is located in Appendix so titled. H.RES.164 of 1987 is located in Appendix so titled. To me it is unbelievable that these two house resolutions could have emanated from our very own Department of Justice in whose integrity for truth I had never reason to question before being involved in the this case. The gross allegations against Rudolph, in my mind, would surely have been of great concern to any responsible official involved, to raise the question: "where are the facts to substantiate such a statement?" And most surely to have such a statement, involving such a controversial subject and such a prominent former American citizen, before having it passed to a member of Congress, should elicit and require some form of verification. This evidently did not occur, as the misrepresentation of facts happened twice in two years!

Now I wish to refresh your memory a bit about how the same DOJ officials, and I can quote four, handled inquiries concerning the Rudolph case. In his letter dated January 29, 1987, to Senator Pete Wilson, Assistant Attorney General John Bolton, in paragraph three, stated that: "Let me assure you that before proceeding in cases such as the Rudolph matter, we at the Department of Justice carefully review the evidence and weigh its credibility. We proceed only after we are convinced that the evidence supports allegations."

The other officials, as noted above, and not in the OSI, have used similar or almost identical language in their responses to Congress, or others, in reference to the Rudolph case. In my opinion, these officials, evidently depending on the veracity, integrity and honesty of the information that they received from the OSI were duped into putting out false and misleading information.

One of the foremost literary works, which portrayed the contamination of this nation's early history in space came from an almost unbelievable source, the guardian of our nation's history, the Smithsonian Institution! The book, *The Rocket and the Reich*, was copyrighted by the Smithsonian in 1995. Another great surprise was that the author, Michael J. Neufeld, was the Curator of the Smithsonian Air and Space Museum. A further surprise is that Neufeld is not even an American citizen but a citizen of Canada! According to valid legitimate documentary evidence, the very first item, the dedicatory statement contains a gross lie, and the quote is "To the tens of thousands of prisoners who suffered, died or survived Dora and the other concentration camps of the V-2 program. May their sacrifice never be forgotten!" Evidence reveals that there was not one death on the V-2 line due to production personnel responsibility. The reference to "tens of thousands of prisoners" relates to the same type of information contained in the two House resolutions previously referred to in the book. [See Appendix titled Stuhlinger open letter to Neufeld for further comment from one of the Old Timers.]

Mr. Neufeld fails to accurately describe the scope of the operations which occurred at the Dora/Nordhausen complex. He indicates that all deaths occurring at that installation were on the V-2 line. Evidence reveals that there were tunnel-digging operations in progress, where many deaths took place. There were additional production lines where the work indicated that skilled labor was required to produce the V-1 missiles, the jet engines for aircraft, and the V-2 guided missile. Arthur Rudolph's sole responsibility was as production manager of the V-2 line.

It truly is amazing that Mr. Neufeld lacked the rendition of common ordinary logic in his book when he claims that thousands died while producing the V-2. The V-2 was a very complex guided missile, the top product of technical development at the time, and which required highly skilled workmanship to produce. What kind of logic would it be for a production manager for a vitally needed weapon, at least from the German point of view, to deliberately sabotage the war effort, and willfully kill off his highly skilled workforce? Indeed had he done so, he himself could have been executed for high treason for sabotaging the war effort!

Evidence reveals the truth that Rudolph, in trying to meet almost impossible production demands, was very much concerned over the welfare of the camp inmates who worked on his production line. He managed to get them additional rations, better medical help, and better clothing. His proactive performance in doing this far outshines the performance of Schindler as portrayed in "Schindler's List." Schindler only passively befriended about 1000 camp inmates, and Rudolph's crew was about 5000!

The Allied forces, immediately after the war, quickly recognized that war crimes had been committed at the Dora/Nordhausen complex. Intensive investigations were begun. In 1947, a war crimes court was convened in Dachau, Germany to specifically determine who was responsible for committing such crimes at Dora. At that time there were thousands of legitimate prosecution witnesses available very eager to testify against the persons who caused them so much grief. The court found that all rocket scientists who were defendants were not guilty of any war crime, and Rudolph's immediate supervisor was a defendant. Rudolph was not a defendant at the trial for the simple reason that there was not a single complaint from any of the camp inmates who worked on the V-2 line against him.

Another error by Mr. Neufeld in the dedicatory statement of his book is that "camps" were involved in the production of V-2s. Evidence reveals that Camp Dora of the Dora/Nordhausen complex was the only location of the V-2 production line.

We now have evidence, 58 years after the outcome of the war crimes trial at Dachau. Mr. Neufeld does not present one shred of supportive evidence in his book, *The Rocket and the Reich*, to substantiate his allegation contained in the dedicatory statement. I therefore contend that, with the evidence that has evolved, Mr. Neufeld, willfully, knowingly, and with aforethought, deliberately tried to discredit one of America's space pioneer heroes, and in doing so, contaminated our early history in space.

This turn of events, wherein false information is appearing on our library shelves concerning events in the history of our country, should be of great public concern. I believe that most Americans would strongly object to false information entering their history books, especially if it is done on an intentional basis to satisfy either a personal agenda, or contribute to a political cause.

Thus, we now have another almost unbelievable situation. Here the venerable Smithsonian Institution, the guardian of our nation's history, and the prime source of information for historical scholars, finds itself involved in copyrighting a book containing false information about our nation's history.

Another book, disseminating incorrect "facts" concerning the wartime role of Arthur Rudolph in Germany, is titled *Prosecuting Nazi War Criminals*, written by Alan S. Rosenbaum, and copyrighted in 1993. It does not go into much detail about Rudolph, but it references the same type of language as is contained in the two House Resolutions, namely, and very erroneously, that Rudolph "accepted slave labor brigades totaling some 60,000 individuals." However Rosenbaum comes up with a quote which indicates where most of the deaths at Dora occurred and is contradictory to Neufeld's indication that they occurred on the V-2 line. Here is Rosenbaum's statement: "Upward of 25,000 people apparently died, mainly from excavating underground tunnels under conditions of light, air, food, and medical deprivation."

To my recollection, one of the first TV shows which contributed to the contamination of space history was presented by "Frontline TV News" in a feature length commentary titled the "Nazi Connection." It was in two parts, the first part featured the work of Dr. Wernher von Braun and Arthur Rudolph encompassing their wartime role in Germany and later in the U.S. The second part of the program involved medical research by German doctors during the war and thus had no connection with von Braun or Rudolph. The main elements concerning von Braun and Rudolph in the discourse were their involvement in the V-2 program in Germany, and their accomplishments after coming to the United States being instrumental in sending U.S. astronauts to the moon.

The program consisted of a number of interviews with both von Braun and Rudolph wherein both were questioned about what they did, and their opinions or views on certain matters. It also consisted of interviews with other persons who obviously were not 'targeted' as possible war criminals. One thing that appeared quite strange to me during these interviews was that the interrogator or questioner was never identified or seen on the television screen. Normally it would appear to me that occasionally the one who is asking all of the questions would appear, at least briefly, on the screen.

Between the interviews, there would appear on the screen photo views of events or locations of scenes in Germany where war crimes evidently occurred. A number of the scenes showed piles of corpses, presumably taken at or near the Dora/Nordhausen complex where the V-2 production line was located. In reference, this was the same scene observed by Milton Hochmuth, the first U.S. Army intelligence officer who arrived at Dora/Nordhausen when U.S. troops captured the place. However, Hochmuth states that Rudolph was not responsible for what caused the corpses to be there.

In the beginning of this TV program, a comment was made that the program was initiated after "years of investigation." It is evident that the producers failed to dig deeply enough into historical information that was readily available. Specifically into those events which addressed what happened at Dora/Nordhausen.

There was not a word mentioned about the outcome of the war crimes trial that occurred at Dachau, Germany, in 1947, wherein all rocket scientists were found not guilty of any war crimes. This included a Mr. Rickhey, Rudolph's immediate supervisor. Rudolph himself was not a defendant at that trial because there had been no complaints filed against him. Neither was anything mentioned about the testimony of camp inmate survivors of the V-2 production line who swore that Rudolph was innocent. Moreover, apparently the producers were not interested in what the first Army intelligence officer on the scene had to say about the matter, as Hochmuth's name was not mentioned.

In the program involving von Braun and Rudolph, they were portrayed as war criminals due to association with the production of V-2s. The program did not present one piece of tangible or direct evidence to legitimately substantiate these allegations. In the closing few moments of that portion, evidence was revealed as to who was responsible for instigating the program. Eli Rosenbaum, the current director of the OSI, was presented in his office. This was the same individual who was involved in advertising for witnesses against Rudolph in the news media after Rudolph had left the U.S.

A considerable number of articles concerning the contamination of space have appeared in a number of ways into the news media network. Dr. Walter Haeussermann and Marsha Freeman, coordinated a second reply to Dr. Roger D. Launius, editor of *Space Times* concerning their earlier reply to a letter to "Dr. M. Neufeld's letter to the editor of *Space Times*, January-February, 1996."

TO THE EDITOR:

It is most unfortunate that Michael Neufeld, claiming to be an historian, high-handedly chooses to disregard direct evidence and corroborating witnesses regarding Dr. Arthur Rudolph and the operations of the V-2 Rocket facility in Nordhausen. We are most offended at his casual dismissal of the facts given in our letter to the Editor in Space Times of May/June 1995 as "false and egregious."

There are compelling statements from other authorities who have direct knowledge of the circumstances surrounding the V-2 facility in Nordhausen. An historian true to his calling would consider such direct testimonials as pieces of a puzzle requiring further investigation, rather than simply discrediting them because they do not fit into his preconceived theory.

The following citations are from authorities who have direct knowledge of the WWII environment in Nordhausen.

They provided in addition previous historical data to set the record straight:

Colonel Milton Hochmuth U.S.A (ret). Letter to Senator Sam Nunn, November 8, 1984: Certainly, no one was closer to the events than I concerning the Nordhausen underground plant. I was the only officer in the first U.S. Army directly concerned in gathering intelligence, hardware, people, etc. concerning the V-2s, V-1s, other guided missiles and rockets, etc. I arrived in Nordhausen a few hours after an infantry regiment occupied the town and vicinity. I inspected the plant... I interviewed several Germans, and as I recall, at least one "haeftling" or slave laborer... I was surprised at seeing numbers of apparently well-fed, healthy "haeft-linge."

On the first day at Nordhausen, I was shocked by the horrors of one concentration camp where bodies were stacked in piles, etc...But I am fairly certain there was another concentration camp near the underground plant where whatever "slave-labor" worked nearer the [V-2] plant came from. I recall interviewing an East European lathe operator in striped clothes they wore. He was well fed and I got the impression that those who worked in the plant were not mistreated as were those in the other camp.

As far as I could determine Rudolph was not more guilty of slave labor supervision than anyone on the vast German War machinery. I know the man. Of all the Germans we brought over, he was the mildest, soft-spoken, and non-authoritarian. He could not hurt a fly."

2. Milton Crook. Member of the U.S. Legal Staff in the Dachau War Crimes Trials, 1947.

Letter to the Baltimore Sun, November 17, 1984.

"War crimes investigations were commenced in 1945 involving slave labor at Dora-Nordhausen and upon completion some of the scientists so recruited by us and working in U.S. installations were formally accused of such crimes and returned to Germany for trial at Dachau. Likewise accused and joined in the trial were various camp officials, guards, and other personnel. After a long thorough trial the war crimes court considered the evidence and testimony introduced by the parties and adjudged the scientists not guilty of all charges."

Readers should be aware that Neufeld has interpreted only selective material. Intellectual integrity in historical as well as scientific inquiry requires consideration of all aspects of a phenomenon, not just material, which on the surface appears to confirm a preconceived notion. Neufeld seems to be unwilling to consider the range of direct sources available to him, which, indeed, compellingly refutes his theory. There is sufficient, if not altogether overwhelming evidence that Arthur Rudolph did not commit war crimes, as Neufeld claims.

Marsha Freeman, Author Dr.-Ing. Walter Haeussermann
"How we got to the Moon: AAS Fellow
The Story of the German Space Pioneers"

The contamination of our space history not only involves the Arthur Rudolph case but developments have evolved wherein Dr. Wernher von Braun, the leader of the space team in which Rudolph was involved, has been publicly and erroneously criticized for his wartime role in Germany.

At this time I wish to point out that the *Huntsville Times* had in the past, and has been publishing articles concerning members of the von Braun rocket team that have been other than complimentary. The source of such information has been the *Times* Washington correspondent Brett Davis. In my opinion, Mr. Davis has been in touch with officials of the OSI and has been following their line of propaganda without fully investigating the facts available from local sources, such as leading citizens of Huntsville, and members of the rocket team with first hand knowledge of the facts.

The following is a news item by Brett Davis, the *Times* Washington correspondent, and dated Monday February 28, 2000.

V-2 Plant Survivors Publicize their Story
By BRETT DAVIS

Times Washington Correspondent

WASHINGTON—During World War II, a group of German engineers, led by the brilliant Wernher von Braun, developed the V-2, the world's first ballistic missile.

At the war's end, U.S. and Russian forces scrambled to get those German engineers and their knowledge. The U.S. Army won most of the race, spiriting von Braun and 128 of his compatriots to America.

They settled in Huntsville and transformed the Nazi wartime technology into a series of space vehicles, beating the Russians to the moon and helping the world dream of space travel. In two decades, they became American heroes.

That is the version of the story most people remember, but a group of survivors of the underground plant where the V-2 was built want to add something to that history.

V-2 factory workers who live in America are forming a loose-knit group to share their memories. They don't want the V-2 to go down in history as just a brilliant product the Nazis devised that was later put to good use by America.

They also want people to remember the V-2s were built by slave laborers from concentration camps worked to death by Nazis desperate for a weapon to turn back the advancing Allied armies.

"People have now started to realize what happened there," said Alex Baum, who was a member of the French Resistance and was captured and sent to the underground V-2 plant. He now lives in California.

"We want to make the public more aware," Baum said.

The president of the group is an anthropology professor from American University, whose husband had a relative who died in the Holocaust.

Gretchen Schafft and her husband decided to find out about the relative, who they thought had died in the notorious death camp Buchenwald. Instead, they learned he died in a place called Dora.

"We didn't have any idea what Dora was," Schafft said in a recent interview at her home in Silver Spring, Md.

Ernst Stuhlinger, a Huntsville rocket team member who co-wrote a 1994 biography of von Braun titled "Wernher von Braun: Crusader for Space," said von Braun gets a lot of blame he does not deserve from Holocaust survivors.

"They remember von Braun because he made a name for himself after the war," Stuhlinger said. "They are inclined to put all the negative aspects of the Nazi regime on von Braun."

In his book, Stuhlinger quoted von Braun as saying he was powerless to improve conditions for the workers.

Schafft said the Dora survivors she met told her what it was: hell. (In fact, Stuhlinger's biography quotes von Braun as calling the place "hellish.")

In the early years of the war, von Braun and his rocket team developed the V-2 at a Baltic Sea site called Peenemünde. When the allies learned of the site and bombed it, the V-2 factory was moved underground to a series of tunnels carved into the Harz Mountains.

The place was run by a government-owned company euphemistically called the Mittelwerk, or "central works." It was fueled by prisoners from nearby concentration camps, including Dora.

Thousands died. In fact, more people died building the V-2 than did being hit by it.

Baum was a teenager active in the French Resistance when he was captured and sent to Buchenwald, and then to Peenemünde, where he and about 400 fellow prisoners worked on the rockets.

"We had to work very, very hard, constant running, schnell, schnell, but we had soup and we had a decent facility where we could sleep," Baum said. "We worked 12 hours a day and then 12 hours rest, seven days a week."

And then things got worse. Peenemünde was bombed and Baum went to Mittelwerk, where he helped build the tunnels, a grueling process that killed thousands.

"Dora was a hell," said Baum. "We had to build the tunnels. Imagining it, it is not even possible. We lived there in the tunnels in the beginning . . . we had to sleep underground, day shift or night shift there was mining, explosions, you lived under tremendous dust.

"We didn't have showers for maybe six to eight months. We had one cup of water to drink a day, and we had a cup of coffee, a piece of bread and soup, that is it. We lost a tremendous amount of people."

Ed Wynschenk was born in Holland and sent to the camps at 15 when the Nazis invaded. He went from Auschwitz to Birkenau and then, at the end of the war, to Dora, where his toes had to be cut off because of gangrene.

On April 11, 1945, all the inmates were forced on a death march as the Nazis abandoned the V-2 tunnels in the face of the advancing Russian and American armies.

Because he could not walk, the Nazis left him behind.

"The soldiers came the next day, the 12th. Many cried. The American soldiers were trained to fight other soldiers," Wynschenk said. "They were not prepared for what they saw and smelled when they opened the gates of hell."

Ragene Farris was one of those liberators. He was with the 329th Medical Battalion. He had seen V-2s flying overhead but was not prepared for seeing them in the tunnels, with so many half-dead walking skeletons around.

My comments about the previous article follow:

Brett Davis, *The Huntsville Times* Washington correspondent, in my opinion, is again following the propaganda line of OSI officials in trying to bring discredit to members of the German Rocket team, who have made their home in Huntsville since 1950. It was through the efforts of this team, which designed and developed the V-2 guided missile in wartime Germany that brought them to Huntsville after the war.

In 2000, several months prior to the University of Alabama, Huntsville, dedicating the Dr. Wernher von Braun Research Hall, several articles appeared in the *Times*, which concerned members of the team. This foregoing article, by Mr. Davis, is a point of issue. The very title of the article is so misleading in fact that it is almost a lie in my opinion. It reveals that Mr. Davis has failed to fully research or understand the facts concerning the location and scope of operations that actually occurred on the V-2 production line.

This article refers to the underground plant, indicating that only V-2s were produced there. With some research, Mr. Davis would have discovered that the underground complex consisted of four different operations. There was tunnel digging requiring unskilled labor, and evidently, here thousands died. Then there were the manufacturing lines where jet aircraft engines, V-1s and the V-2s were produced.

There was not one "survivor" mentioned in the article who worked on the V-2 production line in the plant, therefore the context of the title of the article is false. From what is quoted in the article, they all worked on the horrendous job of digging tunnels which was not under the responsibility of the production manager of the V-2 line.

It appears that much of what is released from the press concerning the production of the V-2 missile in Germany is associated with war crime allegations. The true fact is; if Mr. Davis had dug a little deeper into legitimate historical records he would have an amazing story to tell. Arthur Rudolph, as manager of the V-2 line, was faced with work force shortages of the high skilled labor necessary to meet almost impossible production schedules. As a result, he was very much concerned about the welfare of his prison inmate workforce. He managed to obtain supplemental rations, better medical attention, and other benefits.

Thus the true story about Rudolph's involvement concerning V-2 construction in Germany was; if you were a prisoner in a concentration camp, just hope that you would be transferred to the V-2 production line, because there you will be assured of better treatment, and a longer life.

The following is an article which appeared the very next day, February 29, 2000, in *The Huntsville Times* concerning von Braun, and which indicates that von Braun was involved in war crimes, however evidence reveals that he was not. It is as follows:

Von Braun: A Life in Full

To understand the legendary scientist, you have to accept his role in Nazi Germany and note his contributions to Huntsville.

"Much as we often wish it otherwise, ours is not a black-and-white world in which good is always a pole apart from evil. That is particularly true among people; we are amalgams of frailties and good intentions, occasionally marked by transcendent moments of righteousness.

An excellent case in point is Wernher von Braun: the man who almost single handedly turned Huntsville from a sleepy agricultural market into the South's high-tech diamond, the mastermind of humanity's greatest adventure in exploration-and, according to survivors of slave labor in Germany, a pawn of the Nazis who bragged about eventually being able to destroy the United States with missiles.

Early Space History

Brett Davis, The Times' Washington correspondent, detailed on Monday the claims of historians, survivors of the underground plant where the V-2 rockets that bombarded Great Britain were built, and relatives of survivors. Some officials say more laborers died building the complex than were killed by the missiles the plant eventually produced.

This is not something many in Huntsville want to hear in the best of times-but this seems a particularly bad one. A festival celebrating Von Braun and his rocket team's contributions to science and art and the 25th anniversary of the Von Braun Center are scheduled. (So, too, coincidentally, is a Huntsville Museum of Art show featuring contemporary art about the Holocaust.)

For Von Braun's supporters, Ernst Stuhlinger, a rocket team member and Von Braun's biographer, has offered a consistent explanation: Von Braun was an unwilling piece of the German war machine that had no effective way to protest the treatment of the slave laborers.

Did Wernher von Braun help one of the most evil regimes in humankind's history become even more destructive, in an effort that killed hundreds of laborers?

Did Wernher Von Braun lead humankind to the moon and help shape prosperous present-day Huntsville?

The answers are yes and yes. In addition, it is understandable that most folks in Huntsville would prefer to accentuate his role in America's great scientific achievements rather than his V-2 efforts. But no matter which you emphasize, you can't appreciate and understand his legacy without taking his entire life into account."

I wish to make a comment about Mr. Davis's comment quoted in the paragraph immediately above. In my opinion, Mr. Davis's answers should have been no for the first question and yes for the second question, instead of yes and yes.

There is no evidence to support the allegation that von Braun was in any way involved "in an effort that killed hundreds of laborers."

To me it is most puzzling why *The Huntsville Times* has engaged in writing so many articles that tend to discredit the accomplishments of the German rocket team, which was so instrumental in transforming the sleepy southern town, of about 15,000, which depended on cotton crops to the high-tech city of today. Evidently, a number of the leading citizens of Huntsville have strongly objected to this and here is an article about their feelings on the matter, which appeared in the *Times* on December 24, 1999:

Rudolph Backers Rebut Papers Say Scientist Done "Injustice"
By MIKE SALINERO and KEITH CLINES
Times Staff Writers
Friday, December 24, 1999

Friends of Arthur Rudolph on Thursday said publicity surrounding the recent release of more U.S. government documents on the German rocket scientist did a "great injustice" to an innocent man.

Supporters of Rudolph, who was labeled a Nazi war criminal after his NASA career ended, held a press conference Thursday to rebut again any allegations that Rudolph was connected with the deaths of thousands of slave laborers in German camps during World War II.

"This is our neighbor and friend, and people should be making sure accuracy is shown," said Joe Moquin, a longtime friend of Rudolph. "It was devastating to harp on all these issues that I thought had been pretty well put to bed."

Rudolph was a member of Wernher von Braun's German rocket team that was brought to America by the U.S. Army after World War II.

The team was eventually assigned to Redstone Arsenal, where it developed the Saturn rockets for NASA.

However, after Rudolph's retirement from NASA, the Justice Department's Office of Special Investigations (OSI) accused him of war crimes for his involvement in German V-2 rocket plant during World War II.

Rudolph was accused of helping run a program that worked thousands of slave laborers to death, but he contended that he only managed the assembly of the rockets, and had nothing to do with the care of prisoners.

The U.S. Justice Department contended that as many as 20,000 slave laborers died from mistreatment in the tunnels of the rocket plant and nearby concentration camp.

In 1984, Rudolph relinquished his U.S. citizenship and returned to Germany to avoid possible prosecution. He died in Germany in 1996 at age 89 after years of unsuccessful attempts to prove his innocence. A Saturday article in The Huntsville Times was based on military records recently released by the National Archives. The records were made public by an act of Congress, which mandates the release of Cold War-era government information about suspected Nazi war criminals. The article said that the records shed little new light on Rudolph's career. It quotes an unknown Army intelligence source who described Rudolph as 100 percent Nazi, dangerous type, security threat. Suggest internment."

The Army later concluded that Rudolph was not a security risk.

Moquin took exception to information in the documents that indicated Rudolph was under light surveillance while on a trip to Europe in 1958. At the time, he was technical director of the Army's Redstone rocket program.

His friends on Thursday characterized that the government monitoring was being used for Rudolph's protection.

"You related to this trip he made; it made it sound like he had Nazi affiliations after he came to America," Moquin said. If all your population, essentially all professionals, have to belong to the party, why would you harp on it?"

Moquin said information in the article "maligns (Rudolph's) integrity and reputation, and it's not accurate." He also said such information reflects on the surviving members of von Braun's rocket team.

"It devastates them to have those statements made about their association with Arthur Rudolph," Moquin said.

Gerhard Reisig and Walter Haeussermann, original members of von Braun's rocket team, knew and worked with Rudolph in Germany and in Huntsville.

Haeussermann said he was upset that The Times published an article that did not present any new evidence against Rudolph. He said it is "utter nonsense" to say that Rudolph was responsible for workers deaths and insisted no workers died at the factory that Rudolph directed.

"What has been done to him by the OSI (Office of Special Investigations) is a crime," Haeussermann said.

Reisig said the article was "a very bad representation of the facts."

"The whole issue accusing him of killing 20,000 detainees was a stinking big lie," Reisig said.

Former Huntsville Mayor Steve Hettinger attended the press conference.

Hettinger said he had always supported the efforts of Rudolph's friends to get Rudolph back to the United States to try to clear his name.

"When I was mayor, I was supportive of their efforts defending Arthur Rudolph ... to allow him to tell his story the right way."

Here is an article that appeared on the front page of *The Huntsville Times* on June 18, 2000, wherein von Braun team members and friends had their say and is as follows:

When retired Huntsville aerospace CEO Joe Moquin talks about his friends among the city's, German rocket pioneers—the so-called Old Timers—his eyes get watery his voice goes from scratchy to a near-shout and he's known to repeat himself.

"It's wrong. It is just wrong. It's not right," he'll say of those who want his story to stress the Germans role in building V-2 missiles for Adolph Hitler as much as their leadership in America's moon race.

Engineer-turned-author Hugh McInnish, another ardent team defender, sneers at sentiment. He wields the sword of his own research to say the Germans did not do what the critics claim. He wrote a book about it.

"It's not about feelings," McInnish, said recently. "It's about facts." They are both right. The ongoing discussion about the Germans is about right and wrong in both a moral sense and a factual sense. It is about the facts of Wernher von Braun and his band of rocket pioneers. It is about how we feel about the way we have treated them.

Why do Moquin and company feel so deeply? Why must they show up to challenge every critical report, every addition to the record and every new allegation from historians, Holocaust survivors, Nazi-bunters? Why can they not agree that the Germans were complex figures—?

—American heroes and German warriors—and just move on?

It is because there is almost desperation now, a feeling that the old, familiar story is slipping out of control, being rewritten by people who dismiss our long-accepted version as mere "Huntsville history."

Moreover, the team's defenders insist, the new story is badly flawed.

The defenders raise two basic questions.

First, what if the accusers are wrong? What if the team did not mistreat forced workers at the German rocket plant during the war? That is what the team members themselves say.

It is what some survivors say, too, although other survivors say otherwise. If the matter is in doubt, why is our government now acting as though it were not, threatening to investigate team members, keeping files on them? Especially given what happened between the government and the Germans during and after the war?

That leads to the next question.

How could we bring the Germans here, use them to beat the Soviets in both the arms and moon races, grant them citizenship, then turn around years later and go after them?

In Huntsville, people know a lot of the story firsthand. They do not know everything. No one here was at the German missile factory, and that is a big gap. However, they knew the generals, many now dead, who brought the Germans here. They knew the politicians, also dead, who OK'd each step along the way.

The Germans were "a war trophy" when they arrived at Fort Bliss, Texas, after the war. They were our trophy because we won the first race with the Soviet army to find them.

People here say our generals knew a lot even then about the V-2 missile plant. The German team told us, for one thing, and the Army interviewed people rescued when it was liberated.

The Germans were years ahead of us in missile expertise, and our generals wanted what they knew. That is why, along with the team, we brought 100 captured V-2 rockets to Texas.

It is why we handpicked the German contingent to include experts in guidance, propulsion ordnance—everything that makes a rocket go.

Perhaps significantly, we brought only one production expert, one man who knew how the Germans ran their rocket assembly line.

At Fort Bliss, the Army basically went to rocket school, with the Germans as willing teachers. We launched more than 70 V-2s and studied every flight.

Why were the Germans so willing to teach? They were doing what they loved, and they did not have to do it in the communist Soviet Union.

Even then, some people did not like the Germans here. Nevertheless, the criticism stopped abruptly in 1949 when one thing happened. One really big thing.

The Soviets exploded an atomic bomb.

Suddenly, it was a colder world. That is even what they called the period: the Cold War.

The Germans were our secret weapon, and the very next year the Army brought that secret weapon here, to a place described as a "small, Southern cotton town." That phrase is famous hereabouts. Families that date back to the era are the local equivalent of the Mayflower Society.

Why here? There was a big arsenal, Redstone, with miles and miles of empty space where missiles could be tested.

The Army's plan? Build a new generation of V-2 rockets that could carry atomic bombs.

The plan worked, too. With the Germans heading the laboratory teams, America built a series of bigger, better missiles.

In the early years, the Army had to assign officers to watch the Germans. Not because they were a security threat—they were actually happy as clams and became American citizens en masse in the mid-1950s—but because von Braun kept pushing his own plans. Military rockets were never what excited von Braun. He wanted to go to the moon. He wanted Mars.

The Army was interested in the moon, too. As the site for a military base. However, von Braun found a kindred spirit in President Kennedy, who vowed America would reach the moon, peacefully, during the 1960s.

The new civilian space agency, NASA, took on the job in Huntsville. Just as he was for military rockets during the arms race, Rudolph was in charge of Saturn V production. The rest, as they say, is history, Huntsville history. American history, World history.

The Germans who led the way lived here, never cashing in, retiring on government pensions. Their children attended public schools many still live here.

The Germans did not stay in a compound, either. They made Huntsville better. You can still visit the observatory von Braun helped students build on Monte Sano. You can hear the symphony they helped start Huntsville's love affair with the Germans probably peaked in the famous downtown celebration in 1969, right after the first moon landing. Community leaders carried von Braun on their shoulders. The people cheered.

Huntsville is still cheering. We spent a good part of this year observing the von Braun Celebration of the Arts and Sciences.

However, each year, the cheering section seems a little smaller. More and more people are inclined to look for the "whole story," not just the hero story.

That is appalling to the team's defenders. For the rest of us, it is the way these things go.

At this time I wish to add a bit of news to the editor of *The Huntsville Times* regarding the contents of the second paragraph above. I believe that this book contains the "whole story" concerning the association of Arthur Rudolph and Wernher von Braun with the production of the V-2 rocket at the Dora/Nordhausen complex. And as referred to earlier in this book, Rudolph, instead of being a Nazi war criminal, as indicated in some of the past articles published in the *Times*, was a hero to the prison inmates who worked for him. I disagree with the comment about the statement indicating that the team mistreated forced workers at the rocket plant during the war.

The comment in the article states: "It's what some survivors say, too, although other survivors say otherwise." I have failed to see an article in the *Times* describing a story by an "otherwise" survivor who actually worked on the V-2 line. The only statements made by "otherwise" survivors, as printed in the *Times*, was under the erroneous heading of the news article printed February 28, 2000, titled: "V-2 plant survivors publicize their story." These "survivors" worked in the tunnel digging operations and had nothing to do in producing V-2s.

At the beginning of this chapter, I stated that the main source of the contamination of our space history is contained in the two congressional resolutions, which were introduced into Congress in 1985 and 1987. The following information supports that allegation. On August 8, 1998, a program was presented on the biography of Dr. Wernher von Braun on the "History Channel," titled "Threshold to the Stars," with Jack Perkins officiating.

The program was very well presented until about the last 30 seconds, when Jack Perkins suddenly came up with the words to the effect that, "but there is another one who did not outlive his Nazi past, Arthur Rudolph, manager of the Saturn V program, who surrendered his NASA Distinguished Service Medal, gave up his citizenship, and returned to Germany, because he was involved with supervising 20,000 slave laborers in Germany. He died this year." Jack Perkins was wrong on three counts, Rudolph did not surrender the medal he received from NASA, and he only utilized 5,000 slave laborers provided by the SS.

This quote by Jack Perkins clearly reflects the information contained in the House resolutions. The resolutions begin with "Expressing the sense of the House of Representatives that the NASA Distinguished Service Medal should be taken away from Arthur Rudolph." Then in paragraph four of the resolutions is the quote: "estimated 20,000 to 30,000 workers."

One of the most shocking, in my opinion, TV programs concerning the contamination of our space history, appeared on "Inside Edition," as an 'Extra,' at 6:00 PM, PST, on February 8, 1993. There was about a 20-minute portion, evidently tailored for the character assassination of Arthur Rudolph. One of the leading statements by Neal Sher, I believe OSI director at the time, was that Rudolph was an "unmitigated liar."

Arthur Rudolph appeared in a number of scenes, being questioned by Nancy Glass. Between the scenes were a number of photographs presented, depicting piles of corpses, presumably at or near Camp Dora. He was questioned about the origin of the corpses, and whether he had anything to do with them, in which he flatly denied that he was not guilty of any war crime. Rudolph was faced with the question of why he signed "The Agreement." He responded several times that he did it because he was under duress. Both Neal Sher, (recently disbarred for stealing from a Jewish non-profit organization) and Eli Rosenbaum another OSI prosecutor, came on intermittently, accusing Rudolph of killing thousands of prisoners. Rosenbaum finally, in a contemptuous voice, called Rudolph a "beast."

The commentator, Nancy Glass, repeatedly asked Rudolph if he had an apology to offer, and whether he was sorry, with the air that he had committed a war crime. Rudolph stated that no one was killed on the V-2 line where he was production manager. Ms. Glass asked Dr. Rudolph: "How was it possible that you could not see the bodies?" referring to the piles of corpses. Rudolph simply stated that he was not in the vicinity of the bodies. Nancy Glass again asked Rudolph if he had any apologies to offer, and whether he was sorry for what had happened. Rudolph indicated again that he had no apology to offer, because he was not guilty of any war crime. The sense of the program was that he was guilty of a war crime, and that he was lying.

The most disgusting element of this television program was that both Neal Sher, and Eli Rosenbaum, vociferous in denouncing Rudolph as a war criminal, were fully aware of the outcome of the Dora/Nordhausen war crimes trial, which was held in Dachau, Germany, in 1947. They positively knew that the rocket scientists were found not guilty. Now 47 years later, as officials representing our Department of Justice, appear on a public TV program castigating a distinguished former U.S. citizen as a war criminal. (Both Germany and Canada found Rudolph innocent using old and so called new evidence.) Evidently, the TV staff did a very poor job on historical research, possibly only referring to the House resolutions and other OSI propaganda. There was not a shred of information on the program relating to the Dachau trial or new findings of innocence by German and Canadian legal systems.

What a gross and ludicrous situation!! Here was Sher, one of our Department of Justice officials, calling Rudolph a liar, when he himself, failed to produce one shred of legitimate evidence to the West German prosecutor to substantiate his allegations against Rudolph. To me, that represents a lie, which as a result, was cause of an embarrassing black eye in the face of the administration of American justice. Moreover, Rosenbaum, who lied to a member of the Senate, when he indicated that the OSI was not involved in contacting the East Bloc in the Rudolph case, was a participant in this character assassination of Rudolph on this TV program.

This exhibition by officials of our very own Department of Justice is again an almost unbelievable event were it not for the evidence that it actually occurred.

The Huntsville Times, the only newspaper in the city where the German rocket team finally made its home in the U.S., went to great lengths in its Sunday edition of June 18, 2000, in describing the mission of the OSI and other articles about Arthur Rudolph. On the front page, in 2-1/2 inch letters were the letters: "OSI," immediately below was the word in smaller script: "FOREVER." This news clip follows:

> *WASHINGTON—A special Nazi-hunting agency within the U.S. Justice Department has always been thought to have a finite life span.*
>
> *Its mission to hunt down war criminals in the United States and deport them should obviously end when all the potential criminals of that era are dead. If some lawmakers in Congress have their way though, the*

Office of Special Investigations, as it is named, may get a new lease on life.

Legislation moving through Congress could give the agency the authority to pursue war criminals beyond just World War II: those from Haiti, Rwanda, Yugoslavia and anywhere else where torture or genocide was committed and the perpetrators seek to vanish into American anonymity.

"If we get the jurisdiction, it will mean, alas…that this mission will go on indefinitely, since humankind shows no indication that it is going to stop perpetrating crimes against humanity." said the OSI's director, Eli Rosenbaum.

"This is an ongoing nightmare around the world."

If the agency does get the new mission, it will be hailed by some lawmakers and civil rights advocates who say the move is overdue.

"We should not repeat the mistake of waiting decades before tracking down war criminals who have settled in this country," Sen. Patrick Leahy, D-VT., said on the floor of the Senate last year when he introduced the bill to expand the OSI's authority.

"No war criminal should ever come to believe that he is going to find safe harbor in the United States."

At this point, I cannot but help to introduce some information, which I am quite positive that Senator Leahy does not know about. It is very evident that the senator is basing his faith on the integrity of the information which he receives from the Department of Justice about the matter. So what do the real facts reveal? It reveals the gross horrendous lies contained in the two House resolutions, which were perpetrated by our Department of Justice!!!

Now I will say a few words: Had the Senate Judiciary Committee or the House Judiciary Committee conducted oversight hearings into the case, as I had previously requested, evidence would have surfaced which would have revealed the criminal, and gross prosecutorial misconduct of the OSI in both the Rudolph and John Demjanjuk cases. Thus, the activities of the OSI have been kept more or less secret because my requests to Congress were ignored. I suggest that Senator Leahy obtain the results of the war crimes court, which was held at Dachau, Germany, in 1947, and then rescind his bill, and after sponsoring an oversight hearing into the matter, and cleaning house at OSI, reintroduce his bill if it is warranted. The news clipping continues:

The new mission will be derided by foes of the agency who criticize some OSI lawyers as legal thugs who railroad old people out of the country on trumped-up charges.

Hugh McInnish is a local engineer who has been one of the most ardent supporters of former NASA engineer Arthur Rudolph, a past OSI target.

"I think it's a thing that sounds legitimate, but based on the past performance of the OSI, I think there's a great deal of danger of abuse," McInnish said.

The OSI is currently investigating 233 people and has 18 cases in court. It has finished more than 1,261 investigations since its inception in 1979 and has stripped 63 people of their U.S. citizenship on grounds they were war criminals. It has had 53 people deported or removed from the United States and has denied another 157 people entry into the country.

More than 60,000 people are on watch lists, meaning OSI officials are alerted when they try to enter the country.

The agency has stirred up complaints wherever it goes, chiefly among family members or friends of those accused of Nazi-era charges.

In the 1980's, the agency roiled Huntsville by investigating Rudolph, a star member of Wernher von Braun's rocket team.

The OSI contended Rudolph helped persecute concentration camp labor during World War II by ordering slave laborers from the Nazi SS to work on the V-2 rocket.

Rudolph denied it and maintained his innocence, but he reached an agreement with the OSI: He left the country and gave up his citizenship rather than face a court fight. Once back in Germany, he regretted signing The Agreement and fought to clear his name.

According to Rosenbaum, the fight over the wartime activities of members of the von Braun team may not end any time soon. He said the OSI is investigating other members of that rocket team.

"I can't say who, what, but there are still individuals from the World War II V-2 missile program, and other Paperclip experts as well, who remain under investigation by our office," Rosenbaum said in an interview.

Paperclip was the U.S. government's code name for getting German scientists to America at the close of the war before the Soviets got them.

"What we've found over the years is after the Rudolph case was public, most of the Paper-clip scientists whom we sought to interview refused to speak with us," Rosenbaum said. "So the wagons have been circled, and for the most part, they won't talk."

Huntsville attorney Pat Richardson said he represents two rocket team members the OSI wanted to question in the wake of the Rudolph case. Richardson wrote to the OSI and said he would consider questions in writing and would have them answered in writing. That was more than a decade ago; Richardson said he has heard nothing since.

"They tried to bulldoze us into giving us an interview," Richardson said. "They wanted to browbeat these men. Nothing is going to happen."

Von Braun died in 1977. His role in the use of labor has also been debated by historians. Rosenbaum said he does not know if von Braun could be deported if he were still alive.

"I don't like to speculate on that because it's not fair; he's not here to defend himself," Rosenbaum said. "Obviously, he would have been the subject of some inquiry."

Rosenbaum did say that if von Braun were still alive, things might have gone differently for Rudolph.

"Rudolph's first call would have been to him (von Braun)," Rosenbaum said. "Von Braun was an individual who could call presidents of the United States directly and talk with them. What that might have led to, I hope it would have led to exactly nothing, but one never knows. He (Rudolph) certainly would have had a very high-profile defender."

Although the Rudolph case earned the OSI the enmity of many in Huntsville, where the rocket team is revered, Rosenbaum said the case was big for the agency because it showed that no potential criminals were safe from investigation.

"I suppose what it did do is help establish our bona fides as an agency that was not going to avert its gaze from individuals who were used by the U.S. government. I think for the survivors in particular, that case helped establish our credibility in a large way," Rosenbaum said.

Another big OSI case had the opposite effect. In 1981, the OSI deported Cleveland autoworker John Demjanjuk, accused of being "Ivan the Terrible" of the Treblinka death camp in Poland, an unusually savage guard who helped run the camp's gas chambers.

Demjanjuk then stood trial in Israel and was sentenced to death. During his appeal of that ruling, evidence surfaced indicating that another man, not Demjanjuk, was actually Ivan the Terrible.

Israel sent Demjanjuk back to the United States. The U.S. 6th Circuit Court of Appeals investigating the charges against Demjanjuk and concluded the OSI had evidence that could have exonerated Demjanjuk of the charge of being that particular guard.

[Author note: In the 6th U.S. Circuit Court of Appeals hearing Demjanjuk vs. Petrovsky 10F 3d 338, of November 17, 1993, concluded after judges in February 1994 that the OSI had engaged in "prosecutorial misconduct" and had committed "fraud on the court," which had "seriously misled the court."]

A U.S. district judge investigated the OSI's behavior in that case and concluded that its attorneys played "hardball" and did not turn over evidence that another man was actually Ivan the Terrible. The judge said some of that information had been in government hands as far back as 1978, before the OSI was even founded.

The judge ultimately concluded that OSI attorneys had made these errors inadvertently and not out of an "evil intent" to get Demjanjuk, but the chief judge of the circuit overruled that conclusion and said the OSI had indeed acted recklessly.

"We hold that the OSI attorneys acted with reckless disregard for the truth and for the government's obligation to take no steps that prevent an adversary from presenting his case fully and fairly," the Circuit Court ultimately ruled.

Rosenbaum said the OSI disputed that conclusion, but it stands.

"You have to live with that," Rosenbaum said.

Now I will say a few words: With these callous words, Rosenbaum reveals his mindset concerning the administration of justice, not the American way, but Gestapo style. Here the OSI was caught by an American court willfully withholding exculpatory evidence about Demjanjuk, which directly led to his conviction by an Israeli court, with the result of a sentence of death by hanging. Thus, this evidence reveals that the OSI is guilty of obstruction of justice, which is a felony, punishable by imprisonment of responsible officials. Also, in my opinion, had the hanging actually taken place, would the OSI officials not be responsible as an accessory to murder? The news clipping continues:

> *He did say the case changed the way the OSI does business. Its operatives now bend over backward to give evidence to the opposing side, Rosenbaum said. "Our attorneys spend more time pursuing their disclosure obligations…than they do doing anything else in their job, investigating, litigating," Rosenbaum said. "It's far beyond anything that a court has required us to do. We think under the circumstances it's prudent to operate that way."*

> *Despite that change, the agency has not backed down in the Demjanjuk case. It is again seeking to deport him. He is no longer accused of being Ivan the Terrible of Treblinka, but instead being a Nazi guard at other camps, including Sobibor.*

> *Demjanjuk has sued the OSI charging it with "torture" for its efforts to again strip him of his citizenship and deport him.*

Congress Plows Ahead

> *Despite the OSI's legal fight, the new push to extend the agency's mission is meeting little opposition in Congress.*

> *The move was started by Leahy's bill, which was co-sponsored by conservative Sen. Orrin Hatch of Utah. No other senator objected, so the bill was deemed passed unanimously on a voice vote in November.*

> *A companion version is pending in the House before the Judiciary Committee. A subcommittee of that panel has held hearing on it, but the bill has not been approved there.*

Those bills would make the OSI a permanent part of the Justice Department. Until now, the agency has technically existed at the discretion of the attorney general.

Now I will say a few words: Before Congress passes any new law concerning the extension of the OSI charter, they should recognize the great problem that still exists, which is their direct responsibility for the contamination of early space history. There are the two House resolutions in effect as public documents, which contain gross horrendous lies, which were perpetrated upon Congress by the OSI, and which are evidently being used by historians as a source of historical reference. Had members of Congress heeded my pleas and requests for oversight hearings into the matter, evidence would have revealed the truth about the situation, and we would not currently be faced with the fact that publications are appearing on our library shelves which contain lies about our emergence as a leader in the exploration of space.

Now the news clipping continues:

However, there has been some debate in Congress about whether this new jurisdiction should be given to the Immigration and Naturalization Service not the OSI

Richard Krieger, president of International Educational Missions Inc., a nonprofit group, told a House Judiciary Committee panel in February that OSI should get the work.

"In the 35 years between the end of World War II and OSI's creation, the INS succeeded in removing just one Nazi criminal from the United States," Krieger said.

Rep. Mark Foley, R-Fla., who wrote the House version, also favors the OSI. Foley press aide Sean Spicer said, "Everybody is pretty much in agreement that this is a good bill," but the question of which agency should get the jurisdiction is helping hold it up.

Rep. Bud Cramer, D-Huntsville, said he is not familiar with the legislation and does not know how he will vote. A staff representative for Rep. Robert Aderholt, R-Haleyville, said Aderholt also is undecided.

If the OSI does get the mission, it would have to beef up its current staff of 35, which includes 12 lawyers and 11 historians—workers Rosenbaum said are swamped by their World War II era investigations.

Rosenbaum has been with the agency for more than 15 years. He works from a paper-choked office equipped with overstuffed chairs that he has dubbed "New Orleans cathouse furniture."

Rosenbaum started as the office's first summer law intern in 1979. After years away at a Manhattan law firm and at the World Jewish Congress, he returned to the OSI in 1988 and has been there ever since. He became director in 1995.

His deputy, Susan Siegal, has been with the agency for 11 years and has been the principal deputy director for nearly four years. She is a Birmingham native who went to Georgetown law school in Washington.

"It's the kind of job that many people who go to law school dream of," Siegal said "It's incredibly interesting, you feel like you're helping people and you get to practice law at the same time." She visits Birmingham regularly but has not been to Huntsville since she started working at OSI. Siegal handled some of the paperwork on claims that Rudolph filed against the agency seeking to have his agreement with the OSI nullified on the grounds it was coerced, claims that courts ultimately dismissed.

"I was a little chagrined there was a sizable community in Huntsville that supported Rudolph after it was clear what he had done," Siegal said. "He contributed to the space industry but this is the man who conceived the idea of slave labor to advance the German missile search."

Rudolph denied that, and supporters insist there is no evidence to support the charge, which surfaced after he left the United States.

If the OSI is given its new mission, it faces even more work.

Allegations of war crimes and torture have arisen from places like Haiti and Yugoslavia, and the Center for Justice and Accountability, a California-based human rights group has estimated that as many as 60 alleged perpetrators of the crimes could be deported by an expanded OSI.

Those are people who have already been convicted of crimes elsewhere, who have committed torture, or whose complicity in torture or other crimes against humanity are well known, according to the group.

The total number of such criminals hiding in the United States since the end of the Vietnam War could reach into the thousands, the group says.

Rosenbaum said the OSI pursuit of Nazi war criminals, despite their age and the length of time that has passed since their crimes, sends a clear message to war criminals now. "If you dare to get involved in these kinds of crimes, there is a very real chance that what remains of the civilized world will pursue you forever, if necessary for the rest of your life and if necessary to locations thousands of miles away from the scene of the crime," Rosenbaum said.

"Are we going to say to Slobodan Milosevic, just wait out a few years or few decades, and then you can come to Disney World? I hope not. That's almost what we did in the Nazi cases."

I commend *The Huntsville Times* for presenting this in-depth news clipping to inform the public concerning both sides of the controversial issue of suspected war criminals versus the conduct of American prosecutors in pursuing their mission. This release was aptly timed in that the University of Alabama, Huntsville, dedicated the Dr. Wernher von Braun Research Hall at the same time.

After returning from Huntsville, and being shocked by the news contained in the *Times* clipping concerning the fact that the Senate had already passed an extension of the OSI charter, I promptly wrote a letter to my Representative Elton Gallegly. Due to the fact that I felt this to be a crucial issue, I hereby present the letter, without enclosures, in its entirety:

The Honorable Elton Gallegly
2427 Rayburn Office Building
Washington, DC 20515   *June 26, 2000*

Dear Elton:

Enclosed is news clipping from the Huntsville, Alabama Times, dated June 18, 2000.

The OSI, Office of Special Investigation of the Department of Justice, is featured in the page one headlines, indicating that the possible extension of their charter is being considered in Congress.

Your attention is invited to the third column on page A9. I highlighted the portion where it indicates that the OSI was guilty of criminal action in their prosecution of the John Demjanjuk case. It reveals how they withheld exonerating evidence from the court before Demjanjuk was extradited to Israel, there where with further aid from the OSI, Demjanjuk was sentenced to death by an Israeli court, Shortly before the execution date, the Israeli Supreme Court, considering new evidence, overturned the sentence, and turned Demjanjuk free.

Prior to the action of the Israeli Supreme Court, the OSI had bragged about their actions concerning the case as one of their greatest accomplishments. This is almost unbelievable, wherein OSI officials, knowingly and willfully subject a U.S. citizen to the death penalty by withholding exonerating evidence. This embarrassing situation is painfully reminiscent of the operating tactics employed by the Gestapo in Hitler days. Eli Rosenbaum in his reaction to a later ruling by a U.S. Circuit Court that the OSI had acted recklessly had the response; "You have to live with that," this is truly unconscionable.

I have previously submitted incontrovertible documentary evidence of criminal action by the OSI in their conduct of the Arthur Rudolph case. Particularly about their role in the introduction of the House Resolutions, H.RES.68 of 1985, and H.RES.164 of 1987. These resolutions contain gross lies. It has become increasingly evident that a thorough, unbiased, and impartial oversight investigation of the operational tactics employed by the OSI in their conduct of the Rudolph case will reveal that malfeasance of office, obstruction of justice, and contempt of Congress has been committed.

Congress passed the Nazi War Crimes Disclosure Act, which took effect in January, 1999. This Act, in effect, countermands the Freedom of Information Act insofar as the OSI is concerned. This Act specifically exempts the OSI from furnishing any information requested by citizens under the provisions of the Freedom of Information Act, which may reveal misconduct or other aberrational behavior. This is totally against the spirit, and purpose, of the Freedom of Information Act.

This evidence as referred to in the enclosed news clip, and the documentary evidence which I have previously submitted to you, should make it incumbent upon you to take immediate action to stop any further action in Congress to extend the charter of the OSI. As my

Representative, I hereby request that you take such action. An oversight hearing by the House Judiciary Committee on the past performance of the OSI is long overdue. If indeed, the Congress feels the need that the charter is to be extended, let a hearing be the first priority. First, determine whether crime(s) has been committed, and if it has, see that appropriate action is taken so that the operational tactics employed by the OSI in the future will no longer be an embarrassing chain of events involving the administration of American justice.

Please give me a response to my request, as you state in the local newspaper that you give prompt attention to all correspondence.

Sincerely,
William E. Winterstein, Sr., LTC. Army (Ret.)

I have received no response from Rep. Gallegly concerning my request that he take immediate action to stop any extension of the OSI charter, pending an oversight hearing into the past performance of the OSI. I hope that he has taken such action, and not to have ignored this as just another request from Bill Winterstein.

Much has been discussed about the OSI, and their continued pursuit of certain members of the von Braun rocket team, who were instrumental in placing Huntsville on the map. I believe that had the *Times* spent a little more time on researching historical records concerning Nazi war criminals right after the war, that much of this discussion, especially about Arthur Rudolph, would have taken a different direction.

There was not one word uttered about the outcome of the war crimes trial which was held in Dachau, Germany, in 1947, wherein all rocket scientists involved in the manufacture of V-2s were found innocent. Nor was there one word mentioned about the **fact that the OSI officials had full knowledge of this before they began the prosecution of Rudolph.**

As a result of the very lengthy and informative article in the *Times*, I wrote the editor, Mr. Joe Distelheim, a rather lengthy letter, giving him a more comprehensive coverage on certain aspects of the situation as they were discussed in the news clipping. I am therefore disclosing at this point the entire content, without the enclosures, of my letter:

Mr. Joe Distelheim
Editor The Huntsville Times
Huntsville, Alabama 35801   July 12, 2000

Dear Mr. Distelheim:

Your very lengthy article concerning the Office of Special Investigation
(OSI) Department of Justice (DOJ) in your June 18, 2000, issue was of
great interest to me. The article initially deals with the possibility of an
extension of the Congressional charter of the OSI. The article then goes
into some detail of the Arthur Rudolph case.

However, the item concerning the John Demjanjuk case was of special
interest. You mention it briefly, however OSI officials were involved in
a criminal action in this case, however you failed to mention it as such.
As stated, the OSI was guilty of withholding exonerating evidence on
Demjanjuk, prior to his being deported to Israel. There he stood trial,
and was sentenced to death based on false evidence furnished by the
OSI. Prior to the execution date, Demjanjuk filed an appeal. The Israeli
Supreme Court found that Demjanjuk was falsely charged by the OSI
investigation and set Demjanjuk free.

I wish to add that, prior to the ruling of the Israeli Supreme Court, the
OSI complimented themselves that the Demjanjuk case was one of their
greatest accomplishments. This is almost unbelievable, wherein OSI
officials, knowingly and willfully subject a U.S. citizen to the death
penalty by withholding exonerating evidence. This embarrassing
situation is painfully reminiscent of the operating tactics of the Gestapo
under Hitler. As stated in your article, Eli Rosenbaum, the current
director of the OSI, in his reaction to a later ruling by a Circuit Court
that the OSI acted recklessly, responded, "You have to live with that."
This is truly unconscionable on the part of Rosenbaum.

Now I wish to furnish you further information concerning evident
criminal activities of officials of the OSI in their prosecution of the
Arthur Rudolph case. I have been investigating and attempting to get
truth and justice resolved in that case for over 15 years. The actions by
the OSI after Rudolph returned to Germany are almost completely
unbelievable were it not for hard legitimate documentary evidence
which proves otherwise. I will furnish you only a portion of such
evidence as it would be too voluminous to cover the full story by
correspondence. Twice I requested the Department of Justice reconsider
the Rudolph case, furnishing them with new legitimate evidence, which

fully justified reconsideration. My first request in 1985 was ignored, and the response to my second request in 1987 was that I did not offer evidence for reconsideration.

Enclosed is a copy of a letter, dated July 23, 1985, from Eli Rosenbaum to a member of the Senate concerning the Arthur Rudolph case. Rosenbaum identifies himself as the chief prosecutor of the Rudolph case. The text of the letter implies that Rosenbaum has a tight open and shut case on the matter. I have evidence that reveals a number of inaccuracies in the letter; however, the most obvious lie I invite your attention to is in the last paragraph of the letter, which evidently denies East Bloc involvement in the case.

At this time, the Communist East Bloc was known as the 'Evil Empire.' This then was evidently an outright lie to Congress, which is a felony. The copy of the letter is marked Encl. 1. To substantiate this allegation, I am enclosing a copy of Diplomatic Note No. 433, dated July 15, 1983, from the U.S. Embassy in Berlin, to the East German prosecutor. This definitely links the OSI with the East Bloc concerning the Rudolph case. This note is marked Encl.2.

At this time, I wish to make a comment regarding this action about the note. The East German prosecutor, Guenter Wieland, in his response, dated December 15, 1983, to the note, gave exculpatory evidence in that no incriminating evidence had been found concerning Rudolph. Mr. Neal Sher, then director of the OSI, in his letter, dated April 26, 1985, to the West German prosecutor failed to include this document in his presentation on the Rudolph case. This withholding of exculpatory evidence is obstruction of justice, a felony on part of the OSI. Mr. Sher's letter will be mentioned later on in this discourse.

The following covers two House resolutions, which constitute some of the most gross, and contemptible lies, in my opinion, ever perpetrated upon the American public. I am referring to H.RES.68 of 1985, and H.RES.164 of 1987. Copies of these resolutions are enclosed and marked End. 3, and 4, respectively. Further evidence will reveal justification for the allegation expressed above. The texts of the resolutions are identical, and place the source of the information contained therein squarely on the Department of Justice and the OSI. The resolutions imply that Rudolph was responsible for the deaths of 20,000 to 30,000 workers, or concentration camp inmates. Evidence now reveals that there were about 5,000 camp inmates on the V-2 line, which was Rudolph's sole responsibility for production activities only.

Further that there was not one death on the V-2 line due to misconduct by Rudolph, or any of his 500 civilian staff.

Due to the highly complex nature of the V-2, requiring extremely close tolerances, etc., Rudolph was quite concerned about his workers welfare. As a result, he managed to get supplemental rations, better medical service, and clothing. Therefore the workers on the V-2 line, under Rudolph, were far better treated than those who worked in the tunnel digging operations, which were not part of Rudolph's responsibility, and where evidently many died.

*The above resolutions, though they did not pass, are still on public record, and are evidently being used as reference material by historians. One evident example of this is contained in a book, "The Rocket and the Reich," by Michael J. Neufeld, which was copyrighted by the Smithsonian Institution in 1995, our prime repository for U.S. history. The book contains many references to Rudolph; however, the greatest misstatement of fact is in the very first part of the book. The statement of dedication; "To the tens of thousands of prisoners who suffered, died—or survived—Dora and the other concentration camps of the V-2 program May their sacrifice never be forgotten" There evidently was only **one** camp involved in the V-2 production, Dora, and there were **four** operations taking place at the facility. There was tunnel digging, the jet engine line, the V-1 line, and the V-2 line; however, Neufeld places all the blame on the V-2, where there was not one death due to misconduct by Rudolph or his staff.*

Further, these two House resolutions, perpetrated upon a former distinguished U.S. citizen, were horrendous, contemptible lies, and being placed in public record, caused Rudolph and his family great stress and mental anguish for many years. Martha Rudolph, his widow, in a letter, dated November 19, 1996, to Chairman Henry Hyde, of the House Judiciary Committee, stated that the anguish, stress and despondency ultimately shortened his life. He died of a massive heart attack on January 1, 1996.

When Rudolph returned to Germany in 1984, the West German prosecutor promptly asked the Department of Justice for their file on Rudolph. He had to repeat this request several times due to the delays by the Department of Justice. The cause for the delay was evidently due to the action of the OSI, which in the meantime, was advertising in the news media for witnesses against Rudolph. A copy of news clipping concerning this is enclosed and marked Encl. 5.

Evidently, because of this advertising a Mr. Frank Barwacz, a former prisoner on the V-2 line, answered a questionnaire from the OSI. On page 5 of the questionnaire, he stated that he would gladly testify against the SS but not against any German civilians. He stated that all the German civilians were very kind to the prisoners.

This exculpatory evidence was not included in Mr. Sher's submission of documents, or listed Mr. Barwacz as a witness, to the West German prosecutor. This was another count of obstruction of justice by the OSI, another felony. A copy of Barwacz's statement is marked Encl. 6.

Mr. Sher finally responded to the West German prosecutor's request on April 26, 1985, just over a year after Rudolph left the U.S. He listed nine witnesses and some documentation. Upon interrogation by the West German prosecutor, four of the witnesses did not know Rudolph, one testified for him, two contradicted themselves, and two were mentally incompetent. This embarrassing situation revealed that the OSI failed to provide even one legitimate prosecution witness to substantiate their allegations. The documentation also failed to support the allegations. Where were the many witnesses, and legitimate documentation, that the OSI implied that they had when they evidently coerced Rudolph into signing The Agreement in November, 1983?? Due to the unusual nature of the case, the West German prosecutor conducted a very intensive investigation of the matter. After over two years, the interrogation of 65 witnesses, or depositions, and over 2300 pages of transcript, Rudolph was found not guilty of OSI allegations.

Rudolph was then granted citizenship in West Germany.

*This episode gives evidence of what evidently was contained in the OSI prosecution file on Rudolph, and which related to legitimate evidence concerning the case. This indicates that there was no such evidence. This is borne out by the **fact** that instead of making a prompt reply to the West German prosecutor, and giving him substantial evidence, the OSI advertised for witnesses against Rudolph, and a year later, failed to furnish him legitimate evidence to support their allegations. This also contradicts the implication in Eli Rosenbaum's letter; reference End .1, that he had a firm case against Rudolph.*

When the West German government found Rudolph not guilty of any war crimes in 1987, the OSI proclaimed to the news media that Rudolph was still a war criminal. Mr. Sher, then director of the OSI, further evidently lied wherein he stated that Rudolph and his 500 civilians were involved in the crimes by the SS troops or others. A copy of a news clip, dated March 19, 1987, from the San Jose Mercury News is enclosed, and marked Encl. 7. At the time, Rudolph had not ever been indicted, tried, or convicted as a war criminal.

I am enclosing a copy of a letter, dated may 20, 1985, from Mr. Frank Barwacz to President Reagan. Barwacz was evidently the only American citizen, who as a concentration camp inmate, worked on the V-2 under Rudolph. He emphatically states that Rudolph is 100% innocent, and that his life was saved several times by action of Rudolph's subordinates. This letter is marked Encl. 8.

Also enclosed is a copy of an affidavit dated September 1, 1985, from Mr. Gerhard Schramm, who also as a camp inmate who worked on the V-2 line under Rudolph. He also emphatically states that Rudolph treated the camp inmates well, got them additional rations, and "we prisoners had esteem and respect for Mr. Rudolph and I heard never a complaint about him from another prisoner." I have additional affidavits from other former prisoners who offer additional exculpatory evidence. A copy of Schramm's affidavit is marked Encl. 9

*In addition to the above, I have copies of two rather lengthy letters from Milton S. Hochmuth, who was the first U.S. Army intelligence officer who was on the scene when U.S. forces captured the V-2 facility. He also states that Rudolph is innocent. However he also states that; "I was so shocked to see the dead and the dying **ELSEWHERE** in the Nordhausen area," and he adds, "that there were at least two camps I know, and I remember concluding that the camp where the workers came from were not ill treated as were those in what were apparently near-by murder camps." Hochmuth completely clears Rudolph of any wrongdoing.*

The OSI evidently was not the only source of lies or misstatements of fact emanating from the Department of Justice concerning the Arthur Rudolph case. Because the OSI had advertised for witnesses after Rudolph left the States, I was intrigued by statements made by Assistant Attorney General John R. Bolton, in a letter, dated 29 January 1987, to Senator Pete Wilson. This is the same letter wherein Mr. Bolton invited me to present any new legitimate evidence concerning the Rudolph case. In paragraph three is the quote, "and when faced with incontrovertible evidence." Paragraph four reveals the following; "Let me assure you that before proceeding in cases such as the Rudolph matter, we at the Department of Justice carefully review the evidence and weigh its credibility. We proceed only after we are convinced that the evidence supports the allegations."

In a letter, dated December 7, 1995, I requested under the Freedom of Information Act, a copy of the documents which reveal the "incontrovertible evidence" referred to in Mr. Bolton's letter. The response from the Department of Justice, received by undated letter on July 22, 1996, consisted of a full three-inch thick stack of documentation. Most of it consisted of the sworn testimony taken by the OSI of the two interviews of Rudolph in 1982 and 1983, and was therefore mostly exculpatory evidence. After very careful examination, I could not find any incontrovertible or unimpeachable evidence of wrongdoing by Rudolph. Therefore, I contend that Mr. Bolton's reply is false on two counts; first, that Rudolph was not shown any "incontrovertible documentary evidence," because there evidently was none, and due to that fact, how could the Department of Justice "carefully review the evidence"??? This is indicative that the OSI obtained Rudolph's signature on The Agreement through coercion and duress.

The FBI has the responsibility of carefully investigating all personnel who are granted security clearances involving work on classified government programs or projects. The FBI granted Rudolph a TOP SECRET security clearance, evidently in the 1950's when he was working on the Pershing missile, which was designed to carry a nuclear warhead. Had any evidence surfaced during their very intensive background investigation, which I have been informed, included a lie detector test, the FBI could not have lawfully granted Rudolph that clearance. The FBI was also a recipient of my request under the Freedom of Information Act for information on the Rudolph case. The response, dated August 12, 1998, consisting of 107 pages of documentation, completely rebuts the OSI allegations. Now we have the embarrassing situation of two elements within the Department of Justice contradicting each other!

That war crimes did occur at Dora/Nordhausen was immediately recognized by the Allies. Intensive war crimes investigations were commenced in 1945 immediately after the war. After a long, thorough trial, the war crimes court found that the scientists were not guilty of all charges. The other defendants were all found guilty as charged and duly sentenced. A copy of news clipping from the Baltimore Sun, dated November 17, 1984, is enclosed and marked Encl.10.

This was written by Mr. Milton Crook, who was a member of the U.S. legal staff, and participated in the trial, which was held in Dachau, Germany, in 1947.

*It has become very evident that the outcome of this trial is a crucial element concerning the history of the Rudolph case. He was not even a defendant at the trial. As production manager of the V-2 line, he did have a sizable workforce of camp inmates, who were working on a very important item for the German Army. The reason that he was not a defendant was evidently very simple. There had not been **one** complaint filed against him from any of his 5,000-inmate workforce. Mr. Schramm, a former camp inmate, confirms this in his affidavit, see Encl. 9. In addition, the OSI was totally cognizant of the purpose and outcome of this trial. I again invite your attention to Diplomatic Note No. 433, Encl. 2.*

I now contend, that due to the fact that the OSI has failed to produce either witnesses, or legitimate documentary evidence to substantiate their allegations, and that the action of the FBI rebuts their allegations, and that the outcome of the war crimes court negates their actions, that the OSI did not have a logical justification to initiate an investigation of Rudolph.

At this point, my concern in this matter is in the public interest. It is my belief that the public wants the truth to be reflected concerning the emergence of this nation as the leader in the exploration of space. It has become very evident that inaccuracies and outright lies have surfaced which has contaminated that history from a number of sources. In this discourse, I have revealed that one of the main sources is the information emanating from the OSI. I believe that most people believe in the integrity of the Department of Justice, and that any information given out can be depended upon as being essentially truthful. However as revealed in this letter, the eminent stature of the Department of Justice has been badly flawed by the actions of the OSI concerning the Rudolph and Demjanjuk cases.

I am in possession of a number of news clips from the Huntsville Times, concerning V-2 production involving Dr. Wernher von Braun and Arthur. Of particular interest to me was a clipping, dated February 28, 2000, which was written by your Times Washington correspondent Brett Davis. In my opinion, Mr. Davis had some contact with the OSI, and as a result, evidently relying on the integrity and honesty of the OSI, believed that the information he was getting was correct. Because of this, there appears a statement in the second column of the clipping, and whatever the source, is a gross misstatement of fact; "Thousands died. In fact, more people died building the V-2 than did being hit by it." Another individual, Representative Green, who introduced the two House resolutions, which contained gross lies about Rudolph, was also evidently deceived by the OSI. Evidence previously given before in this dissertation supports my allegation above.

It is hard for me to understand the apparent lack of logic exhibited by some writers when they talk about the thousands that died during the manufacture of the V-2. They evidently did not understand that the V-2 was a very highly complex missile requiring highly skilled workmanship. Now how could a production manager, trying to meet almost impossible production schedules, willfully mistreat or kill some of his highly skilled workforce???

It is my belief that the American public has a right to know the truth about the beginnings of their history in the exploration of space. As I have referred to, there has been too much contamination of this information. I have much evidence in my files to support this statement. It has entered into TV presentations, magazine articles, and newspapers.

I am quite confident that the citizens of Huntsville would appreciate the truth about the space pioneers who turned their small town into a high tech city.

Sincerely, (Signed)
William E. Winterstein, Sr.
LTC Army (Ret.)

In my attempts to stem the contamination of our space history, I wrote my Senator, Diane Feinstein, a letter dated October 2, 2000, in which I referred to the two House Resolutions, 68 and 164, which I have previously discussed. The full content of this letter, without enclosures, is as follows:

Reference: House Resolutions; H.RES.68 of 1985, H.RES.164 of 1987.
October 3, 2000
The Honorable Diane Feinstein
U.S. Senate
Washington, D.C. 20510

Dear Senator Feinstein:

As my representative in the Senate, I wish to inform you of a serious problem that is now affecting the public interest of all American citizens. This problem is the current contamination of the early history of the United States of America in the emergence of this country as the world leader in the exploration of space.

The main reason I am coming to you is that I understand that you are a member of the Senate Judiciary Committee, and in my opinion this problem can only be solved by Congress, as evidence reveals that the Department of Justice (DOJ) has issued gross false information to Congress concerning the matter at hand. The secondary reason is that I am a duly recognized member, by Certificate of Achievement, NASA Headquarters, Washington, DC, as a member of the Apollo Team, which put U.S. astronauts on the moon in July 1969. As a member of this Team, I strongly oppose the contamination of our space history.

Briefly stated, the above referenced House resolutions contain gross lies about Arthur Rudolph, a former patriotic and distinguished American citizen, who as manager of the Saturn V Program, was instrumental in placing U.S. astronauts on the moon. The purpose of the resolutions, as indicated in the texts1 was for NASA to rescind the Distinguished Service Medal awarded to Arthur Rudolph in 1969. The resolutions, though they did not pass, are still public documents, available to the public. The source of the information, which constitutes the lies, is clearly revealed in the texts; the Department of Justice (DOJ) and the Office of Special Investigation (OSI). Thus the existence of the resolutions is evidently that Representative Green, who introduced the resolutions, relied on the honesty and integrity of the information furnished by the DOJ to be accurate, inadvertently lied to the American public by introducing the resolutions to Congress.

The House resolutions reflect the most current problem concerning history. However the background of the Rudolph case, wherein firm legitimate documentary evidence reveals gross and evidently criminal conduct on the part of certain DOJ officials involved in the case, evolves into an almost unbelievable story, were it not for the evidence. The question is; how could this possibly happen in the United States of America, wherein a devoted and patriotic citizen, who contributed so much in the defense effort of this country during the Cold war and later to the exploration of space, and then be exiled from the U.S. by duress and coercion, on false charges? This is painfully reminiscent of the tactics employed by the Gestapo and the KGB.

In my fifteen years' involvement in the Rudolph case, it has evolved from a very simple issue: whether the DOJ would reconsider the case, based on new and legitimate evidence substantiating reconsideration. Now the public interest of this nation, in a truthful rendition of a glorious event in the history of humankind is involved.

The DOJ has flatly and repeatedly refused to reconsider the case, even when furnished new and incontrovertible documentary evidence. The DOJ knew then that the innocence of Rudolph was settled in the course of war crimes prosecutions in Dachau, Germany in 1947, specifically dealing with atrocities at the prison camp Dora/Nordhausen. All scientists tried were found not guilty of any war crime. Many thousands of percipient witnesses were readily available at the time, however Rudolph was not even made a defendant at the trial, even though he was production manager of the V.- 2 line. There was not one complaint filed against him from any of the 5000 camp inmates who worked under him. Rudolph had been very much concerned about the welfare of his workers, trying to improve the working environment. He managed to provide them with supplemental rations, improved medical care, and clothing, all at risk to himself at the hands of the SS.

I have much evidence in the way of news clippings, references to TV programs, and magazine articles, by which those who wish to denigrate members of the German Rocket Team by issuing false and misleading information, or plain lies, have had their say. Without the combination of the Dr. Wernher von Braun and the President Kennedy affiliation in 1961, it is doubtful that the U.S. would have placed man on the moon.

Copies of the two House resolutions, H.RES.68 of 1985, and H.RES.164 of 1987 are included as enclosures No. 3, and 4, in my letter, dated July 12, 2000, to the Editor of the Huntsville (Alabama) Times, which is enclosed. This letter with its enclosures, gives direct evidence supporting my allegations of the contamination of space history. This very recent event is only a brief indication of what has happened in the past. I have documentary evidence concerning the contamination of space history in the past. However, the most significant rendition of this falsehood is that which is contained in the book, "THE ROCKET and the REICH." This book, authored by N.J. Neufeld, Curator of our Smithsonian Air and Space Museum, was copyrighted by no less than our guardian of American history, the

Smithsonian Institution in 1995. This book, in its very first part, the dedicatory statement, contains a gross lie. It indicates that "tens of thousands of prisoners" died as the result of building V-2s. This is essentially repeated later on in the book. This directly reflects the same kind of language as expressed in the texts of the house resolutions. Evidence contained in the enclosures to my letter to the Editor of the Huntsville Times reveals that not one death occurred in V-2 production due to misconduct of supervisory personnel.

The continued existence of the two House resolutions, evidently continue to be a threat to the validity, and the integrity of our history in space. Since they continue to be public documents there is evidence that some historians have evidently used the information as reliable historical reference material.

As my Senator, I hereby request that you take action to have House Resolutions, H.RES.68 of 1985, and H.RES.164 of 1987, either eliminated or nullified, and that the public be notified that they should no longer be available as a truthful source for historical research. I make this appeal to you, because Chairman Henry Hyde, of the House Judiciary Committee, has inexplicably ignored my requests to take this action.

Your assistance in this matter is respectfully requested. Please let me know what action you intend to take concerning this important matter.

Sincerely,
William E. Winterstein, Sr., LTC Army (Ret.)

Senator Feinstein ignored my request to take action on either eliminating or nullifying the two House resolutions, which apparently are one of the main sources of contamination of our space history, as I have not received a response to my request. Thus it has become quite evident that no member of Congress, either Republican, or Democrat, wants to assume responsibility in resolving truth and justice concerning the matter brought before them.

I have made a number of requests to my Congressman Elton Gallegly concerning the same issue of either eliminating or annulling the House resolutions, with the same result of being ignored, with the exception of receiving an informal note from his Chief of Staff of his home office, Brian Miller. This note is quoted: "Mr. Winterstein, Enclosed please find a copy of the response we received from the congressional record service regarding your concerns of H.RES.68 and H.RES.164. I hope this helped," signed Brian Miller.

I responded with the following letter, without enclosures, which in my files I have labeled as my final request for action on H.RES.68 and H.RES.164:

> *The Honorable Elton Gallegly*
> *2441 Rayburn Office Building*
> *Washington, D.C. 20515*
> *August 12, 2000*
>
> *Dear Elton:*
>
> *The memorandum, dated June 28, 2000, you received from the Congressional Research Service, addresses only that, since H.RES.68, 99th Cong., and H.RES.164, 100th Cong. were not approved, that the resolutions lacked legal impact. Therefore, there is no need for the House to take any action to rescind them.*
>
> *As indicated in my letter, dated May 1, 2000, to you, I stated that the existence of the two resolutions has an impact as a source of information for those eager to contaminate our early history in space. This item was not mentioned in the memorandum referred to above.*
>
> *Having truth reflected in any phase of this country's history is of prime public interest. Therefore, the "facts" purporting to underlie these two resolutions should be reconsidered and appropriate action taken to erase their impact and nullify their asserted historical value.*
>
> *These resolutions do exist and are available as public documents, and which were presented to the House. For ready reference a copy of each is enclosed, and marked End. 1, and 2, respectively. You have been previously furnished firm, conclusive, and legitimate documentary evidence that the allegation in paragraph four of both resolutions is a gross lie. That it is a lie is substantiated by the verdict(s) of a war crimes court, the statements by former prisoners who worked under Arthur Rudolph on the V-2 line, and the action by the FBI in granting Rudolph a TOP SECRET security clearance.*
>
> *As stated in the texts of the resolutions, the source of the information consisting of the lie is the Department of Justice and the Office of Special Investigation (OSI). I believe that the average citizen has the*

general viewpoint, due to the aura and eminence of the Department of Justice as our defender of truth and justice, to accept any information coming from there as the truth. It would be almost unbelievable that a gross contemptuous lie could come from that same source.

However, since the resolutions are public documents, it has become very evident that they have become a source of contamination of the history of this nation's eminence as the leader in the exploration of space. The book, "The Rocket and the Reich," by Michael Neufeld, curator, of **World War II History for the National Air and Space Museum,** *and copyrighted by the Smithsonian Institution in 1995, echoes the allegations in the resolutions. In the very dedication of the book is this statement, "To the tens of thousands of prisoners, who suffered, died— or survived—Dora and the other concentration camps of the V-2 program." This statement is false as there was only one camp involved in the V-2 program, and there was not one death on the V-2 line due to misconduct by production staff members.*

Another statement by Mr. Neufeld which directly links the allegations in the resolutions to public media disclosure is contained in an article in the Huntsville, Times, dated November 18, 1998, a copy of which is enclosed and marked Encl.3. In the early part of the article is the reference made to "the deaths of 20,000 prisoners."

Enclosed is another clipping, dated December 24, 1999, from the Huntsville Times which repeat the number of prisoners who died in reference to the V-2 plant. This clipping is marked Encl. 4.

One of the more recent news clippings, dated February 28, 2000, was written by the Times Washington correspondent, Brett Davis, is enclosed and marked End. 5. This article states; "Thousands died. In fact, more died building the V-2 than did being hit by it." The title of the article is grossly misleading; "V-2 plant survivors publicize their story." Your attention is invited to the bottom of the second column. The statement is attributed to a Mr. Baum; "where he helped build the tunnels, a grueling process that killed thousands," is not related to the activities on the V-2 line. At Camp Dora there were four activities going on at the same time, tunnel digging, jet engine production, V-1 production, and V-2 production. Almost all of the deaths were the result of the murderous methods employed in tunnel building activity, in which Rudolph had no part at all. It is absurd to suggest that all the blame for the deaths is on V-2 production.

What is truly amazing is the evident lack of knowledge exhibited by some writers in their discussion of "thousands" of deaths being attributed to the production of V-2s. The apparent total lack of honest common sense and just plain logic is ludicrous in face of the real facts, which were associated in the fabrication of the V-2. The V-2 was a very highly complex missile, about 46 feet long and weighing 14 tons. It required very highly skilled workmanship, involving very close tolerances, to produce. In particular, the propulsion and the guidance systems were highly innovative in design and fabrication, and the techniques used to produce them were not then mastered by any other engineers in the world. Therefore, a production manager would have severely countered his own efforts in producing V-2s for the German Army by willfully killing any of the highly trained, and scarce, workforces.

It can be clearly seen that the continued existence of the two House resolutions support the distortion of our early history in space, and are therefore contrary to the interest of the American public.

The audacity of the government official(s) who perpetrated this gross insult to the face of American truth and justice thirty-eight and again forty years after the matter was resolved by a war crimes court, must be guilty of gross abuse of and malfeasance in office.

Since the proposed House Resolutions are in the Record, it is incumbent upon the House to recognize their falsity. Therefore as my Representative, I request that you introduce a House Resolution, which in essence states that, the resolutions H.RES.68 of 1985, and H.RES.164 of 1987, are erroneous, and should not be referred to for historical or other purposes as fact. Further, that this action be pursued to the point where your resolution is passed. This should remove, or substantially nullify, the cloud of deceit wherein false information has been creeping into our history from a source which leads to our House of Representatives.

The continuing contamination of our history in space is very definitely against the public interest. To unduly delay, or ignore, corrective action concerning this matter would be unconscionable.

Please inform me on the action you intend to take in this matter.

Sincerely,
William E. Winterstein, Sr., LTC Army (Ret.)

Again I was ignored by my Congressman, as I did not receive a response concerning this important matter relating to our history. Because of my loss in appealing to the U.S. District Court, District of Columbia, in attempting to obtain, under the provisions of the Freedom of Information Act, the Prosecution Memorandum on the Rudolph case from the Department of Justice, I requested a meeting with Brian Miller, chief of staff of Rep. Gallegly's home office, in Oxnard, California. After the meeting, I made a Memorandum for Record, which follows:

MEMORANDUM FOR RECORD

February 20, 2001

This morning at 9:00 AM I met Brian Miller, Congressman Gallegly's chief of staff, from his home office in Oxnard, and with Joe Kern, my lawyer, in the City Hall in Fillmore, California.

The subject of the conversation centered around the amendment to the Nazi War Crimes Disclosure Act, sponsored by Senator DeWine on November 5, 1997. This amendment was a key factor, which caused the U.S. District Court, District of Columbia, to deny my appeal for copy of the prosecution memorandum on the Arthur Rudolph case from the Department of Justice. In addition, this ruling by the Court denied me the right to appeal to a U.S. District Court of Appeals, which in my opinion was unconstitutional. In addition, the amendment nullified the intent of the Freedom of Information Act. The text of the amendment also specifically exempted the Office of Special Investigations (OSI), Department of Justice, from disclosing any records that it had in its custody.

Mr. Kern pointed out the obvious contradiction of the matter and suggested that some congressional action be taken to investigate the operations being conducted by the OSI, since they have been involved in very questionable incidents in the past. This would be an effort to curb any further malpractice on part of the OSI in the future. Mr. Kern indicated that the amendment be withdrawn or eliminated.

Mr. Miller indicated that it would be very difficult, at the present time, to get any action taken on the subject. Congress is focused on taking action on the many areas brought up during the recent presidential campaign. Such as, tax cuts, health reform, education, and so forth. He pointed out that to get any action would be to get the members of Congress acquainted with the issue. He suggested that I write a detailed history of the matter so that Gallegly could endorse it and forward it to the proper committee for investigation.

Brian heartily agreed with my suggestion of me writing a book about the Rudolph case. That should arouse public reaction, and then Congress would be more assured to take action. I had indicated that the main obstacle in the case was the evident influence of certain political groups who did not want the truth to emerge concerning the Rudolph case. I suggested that the title of the book should be rather somewhat sensational, however reflect upon the truth of the matter, he agreed. There were also suggestions made that I write articles to scientific journals concerning the Rudolph case. I indicated that all my current efforts are in the public interest in trying to get truth reflected in our early space history and eliminate the current contamination of that history from our library shelves.

The above ended my Memorandum for Record concerning my meeting with Brian Miller, with Joe Kern.

After 20 years, from May 30, 1985, in which I attempted to resolve truth and justice in the Rudolph case through administrative, and a bit of judicial channels, without success, I decided to write this book. My initial efforts were on a very simple approach in attempting to convince the Department of Justice to reconsider the case on new and legitimate evidence, which had emerged since Rudolph returned to Germany. However, the adamant stand of the Department of Justice "stonewalled" me on that issue. Therefore, as evidence that is more legitimate evolved, the situation became a 'Pandora's Box' of political intrigue, which in my opinion is unbelievable that this happened in the United States of America.

It has become very evident, that in general, with only minor exceptions, that all Members of Congress have ignored my requests to take positive action in resolving truth and justice in the Rudolph case. I realize that it is a controversial issue when approaching issues related to allegations concerning Nazi war crimes. However, here we have incontrovertible evidence, which has surfaced wherein a former distinguished American rocket scientist, has been unlawfully prosecuted, and later persecuted, by a small organizational element within our very own Department of Justice.

By following the beginning of the contamination of history of this country's emergence into the exploration of space. I wrote a letter dated January 8, 2001, to the Secretary of the Smithsonian Institution, concerning an item of public interest. It referred to the gross misrepresentation of our early space history as represented in the book, *The Rocket and the Reich*, by M.J. Neufeld. Because of the Smithsonian's importance, that of providing information as our guardian of national history, I am furnishing the entire context of the letter including the enclosures:

January 8, 2001
Mr. Lawrence M. Small
Secretary, Smithsonian Institution
1000 Jefferson Drive S.W.
Washington, D.C. 20560

Dear Secretary Small:

I wish to bring to your attention, a matter of concern that affects the public interest; that is the contamination of early space history as represented in the book "The Rocket and the Reich" by M.J. Neufeld, copyrighted by the Smithsonian in 1995.

There is no doubt that the first part of the book contains three serious misstatements: (1) the allegation that "tens of thousands of prisoners" died while working directly on the production line of the V-2 rocket, (2) that those persons involved in the production of this rocket were guilty of war crimes, and specifically that (3) Arthur Rudolph was a war criminal" at the same time that he was production manager at Dora/Nordhausen. Simply stated, this re-write of space history as conceived by the author is not only historically incorrect, it also does a grave disservice to those members of the scientific community who gave so much of their remarkable talent to the United States space program. I will address each allegation briefly:

There was never even one complaint filed against Rudolph by any one of his 5,000 camp inmate workforce.

During the war crimes trial held in Dachau, Germany in 1947, Arthur Rudolph's innocence was clearly established. He was not even a defendant at that trial.

In 1987, the West German war crimes prosecutor found Rudolph not guilty.

In 1990, a Canadian Court found Rudolph not guilty.

The FBI conducted a thorough background check of Rudolph, which cleared him, and resulted in a Top Secret security clearance.

The evidence has concluded that Rudolph was not guilty of any war crime. Mr. Neufeld failed to reveal any direct evidence to support his allegations, also, he failed to give a comprehensive account of what actually occurred at the Camp Dora Complex.

I received 704 pages of documentation from the Department of Justice concerning the Rudolph case under the Freedom of Information Act that revealed much exculpatory evidence for Rudolph. I am sending copies of this letter to three members of Congress.

I have previously furnished them with evidence concerning Rudolph's innocence, and I will gladly furnish you with the same evidence.

Enclosed is a letter from Dr. Walter Haeussermann, the rocket expert who designed the analog computer to test the control system of the V-2 rocket. He was also responsible for the entire electronic and electrical system, which included the guidance and control system for the Saturn V launch vehicle for the lunar missions. He concludes that portions of the "Rocket and the Reich" contains numerous errors and senseless statements." A copy of this letter is marked Encl. 1.

Another example of Mr. Neufeld's apparent proclivity to denigrate the character of another great NASA space pioneer is contained in a critique by Dr. Gerhard H.R. Reisig, concerning a presentation by Mr. Neufeld, about Dr. Wernher von Braun, at a lecture at the University of Alabama, Huntsville, Alabama. A copy of this is enclosed, and marked Encl. 2.

It is my fervent hope that you may address this serious matter and respond to this letter at your earliest convenience.

Sincerely,
(Signed)
William E. Winterstein, Sr., LTC. Army (Ret)

2 Enclosures: Encl. 1, Ltr. Dr. Haeussermann Encl. 2, Critique, Dr. Reisig
cc: Sen. Diane Feinstein   Rep. Henry Hyde, Chrm. House Judiciary
Rep. Elton Gallegly   Daniel Goldin, Hq. NASA

The following is Encl. No. 1 Ltr. Dr. Haeussermann;

2/27/95
Subject: The Rocket and the Reich, *by M.J. Nuefeld, Curator SASM.*

Dear Mr. Heyman:

The Rocket and the Reich *contains a remarkable list of documents generated during WWII, books on the subject by various authors, and interviews by Neufeld with former Peenemünde employees.*

The book has received the AIAA History Manuscript Award mainly through the recommendation of historians, including NASA Chief Historian R. D. Launius and NASM Curator Von Hardesty.

Enclosed I am sending you my comments to some statements in Mr. Neufeld's book. The technical descriptions and conclusions contain numerous errors and senseless statements, despite the fact that Neufeld's interview questions were very thoroughly answered, most obligingly and colloquially. It is difficult to comprehend that not one of the Award nominators became aware of the erroneous statements or tried to obtain a review from competent persons.

The author's assessment of the non-technical part (some examples are given on page 2 of my comments) is equally deficient, and incomplete. His often-speculative assessments are in my opinion unworthy for an historian.

It is difficult to comprehend that the AIAA History Manuscript Award was approved after only a most superficial review and without the judgment of competent members from institutions or NASA.

I withdraw herewith permission to Mr. Neufeld to use the manuscript of his interview with me of January 24, 1990. *Further his assessments in the subject book have convinced me that he will be similarly incorrect and tendentious should he be allowed to use the manuscript in the future. I would appreciate if you would assure me of proper corresponding action taken.*

Sincerely,
(Signed) Walter Haeussermann
Enclosed: Comments to some erroneous and senseless statements in the, book "The Rocket and the Reich" by Michael Neufeld.

Feb. 20, 1995

TO WHOM IT MAY CONCERN:

Subject: Comments to some erroneous and senseless statements in the book "The Rocket and the Reich" by Michael J. Neufeld.

#1. Page 66, last sentence: The signals from the rate gyros were only able to dampen the motion of the rocket but not to push it back into its initial attitude.

#2. Page 70. The description of the interaction of the stable platform and the rocket does not make sense: the stable platform must remain space-fixed and means have to be provided that the rocket can turn with respect to the platform. The rotational freedom about the roll axis was not provided, nor was roll attitude control incorporated. These shortcomings caused the control failure. The author does not know the difference between "guidance" and "control" and uses the words arbitrarily.

#3 Pages 96: There is no "contrast" in obtaining the attitude signals on the Sg 52 and the A-3 platform Sg 33.

The author uses the words "position," "attitude," and "guidance" confusingly.

#4. Page 97, last sentence; an incomplete explanation, which does not make sense.

#5. Page 98, end of second paragraph: The author again shows that he has not understood the "stabilized platform," because the platform is space stabilized by its gyros and the missile pitches around the platform. The "complexity" was to provide the Cardin suspension of the platform for the missile rotation.

#6 page 162, last; paragraph: The author compares the flight results of the A4/V2 with the failure of the A-3. He concludes that the A4/V2 failure was "just as in the case of the A-3s," an absolutely illogical

comment of the author, who described the very different control systems of the two missiles in other parts of his book obviously without any comprehension.

It should be expected that an author, employed as curator at the National Air and Space Museum of the Smithsonian Institution attempts to give an unbiased historical account. His one-sidedness is evident throughout his book. A few examples are as follows:

One of the pictures between pages 210 and 211 carries the inscription: "A-4 production led directly to the deaths of thousands of prisoners at the Mittelwerk and elsewhere." The fact is that not a single death, not even a deadly accident occurred because of manufacturing in the Mittelwerk, for which supervising German technical personnel were responsible. Actually, in the original Nordhausen war crimes trial at Dachau, Germany, the court adjudged the scientists not guilty of all charges. Enclosure 1 is a publication by Mr. Milton Crook, a member of the legal staff, who participated in the original war crimes trial at Dachau, Germany, in 1947. His statements are known to OSI, but are not mentioned in Neufeld's book.

On page 184 Neufeld writes: "After the war the Peenemünders made the SS a scapegoat for all the crimes associated with the rocket program, yet the initiative for this action came not from the SS but from the A-4 Special Committee and Arthur Rudolph." One page later Neufeld writes that "Degenkolb [as a member of the Armament Ministry] formed the A-4 Special Committee"! Then Neufeld mentions that Mr. Jaeger headed a Labor Supply Committee for Degenkolb, who belonged to the Staff of Speer, Minister of Armament. Jaeger visited Peenemünde on April 8/9 and recommended the employment of concentration camp inmates. Consequently, Rudolph had to join the A-4 Special Committee to visit the Heinkel Aircraft Works in Oranienburg, where in only 8 months Heinkel had increased the number of prisoners from zero to four thousand. The matter-of-fact report from the visit with the conclusions of the Committee does not show in any way that Rudolph was "enthused" (as imputed by Neufeld) about the "advantages" (again a Neufeld invention) of concentration camp labor. Obviously, Neufeld, like OSI employees, cannot imagine what it means to live in a dictatorship during a war. When Rudolph was requested by a member of the armament ministry to join the committee to visit Heinkel Aircraft Works he could not refuse without being reprimanded, if not penalized seriously.

Neufeld must have neglected intentionally whatever is contradicting OSI claims. The letters of Professor Milton Hochmuth to Senator Sam Nunn are just one example. Enclosure 2 is a copy of one of his letters. I shall be glad to give numerous additional examples.

*Throughout his book, Neufeld gives assessments degrading motives of Peenemünders. He takes for granted the claims of OSI without any attempt to find out whether or not they are correct. **A typical example is that Sawatzki's secretary testified that sabotage reports did go through the production manager's [Rudolph's] hands. Actually, OSI did not obtain any confirmation when the OSI investigators contacted the secretary. She clarified in a follow-up letter her statement, which she had given in the interrogation about Sawatzki.***

(Signed) Walter Haeussermann

An additional comment in an open letter to Neufeld from Ernst Stuhlinger may be found in the Appendix titled Stuhlinger open letter to Neufeld. The following is Encl. No. 2, a memorandum from Dr. Reisig; (The memorandum concerns a lecture held at the University of Alabama, Huntsville.)

About Wernher von Braun's Ethical Integrity

On November 17, 1998, M. Neufeld (Smithsonian NASM; author of "The Rocket and the Reich") presented at UAH a lecture on a historical period of the German genesis of rocket technology. This lecture was limited by the Department of History, UAH, as a "History Forum." The topic of this lecture was chosen as "Wernher Von Braun and the Third Reich." It is not known whether this subject was selected by the lecturer Neufeld, or whether it was proposed by the UAH Department of History.

As a matter of fact, Mr. Neufeld undertook to prove that Wernher Von Braun had a split personality, "neither solely black nor white." This, allegedly, makes W. v. Braun guilty of the lack of moral responsibility with regard to the employment of forced labor at "Mittelwerk." These laborers' most deplorable, physical, and mental suffering was caused by their rude use for manufacturing of weaponry in the "Mittelwerk," the ill-famed underground factory in Northern Thuringia (Germany).

Thus, Lecturer Neufeld explained his concept of Wernher von Braun's alleged split personality as:

"White" for W. v. Braun's unquestioned genial leadership as the most outstanding promoter of rocket and space technologies, and as a space visionary during his entire adult lifetime.

"Black" for W. v. Braun's alleged approval of employing forced labor for the manufacturing of War materials, and his lack of effecting the proper living and working conditions of each human individual.

The emphasis of the Forum lecture was concerned with the "black" side of W. v. Braun's personality. At this point of personal analysis, as reported in the three mentioned commentaries, esteemed H. Lowers "hits the spot": Author Neufeld may be a good writer, but he definitely is not a competent, professional historian.

*His concept of "History" fails by the same ill conceived attitude of **many so called "historians" who try to explain the intrinsic meaning of historical events, rather than to just report historical events as far as they are reliably documented.** From this tendency result too many distorted explanations of factual documents in Mr. Neufeld's writings.*

Mr. Neufeld lives in a too distant time period from the "Third Reich" to have the slightest feeling amid proper appreciation of the meaning of living under a cruel dictatorship. Any individual living at that time knows only the merciless alternative "Do (and think!) as ordered or risk your life."

*As to W. v. Braun's alleged "approval" of the use of forced labor: Mr. Neufeld again seems to miss the historical fact, that W. v. Braun was the technical director of rocketry developments at Peenemünde. In his position in the organizational order, he had no authority of deciding on the employment of forced labor. **He had to report his pertinent objections to the "Executive Director" of Peenemünde, General Dornberger. However, even this General had to report about such fundamental matters to A. Speer, Minister for Armament Production. Nevertheless, here surfaces the critical point about A. Speer's authority: He was the archenemy of Himmler, the High Commander of the SS, who hated Speer just as much as Speer hated him. Himmler managed to obtain Hitler's approval for the employment of concentration camp prisoners in the Mittelwerk productions. How could W. v. Braun act directly against Himmler in the matter of forced labor?***

In spite of being appointed an "Honorary SS Officer" by Himmler, W. v. Braun ended up in prison, having been seized at night by Himmler's justice negating "Gestapo." This craven act was Himmler's revenge for W. v. Braun's unshakable loyalty to General Dornberger. This steadfastness of W. v. Braun to his immediate superior, in itself proves W. v. Braun's moral integrity.

The only activity required of W. v. Braun at the Mittelwerk was the inspection of the quality of the end product, the complete A-4-Rocket (Göbbels: "V-2"). His Staff personnel for these control functions were members of his Peenemünde development team who were, of course, independent of the permanent technical staff of the Mittelwerk.

*Hypothetically, that W. v. Braun could have requested the manufacturing of the A4-Rocket be done by skilled German workers, instead of the less qualified and less reliable forced labor (detainees), in order to procure top quality rockets. However, to no avail! **There were no such German skilled workers available. Hitler had drafted this most valuable workforce only to have it slaughtered in the hopeless fighting conditions on the Russian front, as I witnessed from my own deployment in Russia in 1943.** Hence, the forced workers were the only manufacturing crews the Ministry of Armament could supply.*

In certain publications, W. v. Braun has been accused of being a war criminal, and finally the whole Peenemünde team was included in this most heinous category. In his commentary of November 22, 1998, the staff writer M. Burkey of the Huntsville Times dared to state: "The issue of whether Wernher von Braun or members of his team were war criminals is not likely to be settled any time soon." If the developers of a long-range, self-controlled rocket are defamed "war criminals," then the same defamation holds true for the designer of a "tank," or for a designer of a fighter plane, or even for a woman manufacturing artillery shells at a lathe. This scornful classification of people serving their country was positively cleared by the British shortly after the last world war. Consequently, General Dornberger was cleared of all charges; otherwise, he, a prisoner of the British, would have been hanged as a war criminal.

*In conclusion, as I mentioned in my remarks during the discussion period after Mr. Neufeld's lecture, I worked with W. v. Braun for 33 years and had ample opportunity to get familiar with von Braun's personality; certainly far more so than Mr. Neufeld who never met him. Mr. Neufeld's judgment of W. v. Braun's "black-white" split personality might be qualified as willful nonsense by a **poorly substantiated "Quasi-Historian." Mr. Neufeld's "standing" is too "small" to touch Dr. von Braun's integrity.***

The above is the end of Dr. Reisig's memorandum on his comments of Mr. Neufeld's lecture at the University of Alabama, Huntsville.

Also to be noted is that **Mr. Neufeld is a Canadian citizen** acting as curator for the Smithsonian!

As a member of the NASA Apollo Team which put U.S. astronauts on the moon. I was very much concerned about what was appearing in the news media, and other publications concerning this country's history in space. The following is a letter, dated January 8, 2001, that I sent to NASA Headquarters with the suggestion that NASA become more involved in what is appearing concerning NASA's history:

January 8, 2001
Daniel S. Goldin
Administrator, NASA Headquarters
300 E Street S.W.
Washington, D.C. 20546

Dear Mr. Goldin:

The reason for my letter is to bring to your attention the fact that some events concerning our early history in space exploration have become contaminated. One of the most recent examples of this is the subject of my letter to Mr. Small, a copy of which is enclosed. This denigrates the glorious and historical role of NASA in placing the United States of America as the world leader in the exploration of space.

There have been a number of such incidents in the past. I have accumulated evidence concerning such contamination as related in the book, "The Rocket and the Reich," in TV programs, newspapers, books, and magazine articles.

As a member of the Apollo Team, I was rather shocked to learn that Mr. Neufeld was the Curator of the Smithsonian Air and Space Museum. His lack of common sense logic as displayed in the book was amazing. He did not indicate that the V-2 was a very highly complex missile, weighing 14 tons, 46 feet long, and that it required highly trained workers to fabricate it. However he claims "tens of thousands died" while working on it. Firm evidence reveals that no one died on the V-2 line due to supervisory management, and that the entire workforce of camp inmates involved was only 5000.

I suggest that NASA takes a more critical role in determining what is coming out and appearing on our library shelves, and news media, concerning our history in space.

As a retired member of NASA, I consider this proliferation of false and misleading information concerning the history of our country in the exploration of space a very serious matter of public concern. The public expects, and deserves, to receive a truthful rendition of historical events.

I will be happy to furnish you with additional information concerning this matter.

Sincerely,
William E. Winterstein, Sr., LTC. Army (Ret)
One Encl. Cpy. Ltr. Mr. Small

I received a quite prompt response from the Smithsonian, dated February 20, 2001, to my letter, Here is the reply, verbatim:

Smithsonian
National Air and Space Museum
Division of Space History
February 20, 2001

Dear Mr. Winterstein:

Secretary Small has forwarded to me your letter regarding the work of Dr. Michael Neufeld. As Chairman of the Division of Space History of the National Air and Space Museum, I am most directly concerned with the issues you raise. NASM and the Smithsonian recognize their special responsibility to make sure that exhibits and public programs provide accurate and balanced accounts of the subjects and issues they present. As for the individual work of our professional staff, we also recognize that we must hold our curators to the highest professional standards.

I have reviewed the points made in your letter and respect the deep concern and the amount of work I can imagine has gone into its preparation. That said, I would also like to express my confidence in and respect for Dr. Neufeld, his scholarship and the enormous contributions he has made and continues to make to the Museum, the Smithsonian, and to the historical profession.

I recognize that some of Dr. Neufeld's work challenges some long-held and deeply felt beliefs and that, as in the case with all scholarship, further evidence, analysis or argument may well lead to the revision or even the overturning of some of his conclusions. Future research, on the other hand, may well confirm, and strengthen what he has written. To his credit, Dr. Neufeld's submissions were subject, in advance, to rigorous professional review. His book won the AIAA History Manuscript Award for 1995 and the Dexter Prize of the Society for History of Technology for 1997.

Those accomplishments aside, I do appreciate your perspective on these matters is quite different from Dr. Neufeld's. I also know that issues much like those you raise have been discussed in the published literature. I do follow such discussions with interest.

Sincerely,
(Signed) Allan A. Needell, Chairman
Cc: J. R. Dailey, Director NASM
Secretary Small

The following is the response from NASA Headquarters to my letter to Mr. Goldin.

National Aeronautics and Space Administration
Headquarters Washington, DC 20546-0001
January 30, 2001

Reply to Attn of:
William E. Winterstein

Dear LTC. Winterstein:

Thank you for your letter of January 8, 2001, to NASA Administrator Daniel S. Goldin regarding your concerns about recording the history of the role played by Wernher von Braun, Arthur Rudolph, and others in developing the V-2 during World War II. To be sure, there is a debate-taking place concerning the moral implications of developing rockets for use in warfare, and specifically of the Nazi use of concentration camp inmates to build the V-2. The work of Dr. Neufeld that you object to is well known, but he will certainly not have the final word on the subject as other writers are also making their cases. In this process of point and counterpoint, additional historical understanding should emerge in the marketplace of ideas. The place of Wernher von Braun and his rocket team in this marketplace will no doubt remain secure, for they successfully built the first operational rocket.

I would encourage you to present your understanding of this issue as articles in historical and spaceflight periodicals, for it is an important historical debate in which all voices should be heard. NASA is confident that aerospace history benefits from the free and open debate among informed individuals.

Thank you for your interest in NASA and its history. If you have questions, please feel free to contact the NASA Chief Historian, Dr. Roger D. Launius.

Sincerely,
(Signed) Beth M. McCormick Associate Administrator for Policy and Plans (Acting)

The extensive article referred to in the following letter appeared, beginning on the front page of the *Wall Street Journal*, on November 10, 2004. The vilifying remarks in one of this nation's most highly respected and honored newspapers concerning America's two top space pioneers and heroes, is increasing evidence of the trend of a hate crime being perpetrated against our distinguished scientists because of their ethnic origin of being German. The letter clearly reveals the evident ignorance of past historical events being ignored, and utter stupidity regarding the very complex construction of the worlds first guided missile. This situation concerning a treasured important national heritage demands immediate action by our government, evidently by oversight activity by our Congress, as the Department of Justice, and the Smithsonian Institution, are involved in this national disgrace of political parody.

William E. Winterstein Sr,. LTC Army (Ret.)   *November 30, 2004*
EDITOR
The Wall Street Journal
World Financial Center
New York City, New York 10281
Re: "Huntsville, Alabama Rocketeers' Legacy Has Complex Echoes"
(Journal, November 10, 2004)

Sir:
As I read this piece, some words of Rev. Dr. Martin Luther King Jr. come immediately to my mind, words neatly applying to the views of those

quoted in the article vilifying members of the rocket team led by Dr.
Wernher von Braun: "Nothing in all the world is more dangerous than
sincere ignorance and conscientious stupidity."

It is easily evident that the people quoted are ignorant of the results of
the war crimes trials conducted at Dachau, Germany, in 1947,
specifically relating to abuses at the Dora/Nordhausen complex. Upon
the facts determined after intensive investigation and while
recollections were fresh, the court found all of the rocket scientists not
guilty. Beyond that, Arthur Rudolph, the manager of the V-2 production
line was not even a defendant there, or any other proceedings. Why?
Rudolph was something of a hero to his 5000 man camp inmate
workforce, providing them with supplemental rations, improved medical
attention and clothing. There was not one complaint against him.

Rudolph's story ranks with, and even exceeds, Schindler's. The hero of
"the list" befriended about 1000 camp inmates and did nothing for the
United States. Rudolph brought relief to about 5000 camp inmates and
helped give America a technological victory in the midst of the Cold
War and helped turn the balance of world power in favor of his beloved
adopted country.

The sources in your article were apparently also unaware that there
were four distinct operations going on at the same time at the
Dora/Nordhausen site:1) V-1 production, 2) V-2 production, 3) jet
aircraft engine production, an 4) tunnel digging. Each was separate
from the others. Many prisoners did indeed die in the tunneling, as Mr.
Baum says, under horrendous conditions, but none of that operation
was under the supervision of any of the rocket scientists.

Your sources are also wrong about Jewish prisoners involved with the
manufacture of the V-2. The only American citizen/prisoner who worked
on the V-2 line gave testimony that no Jews were present there.

Bob Ward is quoted in the latter part of the article about "Dr. von
Braun's flaw." I was custodian of the German rocket team at Fort Bliss,
Texas in 1945. It was von Braun's intense desire to get started on missile
defense immediately. He correctly perceived a Russian threat to
America because of the surrender of the V-2 plant and the Soviets'
capture of a number of German rocket scientists. von Braun did exhibit
one flaw in wartime Germany: he was arrested by the Gestapo for being
inattentive to the Reich's war effort.

I would very much like to see a clear declaration on your front page stating that Arthur Rudolph's innocence of crime was established by war crimes prosecutors at Dachau, Germany, in 1947. I am requesting that the Wall Street Journal, as one of the most respected newspapers in the country, take up the task of restoring truth and respect to the glorious patrimony of this nation. The history of our entry into the space age, and of those scientists who made it possible, will be deeply appreciated by every American who wants our history straight and uncontaminated. Let me suggest also that you investigate the current trend toward defaming our nation's top space pioneers, von Braun and Rudolph. That our Department of Justice and even the Smithsonian Institution are involved amounts to a national disgrace.

Sincerely yours, William E. Winterstein, Sr.

On December 20, 2004, at 11:00 PM, Pacific Time, the "History Channel" presented an hour long program titled: *Conspiracy—the CIA and the Nazis*. Basically the program was in two parts. The second part dealt with the "Paperclip" rocket scientists, and specifically with Arthur Rudolph. The tone of the whole program was that nothing was gained from the Germans by the U.S. whether it be intelligence or scientific or engineering in nature that was of any value. The slanderous remarks against Rudolph were through repeated interviews with ex-Congresswoman Elizabeth Holtzman and OSI Director Eli Rosenbaum. Finally after claims that 20,000 slaves died as a result of Rudolph's actions, the statement was made that Rudolph was really a CEO, managerial type, not an engineer or scientist. Thus, like many "Paperclip" war criminals, had nothing of a technical or engineering skill to offer the U.S.

The "History Channel" is one of if not the most popular of television channels where American citizens go to for a source depicting truthful history. This is further prima-facie evidence that the program referred to above is a gross contemptuous lie perpetrated by direct aid of the OSI upon the American public. As referred to in other parts of the book, this adds to the contamination of this nation's space history.

This act of national disgrace, follows similar acts this year involving insults against our national space heroes. The first by television program "Jeopardy" on March 1, 2004, followed by the *Wall Street Journal* on November 10. **Will these hate crimes, based on senseless stupidity, continue?**

.

20

Where Is America's Lunar Landmark?

Where in America is the nationally recognized monument dedicated as the spot where this country achieved the victory of performing the greatest technological feats of humankind, man's first journey to the moon? Not one brick has been laid to commemorate that historic national event. True, there has been action by the City of Titusville, Florida, the gateway to the Kennedy Space Center, to commemorate the event, however this falls far short of the nationally recognized location of where the moon mission was actually engineered.

History clearly defines the exact spot where the moon mission was engineered and successfully carried out, and reveals the names of this country's two top space heroes and pioneers. At the time President Kennedy proclaimed that America was going to the moon "in this decade" in 1961, Marshall Space Flight Center in Huntsville, Alabama, was given the assignment, to engineer and produce, the giant rocket boosters which took our astronauts to the moon. Dr. Wernher von Braun was director of Marshall Space Flight Center at the time. Arthur Rudolph, under von Braun, was manager of the Saturn V Program, which produced the rocket boosters.

The Kill Devil Hill Monument National Memorial, established at Kitty Hawk, North Carolina, on March 2, 1927, commemorating man's first powered air flight is a fitting historical edifice to American ingenuity. The establishment of this monument was accomplished just 24 years after the event.

It took about 50 years of slow development after the event in 1903 at Kitty Hawk, for humankind to reap significant benefits, such as air travel affordable to the average person. The delivery of mail by air, introduced in the mid-'20s, was an earlier benefit.

The total lack of a national monument commemorating humankind's greatest technological achievements, engineered by the United States of America, for the world to behold, exhibits a gross flaw in American history. In the year 2004, it has been *35 years after the event* without one brick laid for the occasion. A thinking man must ask; "Why is not a national monument erected for our piece of American heritage which has set us up as the world leader in the exploration of space"?

Here is but a glimpse of what a foreigner's opinion of the situation is: Dr. Ernst Stuhlinger, currently the top living rocket scientist in the world today, was visiting the Huntsville, Alabama, Space and Rocket Center, in May 2000. He was greeted there by a young member of the Russian space program. During the conversation, this subject came up. The Russian made this comment; "There is one profound difference between your space programs and ours: in Russia, our space pioneers are heroes, and we build monuments for them. **The Germans and the Americans treat their most prominent space pioneers as war criminals. We in Russia could never understand that. Why are they doing this?**" See complete recollection in Appendix titled A Visitor from Russia

The question by the Russian truly 'hits the nail on the head' for a prudent logical minded man to ponder. "Why are THEY doing this"? From my experience in writing this book, and with the abundance of legitimate documented evidence that I have on hand, the facts are startling to say the least. The word THEY opens up a huge Pandora's Box of apparent national and international intrigue. The question now focuses on who are the individuals who are the guiding force behind THEY?

It has become apparent to me that there is an insidious and evasive force in the U.S. whose motive is to try to subdue the true facts of American space history and vilify our space pioneers and heroes. Their target is members of the rocket team led by Dr. Wernher von Braun which placed U.S. astronauts on the moon. The cause for this vendetta is of the ethnic origin of the team members, which is German.

Clear evidence of the work of this insidious force surfaced on March 1, 2004.

On the popular televison quiz show "Jeopardy," the question was asked: "What rocket scientist, a Nazi war criminal, gained entry to the U.S. by Operation Paperclip." The immediate response was "Wernher von Braun." Because of the fact that Wernher von Braun was never tried, convicted, or officially accused of a war crime, and being the No.1 space pioneer and hero of our country, I found this answer an inexcusable perpetuation of a lie. I filed a complaint with Attorney General John Ashcroft to investigate and prosecute this as a hate crime. Again the very serious question arises which directly affects the truth, integrity, and destiny of our national space history. How much perversion has this insidious force affected our news media and library shelves to cause unsuspecting citizens to lie to the American public?

This literary cancer affecting the integrity of our historical heritage must be removed to ensure that truth will endure as a cornerstone of American belief. A copy of my letter to Attorney General John Ashcroft is in the Appendix so titled.

Last year, 2003, I perceived another inkling on the scope and power that this insidious force has on the lives of the American public. I intended to go to the American public in pursuing my quest that a nationally recognized monument should be established in commemorating of our glorious victory of the lunar mission. I thought that it would be appropriate to do this during the 100th anniversary year of Kitty Hawk, man's first powered aircraft flight. A letter to the Editor has been a time-honored means for the common citizen to have his opinions known to the general public. I wrote 143 'letters to the editor' to at least two major newspapers of every state in the Union, from Alaska to Florida, from Maine to Hawaii. I clearly outlined the desirability and need of a nationally recognized monument commemorating our country's great technological gift to humankind, and to preserve this historical heritage for future generations of Americans to observe. I do not know what happened to any of these letters, as I did not receive a single response concerning this important subject of the truthful preservation of American space history. The question then occurred to me; does this insidious force, which has evidently contaminated our space history, have any control over the national press or mail delivery process? A copy of my letter, which I mailed to the editors, is Appendix titled Letter to Editors.

On June 7, 2003, I wrote President Bush a letter to accompany a presentation of a copy of my first book, *Gestapo U.S.A.—When Justice Was Blindfolded*. Since this was the 100th anniversary year of Kitty Hawk, I requested that it would be most appropriate that the lunar landing of American astronauts be also commemorated within the 100-year period, as it was also the 34th anniversary that the moon mission was successfully completed. I suggested that this be accomplished by his issuing an Executive Order. I commented that all Americans should be very proud of the historical fact that their country achieved both Man's first air flight and Man's first voyage to the Moon within the same century (actually within 65 years)! Indeed, what a magnificent historical legacy that we will hand down to future generations of American citizens. A copy of my letter to President Bush is later in this chapter.

In almost a year, I have not received a response from the White House concerning the huge void in American history that a nationally recognized place has not been designated as the origin of America's greatest technological victory and humankind's leap into outer space.

This huge void in American space history has been of much concern to me as a member of the Apollo team, which put our astronauts on the moon, and now a member of NASA Alumni League. As indicated before, the fact is, this country's two top space heroes, Dr. Wernher von Braun, and Arthur Rudolph, have been portrayed to the American public as Nazi war criminals, when legitimate evidence reveals the exact opposite facts. von Braun was jailed in wartime Germany by the Gestapo for being inattentive to the German war effort. Rudolph, as manager of the V-2 production line was hero to the 5000 camp inmates who worked on the V-2s, by providing supplemental rations, clothing and medical attention for them.

Rudolph's story far surpasses that portrayed in "Schindler's List."

The question now arises, after 36 years why do we not have a monument to our moon mission? In my opinion, it arises from an ethnic vendetta against the origin of the rocket scientists who made the United States the leader among nations in space exploration. The fact is that the scientists were of German ethnic origin. An indication of who may be behind the driving force in attempting to suppress a national monument for America to venerate its space heroes is revealed in newspaper clipping from the

Las Vegas (Nevada) *Israelite*, dated, January 11, 1985. On this occasion, the Department of Justice has asked the World Jewish Congress in locating survivors among laborers who worked in the V-2 factory. Evidence has revealed that this incident must be one of the most disgusting black marks on the face of American justice in its history. At the time, the Department of Justice was frantically trying to assemble witnesses *against* Arthur Rudolph who they exiled from country the year before without one shred of legitimate evidence to substantiate their act. The Department of Justice had accomplished this involuntary exile of Rudolph by convincing him that they had a solid case against him. Department officials had stated to Rudolph that the witnesses and documentary evidence they possessed was firm evidence against him. After Rudolph's return to Germany the West German war crimes prosecutor had asked the Department of Justice for the criminal file on Rudolph. Instead of promptly handing over a legitimate file, Department officials were scrambling for witnesses to substantiate their allegations. The net result of the Department's search for witnesses against Rudolph in the news media was zero. In fact, two of the witnesses were for Rudolph, one a very strong supporter.

My question about this incident is what role is the World Jewish Congress playing in this affiliation with the Department of Justice concerning a matter of space history of this country? It is my hope that Attorney John Ashcroft conducts an unbiased investigation into who perpetrated the hate crime against Wernher von Braun. The very words, the '**World**' Jewish Congress, bear an ominous overtone. What entity in the world do they govern?

As a U.S. citizen, I would assume that the Smithsonian Institution, our guardian of this country's history would be instrumental in sponsoring the erection of a memorial for a history-making event. This definitely was not in the course of events regarding America's first journey to the moon. Instead of praise emanating from that institution, a book copyrighted by the Smithsonian in 1995, strongly vilified this country's No. 2 space hero, Arthur Rudolph. In his book, *The Rocket and the Reich*, Michael J. Neufeld, Curator of the Smithsonian Air and Space Museum, previously mentioned in the chapter on Contamination of Early Space History.

Currently there is evidently a vibrant need for the establishment of a national memorial commemorating America's, great technological achievement, and great gift to all humankind, man's first voyage to the moon. This precious national historical heritage must be preserved for future generations to observe in dignity and truth. It should not be obscured in an ominous cloud of deceit, acrimony, and viciousness engendered against our space heroes by evidently a foreign influence because of their ethnic origin being German.

America must protect her historical heritage before it is lost.

The following letter was sent to President Bush with no response.

William E. Winterstein, Sr., LTC. Army (Ret.)
Reference: A void in American history.   *June 7, 2003*
The Honorable George W. Bush
President of the United States
The White House
Washington, D.C. 20500

Dear President Bush:

As a member of the Apollo Team who put our astronauts on the moon in 1969, I am presenting you with a copy of my book; Gestapo USA— When Justice Was Blindfolded.

This book reveals the true history wherein two of the greatest, and distinguished, American space heroes and pioneers, brought the United States from humiliating defeat by the Soviet Union, due to Sputnik, to be the leader in the world in the exploration of space. I am speaking of Dr. Wernher von Braun, and Dr. Arthur Rudolph.

It also is an intriguing story of how the 118 German rocket scientists who designed and fabricated the first guided missile in the world, the German war-time V-2, were invited by President Truman to come to this country immediately after WWII to assist our nation in research for missiles for our own defense. This rocket team was headed by Dr. Wernher von Braun. I was very fortunate in being selected as custodian of this group during the very critical first year after their arrival in this country.

This year in December this nation will be celebrating the 100th anniversary of man's first flight by aircraft. The name and location of this event is nationally recognized as Kitty Hawk, North Carolina. The people responsible for this achievement are nationally recognized as Orville and Wilber Wright. This historical fact has been nationally recognized for many years.

*Yet this year, 34 years after the event, there has been no nationally designated location of where man's first flight to the moon **originated**, that is, where did the plans and designs of the moon mission take place, and who were the primary persons responsible for the event? We know that the vehicles departed from Cape Kennedy, and that the astronauts rode them to the moon, but without the vehicles there would be no footprints of U.S. astronauts on the moon today.*

My book contains the documented evidence to support the following suggestion which would eliminate a void in the history of the United States of America. I suggest that you execute, by Executive Order, a Proclamation that the Marshall Space Flight Center in Huntsville, Alabama, was the focal point of man's first flight to the moon. Further, that Dr. Wernher von Braun for his technical and administrative expertise, and that Dr. Arthur Rudolph, for his outstanding performance as manager of the Saturn V Program, be named as national heroes in accomplishing this event.

Indeed that glorious moment in history wherein our country leaped ahead of the world in performing the greatest technological achievement of all mankind should be duly recorded in proper manner. All Americans should be very proud of the historical fact that their country achieved both man's first air flight and man's first voyage to the moon within 100 years! Indeed, what a magnificent historical legacy that we will hand down to future generations of American citizens.

Your kind consideration of this suggestion should be appreciated by every American citizen.

Sincerely, signed William E. Winterstein, Sr.
Two enclosures: :1 book, 1 book review

21

U.S. Space Heroes Betrayed

The most incredible chapter in the lives of the original rocket team, hand picked to be brought to this country by Wernher von Braun, is how dedicated they were and that they stayed with the team. Also how those who later joined his tightly knit team became dedicated to the task at hand. That the unbelievable treatment that they received from U.S. institutions and governmental departments after they presented the United States its greatest technical achievement in all humankind. Their patriotism and dedication to the well being of their adopted country, far exceeded that of the average American citizen. They each forfeited a personal financial fortune to remain employed as civil servants and remain intact as a team rather than go to private industry at higher pay. The main reason for remaining as a team was their lifelong ambition to be pioneers in the exploration of space.

The chronicles of their times clearly identify America's two top space hero-pioneers: Wernher von Braun and Arthur Rudolph. President Kennedy announced to the world in May 1961 that Americans would go to the moon "in this decade" and Marshall Space Flight Center at Huntsville, Alabama, was shortly thereafter assigned the task of conceiving and preparing the rocket boosters for the mission. Dr. von Braun was Director of the Center and Rudolph was manager of the rocket booster Saturn V Program. The two carried out their assignments brilliantly together and brought off the greatest technological achievement yet seen, the first successful human visit to another part of the solar system.

I have been involved and at work for twenty years in trying to get the truth revealed and justice done in the Rudolph case. That long labor has left me a bit weary and with little confidence in those who mean to guide the account of history of our times, I was again stunned over the misrepresentation of history as presented on the television quiz program "Jeopardy," as related previously.

This type of incident seems to happen all too frequently from sources of supposed credibility resulting in people, and especially our children, being misinformed about history.

Why and how is this allowed to happen? We should have laws protecting history's accuracy just like we have laws protecting an individual from words of malice and defamation; history should be protected from misuse and promoting an individual or group's agenda.

As a very close friend to von Braun immediately after the war, I knew of his drive to build our country's defenses and advance its prestige in space. I knew him to be a deeply good man, incapable of crime. What could have prompted the American Broadcasting Company writers and producers to come up with the question and the false answer? Dr. von Braun was never tried as, or ever officially accused of being, a war criminal. He was never accused of any misdeeds at all. How was it that the contestant, apparently an ordinary American, perhaps a great deal more intelligent than most, gave so prompt a response with such a wrong and defamatory answer?

The abuse heaped on Arthur Rudolph, both during his life and posthumously, came from the zealots in the Office of Special Investigations of our Department of Justice, who have benefited from the assistance of the World Jewish Congress. Their work has apparently permeated our entertainment media and is on its way to becoming fixed in a sort of folkloric history, which is all most Americans will ever know. Dr. von Braun, out of his devotion to his science and a keen desire to promote the cause of the West, declined many offers of better-paying employment and worked faithfully towards America's moon victory. Now, without a shred of evidence to support it, he is vilified in at least some quarters of popular opinion, and his work, this American achievement, thereby denigrated.

When taken together with the evidence of the baseless prosecution of the Rudolph case, laid out earlier in this book, the facts here impel one to conclude that something very like a hate crime continues to be perpetrated against these two men. Well-funded government officials still carry on in their effort to disgrace our space heroes before Congress and public American opinion, simply because these two men happen to have been ethnic Germans. This was the thrust of my March 26, 2004, letter to U.S. Attorney General John Ashcroft. In it, I cited the Jeopardy incident as another product of and contribution of the Black Legend created and disseminated by over-zealous Nazi-hunters who are running out of living Nazis to hunt. I briefly mentioned other examples of attempts to rewrite history, detailed in this book, including the libels of Rudolph in Michael J. Neufeld's *The Rocket and the Reich.* My request to the Attorney General to investigate and prosecute the hate crime was rebuffed on June 10, 2004, in a *non sequitur* and almost comic response:

> *"Thank you for your letter to the Attorney General. Federal law authorizes officers of the Department of Justice to give opinions or to render legal services only to Federal officials charged with public responsibilities. After a review of your letter, we have determined that the agency listed below (The Federal Communications Division) can best address your concern."*

—an odd reply to notification of an offense against federal law.

The timidity of the Attorney General is in line with that displayed in other official quarters, when faced with the clear evidence of the Rudolph case. It happened a long time ago and present issues are, perhaps conveniently, much too pressing to allow time to correct errors about the dead. However, it is most surprising that NASA Headquarters remains totally silent, oddly timid about defending the reputation about von Braun, its very founder. It was von Braun's team who launched America's first satellite, Explorer I, and the National Aeronautics and Space Administration was founded as a result of that success. I called the matter to the attention of Daniel S. Goldin, then Administrator of NASA, with a letter in January 2001. I suggested that his agency take a more active role to affect positively what is appearing on our library shelves and news media concerning U.S. space history. I know of no action taken that was taken. Somehow, the opinion-forming sector of our population has persuaded itself, without evidentiary basis, that our space pioneers were war criminals and that our space program therefore originates in their crimes. Therefore, popular history is contorted and badly contaminated for the citizens of the United States of America, whose founding fathers dedicated this land to be a place where truth, justice, and fairness will prevail.

Also in January 2001, I wrote a letter to Mr. Lawrence Small, Secretary of the Smithsonian Institution, explaining in some detail the historical misrepresentations of Michael J. Neufeld (at that time curator of the Smithsonian Air and Space Museum) in his book *The Rocket and the Reich*. Neufeld's rendition of events concerning Arthur Rudolph's work in Germany was contrary to the easily obtainable facts. He passes off as fact the statement that Rudolph was guilty of the death of tens of thousands of prisoner-slaves working on the V-2 missile production line. As previously stated there was not one death due to supervisory misconduct on that production line so long as Rudolph was in charge of it. Several of the 5000 camp inmate workers reported that Rudolph was a good friend to them and did what he could, when he could, to ease their condition.

There were two enclosures with my letter to Mr. Small. The first was a letter (February 1995) from Dr. Walter Haeussermann, one of the top rocket scientists in the world, a specialist in guidance and control of space vehicles. It was directed to Mr. Heyman, an official with the Smithsonian. Haeussermann was furious at the lack of technical knowledge displayed by Neufeld in his book, and wrote: "The technical descriptions and conclusions contain numerous errors and senseless statements, despite the fact that Neufeld's interview questions were very thoroughly answered (by me), most obligingly and colloquially." Haeussermann concludes his letter: "I withdraw herewith permission to Mr. Neufeld to use the manuscript of his interview with me of January 24, 1990."

How far did Neufeld ignore good science and abandon good sense? And also, as previously mentioned the V-2 was a sophisticated guided missile, a masterpiece of engineering and workmanship, unequaled by the best the U.S. or any allied nation could attain at the time. Its complex parts demanded the most highly skilled machining and assembly work. Micro-tolerances were called for throughout the machining processes. Neufeld declares that the work was done by unskilled, and therefore expendable, workers. However, look at the desperate situation of the Germans at the time. The Reich was demanding far more V-2s than Rudolph's crew was able to produce. If Rudolph was killing off by tens of thousands, the very workforce that was producing Hitler's most highly- prized weapon at the time he would have been shot for treason, probably without trial. The whole thrust of logic is against Neufeld's inventions.

The second enclosure was a critique by Dr. Gerhard Reisig, a prominent rocket engineer, of the lecture given by Neufeld (November 17, 1998) at the University of Alabama, Huntsville. The lecture, one in the University's "History Forum" series was titled *Wernher von Braun and the Third Reich*. Reisig deplored Neufeld's failure to refer to reliably documented historical fact, accentuated by reliance on mere conjecture. He could explain it only as a deliberate attempt to destroy von Braun's ethical integrity. He found it obvious that Neufeld had no concept of life under a cruel dictatorship. Reisig mentioned that von Braun himself was imprisoned, after a nighttime arrest, by the Gestapo. The ground for the action (not mentioned in Reisig's critique) that von Braun displayed some indication that he was insufficiently enthusiastic about the German war effort. In Reisig's opinion, Neufeld "may be a good writer, but definitely is not a competent, professional historian."

A response to my letter to the Smithsonian came promptly from the hand of Allan A. Needell, Chairman. Judge from the following extracts how that venerable institution guards this part of our history:

First—

> *"As Chairman of the Division of Space History of the National Air and Space Museum. I am most directly concerned with the issues you raise. NASM and the Smithsonian recognize their special responsibility to make sure that exhibits and public programs provide accurate and balanced accounts of the subjects and issues, they present. As for the individual work of our professional staff, we also recognize that we must hold our curators to the highest professional standards."*

Then—

> *"I have reviewed the points made in your letter and respect the deep concern and the amount of work I imagine has gone into its preparation. That said, I would like to express my confidence in and respect for Dr. Neufeld, his scholarship, and the enormous contributions he has made and continues to make to the Museum, the Smithsonian, and to the historical profession."*

—a reply that confirms the stereotype of the entrenched Washington official **when truth will not be recognized**.

The book had been published and nothing was to be done about its falsities. Why would the directorship of the Smithsonian lend Neufeld such vigorous support in committing a hideous historical blunder?? There it was in the dedicatory statement to the book: "To the tens of thousands of prisoners—who perished at the hand of Rudolph." However, the whole number of prisoners who ever worked on the V-2, according to the only evidence, did not exceed 5000. To say the least that would demonstrate Neufeld's lack of research. The whole record of the Dachau trials, convened promptly after the war to prosecute crimes committed at the Dora/Nordhausen prisoner complex, which supplied the workers for the V-2 line, argues against Neufeld's accusations. The prosecutors had thousands of prisoners eager to testify against the real criminals. Rudolph was never a defendant at that or any other war crimes trial. Not one complaint had been raised against him from any of those 5000 prisoners.

Puzzling questions arise: Did Neufeld consciously contort the record available to him? On the other hand, is he simply a poor historian, exercising his imagination and eager to sell a sensational book? If the first question gets a "yes" response, then he ought to be forever disregarded as a serious historian. If he is simply fictionalizing in the manner of *The daVinci Code*, then his book ought to be plainly identified as a sort of period fantasy. Whatever the case, vigorous action still needs to be taken in the world of public officialdom, and in academic circles to restore and protect the truth about the United States Space Program, and its originators. Moreover, the reputation of this country is at stake, both the scientific development and the unselfish application of science for the benefit of all humankind.

Dr. Ernst Stuhlinger, in an open letter to Dr. Neufeld, had this to say:

> *"When your rocket book appeared in 1995, I immediately bought and read it. I was delighted when I read that as a teenager in the 1960's you "lived and breathed space flight and that you planned to become a space engineer. But then, reading further, I was shocked to realize that you soon discarded the noble endeavor to become a space aficionado when you discovered—perhaps stimulated by others who had made the same discovery before—that there was a cheap opportunity of a short cut to fame and fortune by denigrating and vilifying those who had*

spent their lives' work making space flight and space exploration possible.

*It is a great pity that you dropped your early plans to help space age come to life. For us Old Timers in the rocket and space program who have become the targets of your attacks, it is very difficult to understand how you could choose such **a strange and negative activity as your life career**. Rather than indulging in a study of the technology and science of rockets and space flight, you put the cruel and chaotic undertakings of Nazi dictatorship to the feet of von Braun and his co-workers. You hate and deplore them as if they had invented and operated the concentration camps. You base your arguments on unproven rumors, on questionable documents, and on notes and reports that you misinterpreted and misunderstood. **Consequently, your von Braun is not the real von Braun and your Peenemünde never existed.** A sad accomplishment indeed. If you should ever have a chance to leaf through the two volumes of the Century of Space Science (I'm sure the Smithsonian's library will acquire them), you may realize what has been accomplished by those who have remained faithful to their early love of rockets and space exploration."*

The most puzzling question still remains: Why did Neufeld attempt to contort history when the true story, as previously referred to in this book, of Rudolph presents a magnificent epic, which far transcends the thrust of *Shindler's List*? Moreover, indeed Rudolph was a great hero to the workers on the V-2 line, and remains a much greater one for the prestige of the United States of America.

In July of 1969, immediately after the successful moon mission, the von Braun team enjoyed the praise of the public for an outstanding job well done. Arthur Rudolph received NASA's highest award, the Distinguished Service Medal. Von Braun was sought out by foreign heads of state, after a huge celebration in Huntsville, Alabama, where he was carried on the shoulders of city officials.

However, this adulation did not last for long, as referred to earlier in the book in the chapter about the break-up of the rocket team; a few months later, NASA was planning on the break-up of Wernher's dream team. After von Braun's transfer to NASA Headquarters in 1970, and later resignation in 1972, most of the team had retired from Marshall Space

Flight Center. It appeared that everything was going to be peaceful in their retired life.

Not so, as referred to earlier in the book, disaster struck in 1983 when the Department of Justice, through the OSI, pounced on Rudolph, which forced him into an unjust exile from the U.S. This affected the surviving members of the rocket team with a sense of helplessness and surprise at what the government that they sacrificed to work for would allow to happen.

Thus the tightly knit rocket team of von Braun who completed the moon mission suffered the sacrifice of "loss of face," or integrity, by the rather ignominious break-up of the team presumably because they were ethnic Germans associated with the development of the V-2 for wartime Germany. And that they all wished a peaceful use of space! (See chapter on breakup of team.)

Thus most of them were very reticent in coming out in any defense of Rudolph as who would want to get embroiled with the power exercised by the OSI, which evidently appeared to them the same as exercised by the Gestapo who they hated and had more then enough of that environment in their life.

Thus the legacy in history, as it appears in the public record now, aided by Congress, the Department of Justice, the Smithsonian Institution and certain in the literary field, and also in the news media, that this great country gives to its top two space pioneers is that they are war criminals. Thus the rest of the team are guilty by association. All of this without one shred of legitimate evidence to substantiate such a deplorable situation. What a sacrifice to make for your beloved, and adopted country!!!!

The solution to this un-American situation is clear. The power to restore decency to eliminate this blot on the face of America resides in the Administration and Congress.

U.S. citizenship should be restored to Arthur Rudolph posthumously. Further, that a National monument should be erected at Marshall Space Flight Center, Huntsville, Alabama commemorating humankind's greatest technological achievement.

Thus, in summation, and as revealed in this book the following entities in the American fabric have betrayed our two top **American** space heroes and pioneers and defamed the **entire** scientific team by association:

1. Our Department of Justice.
2. Responsible members of Congress.
3. The Smithsonian Institution.
4. Certain news media, including TV and publications.

The Wall Street Journal published an article titled *In Huntsville, Ala., Rocketeers' Legacy Has Complex Echoes* on November 10th 2004 written by Jeffery Zaslow, Staff Reporter of *The Wall Street Journal.* This article was distorted and confused basic facts. The following is a letter from one of the people that was interviewed. This person (Bob Ward) himself has been a reporter for over 40 years and now regrets that he ever allowed himself to be in a position where his words could be taken and twisted. Bob Ward is also quoted in the book chapter "Humor on way to The Moon." Here follow extracts of the letter from Bob Ward to the author:

> *Larry Capps was kind enough to copy me on your excellent Letter to The Wall Street Journal. (By the way, was your letter, or any other such protesting letter [such as the one by Huntsville's George McCanless that I am aware of] regarding the reprehensible Jeffrey Laslow article, was published by The Journal?). Your letter mentioned me, and I feel compelled to offer you an explanation and background information.*
>
> *First, I want to say "Amen" to the sentiments you expressed to The Journal. I was one of the Huntsville sources who consented in good faith to speak with Mr. Laslow last fall and have now lived to regret it. He proved to be a writer-with-an agenda, and it **was not to get the truth.***
>
> *By the way, he did not use a tape recorder and took only the sketchiest notes during the long interview (90 minutes). That concerned me as a former 43-year daily newspaper journalist with The Huntsville Times.*
>
> *A year ago, or more, I purchased and read your most interesting and much-needed book, "Gestapo USA," and have cited it in the end notes to my forthcoming book. I have spent seven years researching and writing a fresh biography of Dr. von Braun. It will be published this coming April in hardback by the Naval Institute Press.*
>
> *Please keep up the good fight.*

The reader is again referred to the author's letter to the Editor of *The Wall Street Journal* at the end of the chapter on Contamination of Early Space History. This letter is very important in dealing with several aspects of what this book is trying to address and is very relevant to this subject now.

The article in *USA Today* just a month later was done well and spoke the truth. The author commends them for doing an excellent job in their effort to portray the truth. That article appeared titled as "Last Rocketeers Set Sights on Mars" by Kevin Maney, in Huntsville, Alabama, *USA Today* December 7, 2004. The following is the author's letter to the editor of *USA Today*.

LTC. William E. Winterstein, Sr,. Army (Ret.)

January 3, 2005

Editor USA Today
7950 Jones Branch Drive
McLean, Virginia 22108-0605   Attn: Kevin Maney

Re: Hate crimes against U.S. space heroes.

Dear Sir:

It indeed was with great pleasure that I read your article "Last rocketeers set sights on Mars" in your December 8 edition. This is the first article in a major newspaper that I have seen in 20 years that spoke the truth about who put America on the moon. I am a member of the Apollo Team that put U.S. astronauts on the moon in 1969. My participation in the beginning of the space age for America began in late 1945 when I was custodian of the German rocket team when they arrived in this country at Fort Bliss, Texas.

Enclosed is a copy of my letter to Senator Feinstein requesting that action be taken to curb the hate crimes which have begun to proliferate this year against America's two top space heroes. The rendition by the History Channel on December 20 was utter ridiculous. They went so far from the truth to imply that Arthur Rudolph was sort of a CEO type and had nothing of a technical or engineering-skill nature to offer the U.S.. As manager of the Saturn V Program Rudolph engineered the design and fabrication of the giant rocket boosters that placed our astronauts on the moon.

I hope that this gives you a bit more information concerning events surrounding this country's entrance into the space age. I have much more documentation, which I believe has not been previously revealed concerning our early space history which should be of interest to our citizens and the world.

Please use this information as you may see fit for the national good and benefit.

Sincerely, William E. Winterstein, Sr.

Due to the nature of the article from the *Wall Street Journal* the author wrote a letter to Senator Feinstein feeling that a Hate Crime has been committed.

December 31, 2004

Honorable Diane Feinstein
331 Hart Senate Office Building
Washington, D.C. 20510

Re: Hate crimes against U.S. space heroes.

Dear Senator Feinstein:

I was a member of the Apollo Team that placed U.S. astronauts on the moon in 1969. The thrill of that achievement must stir still in the heart of any American alive and aware at that time. Lately, I have been appalled by the spread of false information reported in the public news media vilifying our top two national space heroes-pioneers.

Following President Kennedy's declaration to the world in May, 1961, that this nation would put men on the moon "in this decade," Marshall Space Flight Center in Huntsville, Alabama, was selected to design and engineer for the lunar mission. Dr. Wernher von Braun was the Director of the Center and Arthur Rudolph was Manager of the Saturn V Program to design and fabricate the giant rocket boosters which propelled our astronauts to the moon.

Within the present year these two national space heroes have, again, been grossly defamed without justification in three nationally respected news media. The gist of these falsities is that both von Braun and Rudolph were war criminals, in that they were involved in the manufacture of the V-2 missile in wartime Germany. A military war-crimes tribunal convened at Dachau, Germany, in 1947 had determined that all rocket scientists involved in the manufacture of the V-2 were found not guilty.

There was never any worthwhile evidence, then or later, to suggest guilt of either man. It is evident that there is a powerful influence, from within the Office of Special Investigations in the Department of Justice, infiltrating our news media and attempting to disfigure or destroy the story of one of this nation's most glorious moments. The first voyage to the moon embodied mankind's greatest technological achievements. Happening in the midst of the Cold War, it tipped the balance of world power in our favor.

Briefly I will recall the facts of the hate crimes directed at our top space heroes who were ethnic Germans. On March 1, of this year, von Braun was referred to as a war criminal on the TV Jeopardy program. Then, on November 10th Rudolph and von Braun were described as war criminals on the front page of the Wall Street Journal. The third offense occurred in an hour-long History Channel program on December 20th, wherein German rocket scientists working in this country were denounced as criminals, particularly Rudolph. He was accused for the death of 20,000 "slave" laborers, the same number as mentioned in the House Resolutions referred to below. Unbiased investigation will reveal that this allegation is totally false in that not one death occurred on the V-2 line due to managerial misconduct.

The newspaper USA Today, on December 8th, in a long article beginning on the front page completely refuted all three of the aforementioned instances of falsities and published the true circumstances of how America got to the moon, relating the facts about the German scientists, then dedicated American patriots and citizens, who made it possible. In the headlines on the article are the words "German pioneers lassoed moon for U.S."

One often-cited source for the defamatory stories is a pair of identical Resolutions of the House of Representatives (No. 68, of 1985 and No.164 of 1987, copies enclosed). This is what was dealt to Arthur Rudolph, hero-pioneer. A single Congressman, at the suggestion and under the influence of a determined operative in the Department of Justice, blazoned Rudolph as a low criminal, without a single shred of legitimate evidence to support any charge, and imposed on him and his family a lifetime of unjustifiable disgrace and lasting national ridicule.

A horrendous and terroristic depiction of American life. Despite the fact that both Resolutions were roundly defeated in the House, they remain in the Public Record and continue to be cited as high authority for rank deformation.

This matter can only be put to right by an over site investigation by the Senate Judiciary Committee, as the Department of Justice is involved at the bottom of the matter.

I request that you, my Senator, exert your influence among your fellow members of the 109th Congress to carry on such an investigation and to adopt legislation forbidding inclusion in the Congressional Record of un-adopted resolutions (in either House or joint) which directly or inferentially impugn the character or reputation of any person.

Please let me have your response about the action you will be taking to avoid the parody of American justice created by the two Resolutions and the ethics-deprived journalists and careless irresponsible historians who use them to falsify and mar great moments in our national history.

Respectfully yours,

William E. Winterstein, Sr.

2 Enclosures: H.RES.68, 1985
H. RES.164, 1987
cc: Sen. Boxer
Rep. Gallegly
USA Today

22

Why the U.S. Should Restore Citizenship to Arthur Rudolph

In 1982, thirteen years after his retirement from NASA, Arthur Rudolph's life was interdicted by representatives of the U.S. Department of Justice. Rudolph and his wife, Martha, were by that time living in San Jose, California, to be near their daughter Marianne.

Then began the later history of Arthur Rudolph, a dedicated and patriotic citizen of the United States and a major contributor to its advancement in the world. That history would be unbelievable, were it not borne out by documentary evidence.

The story of Arthur Rudolph begins with his determination, representing considerable financial sacrifice, to remain on the von Braun rocket team. It was enough for him to have the chance to become America's Number Two space pioneer. It ends with his shameful exile from his adopted homeland, based on unsubstantiated charges brought by interests who had somehow gained the ear, via pressure applied to the careers, of American legislators.

Why should the United States posthumously restore citizenship to Arthur Rudolph? Our government thrust Rudolph into exile and forced him to surrender his hard-won citizenship under duress and coercion, and by threats against his family members—all without adequate legal representation. Evidence presented elsewhere in this book makes clear that the Department of Justice through its Office of Special Investigations had not assembled even a shred of credible evidence to justify initiating prosecution. Hearsay, perhaps. speculation, to be sure. Evidence, not a whit.

As previously mentioned the war crimes trials were held in Dachau, Germany, in 1947, two years after the end of the war in Europe. The trials were to determine the guilt of the crimes committed against slave-laborers at the Dora/Nordhausen industrial complex in northern Germany. Three separate production lines there were manned by conscripted workers from occupied countries. Jet aircraft engines were produced on one line, V-1 buzz bombs on another. Rudolph was in charge of the third, which manufactured V-2 rockets. He was never, throughout the proceedings, called as a defendant. Not one complaint of a criminal act had been filed against him by any of the 5,000-man workforce. The evidence, still available, demonstrated his attention to, and even solicitous care of, his work crew. He saw to it, as often as he dared, that they were provided with supplemental rations, better clothing, and improved medical care.

The Office of Special Investigations began their campaign against Rudolph no less than 35 years later, in October of 1982, when witnesses were dead and memories were faded. The OSI then had before it all of the evidence presented at those trials. However, apparently, things were slow at OSI just then and it was time for the unit to launch another investigation-prosecution. As Nazi-hunters, OSI had not done remarkably well up to then. The basis for their very existence was in urgent need of justification. Other agencies, notably the Israeli Mossad, and the Germans themselves, had done very much better and were far more careful in searching the woodpiles for war criminals.

Confident in his own innocence, Rudolph did not take counsel until late in the development of the prosecution, and then, he made the unfortunate choice of an attorney who had no prior experience in such cases. Dire threats were made by the OSI against Rudolph's wife and daughter, should Rudolph mount a vigorous defense. They too would be stripped of U.S. citizenship and expelled from the country; pension rights would be denied both to him and them. Instead, the OSI offered to allow Rudolph to surrender his citizenship, leave this country and return to Germany, and retain his pension and the survivorship benefits to his wife. His family could remain in America if they chose; the citizen status of his wife and daughter would be unaffected. By this time Rudolph, an old and tired man (the preferred trophy of the bureaucratic scapegoat hunter) capitulated to the overwhelming force of our government's coercion.

The disposition agreement (paragraph 18) specified that OSI would issue only one public statement concerning the case. Nevertheless, the DOJ/OSI, flushed with pride and its foot on the fallen game, trumpeted their 'success.' That promise of our government was violated at least five times in succeeding years:

1. When the OSI, still trying to convict of war crimes, advertised for witnesses against Rudolph in the *Las Vegas Israelite* in January, 1985;

2. When the OSI Director Neal Sher issued his statement to the *San Jose* (California) *Mercury News* in March 1987 that Rudolph was still a "war criminal." (This was after the OSI had embarrassed itself and the U.S. in failing to provide the West German war crimes agency with the identification of a single credible witness or other evidence to substantiate their allegations against Rudolph). The OSI "hoped" Germany would do its job. They were not being nice as they and Arthur Rudolph knew the Germans would investigate. Arthur Rudolph knew he had nothing to fear from a German investigation as he knew he had done nothing wrong;

3. In providing to Congress the grossly false information about Rudolph that found its way into the proposed *but never adopted* House Resolution 68 of 1985;

4. In providing to Congress the same false information embodied in House Resolution 164 of 1987, which likewise failed adoption; and

5. When Neal Sher and Eli Rosenbaum (the later Director of OSI) appeared and aired the case to the American public on the television program "Inside Edition" on February 8, 1993. Both Sher and Rosenbaum denounced Rudolph as a "war criminal," a charge they had never had proved and for which they could produce no evidence.

That last incident took place after the OSI took a particularly vicious swing at the entire Rudolph family. The family members had arranged to meet for a reunion and vacation in Canada for July 1990. The OSI knew of the event and notified Canadian authorities that Rudolph was not allowed into the United States because of "war crimes involvement" (an unproven statement). In consequence, he was held in detention upon his arrival at Toronto Airport. Proceedings in Canadian court revealed the embarrassing fact that the information provided by the OSI was not valid. A false representation had been made to a foreign government by the highest officials of the OSI: Neal Sher and Eli Rosenbaum. The motive was spite at the worst, an unjustified sense of self-importance at best, involving insignificant bureaucrats playing at international affairs. Whatever the motive, that act of misinformation alone was a *crime*. If the falsification was by affidavit, it was perjury. Rudolph was a citizen, with civil rights to due process and full, fair, and open hearings. These events transpired in a closet, and if Sher and Rosenbaum will not come out of the closet, the due process of law should compel them to come. Will this violation of Rudolph's civil rights ever be prosecuted? Will it be mentioned when OSI once again to the Congressional trough for funding? **This is the OSI that operates with a congressional charter and mantle of secrecy, with no obligation to answer to or account for its actions to the people of the United States.**

The evidence is now overwhelming: the government of this country, through the surrogate action of officials in our Department of Justice, unlawfully deprived Arthur Rudolph of his U.S. citizenship and exiled him to a country that initially grudgingly accepted him back. But after investigating and finding him innocent, welcomed Arthur Rudolph as a German citizen. The United States of America is obligated to restore Arthur Rudolph's U.S. citizenship posthumously and place him on America's roll of space pioneers and heroes—some greater, many lesser. Because of American government misconduct, Rudolph died a foreigner. Had he not been enticed to this country at war's end, to contribute scientific knowledge unavailable among the American engineering community at the time. To render a political slap in the face of a former enemy nation by the plundering of its intellectual resources; to worry the Soviets who were at least more direct in their methods of conscripting scientific talent. Had his involvement with America not occurred, Rudolph at least would have died an unmolested citizen of his native Germany! As it is, the man who was essential to the raising of an American flag on the lunar surface died in disgrace without the honor accorded by the presence of that flag—a flag he chose, but which had not, in the end, chosen him.

23
Reviews/Endorsements

Edgar Mitchell was the Lunar Command pilot of Apollo 14.

Secrets of The Space Age is an important addition to U.S. history and to the record of U.S. efforts in space.

Edgar Mitchell, Sc.D.
Capt USN (Ret.) Apollo Astronaut

Col. Winterstein is a courageous patriot and pioneer of America's space program from its birth with the testing of the captured German V-2 rockets to the landings on the moon. He has a great, but sometimes dark, story to tell about America's advance into space and about what became of the men who took us there.

Patrick J Buchanan

Winterstein's book is a must read historical milestone. It begins with the advent of the space age of America. He was custodian of the German rocket team led by Dr. Wernher von Braun, who were invited to come to this country by President Truman immediately after WWII in 1945. He convinced von Braun to keep his team intact. This led to America's space victory in 1969, when von Braun and his team launched humankind into the space age by placing U.S. astronauts on the moon. Thus von Braun's dreams came true for opening up the new frontier for the peaceful use of all humankind. The final days of America's greatest space hero are also revealed in most interesting detail.

Dr. Carol Rosin, President, Institute for Cooperation in Space

Dear Bill:

I found your book interesting and was impressed by the facts concerning the history of the von Braun Team who contributed to our missile activities.

A major goal was established in the early 1960s by President Kennedy, who transferred the Army Ballistic Missile team (led by von Braun), to Marshall Space Flight Center of NASA, except for Dr. Arthur Rudolph, who was kept by the Army to finish the design of the Pershing missile, then he joined the MSFC team at a key management and technical responsibility for our Space Program in the early 1960s.

Joseph C. Moquin (Former CEO of Brown Engineering when Brown was a contractor supporting the Apollo Program)

Immigrants working together in harmony and peace have made America the great nation it is! Lt. Colonel William E. Winterstein, Sr.'s story of Arthur Rudolph is one such story. Rudolph designed the Pershing missile and he was directly responsible for designing and building the huge Saturn launch vehicle, which put man on the moon. This great feat put America into the lead during the Cold War.

However, after Rudolph had dedicated his life to the U.S. space effort, he was wrongly robbed of his honor and citizenship and exiled by the OSI, an agency within our government. This true and "unbelievable" story may be a forecast of things to come for U.S. citizens? Read *Secrets of the Space Age* and be forewarned.

Martin Hollmann, President of Scientists and Friends

Col. William E. Winterstein, the author, merits great commendation for his superb chronicle of the outstanding American rocketry and space travel legacy of Dr. Arthur Rudolph. As stated in the text, the OSI produced no evidence of wrongdoing by Dr. Rudolph pursuant to our request for evidence under the Freedom of Information Act.

Robert Sellers Smith Lawyer involved with Arthur Rudolph's Appeal

Every American who cares about justice and historical truth owes a debt of gratitude to William Winterstein for this first-hand look at the U.S. space program, which he reinforces with valuable research and illuminating insights. The author is a World War II hero and internationally known rocket specialist who rose to the rank of U.S. Army Lt. Colonel. He supervised security involving the 118 German rocket scientists, headed by Dr. Wernher von Braun, who came to the U.S. after the war to help build America's guided missile program. From 1945 through the 1960s, Winterstein worked closely with von Braun and his team.

In perhaps the book's most important section, Winterstein takes a close and courageous look at the U.S. government's persecution of Arthur Rudolph. Few men contributed more to mankind's first landing on the moon than Dr. Rudolph, a German-born scientist who capped a brilliant career as production manager of the giant Saturn V rocket that in 1969 carried three American astronauts to the lunar surface. Praised as one of this country's greatest scientists, he was awarded numerous high honors, including NASA's Distinguished Service Medal.

In 1982, more than a decade after his retirement, the "Office of Special Investigations"—a U.S. government agency set up under Jewish-Zionist pressure to serve narrow, un-American interests—began a campaign to brand Rudolph a Nazi war criminal for his role in Germany's wartime V-2 rocket program. Rudolph was stripped of his U.S. citizenship, and forced to return to Germany. A German government investigation found no grounds for bringing charges against the elderly man, who died in early 1996.

Winterstein untangles the complexities of this politically-loaded case, marshals facts that exonerate Rudolph, and delivers a stern but persuasive indictment of U.S. government injustice.

Mark Weber Director Institute for Historical Review

1) In 1993 the Sixth Circuit Court of Appeal held that OSI attorneys (in the Demjanjuk case) had acted with reckless disregard for their duty to the court and that they had committed "fraud on the court." Yet no one was fired and the OSI is still in operation. Years of observing its activities have convinced me that their approach is fundamentally flawed and incompatible with international human rights standards. In

my opinion the OSI is un-American, undemocratic, unnecessary and a waste of taxpayers money.

2) The German rocket team served the people of America with loyalty and distinction. The American people and all humanity owe them respect and gratitude for their significant contribution to the space program. The uses of science are in the hands of good and bad politicians. Science and technology are apolitical.

Dr. Alfred de Zayas is an historian and author of numerous books including Nemesis at Potsdam *(Göttingen).*

American educated lawyer (Harvard) and former Secretary of the United Nations Human Rights Committee and currently professor of international law.

He is President of the United Nations Society of Writers and Secretary-General of the Pen Club in Geneva, Switzerland.

The author, who worked closely with members of the Wernher von Braun Rocket Team for many years, is highly qualified to present the historical events in the USA. Like many high ranking army officers, who had a direct knowledge of the Team's work during WWII he disagrees with the discrimination and railroad attempts of the Office of Special Investigations that started in 1982. Supported by extensive documentation and logical conclusions he hopes that the injustice will be corrected.

Dr. Walter Haeussermann

The author studied a huge amount of "Rudolph case" documents. He discussed this topic over many years with Rocket Team members and other interested persons. Based on his military and juristic background he concluded that the United States Justice Department has done to its citizen Arthur Rudolph a grave injustice by lying and distorting facts, which led to his expulsion from this country. The book updates the public on the shameful mistreatment that this outstanding scientist received from the country, which he had chosen, as his post-war home and for which he had contributed major advances in technology and management. These unlawful "Justice" Department actions have disgusted thousands of his former coworkers in Government and Industry and they want these illegal actions revoked and the distorted space history corrected.

Konrad Dannenberg

Confirmation of Dr. von Braun's remark about Bill Winterstein

Ernst Stuhlinger
September 13, 2002.
Colonel William E. Winterstein

Dear Bill,

Thank you for your letters of September 9 and 10.—I would like to make three comments:

(1) My remark to Constance of May 2000 in Huntsville should be expanded somewhat, as indicated in my letter to Constance (enclosed).

(2) There were 5 members of the von Braun team who left the team (for greener pastures: Magnus von Braun, joining the Chrysler Corporation; Martin Schilling, joining the Raytheon Corporation, Theodor Buchhold, joining General Electric; Adolf Thiel, joining Thompson-Ramo-Wooldridge; and Hugo Woerdemann, starting his own company.

3). In the summer of 1969, after the three astronauts of Apollo 11 (Neil Armstrong, Buzz Aldrin, and Mike Collins) had returned safely to Earth, I remarked to von Braun that it was really fortunate that he decided in Fort Bliss during the late 1940s not to accept one of the lucrative offers from industry, but to stay with his team and the American Government, and to wait patiently for better times. **"Yes,"** **he said. "The credit belongs to Bill Winterstein. He persuaded** **me, and I believed him!"**

Bill, I hope this will be useful to you. Best of luck for your project!

Sincerest wishes   *Ernst,*   Dr. Ernst Stuhlinger

24

Get Involved

If you have been moved by the story of America's treatment of its space heroes, complete, sign, and detach the direct-mail letter on the next page and send it to the address provided. The author has been one of several voices 'crying in the wilderness' as it were, for many years now. More voices are more easily heard and more quickly recognized. A convenient, electronic form of this 'petition' is available on our website.

www.secretsofthespaceage.com

A letter is set up that you can tear out and mail it if you desire.

- -- -

Appendix 1
Fireball Orders

The Original "Fireball" Orders

APC V WASHINGTON   NR1057

FRCH ORD RES & DEV SERVICE, COL WEAVER SPOTH   4
OCT 45   1914Z

TO COL EDDY SPOTZ-A

                    GR CONF   PRIORITY "A"

            R E S T R I C T E D

GSHLSS

GA

SUBJECT IS IMMEDIATE REQUIREMENT FOR PERSONNEL TO
BE SUPPLIED FROM YOUR ESTABLISHMENT TO SERVICE
QUOTE FIREBALL UNQUOTE PROJECT REQUIREMENTS ARE
AS FOLLOWS\

COMMISSIONED PERSONNEL 1 CAPTAIN JOB DETACHMENT
COMMANDER

1 1ST LT   JOB EXECUTIVE

1 1ST SGT

2 S/SGT WHICH 2 TO BE QUALIFIED FOR MESS ONE MOTOR
MECHANIC ONE DRAFTS MAN

6 T4 ONE MACHINE SHOP SUPERVISOR ONE QUALIFIED
GERMAN TRANSLATOR TECHNICAL

6 T/5 OR CPL   1 CO DETACHMENT CLK   1 ASST SUPPLY SGT
2 DRAFTSMAN 1 MAIL ORDERLY GERMAN SPEAKING, 1
TECHNICAL EDITOR FOR GERMAN

8PFC   3 DRIVERS   1 DINING ROOM ORDERLY 4 MISCELLANEOUS

8 PVT   BASIC

TOTAL PERSONNEL   2COMMISSIONED   31 ENLISTED GRAND TOTAL 33

1ST INCREMENT NEEDED FOR IMMEDIATE MOVEMENT WITHIN 24 HOURS ARE AS FOLLOWS CLN

1 OFFICER

1ST SGT

1 S/SGT SUPPLY

3 T/5 INCLUDING 1 ASST SUPPLY, CLERK, 1 MAIL ORDERLY

3 PFC

4 PVT

TRAVEL WILL BE BY RAIL BASIS WILL BE TEMPORARY DUTY UNTIL FINAL ESTABLISHMENT OF THE CLASS FOUR INSTALLATION DESTINATION VICINITY FORT BLISS TEXAS

UPON ARRIVAL DESTINATION DETACHMENT COMMANDER TO REPORT TO MAJOR J P HAMILL ORD DEPT THROUGH POST COMMANDER FORT BLISS

ANY QUESTIONS GA

IT IS DESIRABLE DUE TO THE NATURE OF THE MISSION THAT IF AT ALL POSSIBLE REGULAR ARMY PERSONNEL BE DETAILED ON THIS ASSIGNMENT AND/OR FXXX SUCH QUALIFIED PERSONNEL AS HAVE OR WILL EXPRESS A FIRM DESIRE TO REMAIN ON DUTY FOR A PERIOD OF AT LEAST 12 MONTHS FROM DATE.

ANY Q

WILL TRY TO LINE UP NECESSARY QUALIFIED PERSONNEL CONSISTING OF THOSE WHO WILL SERVE FOR A PERIOD OF AT LEAST TWELVE MONTHS. I DONT KNOW HOW SUCCESSFUL WE WILL BE BUT WELL DO THE BEST WE CAN AND IF ANY DIFFICULTIES ARE ENCOUNTERED WE WILL LET U KNOW AT ONCE   GA

IF IT NOT POSSIBLE TO COLLECT NECESSARY PERSONEL FROM THOSE WHO ARE GOING TO STAY IN WE HAVE TO TAKE LOW POINT PERSONNEL AS THE OBLIGATION WILL HAVE TO BE MET ONE WAY OR THE OTHER.

WILL APPRECIATE EXPEDITIOUS HANDLING.

R E S T R I C T E D

ACK PLS AND TK U MEG

RECD MSG APG SHC 1930Z TU

Appendix 2
Meritorious Service Unit Plaque

Meritorious Service Unit Plaque

WAR. DEPARTMENT
Office of the Chief of Ordnance.
Washington 25, D.C.

12 September 1946

GENERAL ORDERS
NUMBER 5
   1. Pursuant to the provisions of War Department Circular 54, 22
February 1946. The Research and Development Service Sub office,
(Rocket) Fort Bliss. Texas (9330 TSU), is hereby awarded the
Meritorious Service Unit Plaque for superior performance of duty in the
execution of exceptionally difficult tasks and "for the achievement and
maintenance of a high standard of discipline during the, period 1
January 1946 to 30 June 1946."

   2. The Meritorious Service Unit Insignia may be worn as a
permanent part of the uniform only by those individuals who were
assigned or attached for a minimum total of 60 days during the period
for which the Meritorious Service Unit Plaque was awarded. Individuals
who are assigned or attached to the unit for less than a total of 60 days.
during the period for which the plaque was awarded, or who are
subsequently assigned or attached to the Research and Development
Service Sub office (Rocket), Fort Bliss, Texas (9330 TSU) are not
eligible to war the insignia as a permanent part of the uniform but may
wear it only during the period they are assigned or attached.
BY COMMAND OF MAJ0R GENERAL HUGHES:
R. E. L. JOHNSON

1st Lt., Ord Dept

Distribution: Assistant
3 copies—AGO
3 copies—File
45 copies—9330 TSU
1 copy—Exec Asst, Mil Pers Div, OCO   (Signed)
(A certified true copy)   Joseph D. Hinesley
               (Page 1 of 1)   1st Lt.,Ord Dept

Appendix 3

Letter from von Braun

NATIONAL AERONAUTICS AND SPACE ADMINISTRATION
GEORGE C. MARSHALL SPACE FLIGHT CENTER
HUNTSVILLE, ALABAMA

IN REPLY REFER TO:
M-DIR

OCT 3 1962

Lt. Colonel W. E. Winterstein

Dear Bill:

I was delighted to hear from you again and to learn that you have followed our activities through these many years.

By now I am sure you have heard from Jim Shepherd, our Facilities Engineering chief, with regard to the engineers you mentioned who might be interested in NASA employment. You are right - we are entering on perhaps the biggest non-military project ever attempted, and we need all the competent people we can line up. Our responsibility at Huntsville in this Apollo program is rather great, and, as you know, no part of it is more important or has greater priority than the facilities effort. For that reason, we are looking for additional people and we appreciate sincerely the suggestion you have made.

Again, thank you for your kind comments, and for your thoughtfulness in writing. Please give my regards to Mrs. Winterstein.

Sincerely yours,

Wernher von Braun
Director

Appendix 4
Agreement by OSI for Rudolph

The Agreement Between Arthur Rudolph And The Department Of Justice

---

AGREEMENT

BETWEEN ARTHUR LOUIS HUGO RUDOLPH

AND THE UNITED STATES DEPARTMENT OF JUSTICE

Arthur Louis Hugo Rudolph. on the advice of his undersigned counsel, and in consideration of and in exchange for the statement and commitment of the United States contained herein, executes the following statement and commitment:

1. I was born on November 9, 1906 in Stepfershausen, Germany. I am a citizen of the United States of America, having obtained United States citizenship on November 11, 1954. I entered the United States for immigration on April 14, 1949.

2. From approximately September 1943 to approximately April 1945, I served as "Betriebsdirektor" (Operations Director) of Betriebsdirektion P ("Operations Directorate I") of the "Mittelwerk" underground rocket fabrication plant in central Germany. Forced laborers, including concentration camp inmates, were utilized at this facility.

3. I am familiar with the allegations of the Office of Special Investigations (OSI), United States Department of Justice, that while serving at the Mittelwerk facility, I participated, under the direction of and on behalf of the Nazi government of Germany, in the persecution of unarmed civilians because of their race, religion, national origin, or political opinion.

4. The aforesaid allegations are not contested as to legal actions commenced or contemplated under United States jurisdictions or in United States courts.

5. Those allegations being uncontested, I concede that my U.S. citizenship was illegally procured under 8 U.S.C. Sl427(a)(1), and that I

am therefore subject to denaturalization pursuant to 8 U.S.C. Sl451 (a). Were I a non U.S. citizen, I concede that I would be deportable under 8 U.S.C. Sl25 11(a) (19). 125 1(a) (1) and 125 1(a) (2).

6. I agree permanently to depart the United States by March 29, 1984. at my own expense.

7. Unless already accomplished, I will take all necessary steps to secure a United States passport and any other documents needed to effectuate my departure from the United States and my immigration to another country.

8. On or before June 1, 1984. I shall formally renounce my United States citizenship before an appropriate U.S. official at a United States consulate or embassy. At the time of such renunciation. I: shall deliver and relinquish my certificate of naturalization as a U.S. citizen (No. 7297628) to the U.S. official before whom I effect my renunciation of United States citizenship. At my option, I shall either surrender my united States passport to the said U.S. official or I shall permit him to imprint my passport with a stamp indicating that the passport has been canceled.

9. In the event that I believe that my departure within the agreed-upon period should be deferred as a result of a catastrophic illness or accident, I agree to submit to a medical examination by a physician to be appointed by the United States Department of Justice. The designated physician shall then make a determination as to whether travel will actually endanger my life. In the event that he determines that I am unable to depart at the time stated in paragraph six (6), I agree to submit, at the request of the U.S. Department of Justice, to periodic, subsequent examinations by a Justice Department-appointed doctor to determine whether travel would actually endanger my life. I agree to make all of my medical records available to the Justice Department-appointed physician.

10. I shall comply with requests made by the U.S. Department of Justice designed to verify my departure from the United States and my renunciation of United States citizenship.

11. I agree not to reapply for United States citizenship under any circumstances.

12. In the event that I do not comply with the terms of paragraphs six (6) through eleven (11) above, and the U.S. Department of Justice consequently files denaturalization and/or deportation actions against me, my counsel, George H. Main. Esq. (or his successor)-, is hereby instructed to consent on my behalf to the entry of the orders of denaturalization and/or deportation sought by the United States Department of Justice, additionally designate said counsel as my legal representative, and I authorize him to receive service of process on my behalf.

13. I understand that the United States Government is empowered to place my name on lists maintained by the U.S. Department of State and the U.S. Department of Justice (and its component U.S. Immigration and Naturalization Service) of persons who are to be denied 13.5. immigrant and non-immigrant visas and who are to be excluded from entering the United States.

14. I hereby waive any right to any application for discretionary relief, any appeal, whether administrative or judicial, any petition for habeas corpus in injunctive relief, asylum, parole, or other collateral relief, any legislative action, whether by way of private bill or otherwise and any other procedure of any nature whatsoever that would have the effect of reviewing or contesting either the contents of this document or any orders of denaturalization or de a ion entered pursuant to this agreement.

15. I have entered into this Agreement freely and voluntarily upon consultation with my counsel. This Agreement completely disposes of all of the issues in this case. I have personally reviewed this Agreement and have discussed it freely with my attorney. I am not now, nor have I been, under duress or compulsion of any kind. The United States of America, by its undersigned counsel, an officer of the United States Department of Justice, executes the following binding statement and commitment in consideration of and in exchange for the statement and commitment of Arthur Louis Hugo Rudolph contained herein:

16. If Arthur Louis Hugo Rudolph (hereinafter, "Rudolph") complies with the terms of paragraphs six (6) through eleven (11) of his statement and commitment, supra, the United States agrees as follows:

(a) the United States will commence no litigation seeking Rudolph's denaturalization as a United States citizen or his deportation from the United States;

(b) the United States recognizes that, if Rudolph complies in full with the terms of this Agreement, there is no basis under U.S. law for limiting in any way, by lawsuit or any other means, Rudolph's receipt of federal retirement, health care, and/or Social Security benefits;

(c) Rudolph will be permitted to retain his United States passport after it has been canceled in the manner specified in paragraph eight (8), supra;

(d) At the time Rudolph renounces his United States citizenship in accordance with paragraph eight (8), supra, he will be provided with certified photocopies of all documents executed by Rudolph to effect such renunciation; and

(e) the United States will act with due diligence to provide Rudolph with certified documentary evidence within a reasonable time establishing his loss of United States citizenship.

17. The United States will commence no litigation seeking the revocation of the United States citizenship of any members of Rudolph's family whose citizenship derives from Rudolph's naturalization as a United States citizen.

18. The United States Department of Justice will make no public statement about this case until either June 1,1984 or such time as Rudolph relinquishes his United States citizenship, whichever is earlier. At that time, a press release containing only the text appended hereto as Exhibit A shall be issued.

19. The Department of Justice will make no disclosures inconsistent with the requirements of the Privacy Act, 5 U.S.C. S552a.

20. The United States agrees that this Agreement completely disposes of all of the issues in this case.

On Behalf of the United States Department of Justice:

 signed   Dated: Nov 28. 1983 at San Jose, CA

    Neal M. Sher

Director Office of Special Investigations

Criminal Division United States Department of Justice

On Behalf **of Arthur** Louis Hugo Rudolph:

  Signed Dated: Nov. 28, 83 at San Jose. CA

Arthur Louis Hugo Rudolph

      Signed Dated: 1 1\28\83 at San Jose, CA

    George H. Main, Esq. Attorney for Arthur Louis Hugo Rudolph

Appendix 5

Vegas Newspaper Ad by OSI

Advertisement for Witnesses in The Las Vegas Israelite

Appendix 6
Summary by German Prosecutor

Short summary by West German Prosecutor () & [] items are translator notes

Case of Dr. A. Rudolph: Short summary of witness evaluations by Attorney General Duhn, Hamburg, Fed. Republic of Germany.

General comment: **Mittelwerk** GmbH was a government defense enterprise with headquarter in Berlin; underground manufacturing of the V-2 took place near Niedersachswerfen.

The laborers in the Mittelwerk were Inmates from the concentration camp Dora-Nordhausen, under control of the **Mittelbau** organization and SS.

Conclusion by Attorney General Duhn:

Questioning of the defendant (Rudolph) by the American Government officials have not yielded a sufficient basis for a criminal investigation.

Witness investigations and earlier depositions:

a. Former inmates of the concentration camp Dora-Nordhausen:

a.1 Martin Adler (OSI named witness) deposed that Rudolph had no contact to the prisoners and was not involved in executions.

a.2 Francis E. Barwacz does not remember Rudolph. He deposed that the German civilians had no contact with the prisoners and cannot be blamed for any violence. He further deposed never to have met a Jewish prisoner in the underground facility.

a.3 Vadirn Flodorowitsch Bykadorow (from U.S.S.R.) does not depose any facts about Rudolph, gives clearly wrong information and unsupported conclusions.

a.4 Nikolai Naxlmowitsch Dektjarew (from U.S.S.R.) does not believe he would recognize Rudolph. The deposition of this witness does not give a sufficient suspicion against the defendant. Some remarks discredit the deposition.

a.5 Roman Drung did not work in an underground facility and does not remember anything about Rudolph. He was in the concentration camp Mittelbau-Dora during its existence, became concentration camp eldest end of 1944.

a.6 Georg Finkenzeller obviously did not know Rudolph, especially does not know to have seen Rudolph at an execution.

a.7 Erich Gebauer was not employed in the underground facility and does not know the name Rudolph.

a.8 Hans Gebauer worked in the underground facility on the 'V-2, deposed that the SS forced executions. He did not meet Rudolph, despite the fact, that he was foreman and Kapo (concentration camp police).

a.9 Lothar Gebhardt (deceased) worked in the underground facility and tested components of the V-2 and V-1 (the latter can't be true!)

a.10 Stephan Gebski (lives in Australia) did not recognize Rudolph in a picture. Has no accusations on Rudolph.

a.11 Felix Goldstein (OSI named witness) deposed that Jews were a minority among the prisoners. He never worked underground and did not know the name Rudolph.

a.12 Siegfried Halbreich (OSI named witness). As a former pharmacist he did not work in the underground facility, but in the hospital of the Boelke Kaserne. His depositions are inconsistent and cannot be supported by depositions of other witnesses.

a.13 Roman Maximowitsch Kornehew deposes no facts or details but guesses conclusions. Several remarks are highly doubtful. He does not give sufficient evidence for accusations. [U.S.S.R. deposition. Compare to a.4, which has similar inconsistent depositions and untruths.]

a.14 Richard Kuhl was not directly involved in the V-2 manufacturing. Never heard the name Rudolph, but von Braun.

a.15 Mendel Leben (OSI named witness) deposed that he did not meet Rudolph in the concentration camp Dora-Mittelbau.

a.16 Berthold Linder gave information that he worked in the underground facility but has no facts or accusations against Rudolph.

a.17 Alfred Meinhardt has no comments on Rudolph. Gave untrue statements [e.g. confusing von Braun most likely with Sawatzki].

a.18 David Mietler (anwered with Mittler) (OSI named witness). Interrogation was not accepted by him for psychical reasons. [in a personal letter he wrote: "7 arrived at Dora in Sept. 1944. I do not remember the name of Rudolph, nor can I positively identify him from the picture in the Time magazine article you enclosed."]

a.19 Tadeusz Jan Patzer (South Africa) never mentioned Rudolph in earlier depositions. Does not want additional interrogations.

a.20 Georg Reichenberger worked underground, but does not remember any names.

a.21 George Seleniques (OSI named witness). Jewish witness, who was in the Mittelwerk. does not want to be interrogated for psychological reasons.

a.22 Otto Slawsky (deceased) never mentioned Rudolph in his depositions.

a.23 Abraham Vered (OSI named witness) does not know Rudolph. He did not observe discovery of sabotage. Only SS personnel were responsible for executions.

a.24 Alfred Waldner (OSI named witness) deposed he did not meet Rudolph.

b. Former coworkers of Rudolph in the Mittelwerke GmbH:

b.1 Erich Ball Worked in the underground facility. He could not give a deposition because of poor health (physically and psychologically).

b.2 Felix Boese has no comments against Rudolph, whom he knew from Peenemünde.

b.3 Magnus von Braun describes Rudolph as a personality of highest ethical standards: brutalities would have been impossible for him.

b.4 Broszat. Witnessed could not be located, may be deceased. Like other civilians Kuhlmann, Raschdorf, Stuhlfauth and Weckbrodt he was involved in the employment of prisoners. Despite several attempts none of them could be found except that it was learned that Raschdorf is deceased.

b.5 Erich Daenicke was an engineer in the underground facility. Gave extensive descriptions of the executions by the SS; did not know anything about the justification for the executions. He never mentioned Rudolph.

b.6 Gertrud Deul deceased.

b.7 Paul Hermann Figge claims that Rudolph was not involved in any reprisals to the prisoners, but that he had been threatened to become a concentration camp prisoner because he stood up for the prisoners.

b.8 Dr. Hans Rudolf Friedrich (deceased 1958) did not give In earlier depositions any facts which would support charges against Rudolph.

b.9 Guenther Haukohl. No depositions requested, because Haukohl might be charged similarly to Rudolph.

b.10 Dr. Kurt Kettler (deceased 1981) described Rudolph to be an excellent technical expert. He gave no other comments with respect to Rudolph.

b.11 Rudi Koenig deposed that the SS arranged for executions. Rudolph had no authority in this matter. He deposed further that Rudolph helped the prisoners, and despite being prohibited, he provided additional food for the prisoners. The SS did not have to become knowledgeable of this.

b.12 Krafft (first name unknown) could not be located and thus not be interrogated.

b.13 Hans Moehring coordinated technical work with the underground facility. Claims not to know Rudolph, but deposes that the accusations against Rudolph are incorrect.

b.14 Hanne-Lore Raufnet. ne Banasch was secretary of Sawatzki. Only her depositions of 1947 show an incriminating tendency towards Rudolph, but she questions [the translation of] the records of 1947. The deposition part in question is "if anybody had signed it sabotage reports] at the Werke, it would have been Rudolph." This is a hypothetical charge, no supporting facts have ever been found.

b.15 Georg Rickhey (deceased) was defendant at the Dachau Military Tribunal (1947) and acquitted. He was a witness in the Essen trial. Neither Rickhey, nor Sawatzki (deceased) deposed charges against Rudolph.)

b.16 Albin Sawatzki (deceased). See b.15.

b.17 Klaus Scheufelen was not involved in Mittelwerk activities. He refers to the letters of Prof. Hochmuth with respect to Rudolph.

b.18 Willie (Wilhelm) Schmidt describes the Mittelwerk as a standard production facility. He has no charges against Rudolph.

b.19 Schuhmacher has no charges against Rudolph.

b.20 Karl Seidenstücker. Shortly before his death he was interrogated by OSI and the (German) Criminal Police in Bad Gandersheim. No accusations can be derived from the depositions.

b.21 Bernhard Franz Vahlhaus deposed that he was only for 2 to 3 months at the Mittelwerk; he did not know Rudolph. Anyway he has the opinion that the defendant (Rudolph) is completely innocent.

b.22 Werner Voss. He could not be reached by mail.

b.23 Rudolf Wackenagel knew the defendant from the time before the war; both were employed in Peenemünde. At an earlier time he gave already two depositions to exonerate the defendant. The witness defines the defendants character and attitude as flawless. Wackenagel **deposed that no Jewish prisoners were employed.**

c. Former SS members.

c.1 Richard Raer (deceased 1963) was in charge of the Mittelbau/Dora. No information available.

c.2 Helmut Bischoff was responsible for executions of prisoners. Rudolph is not mentioned in his depositions.

c.3 Smil Buehring was sentenced to imprisonment for life, died 1963. He never mentioned the defendant (Rudolph).

c.4 Erwin Busta was sentenced to prison for 8 years, 6 months, died 1982. He never mentioned the defendant.

c.5 Otto Förschner died 1946. Depositions are missing.

c.6 Georg Heinrich Porster deceased, no information available.

c.7 Adolf Haeser died 1983. He was stationed at Weimar and probably did not know details about civilians. He never mentioned civilians in connection with sabotage.

c.8 Eberhard Moerbach has been most careful in all his statements; no solid statements can be expected from additional interrogations.

c.9 Franz Hössler (deceased). No depositions available.

c.10 Dr. med. Karl Kahr was first physician at the concentration camp. He does not know Rudolph.

c.11 Dr. med. Alfred Kurzke (deceased) was second physician at the concentration camp. He has been exhaustively interrogated, but never discussed civilians, not even as spectators to executions.

c.12 Hans Moeser was the only one sentenced to death and executed (Dachau military tribunal). No information with respect to Rudolph.

c.13 Heinrich Rudolph no specific Information available. Definitely no confusion possible with the defendant, nor with an SS captain Dr. Arthur Rudolph, born in Schlotheim/Thuringia 8/21/1904, who had never been at the Kittelbau.

c.14 Ernst Sander was sentenced by the jury court Essen to prison. (7 years, 6 months). No true answers can be expected in future interrogations because of self-incrimination; witness was most careful in this respect in the Essen trial. He did not mention any civilians involved in sabotage reports.

c.15 Wilhelm Simon (deceased) received lifelong imprisonment at the Dachau military tribunal. He did not mention involvement of civilians in sabotage cases, nor did he give any names of engineers despite the fact that he knew the names of leading employees at the Mittelwerk, including Rudolph.

The investigation has been stopped for reasons given above according to paragraph 170 II StPo. For the correctness of the summary, extracted from the German Volume 15 of Attorney General Duhn, Hamburg, PRO

A Translation

Dr.-Ing. Walter Haeussermann   January 15, 1989

Appendix 7
Mercury News Article

San Jose Mercury News Newsclip

Rocket scientist Rudolph is still a war criminal, U.S. says

San Jose Mercury News • Thursday, March 19, 1987

By Carl M. Cannon

Mercury News Washington Bureau

WASHINGTON—Despite being granted citizenship by West Germany, former NASA rocket scientist Arthur Rudolph is still considered a war criminal by American officials and will be arrested on sight if he ever sets foot In the United States.

"Whatever West Germany has done is a matter between him and the Germans—it has no bearing on his position vis-a-vis the United States," said Neal M. Sher, director of the Justice Department's Office of Special Investigations. "He absolutely cannot come in this country. Never."

Rudolph, now 81, was brought to the United States along with Wernher von Braun, a childhood friend, after surrendering to American soldiers in May 1945. Von Braun eventually became head of the George C. Marshall Space Flight Center in Huntsville, Ala., and Rudolph the program director there for the Saturn V rocket, which took Americans to the moon. In 1979, Rudolph retired to San Jose.

During World War II, Rudolph was chief of production at a factory called Mittelwerk, in the Harz Mountains of what is now East Germany, which produced the V-2 rockets used by the Germans to bomb London. Operating underground in abandoned railroad tunnels, Mittelwerk used slave labor around the clock in a frantic 20-month effort to build more V-2 rockets.

According to the Justice Department, United Nations reports, testimony at 1947 war crimes trials and the recollections of survivors, many of the slave laborers were starved, beaten, stabbed and sometimes hanged by SS troops who guarded the factory and by the 5000 German civilians—led by Rudolph—who worked there.

The U.N. report estimated that among the 60,000 workers imprisoned at the nearby Dora concentration camp and other satellite camps from the spring of 1944 to the end of the war, at least 25,000 died.

"As chief of operations, this loyal citizen of the Third Reich requisitioned more slave labor and ran the whole program," Sher said. "He admitted this and it was the guts of our allegations."

Sher interrogated Rudolph for several hours in 1983. Rudolph denied then—and still denies—mistreating anyone or even knowing what went on anywhere in the tunnels or camps except on the Mittelwerk assembly line. Sher was unconvinced and Rudolph, faced with impending deportation proceedings, signed an agreement stipulating that he could keep his NASA pension but would have to leave the United States permanently and give up his American citizenship.

When Rudolph moved to Hamburg, he petitioned the West German government to grant him citizenship. This precipitated a three-year investigation by West German authorities that ended last week when they announced that no basis existed for charging him with war crimes and that his citizenship would be restored.

Appendix 8
Letter to Attorney General Edwin Meese

Letter from W.E. Winterstein to Attorney Gen. Meese
Mr. Edwin Meese
Department of Justice
Constitution Ave. & 10th St., N.W.
Washington D.C. 20530
Dear Mr Meese: 30 May 1985

I am deeply concerned about the case of Dr. Arthur Rudolph, one of the
key German scientists who was instrumental in putting man on the moon
for the U.S. and for which he received NASA's highest award, the
Distinguished Service Medal. He was an American citizen from 1955 to
1984, when in my opinion, from documentation recently made available
to me, he was coerced in some degree into relinquishing his U. S.
citizenship.

It is requested that in view of new evidence which was evidently not
available at the tine the Rudolph case was closed in 1984, that the case he
reopened and a reevaluation be made to determine whether the action
taken against Dr. Rudolph be reconsidered.

In my opinion the key elements of the new evidence are in the statements
of Col. Hochmuth the first U.S. Army intelligence officer that was on the
scene when the V-2 facility was liberated or captured, and in the
statements of Mr. Francis Barwacz, an American, who was a slave laborer
at the V-2 production line. Statements from both of these individuals
indicate that Dr. Rudolph is innocent. (See Enclosures 1, 2, and 3)

Dr. Rudolph was one of the 118 German rocket scientists brought to this
country from Germany in 1945 after WWII. This group was initially
housed in Army barracks at Fort Bliss, Texas. I was the first Commanding
Officer of the Army Ordinance Dept., 9330 Technical Service Unit,
(Rocket), which gave logistical support to the German Rocket Team in
the rocket research efforts conducted at Fort Bliss, Texas, and White
Sands, New Mexico. As Commanding Officer of this Unit, which also
had the responsibility of housing, feeding, and security of the German
Rocket Team, I was in almost daily contact with the individual members
of the Team. I was C. O. of the 9330 TSU (Rocket) from October 10,
1945, to October 23, 1946, when my assignment was changed to Plans
and Policies Officer, Hq. Research and Development Sub-Office
(Rocket), Fort Bliss, Texas, from October 24, 1946, to June 6, 1947. In

later years from January, 1963, to January 1971, I was working for the Rocket team in the Saturn V Program (Moon Landing) out of Huntsville, Alabama. In my opinion Dr. Rudolph did not possess the type of personality to have been guilty of war crimes.

It has been well established that the SS under Himmler maintained strict control over the administration of the concentration camp, and were responsible for the housing, feeding, transportation and work assignments of slave labor. Albert Speer in his book "Inside the Third Reich," explains in quite some detail the working of the SS at the V-2 factory site, (pages 369 to 374). Speer also describes in this section the arrest of Dr. von Braun by SS Chief Himmler when von Braun and some of his associates had their minds on other projects rather than full attention on the V-2 war production efforts.

There appears to be contradiction between the statements made in paragraph 4 of the letter to Senator Nunn by the Justice Department dated January 2, 1985, (See enclosure 4) "where prisoners died in large numbers from overwork, disease, malnutrition and brutalities inflicted by the Nazis," and the statements made by Mr. Barwacz stated that the German civilians on the V-2 production line treated the slave laborers kindly, and also Col. Hochmuth's statements that the skilled laborers on the V-2 production lines appeared to be well fed. Col. Hochmuth also states in his letters that there were several concentration camps near the Mittelwerk and at least one was a horror camp. Colonel Hochmuth also makes a most profound logical statement: "It would have been stupid to mistreat skilled workers." (See Enclosure #2) In my opinion one could not expect to get much production out of workers assigned to producing specialized parts requiring the precision fits and extreme close tolerances inherent in the construction of V-2s if the workers were badly mistreated.

In this respect it should be noted that Arthur Rudolph was the Production Manager of the V-2 production line, and that line only. Rudolph further states that not a single death occurred in his group of laborers as a result of inhuman condition. (See Enclosure #5)

In the letter of Dr. Winterberg to Senator Strom Thurmond, dated February 8, 1985, (see Enclosure #6) Dr. Winterberg indicates that members of the OSI had the full cooperation of the Soviet Union, therefore close coordination with the KGB. Dr. Winterberg also states he has located witnesses, after 40 years, who state that the charges against Dr. Rudolph are outright lies.

In my opinion the coordination with KGB elements is understandable, however the KGB is still operating in a similar fashion as the Gestapo and the SS, and probably would not cooperate unless the end product could bring discredit to the U.S., therefore the testimony of any witnesses if supplied by the KGB or similar sources should be highly suspect as to credibility. Colonel Hochmuth also comments on this aspect of the case: "It is well within the realm of probability that the Russians are amusing themselves while at the same time punishing a member of the "Paperclip" exodus by planting false information that cannot be substantiated or easily refuted." (See Enclosure #2)

My primary concern in this case is that a dedicated citizen of the U.S. has been accused for something for which he was not guilty. This, at a time when after 24 years of dedicated service to the country of his choice, being retired, in poor health and with insufficient funds to defend himself.

My second concern in this case is that the outstanding and distinguished service and major contributions to the U.S. by Dr. Rudolph may not have been fully taken into account. (See Enclosure #7) I was there at Fort Bliss in the early pioneering years, when the appropriations from Congress were almost non-existent, when the attitude in Washington, D.C. was: "The war is over, what further need due we have for rocket research and development."

We even considered it a privilege to have access to the Fort Bliss salvage yard. In this atmosphere it took a lot of "guts" for Dr. Rudolph and other members of the German rocket team to stick to their ambition of space travel, in the meantime trying to advance the U.S. defense capability by their expertise. They could have done much better financially by quitting and going to private industry. The pay for Team members at that time averaged about $62 to $240 a month. It took dedication to do that!

It should be noted that the remaining members of the German rocket team, and others associated with them, do not ask for forgiveness or pardon for the crimes that some Nazis committed during WWII, even after 40 years. They only ask for the application of the time honored rule of jurisdictional procedure established as directives and tools in the search for truth and justice. (See Enclosure #9)

Since it is impossible for Dr. Rudolph to appeal due to the binding restrictions in The Agreement he signed with the Justice Department, I, along with many others who feel the sane way, would sincerely appreciate a reconsideration of this case.

The attached enclosures will give a more comprehensive and complete picture of the situation.
Sincerely yours,
(Signed) Lt. Col, W.E. Winterstein (U.S. Army Retired)
Enclosures: (All copies)
Enc. #1, Letter from Colonel Hochmuth to Mr. Ordway dated November 19, 1984.
Enc. #2, Letter from Colonel Hochmuth to Senator Sam Nunn dated April 25, 1985.
Enc. #3, Letter from Dr. F. Winterberg to Senator Laxalt, with an interrogation questionnaire from the Office of Special Investigation to Mr. Francis J. Barwacz attached, dated 18 February, 1985. (Letter only dated)
Enc. #4, Letter from the U. S. Department of Justice to Senator Sam Nunn dated January 2, 1985.
Enc. #5, Memo submitted to me by Dr. Walter Haeussermann on April 30, 1985, outlining Arthur Rudolph's assignments, activities and responsibilities at Mittelwerk. Also attached are the pages headed "Accusations against Arthur Rudolph and Comments." Also attached is an organization chart depicting location of Rudolph in the network.
Enc. #6, Letter from Dr. F. Winterberg to Senator Thurmond dated 8 February, 1985.
Enc. #7, Professional sketch of Arthur Rudolph.
Enc. #8, Declaration of Arthur Rudolph dated March 14, 1985.
Enc. #9, A "To Whom It May Concern" summary of the Arthur Rudolph case as seen by Dr. Ernst Stuhlinger, other members of the German rocket team, and other friends, dated February 18, 1985.
Enc. #10, clipping from the Huntsville Tines (Alabama) dated April 25, 1985, With a front page item titled "U.S Case Against Arthur Rudolph Unjust, Immoral-Medaris." (Major General Medaris is Retired Army)
cc: Senator Pete Wilson   Congressman Bobbi Fiedler

Appendix 9

The Rail Movement of 61 German Rocket Scientists

R E S T R I C T E D
ARMY SERVICE FORCES
FIRST SERVICE COMMAND
HQ ADMINISTRATIVE DET. FORT STRONG
P O BOX 2276, BOSTON 7, MASS

30 November 1945

300
SUBJECT: Orders
TO: Civilians Concerned

1. The fol named civ employees, German, will proceed o/a 3 Dec 1945 from this sta, by rail to Fort Bliss, Texas, reporting upon arrival thereat to CG for TDY. Upon completion of this TDY they will return to this station.

Erich Ball	Johannes Paul
Mangnus V. Braun	Ludwig Roth
Konrad Dannenberg	Heinz Scharnowski
Herbert Fuhrmann	Albert Schuler
Karl Hager	Johann Tschinkel
Walter Jacobi	Oscar Bauschinger
Ernst Klauss	Gerhard Drawe
Hans Lindenmayr	Friedrich Duerr
Josef Michel	Hans-Jochim Fichtner
Rudolf Schlidt	Rudolf Hölker
Wolfgang Steurer	Helmut Horn
Arthur Urbanski	Hans Hosenthien
Walter Wiesman	Johann Klein
Hermann Beduerftig	Kurt Lindner
Rudi Bickel	Helmut Schlitt
Anton Beier	Helmut Schmid
Gerd deBeek	Karl Sendler
Hans Deppe	Carl-Otto Fleischer
Johannes Finzel	Ernst Geissler
Guenther Haukohl	Hans Gruene
Emil Hellebrand	Fritz Mueller
Bruno Helm	Herbert Axster
Oskar Holderer	Martin Schilling
Werner Kuers	Fritz Vandersee

Erich Kashig	Werner Gengelbach
Rudolph Minning	Otto Hirschler
Kurt Neuhoefer	Otto Hoberg
Max Nowak	Hermann Lange
Helmut Zoike	Carl Wagner
Otto Eisenhardt	Hans Hueter
Bruno Heusinger	

2. Per diem of six dollars ($6.00) is atzd in conformance with existing contract.

3.Travel by air, rail or other means of comm carrier is atzd

4.While enroute, civilians will be in custody of competent U.S. Army personnel to be designated by sep orders.

5.TND 212/60425 601-4 P 432-02 S 99—999. Auth: VOCO,

Chief, CPN. Branch, MIS, Washington D.C., 29 Nov 45.

BY ORDER OF LIEUTENANT COLONEL GRIFFIN:

F.R. LENTZNER
1st Lt, Inf
Adjutant

OFFICIAL: (SIGNED)
F.R. LENTZNER 1st Lt, Inf Adjutant

APR. FORM 9 FILE 1146

MISSOURI PACIFIC RAILROAD COMPANY

CONDUCTOR'S REPORT OF TROOPS, NATIONAL GUARD,
NAVY, MARINE CORPS OR OTHER GOVERNMENT PERSONNEL CARRIED

_____ Section, Train No. 7 From _____ To _____ Date 1-5 194_

(Complete run of train or car)

Name of Command or
Description of Movement: _Army Main 46581_

Cars in Movement Number and Kind	Coach	Pullman			Baggage	Kitchen	Other
		Troop	Tourist	Standard			
	Tourist	4086	2311	287			

DESCRIPTION OF TICKETS

Issuing Carrier	Issuing Station	Final Destination	Date of Issue	Form	Number	Number of Passengers		
						1st Cl	Int	Coach
NYC	Boston	El Paso	12-3-4	542	77280			1
—	—	—	—	—	-821			1
—	—	—	—	Del 6	7644	60	1	
—	—	—	—	6550	1501			1

TOTAL NUMBER OF PASSENGERS COVERED BY TICKETS -- ALL CLASSES 64

NUMBER OF PASSENGERS CARRIED ON TRAIN -- ACTUAL COUNT
(To be filled out by Conductors in order)

From	To	1st Class	Int.	Coach	Conductor	Signature and rank of officer or person in charge
O	X166		64		Shore	Well...
X166	X346		64		Nicholas	
X346	X491		64		Murray	

DESCRIPTION OF C.O.D. CHECKS WHEN IMPEDIMENTA CARRIED

Issuing Carrier	Issuing Station	Final Destination	C.O.D. Check Number-Date	List Here Government Bill of Lading Numbers

(Instructions On Reverse Side)

Appendix 10
Revision to Nazi War Crimes Act

Revision to Nazi War Crimes Disclosure Act
Bill Summary & Status for the 105th Congress
5.1379 Public Law: 105-246 (10/08/98)
SPONSOR: Sen DeWine (introduced 11/05/97)
SUMMARY:
(REVISED AS OF 06/19/98 -- Passed Senate, amended)

Nazi War Crimes Disclosure Act—Establishes the Nazi War Criminal
Records Interagency Working Group to locate, identify, inventory,
recommend for declassification, and make available to the public at the
National Archives and Records Administration, all classified Nazi war
criminal records of the United States. Requires that: (1) Group members
include the Director of the Holocaust Museum, the Historian of the
Department of State, and the Archivist of the United States; and (2) the Group
submit a report to the Congress describing all such records, their disposition,
and the interagency Groups activities. Authorizes appropriations.

Requires such records to be released in their entirety, except that an
agency head may exempt from release specific information that would
compromise privacy, national security, or U.S. foreign policy, as
specified. States that in applying the exemptions there shall be a
presumption that the public interest in the release of Nazi war criminal
records will be served by disclosure and release of the records. **Permits
assertion of such exemption only when the agency head determines
that disclosure and release would be harmful to a specific interest
identified. Requires such a determination to be promptly reported to
the appropriate congressional committees, including the Senate
Committee on the Judiciary and the House Committee on
Government Reform and Oversight.** Subjects such exemptions to the
same standard of review that applies to records withheld under the
Freedom of Information Act (FOIA) for matters that are specifically
authorized by an executive order to be kept secret in the interest of
national defense or foreign policy. **Provides an additional exception
from disclosure for records: (1) related to or supporting any
investigation, inquiry, or prosecution by the Office of Special
Investigations of the Department of Justice; or (2) solely in the
possession or control of that office.**

Amends the National Security Act of 1947 to provide that the exemption
from public disclosure authorized under such Act for operational files of

the Central Intelligence Agency shall not apply to information regarding any operational file, or portion of any operational file, that constitutes a Nazi war criminal record.

Provides for expedited processing of FOIA requests for Nazi war criminal records.

4/19/00

Appendix 11
Letter from Mrs. Rudolph to Mr. Hyde

Letter From Martha Rudolph To Chairman Henry Hyde
Reference: Arthur Rudolph case.   November 19, 1996
The Honorable Henry Hyde
Chairman of the House Judiciary Committee
2110 Rayburn House Office Building
Washington, D.C., 20515

Dear Chairman Hyde,

My husband was the late Arthur L.H. Rudolph who died of a massive heart attack in Hamburg, Germany January 1, 1996.

A friend of the family, William E. Winterstein, LTC, Army, (Ret.), has given me copies of several letters, dated July 1, August 1, and August 26, 1996, in which he wrote to you concerning the Arthur Rudolph case. I concur completely with his comments. However, I wish to further comment on my views regarding this case.

In 1983, after coercion and duress by officials from the Office of Special Investigations (OSI), of the Department of Justice, my husband signed an 'Agreement' drafted by the OSI. This Agreement alleged that Arthur Rudolph had participated in the "persecution" of unarmed civilians in wartime Germany. He strenuously objected to the word persecution, but to no avail. I clearly remember his anguish at the time, as he did not wish to sign anything that he knew was false. My husband was an honorable man, and from the beginning I was firmly convinced that he was absolutely innocent of any OSI allegations of persecution or any other crime. Being in very poor health with a heart condition, he did not have the physical stamina or the financial resources for a court battle with the OSI. 'The Agreement' resulted in the loss of his U.S. citizenship. It did, however, provide for future financial stability in granting continuing Civil Service pension and Social Security benefits. In early 1984, at which time he was a retired resident of San Jose, California, he left the U.S. to begin exile in Germany.

In 1985 came another devastating blow perpetrated against my husband by certain officials of the U.S. government. It was the introduction into Congress of House Resolution 68 of 1985. This resolution contained the allegation that Arthur Rudolph had been responsible for the deaths of 20,000 to 30,000 slave laborers in wartime Germany. This resolution directly and implicitly implicates the Department of Justice, and the Office of Special Investigations as the source of the information. The Department of Justice has failed to provide a single thread of legitimate evidence to support this allegation, therefore making it a malicious, gross and deliberate lie. Investigations by three countries, the United States in the early post war years, Germany in the 1980s, and Canada in 1990, have found no evidence to substantiate any of the charges.

Two years later, to further insult and harass my husband, House Resolution 164 of 1987, was added to the public documents. The wording is identical to the text of the previously mentioned resolution. The prime purpose of both resolutions was to strip him of the NASA Distinguished Service Medal. He was awarded this medal for his immense contributions as Program Director of the Saturn V rocket which made the moon voyages possible.

In 1989, Colonel Winterstein requested, under the provisions of the Freedom of Information Act, from the Department of Justice specific information concerning the sources contained in the fourth paragraph of House Resolution 68 of 1985. The response from the Department of Justice was that the Criminal Division did not supply that information to Congress. This evidently is a gross lie, as it is hardly conceivable that a Congressman would concoct a document with such a serious impact without some guidance from a recognizable, reliable source. The response Col. Winterstein received is direct evidence that both House Resolutions referred to above are based on a gross misrepresentation of facts. Copies of both resolutions and the response from the Department of Justice are attached as enclosures No. 1, 2, and 3.

I have further proof that the resolutions are based on lies. My husband had a TOP SECRET security clearance which was granted by the FBI during the many years he was employed by the Army in work vital to the defense of this country, and later on at NASA. The FBI made thorough and intensive background checks of his participation in the German war effort. Had he been guilty of any of the OSI allegations he surely would not have received a top secret clearance.

It has been thirteen years since my husband, and I, began exile. These last years, which should have been some of the happiest of his life, were instead spent in trying to clear his name. This consequently put him under much stress, mental anguish and despondency, which ultimately shortened his life. We have attempted to clear his name through proper channels, which so far has been of no avail. The continued existence of House Resolutions 68 and 164, as public documents, have been a source of deep embarrassment, distress, misery, and unhappiness to my husband and the surviving members of his family, and should therefore be abolished. Since these resolutions originated in the House, it is self evident that the House should take action to have justice restored. Therefore, I am requesting as a citizen of the United States, that the House Judiciary Committee take appropriate action to have House Resolutions No. 68 of 1985 and No. 164 of 1987, refuted and annulled. Also, that the public be notified that the resolutions should not be accepted as historical documents concerning this countries early history in the conquest of space, and the reasons therefore.

I will deeply appreciate your kind consideration of this request.

Sincerely,
(Signed) Martha Rudolph
3 Enclosures:
House Resolution 68, 1985.
House Resolution 164, 1987.
Copy of letter from the Department of Justice to W.E. Winterstein.
cc: Rep. Elton Gallegly
LTC W.E. Winterstein, Sr.

Appendix 12

Letter from Frank Barwacz to
President Reagan

Letter from Frank Barwacz to President Reagan
Frank Barwacz

May 20, 1985

Honorable Ronald Reagan
President, United States of America
The White House
Washington, D.C.

Dear Mr. President:

For the last few weeks in news media, press, TV, radio, there was so much confusion about your trip to Germany. I saw on TV when Mr. Wiesel did receive from you Mr. President the Congressional Medal of Honor in commemorating the Holocaust. Mr. President, I was in that suffering Holocaust too, I did suffer there plenty, and many times I was near death. My blood was spilled there in Germany. I was in four concentration camps, Auschwitz, Birkenau, then Buchenwald, then Dora where we inmates were forced to work on those V2 rockets, then Bergen-Belsen. I was liberated with others by the British Army. Many times before, and lately they were showing on TV the horrors in Bergen-Belsen. They were showing the corpses of the dead and some still alive inmates. I was there and I was near death too, but thanks to God, I survived, and Mr. President I was there as a prisoner, flesh and bones American, born here in Chicago. Mr. President I did write to you before, but you did not answer me. Maybe your aides were holding back my letters, but I do hope Mr. President that you will answer me this time.

When you, Sir, were sworn in, you had your right hand on the Bible, so I am sure Mr. President that you do, as I, believe in the Bible. In the Bible it says: When St. Peter did ask our Lord Jesus Christ, do we have to forgive our enemies 7 times? Jesus answers, not 7 times but 77 times. Christ also said, pray for your enemy and for those who hurt you. And he says: If you have anything against your brother, but want to bring an offering before the altar, first go and make peace with your brother, then take the offering. Now, Mr. President, I did suffer so much in those four concentration camps, that is beyond the human imagination. I was beaten by SS, by Kapos as they were spilling my blood in those concentration camps, and in my thin body, I did not have much blood anyway. There were times in my life after my liberation, I thought how can I forgive, but today my Dear Mr. President I am saying, because I do believe in our Lord Jesus Christ, what the Bible says: I am forgiving all those SS who were torturing me and others, I am forgiving those Kapos, and asking may God to have mercy on their souls. Today I love all those who hurt me so much, today I am praying that Almighty God have mercy on them and forgive them, because I do in my heart forgive them all. Therefore Mr. President, we who suffered so much must forgive. The Bible says: If we forgive those who hurt us and trespass against us, God Almighty will forgive us all in the name of Jesus, His Son, who did pay the high price for us on the Cross. My Dear President I was an American and suffered there terribly, but I do not want any glory, I do not want any medal, all I want and I am asking you our Dear President is justice. Now Mr. President we need friends, we need allies, and they also need us, therefore when you said Mr. President to Mr. Wiesel that you are trying to achieve reconciliation, you are right Mr. President, you Sir must seek reconciliation, and from myself I am adding this one word that we must forgive.

Forgiveness is to me the most important thing. I do forgive. Those SS who died, they already paid their price, but above all, they went before God on the Judgment Day, and I am sure, I am positive, that before they died, they were sorry before God, and if they asked God for mercy, and did ask God for forgiveness deeply from their hearts, I am sure, I am positive, that God granted them His Mercy, therefore we can not judge them, God already did judge them, and some day we will meet them in Heaven because of God's mercy. So let there be no hatred, but forgiveness.

Now Mr. President, I also did ask you Sir for justice. I did ask you Mr. President to bring justice to Mr. Dr. Arthur Rudolph. I did mention before to you Mr. President that Mr. Dr. Rudolph is 100% innocent, and my testimony proves it, because I was in Dora and the V2 rocket plant, and I am repeating, again and again, and again, what I saw in Dora, what I heard from other prisoners, and what I have experienced on my own flesh, I am stating wholeheartedly, that no German civilian high or low group or any scientist-engineers hurt, or harmed me or any other prisoners in Dora, and that is the truth. Nobody can give any better proof for that than me because I was the only American prisoner. When I was forced to work with other inmates on the secret production of the V2 rocket, inside and outside the tunnels, I was beaten there by a Kapo, and an SS guard sent a dog on me and that dog was ripping my body's right leg and right arm, but one German civilian with one arm saved my life.

When I was laying on the ground in blood and the SS man did pull the gun to shoot me and finish me off, this German civilian grabbed his arm and asked the SS man not to shoot me. In doing so he not only endangered himself, but also saved my life. On another occasion, which I forgot to say before in my testimony given already to our Justice Department, I once was told by a German civilian to do a certain job, to separate metal parts and put then in certain places. I made a mistake, a big mistake because I was putting things wrongly. When this German civilian came over to me and saw it that I did wrong, he very kindly and quietly told me that I did wrong. He did not raise his voice, but again showed me kindly. He could have called the SS from nearby, and accused me for sabotage and I would be shot or hanged, he therefore too saved my life. **I never heard, or saw that any German civilian, from the top to the bottom, any German civilian hurt us prisoners, that is the reason why my heart is crying out loudly to you Mr. President to help me that I could prove that Mr. Dr. Arthur Rudolph is innocent.** If only one German civilian would hurt us inmates, I would not fight so hard for Mr. Rudolph. Those German civilians from the top to the bottom were told to do their jobs, or else, and prisoners were told to do our jobs or else. We were victims, and those German civilians were victims in the oppressive hands of the SS even though not all SS men in Dora were mean, some were treating us prisoners fairly.

Once a reporter in a large newspaper here in Chicago asked me these words. Mr. Barwacz were there also Jews In Dora? I said: I did not see any Jewish prisoners in our Kommando, as a matter of fact, nowhere. Then he asked me why I am doing this for Mr. Rudolph. I said: God was good to me, and saved me there, I am repaying now for my neighbor, because I know that Mr. Rudolph is innocent. Mr. President I am not doing this because what Mr. Rudolph with Mr. von Braun did for America, American people already know, I am doing this because **Mr. Rudolph is suffering injustice and I know what it is to suffer injustice**, therefore Mr. President please help to bring and restore honor and dignity to Dr. Arthur Rudolph because he is innocent.

Also Mr. President I want to say this. When I was in Buchenwald, I know that in Buchenwald were German communists as prisoners, also some, I heard, in Dora. If some of them as hard core Communists went to serve communism, and if some of them brought some accusations, then Mr. President, who are you going to believe me as a truly American or you going to believe someone who does not belong to our country, who has maybe some selfish aspirations, or to hurt our beautiful America.

Mr. President, injustice has been done to me here in my beloved America. For many, many years the War Claims Commission, and also the War Settlement Commission in Washington, D.C. were telling me that I will be compensated by the War Claims Commission but nothing from them so far. Now my Dear Mr. President, we silent American majority, are approving your policy in economics, on Defense and on Justice. I still love America, I still love all American people, regardless what origin they are, whites, blacks, Asians, Jewish, Arabic, Germans, Italians, Irish and others. We are all Americans. I would write much more Mr. President, but I know that your time is very valuable, so I am sorry, and God Bless You Mr. President and your family. God Bless America!

> Thank you Mr. President!
> Yours very truly,
> Frank Barwacz

Appendix 13
Letter to President Clinton

Letter from William Winterstein to President Clinton
February 19, 1993

The Honorable Bill Clinton
President of the United States
The White House
1600 Pennsylvania
Washington, DC 20500

Dear President Clinton:

To my knowledge a travesty of justice has occurred in one of our governmental departments, the Department of Justice, concerning a case in which gross prosecutorial misconduct has evidently occurred.

I am referring to the operational tactics of the Office of Special Investigations (OSI), a small element of our Department of Justice. The particular case I am referring to is the one concerning Dr. Arthur Rudolph.

Dr. Rudolph, a U.S. citizen until his exile in 1984, was the project manager of the Saturn V program, which placed U.S. astronauts on the moon in 1969, and returned them safely to earth.

During World War II, Arthur Rudolph, then a German civilian, was employed by a German civilian contractor to build V-2s for the German government. The provisions of the contract was that the German government would provide the facilities and the manpower for this project. The source of the manpower turned out to be concentration camp inmates. Rudolph, prior to his entry into the U.S. in 1945, freely and fully disclosed his wartime role to U.S. officials. He was invited by the U.S. government to come to the U.S. to assist in our efforts to increase our capability in rocket research in which we were so far behind at the time.

The OSI was formed under the provisions of the Holtzman Amendment of 1978, which in fact appears to be an ex-post facto law forbidden by our Constitution.

The OSI has pursued a course of prosecution/persecution of Rudolph from 1983 to the present. In 1983 OSI officials confronted him with allegations concerning the "persecution" of unarmed civilians in the production of V-2s. He firmly denied this at the time, and the OSI did not present firm evidence to Rudolph, or his attorney, to support their allegation. However through devious means such as misrepresentation, duress and fraud, the OSI obtained Rudolph's signature on an agreement in 1983 which resulted in his exile and loss of his U.S. citizenship. Evidence to support these allegations against the OSI surfaced after Rudolph's departure from the U.S. in 1984.

I wrote a letter, dated May 30, 1985, to then Attorney General Edwin Meese. The letter, with ten enclosures, including affidavits of witnesses, requested a reconsideration of the Rudolph case. This letter was ignored, as I received no response to it.

With the assistance of then Senator Pete Wilson, I wrote a letter, dated March 1, 1987, to the Department of Justice. I presented legitimate evidence, including affidavits of former concentration camp inmates who worked on the V-2 production line, and testimony from the U.S. Army Intelligence Officer who was at the site when U.S. troops captured the V-2 facility. This evidence refuted the OSI allegation that Rudolph "persecuted" unarmed civilians. I again requested a reconsideration of the case by the Department of Justice.

I received a letter, dated July 6, 1987, from the Department of Justice stating that I had offered no new legitimate evidence justifying a reconsideration of the Rudolph case.

Upon Rudolph's return to Germany in 1984, the West German government promptly initiated an investigation of Arthur Rudolph. After repeated requests by the West German prosecutor to the Department of Justice for the U.S. file on Rudolph, the OSI sent some documentation and the names of nine witnesses. Upon investigation, four of the witnesses did not even know Rudolph, one testified in favor of Rudolph, two were mentally incompetent, and two contradicted themselves. Thus the OSI did not offer a single legitimate prosecution witness to substantiate their allegation.

Due to the unusual circumstances of the case, the West German prosecutor pursued an intensive and thorough investigation of the matter.

After several years, including the interrogation of over 65 witnesses, or review of depositions, covering over 2300 pages of transcript, the West German prosecutor found that Rudolph was not guilty of allegations as brought by the OSI. Upon this the West German government granted Arthur Rudolph citizenship in 1987.

It has become quite evident that the OSI did not have firm evidence to support their allegation of "persecution" when they first confronted Rudolph in 1983, in San Jose, California. Mr. Robert Smith, Rudolph's lawyer in Huntsville, Alabama, requested a copy of Rudolph's file under the Freedom of Information Act in April of 1989. Now, nearly four years later, the OSI has failed to furnish one shred of legitimate evidence to support their allegation.

My latest attempt to get truth and justice resolved in this case, was in my letter, dated August 28, 1992, to Senator Joseph Biden, Chairman of the Senate Judiciary Committee, a copy of which is enclosed. As you may note, this letter contains additional information concerning prosecutorial misconduct by the OSI, not only in the Rudolph case, but in two other cases with implications far more serious than those in the Rudolph case.

OSI officials have been persecuting Dr. Rudolph since his return to Germany, issuing items to the news media accusing him of being a war criminal or making other highly derogatory or insulting remarks. The latest occurrence, to my knowledge, of this was on February 8, 1993, when two top officials of the OSI appeared on the Los Angeles TV program "Inside Edition" at 6:00 PM accusing Rudolph of being a war criminal, along with other insulting remarks. This program appeared to be a replay of a program aired over the same station on September 5, 1990.

Since I have exhausted my efforts in going through Department of Justice, and Congressional channels, to no avail, I now appeal to you Mr. President, to resolve truth and justice in this matter. That appropriate action be taken to investigate the operational conduct of the OSI in the Rudolph case, and in the other two cases referred to above, and that U.S citizenship be restored to those who have been victims of unconstitutional acts perpetrated upon them by U.S. officials.

Your promise that special interest groups should not have the same influence over our government, as in the past, is most encouraging. It has become increasingly evident that there has been some strong action by special interest to suppress truth and justice in the Rudolph case. The City of Huntsville, Alabama, sent a City Resolution, dated June 20, 1990, to President Bush, requesting an investigation be conducted concerning the Rudolph case. This request was ignored.

I have acted on a voluntary basis, as a U.S. citizen, in my attempt to get truth and justice resolved in this case, and have not received, or expect to receive, any monetary remuneration for my almost eight years of effort.

Your kind consideration of this request will be deeply appreciated.

Sincerely yours,

William E. Winterstein LTC Army (Ret.)
1 Enclosure: Cy of ltr. to Sen. Biden
cc: Sen. Joseph Biden
    Sen. Howell Heflin
    Sen. Richard Shelby
    Rep. Elton Gallegly
    Rep. James Traficant

Appendix 14
House Resolution No. 68 of 1985

House Resolution No. 68 of 1985

99TH CONGRESS

1ST SESSION   **H.RES .68**

Expressing the sense of the House Representatives that the NASA Distinguished Service Medal should be taken away from Arthur Rudolph

IN THE HOUSE OF REPRESENTATIVES

February 21,1985

Mr. Green submitted the following resolutions; which was referred to the Committee on Science and Technology

Resolution

Expressing the sense of the House of Representatives that the NASA Distinguished Service Medal should be taken away from Arthur Rudolph.

Whereas Arthur Rudolph, designer of the Saturn V moon rocket, has been accused by the Department of Justice of working thousands of slave laborers to death while supervising the production of V2 missile for the Nazis during World War II;

Whereas Arthur Rudolph has renounced his American citizenship and returned to West Germany rather than face deportation charges stemming from allegations brought by the Office of Special Investigations, Department of Justice:

Whereas under Rudolph's supervision 60,000 slave laborer, worked in subhuman conditions, resulting in the death of an estimated 20,000 to 30,000 workers;

Whereas Arthur Rudolph was awarded the National Aeronautics and Space Administrator's Distinguished Service Medal in 1969 for his work on the Saturn V rocket project; and

Whereas the Congress, in the National Aeronautics and Space Act of 1958, states that "**it is the policy of the United States that activities in space should be devoted to peaceful purposes for the benefit of all mankind**": Now, therefore, be it

1 Resolved, That the administrator of the National Aeronautics and Space Administration (NASA) should rescind the Distinguished Service Medal awarded to Arthur Rudolph in 1969.

Communications Output Beginning at   14:21:10   17 MAR   1986

1 OF 1   27LINES

DS   ***********99TH CONG. STATUS PROFILE FOR H.Res.68**********

          SPONSOR..................Green
          DATE INTRODUCED.....February 21, 1985
HOUSE COMMITTEE.... Science and Technology
OFFICIAL TITLE..........A resolution expressing the sense of the House of Representatives that the NASA Distinguished Service Medal should be taken away from Arthur Rudolph.
     CO-SPONSORS.....26 CURRENT COSPONSORS --
     Feb 21, 85 Referred to House Committee on Science and Technology. Mar 6, 85 Referred to Subcommittee on Space Science Applications.
CO-SPONSORS   26 CURRENT COSPONSORS—Mar 6, 85 Sensenbrenner, Frank, Fauntroy, Smith (FL), Mrazek, Ackerman, Kaptur, Gallo, Barnes, Boxer, Berman, Horton, Bedell, Heftel (HI) , Reid, Lehman (FL) Apr 3, 85 Schumer, Garcia, Biaggi, Fish, Waxman Levine (CA), Weiss, Saxton, DioGuardi, Addabbo. BD BILL DIGEST. Feb 21, 85. Expresses the sense of the House of Representatives that the Administrator of the National

     Aeronautics and Space Administration should rescind the Distinguished Service Medal awarded to Arthur Rudolph in 1969 (with such rescission to be based in part on such person's renouncing U.S. citizenship and returning to West Germany rather than facing deportation charges stemming from allegations of war crimes brought by the Department of Justice)

Appendix 15
House Resolution No. 164 of 1987

House Resolution No. 164 of 1987

100TH CONGRESS

1ST SESSION   **H.RES.164**

Expressing the sense of the House Representatives that the NASA Distinguished Service Medal should be taken away from Arthur Rudolph

IN THE HOUSE OF REPRESENTATIVES

May 11, 1987

Mr. Green submitted the following resolutions; which was referred to the Committee on Science and Technology

Resolution

Expressing the sense of the House of Representatives that the NASA Distinguished Service Medal should be taken away from Arthur Rudolph.

Whereas Arthur Rudolph, designer of the Saturn V moon rocket, has been accused by the Department of Justice of working thousands of slave laborer to death while supervising the production of V2 missile for the Nazis during World War II;

Whereas Arthur Rudolph has renounced his American citizenship and returned to West Germany rather than face deportation charges stemming from allegations brought by the Office of Special Investigations, Department of Justice:

Whereas under Rudolph's supervision 60,000 slave laborers, worked in subhuman conditions, resulting in the death of an estimated 20,000 to 30,000 workers;

Whereas Arthur Rudolph was awarded the National Aeronautics and Space Administrator's Distinguished Service Medal in 1969 for his work on the Saturn V rocket project; and

Whereas the Congress, in the National Aeronautics and Space Act of 1958, states that "it is the policy of the United States that activities in space should be devoted to peaceful purposes for the benefit of all mankind": Now, therefore, be it

1 Resolved, That the administrator of the National Aeronautics and Space Administration (NASA) should rescind the Distinguished Service Medal awarded to Arthur Rudolph in 1969.

Appendix 16
Stuhlinger Open Letter to Neufeld

Dr. Ernst Stuhlinger   Huntsville, AL 35801.

                                                    December 2002.

Dr. Michael J. Neufeld
Smithsonian Institution
Washington, D.C.

Dear Dr. Neufeld,

When your rocket book appeared in 1995, I immediately bought and read it. I was delighted when I read that as a teenager in the 1960s, you "lived and breathed space flight," and that you planned to become a space engineer. But then, reading further, I was shocked to realize that you soon discarded the noble endeavor to become a space aficionado when you discovered—perhaps stimulated by other who had made the same discovery before—that there was a cheap opportunity of a short cut to fame and fortune by denigrating and vilifying those who had spent their lives' work making space flight and space exploration possible.

It is a great pity that you dropped your early plans to help the space age come to life. For us Old Timers in the rockets and space program who have become the targets of your attacks, it is very difficult to understand how you could choose such a strange and negative activity as your life career. Rather than indulging in a study of the technology and science of rockets and space flight, you put the cruel and chaotic undertakings of the Nazi dictatorship to the feet of von Braun and his co-workers. You hate and deplore them as if they had invented and operated the concentration camps. You based your arguments on misinterpreted and misunderstood. As a consequence, your 'von Braun' is not the real von Braun, and your 'Peenemünde' never existed—a sad accomplishment indeed!

If you should ever have a chance to leaf through the two volumes of 'The Century of Space Science' (I am sure that the Smithsonian's library will acquire them), you many realize what has been accomplished by those who have remained faithful to their early love of rockets and space exploration.

                    Sincerely, Ernst Stuhlinger

Appendix 17
A Visitor from Russia

Huntsville, Alabama, May 2000.

A Visitor from Russia.

By Ernst Stuhlinger

Some months ago, on one of my frequent visits to the Huntsville Space and Rocket Center, I saw a young man standing before one of the rocket motors exhibited in the museum. When I came closer, he looked at me for some seconds, then said, with a slight foreign accent: "Dr. Stuhlinger, I am so happy to meet you! My name is Dimitri, I am a member of the Russian space program in Moscow. I know you well from reading your book on Ion Propulsion, in Russian. It is our bible on electric space propulsion. It is so good to meet you in person!"—Then, we had a long talk on Sputnik and Explorer I, on the MIR space station, on unmanned and manned travel to the moon and to mars, on Braun and the Shuttle, and very extensively on Sergi Korolev and Wernher von Braun, and on the future of space exploration, but also on the founding fathers of space flight, Konstantn Tsiolkovskii, Robert Goddard, and Hermann Oberth. It was most surprising to see how much young Dimitri knew about the European and American space projects. But then, he said: "There is one profound difference between your space programs and ours: in Russia, our space pioneers are heroes, and we build monuments for them. The Germans and the Americans treat their most prominent space pioneers as war criminals. **We in Russia could never understand that. Why are they doing this?**"

Appendix 18

Letter to Attorney General Ashcroft

The Honorable John Ashcroft   March 26,2004
Attorney General of United States
950 Pennsylvania Avenue
Washington, D.C. 20530

Re: Calumnies against the U.S. Space Program

Dear: Mr. Ashcroft:

I witnessed a hate crime, of a kind, committed on a national television
network, ABC, March 1, 2004, at about 7:23 p.m., broadcasting on
Channel 7, Los Angeles. As a faithful viewer of hugely popular
"Jeopardy," I heard host Alex Trebek ask one of the three quiz
participants "What rocket scientist, a Nazi war criminal, gained entry into
the U.S. under "Operation Paperclip?" The answer given, and accepted as
correct, was "Wernher von Braun."

Absolutely untrue, this contribution to the growing Black Legion of
detraction against the U.S. Space Program emanates from a web of
vicious and contemptible lies to besmirch and discredit the achievements
of one of our most glorious national accomplishments. Not only have
"Jeopardy" and ABC unjustly vilified America's foremost space pioneer
and hero; in allowing publication of this falsehood, they have
contaminated the history of this country's and all mankind's greatest
technological achievement. In the midst of the Cold War, von Braun
produced a monumental victory for his adopted country: man's first
voyage to the moon. In 1961, President Kennedy declared to the world
that this nation would go to the moon "in this decade," and Marshall
Space Flight Center at Huntsville, Alabama, took up the task of
designing and building the giant rocket boosters to put our astronauts on
the moon. Dr. von Braun was director of the Center. He and his
teammates accomplished the work brilliantly. To him and them the word
"hero" applies unreservedly.

More amazing than anything else is the Jeopardy segment was that the
(presumably ordinary American) participant gave so promptly such a
wrong and offensive answer. Dr. Wernher von Braun, far from being
convicted, or even declared, a "Nazi war criminal," was never officially
accused of any misdeeds.

I have observed a creeping influence into the public news and
entertainment media intended to denigrate and diminish the country's
heroic space scientists, possibly because of their national origin, possibly

in an effort to debunk the whole notion of space exploration. Another clear example of such an attack is the book *The Rocket and the Reich*, by Michael J. Neufeld, published by the Smithsonian Institution in 1995. Neufeld's portrayal of Arthur Rudolph as a Nazi war criminal is completely false. Rudolph was manager of the Saturn V Program which made the rockets that put us on the moon. All available and reliable evidence reveals that he was savior to many concentration camp inmates who worked under him on the V-2 production line in wartime Germany.

It is appropriate that the Department of Justice look into the origins of Jeopardy's terribly mistaken publication, which amounts to but another contribution to the hate program, the Black Legend directed against German scientists who made America leader among nations in the exploration of space. A formal investigation of this and other elements is called for.

My background concerning this matter is: I was custodian of the 118 member rocket team led by Dr. Wernher von Braun immediately after WWII at Fort Bliss, Texas. In 1963 I was employed by NASA as a member of the Apollo Team, which put our astronauts on the moon in 1969.

I hope to hear from you soon.

Yours very truly,

William E. Winterstein, Sr.

Cc: Rep. Elton Gallegly
ABC

Received from Attorney General Ashcroft June 10, 2004, in a *non sequitur* and almost comic response:

"Thank you for your letter to the Attorney General. Federal law authorizes officers of the Department of Justice to give opinions or to render legal services only to Federal officials charged with public responsibilities. After a review of your letter, we have determined that the agency listed below (The Federal Communications Division) can best address your concern."

Appendix 19

Letter to Editors

William E. Winterstein Sr. LTC. Army (Ret.)

Reference: A void in U.S. history.   September 24, 2003

Editor Huntsville Times
2337 South Memorial Parkway
Huntsville, Alabama 35801

Dear Editor:

As a member of the U.S. Apollo Team who put astronauts on the moon in 1969, I am very much concerned about our history, which achieved the distinction of the U.S. performing the greatest technological achievement of all mankind and which has been clad in obscurity in recent decades. Will a great American heritage be lost to future generations?

Today, in the year 2003, there is a huge void in American history concerning the glorious moment in world history wherein this country achieved man's successful journey to the moon. This great historical event in our history occurred only 66 years after man's first flight by airplane in 1903. This year a number of significant celebrations have occurred commemorating the 100th anniversary of man's first airplane flight by the Wright brothers at Kitty Hawk, North Carolina. Yet I have not observed one word mentioned in the news media about the historical event which far overshadows the accomplishments of the Wright brothers; man's journey to the moon and safe return to earth. Here are only two statistics about these flights:

	Moon Flight	Aircraft Flight
Take-off weight	6,423,000 pounds	605 pounds
Flight distance	over 476,000 miles RT	852 feet

This year, 34 years after the event, there has been no nationally designated location of where man's first flight to the moon **originated**, that is, where did the plans and designs of the moon mission take place, and who were the primary persons responsible for the event? We know that the vehicles departed from the Kennedy Space Center, and that the astronauts rode them to the moon, but without the vehicles there would be no footprints of the astronauts on the moon today.

At the time that President Kennedy announced to the nation in 1961 that we would be going to the moon "in this decade," Dr. Wernher von Braun was Director of the Marshall Space Flight Center, Huntsville, Alabama. Marshall Space Flight Center was given the task of providing the giant rocket boosters for the moon mission. This task was assigned the name "The Saturn V Program." Arthur Rudolph was manger of the Saturn V Program. In that assignment Rudolph received NASA's highest award, the Distinguished Service Medal, for his participation in the lunar mission.

As a member of the Apollo Team who put U.S. astronauts on the moon, I contend that the Marshall Space Flight Center, Huntsville, Alabama, is the focal point wherein the plans and specifications for the journey to the moon were formulated. Thus the Marshall Space Flight Center should be nationally designated, and recognized, as this nation's 'Kitty Hawk' for the moon mission. No other spot in this United States can claim this heritage. Further that Dr. Wernher von Braun and Arthur Rudolph be rightfully, and nationally recognized, as our foremost national space heroes and pioneers of space travel. There is no one else who can justifiably claim these honors.

It is quite evident that many Americans do not readily appreciate the many beneficial items that mankind has received due to the spin-off results concerning the research efforts conducted for the moon mission. Much of the research did not end up on the moon but was of a direct benefit, worldwide, to earth-bound man. It almost revolutionized many manufacturing techniques and gave us many newly developed materials, ranging from kitchen use to medical utilization. One of the greatest benefits that did wind up on the moon was the revolutionary advance of computer technology. This completely changed our lives from laptop computers to the great advances in industry and doing every-day business. There were no such immediate spin-off benefits emerging from the flight at Kitty Hawk, only the beginning of research for improvements resulting in future air travel many years later.

As a member of the Apollo Team I contend that the United States of America has yet failed to claim rightful ownership to a precious national heritage. Where is the corresponding monument, similar to Kitty Hawk, indicating the nationally recognized location of the origin of the journey to the moon???

Indeed that glorious moment in history wherein our country leaped ahead of the world in performing the greatest technological achievement of all mankind should be duly recorded and nationally acknowledged, and celebrated. All Americans should be very proud of the historical fact that their country achieved both man's first powered air flight and man's first journey to the moon within a 66 year period, 1903-1969, all within 100 years!!! Indeed, what a magnificent historical legacy that we will hand down to future generations of American citizens.

I am submitting this information in an attempt that a great American heritage be recognized on a National basis.

Respectfully,

P.S.:
Author's Short Biography:
1915 Born
1934 Enlisted in Army
1943 Selected as Ordnance Technical Intelligence Officer
1945 Selected as Custodian of German Rocket Team
1957 Military Advisor to South Vietnam
1960 Participated in construction of ICBM sites
1963 Selected as Member of Apollo Team Moon Mission
2001 Wrote book on early U.S. rocket history

Appendix 20
Neil Sher Articles

Former OSI lawyer Neal Sher disbarred

Top Holocaust Industry Officer Fired for Embezzling One of the world's prominent figures in both the Israeli lobby and the Holocaust industry has been caught stealing money intended for Holocaust survivors.
By Michael Collins Piper (American Free Press)
November 18, 2002

Exposed as an embezzler, Neal Sher was forced out of his post as chief of staff in the Washington office of the International Commission on Holocaust Era Insurance Claims (ICHEIC). Sher was caught taking "unauthorized reimbursements" on his extravagant worldwide travel expenses for the ICHEIC.

Sher—a longtime leading figure in the worldwide Jewish community and a widely promoted "media star"—was effectively stealing from Holocaust survivors and their heirs by ripping off the ICHEIC.

Another of the growing Holocaust industry's leading forces, the ICHEIC was established jointly by a variety of leading European insurance companies, Holocaust survivor groups, state insurance commissioners, top Jewish organizations and the Israeli government to sort out and resolve claims by Holocaust survivors who allege that insurance companies refuse to pay their family's insurance policies.

Although Sher's resignation was announced on June 20, it was not known until recently that he had been the subject of a highly secretive, top-drawer corruption investigation carried out as the direction of former Secretary of State Lawrence Eagleburger, himself the well paid chairman of the ICHEIC.

The Sher scandal was considered so "sensitive" to Jewish lobby public relations concerns that Eagleberger actually asked William Webster, former director of the FBI and the CIA, to convene a formal high-level review of the secret internal investigation that led to Sher's forced resignation.

Sher's pilfering lends credence to the charge by many that "the Holocaust" has essentially become "a racket," a point driven home by American Jewish Professor Norman G. Finkelstein in his controversial book, *The Holocaust Industry: Reflections on the Exploitation of Jewish Suffering.*

Finkelstein was denied academic tenure for writing that book because he raised questions about the ICHEIC and its profiteering administrators.

Another who has reason to smile at Sher's takedown is former Rep. Jim Traficant (D-Ohio).

For 11 years, until his departure in 1994, Sher was the director of the secretive "Nazi hunting" Office of the Special Investigations (OSI) inside the Justice Department. From his post as OSI, Sher and the OSI for framing Ukraine-born Cleveland autoworker John Demjanjuk, even the Supreme Court of Israel cleared Demjanjuk of the false charges of Sher and the OSI.

After leaving the OSI, Sher went on to serve as executive director of AIPAC, the powerful Israeli lobby unit that listed Traficant—a critic of U.S. favoritism toward Israel—as its number one target.

Ultimately, a clique of Justice department lawyers—using Sher-style tactics—concocted a trumped-up corruption case against Traficant and sent the populist congressman to prison this past year.

As AFP noted on Feb. 18, the late former U.S. Attorney General Eliot Richardson, while serving as the attorney for the INSLAW corporation, discovered that the OSI was responsible for the theft of INSLAW's famous "Promis" surveillance software (which was then turned over to agents of Israel's intelligence service, the Mossad). The INSLAW scandal is ranked as one of the major scandals of the Reagan-Bush era.

Richardson also made the shocking allegation that Sher's OSI operated a covert-operations intelligence unit inside the Justice Department, involved in assassinations and other acts designed to silence American political dissidents.

At the time the INSLAW scandal was coming into the open, The Spotlight newspaper led the media in publicizing the affair. A Justice department attorney who was promoted to a federal judgeship in return for his services on behalf of the OSI thieves—S. Martin Teel—later issued the controversial ruling that killed Liberty Lobby, publisher of The Spotlight.

Despite having confessed to misappropriating Holocaust restitution council funds for his own use, the ex-OSI chief, Sher, will apparently not face criminal charges. Because of his close ties to the Justice department and because of his long-standing services to high-level forces in the global Jewish elite, Sher will not go to prison.

Although the story of Sher's thievery has been reported in the Jewish newspaper, Forward, the major media—radio, television and newspapers—loudly and repeatedly promoted Sher as some sort of "hero" who was "hunting Nazis" and "Protecting the interests of our ally, Israel."

Sher is said to have reimbursed the Holocaust outfit for the fund that he stole. His longtime secretary at the OSI—who still works for new OSI chief Eli Rosenbaum—hung up when AFP called to ask if the OSI would be investigating possible misuse of OSI funds by Sher during his tenure at the organization.

Other articles of interest found at http://www.ukemonde.com/:

The unraveling of Neal Sher—(Ukemonde) Tom Schoenberg reporter for Legal Times wrote article that appeared 09-08-2003

> *"The commission came under fire early on for taking too long to process claims and for its refusal to make its finances public. In May 2001, the Los Angeles Times, citing internal commission documents, claimed that the commission had spent $30 million on salaries and outreach efforts, while paying out just $3 million. Later that year, a House committee held hearings at which Rep. Henry Waxman (D-Calif.) threatened to subpoena commission records. Commission chair Eagleburger, however, maintained that Congress had no authority over the group."*

Restitution exec was probed on spending Neal Sher resigned after inquiry—(Ukemonde)

Top Holocaust Industry Officer Fired for Embezzling (American Free Press)

War Criminals: Can Neal Sher Help Find Them?—(Ukrainian Archive)

Demjanjuk 2001 Denaturalization Trial—(Compiled by Dr. Will Zuzak)

My Campaign for Justice for John Demjanjuk—(Institute for Historical Review)

OSI "rehabilitation" complete?—(Ukrainian Weekly)

The Debate Over Alleged War Criminals in Canada—(On the Record)

OSI COLLABORATES WITH KGB—(LITUANUS—LITHUANIAN QUARTERLY JOURNAL OF ARTS AND SCIENCES)

Who Lied About Demjanjuk? Criticism of Jewish organizations costs judge Supreme Court appointment (UCCLA)

Demjanjuk Files—(Compiled by Dr. Will Zuzak)

John Demjanjuk (The Nizkor Project)

The Loftus Record—(Weekly Planet)

War Crimes Unit proceeding at record pace: (The Canadian Jewish News)

Canada hires Nazi hunter—(BBC On-Line)

Index

Viet Cong war criminals, 225
Vietnam War, 283
von Braun, Magnus, 394
von Braun, Wernher, i-iv, vi, ix-xi,
 1, 2, 5, 6, 9, 14, 17, 21-24, 30,
 34, 35, 38, 39, 43-45, 47-57, 60,
 64, 66, 69, 70, 88, 91-96, 98, 99,
 120, 126, 129, 130-132, 136,
 149, 161, 197, 200, 214, 249,
 257-259, 261-270, 272, 273, 277,
 278, 283, 285, 292, 295, 303,
 307, 309, 312, 314, 315, 317-
 323, 325-327, 329, 331, 332,
 333, 335, 336, 339, 343-347,
 365, 377-379, 384, 389, 410,
 428, 430, 432, 437
von Hessel, 222
Voss, Werner, 380

W

WAC Corporal missile, 11
Wackernagel, Rudolf, 380
Wagner, Carl, 395
Waldner, Alfred, 378
Wall Street Journal, 120, 313, 315,
 333, 335, 336
War Claims Commission, 411
War Department, 24, 33, 364
Ward, Bob, 64, 333
Washington Post, 131
Washington, D.C., vii, 32, 116, 202,
 293, 297, 302, 310, 322, 335,
 390, 404, 408, 411, 428
Watergate, 171
Waxman, Henry, 421, 442
Weber, Mark, 345
Webers, Theodore, 125, 134, 135
Webster, William, 440
Weckbrodt, 379
Weekly Planet, 443
Wehrmacht, 10, 35
Weiss, 421

Wernher von Braun: Crusader for
 Space, 262
West German government, 3
West German prosecutor, 111, 144,
 230, 231, 275, 287-289, 415
West Germany, 9, 166, 222
West New Guinea Campaign, viii
Western Test Range, 36
Whetting, Steve, 201
White House, 149, 160, 197, 199,
 202, 203, 205, 320
White House staff, 149
White Sands Proving Ground, 10,
 30, 37, 39, 50
Wieland, Guenter, 287
Wiesel, 195, 408, 409
Wiesman, Walter, 129, 394
Wifo, 215
William Beaumont Hospital, 10, 38
Wilson, Pete, 122, 123, 128, 138,
 139, 140, 152, 153, 157, 255,
 290, 391, 415
Winterberg, iii, 101, 119, 120, 121,
 122, 125, 134, 135, 137, 138,
 143, 163, 230, 389, 391
Winterstein, David, vi
Winterstein, Elizabeth, iv, ix, x, 34,
 38, 96, 151, 174
Wintestein, William, Jr., iv
Winterstein, Lt. Col. William, Sr., i,
 ii, iv, 39, 45, 46, 49, 51-54, 89,
 122, 123, 128, 138, 168, 169,
 172, 173, 202, 204-206, 231,
 285, 293, 296, 299, 303, 311-
 313, 315, 322, 323, 334, 335,
 343-345, 347, 388, 391, 404-406,
 414, 417, 433, 436
Winterstein-Good, Constance, iv, xi,
 48, 49, 53, 54, 347
Witer, 236
Witzenhausen, 23
Woerdemann, 347